# Communications in Computer and Information Science 533

More information about this series at http://www.springer.com/series/7899

Lorna Uden · Dario Liberona
Tatjana Welzer (Eds.)

# Learning Technology for Education in Cloud

## 4th International Workshop, LTEC 2015
## Maribor, Slovenia, August 24–28, 2015
## Proceedings

Springer

*Editors*
Lorna Uden
Staffordshire University
Stoke-on-Trent
UK

Tatjana Welzer
University of Maribor
Maribor
Slovenia

Dario Liberona
Universidad Tecnica Federico Santa Maria
Valparaíso
Chile

ISSN 1865-0929 ISSN 1865-0937 (electronic)
Communications in Computer and Information Science
ISBN 978-3-319-22628-6 ISBN 978-3-319-22629-3 (eBook)
DOI 10.1007/978-3-319-22629-3

Library of Congress Control Number: 2015945564

Springer Cham Heidelberg New York Dordrecht London


Printed on acid-free paper

Springer International Publishing AG Switzerland is part of Springer Science+Business Media
(www.springer.com)

# Preface

Technologies have impacted the ways we learn and teach. The need for continuous just-in-time training has made learning technology an indispensible part of life for workers. The necessity to disseminate information to large masses in education has led to an explosion of technological innovations in that field. Today, there are various technologies that can be used for teaching and learning. These include tools such as social media, MOOC, big data, and cloud. We are also living in a world of increased mobility where proliferation of mobile technologies is creating a host of new "anytime and anywhere learning" for students. Higher education will vigorously adopt new teaching approaches, propelled by opportunity and efficiency as well as student and parental demands.

The 4th LTEC (2015) conference examined these technologies that are changing the way teachers teach and students learn, while giving special emphasis to the pedagogically effective ways one can harness these new technologies in education. This conference brings together researchers across all educational sectors, from primary years, to informal learning, to higher education across a range of disciplines from humanities to computer science, media, and cultural studies with different perspectives, experiences, and knowledge in one location. It aims to help practitioners find ways of putting research into practice and for researchers to gain an understanding of real-world problems, needs, and aspirations.

The proceedings consist of 24 papers covering various aspects of technologies for learning including:

- MOOC challenges
- Cooperative learning
- Learning engineering
- Learning tools and environments
- STEM

The authors of the papers come from many different countries such as Australia, Brazil, Estonia, Finland, France, Germany, Greece, Guatemala, Japan, Korea, Malaysia, Mexico, Slovakia, Slovenia, Switzerland, Taiwan, and Tunisia, and the UK.

We would like to thank our authors, reviewers, and Program Committee for their contributions and the University of Maribor, Slovenia, for hosting the conference. Our thanks also to Lili Nemec Zlatolas, University of Maribor Slovenia, the local chair, for all her work. Special thanks to the authors and participants at the conference. Without their efforts, there would be no conference or proceedings.

August 2015

Lorna Uden
Dario Liberona
Tatjana Welzer

# Conference Organization

## Conference General Chair

| | |
|---|---|
| Lorna Uden | Staffordshire University, Stafford, UK |

## Program Chairs

| | |
|---|---|
| Dario Liberona | Universidad Tecnica Federico Santa Maria, Santiago, Chile |
| Tatjana Welzer | University of Maribor, Slovenia |

## Local Chair

| | |
|---|---|
| Lili Nemec Zlalotas | University of Maribor, Slovenia |

## Local Organization

| | |
|---|---|
| Marko Hölbl | University of Maribor, Slovenia |
| Saša Kuhar | University of Maribor, Slovenia |

## Conference Officials

| | |
|---|---|
| Amanda Jefferies | University of Hertfordshire, UK |
| Carole R. Beal | FL Online Learning Institute, USA |
| Birgit Feldmann | Fern Universität in Hagen, Germany |
| D'Arcy Becker | University of Wisconsin, USA |
| Dario Liberona | Universidad Tecnica Federico Santa Maria, Chile |
| Dejan Lavbič | University of Ljubljana, Slovenia |
| I. Hsien | National University of Kaohsiung, Taiwan |
| Jane Sinclair | University of Warwick, UK |
| Jeremiah Sullins | University of Mobile, USA |
| Jonathan Kaplan | Lumière University Lyon 2, France |
| Kyparisia Papanikolao | School of Pedagogical and Technological Education, Greece |
| Lorna Uden | Staffordshire University, UK |
| Luciana A.M. Zaina | University of São Carlos, Brazil |
| Manuel Santos-Trigo | Center for Research and Advanced Studies, Cinvestav-IPN, Mexico |
| Michael Vallance | Future University Hakodate, Japan |
| Richard Hartshorne | University of Central Florida, USA |
| Richard Self | University of Derby, UK |

| | |
|---|---|
| Rocael Hernández | Universidad Galileo, Guatemala |
| Sabine Seufert | Universität St. Gallen (HSG), Switzerland |
| Tatjana Welzer | University of Maribor, Slovenia |
| Vello Kukk | Tallinn University of Technology, Estonia |

# Contents

## Learning Engineering



## Learning Tools and Environments

## STEM

# MOOC Challenges

# Engagement Measures in Massive Open Online Courses

Jane Sinclair(✉) and Sara Kalvala

Department of Computer Science, University of Warwick,
Coventry CV4 7AL, UK
{J.E.Sinclair,Sara.Kalvala}@warwick.ac.uk

**Abstract.** Massive Open Online Course (MOOC) provision has proliferated over the past four years and millions of learners have participated. However, it is widely acknowledged that the number of completions is disturbingly low and MOOC drop-out rates have been a prominent issue of discussion. Currently, most MOOC analysis focuses on aspects such as patterns of engagement and prediction of dropout using data obtained by applying learning analytics to the large amounts of data gathered. In contrast, the effectiveness of teaching and learning programs in traditional face-to-face Higher Education (HE) settings is increasingly being assessed by measures linked to the promotion of student engagement. Internationally, student engagement surveys are being used to provide profiles of the effectiveness of teaching and learning within and between courses. In this paper we consider MOOC participation and drop-out issues emerging from the literature, and provide an overview of the student engagement surveys now widely used in HE. MOOC pedagogy is examined from the perspective of student engagement and we identify the need for a similar model adapted to MOOCs which could provide both a framework for course development and an instrument to assess aspects of teaching and learning in existing courses.

## 1 Introduction

The rise of Massive Open Online Courses (MOOCs) in recent years has seen many millions of people enroll on such courses to study a diverse range of topics. Coursera, one of the major platform providers currently has a portfolio of 997 courses and has over 22 million registered students [8]. The not-for-profit edX platform now offers over 300 courses to more than 3 million users [13]. Yet despite the large amount of effort and expense invested by developers and the corresponding commitment of time and effort from learners, the completion rates for most MOOCs remain stubbornly low. This issue has been raised as a topic of concern in many articles and discussions, and commentators have speculated on the reasons and debated the meaningfulness of using attrition statistics as a measure of success.

One reason that drop-out rates are cited so often is that they prove a simple, convenient and easy to calculate measure for an online course. If they were not


L. Uden et al. (Eds.): LTEC 2015, CCIS 533, pp. 3–15, 2015.
DOI: 10.1007/978-3-319-22629-3_1

so dramatically low as they are for most MOOCs they would not have become such a focus of attention. Even if the meaning and relevance of such figures are challenged, the eye-catching headlines still scrutinise and judge MOOCs from the perspective of completion rates. While we may criticise this as being too simplistic, the fact remains that the numbers are startling and that there is currently little else on offer as an acknowledged measure of MOOC "quality" or "success" which can provide a meaningful and inclusive alternative across a wide range of courses.

In contrast to the situation with MOOCs, there has in recent years been a move in Higher Education (HE) to assess courses not only on student experience (which can be a somewhat passive measure and may be weighted heavily towards provisions that please students whether or not they are educationally beneficial [15]) or on learning gain (which can be extremely difficult to evaluate and to compare) but by considering student engagement (SE). Student engagement involves considering what students actually spend their time doing. Certain activities are considered likely to be most beneficial to students and to provide the best opportunities for learning. Time spent engaged in the so-called "high impact educational practices" is mapped and interpreted against a number of benchmark areas to provide an indication of how strongly these areas are addressed across different subjects. Many institutions internationally are now using such data to identify areas of weakness or to develop strategies to better support under-represented groups [25]. While there may be concerns over the interpretation of this data and some of the conclusions drawn [2] it nevertheless seems likely that courses which uncorporate large amounts of "high impact" activities may be more beneficial to students.

There is so far very little research relating MOOCs to student engagement of this kind (indeed, the term is often interpreted rather differently in the context of MOOCs). In this paper we consider both the current landscape of MOOC participation and the use of engagement measures within traditional HE classroom teaching. MOOC activity is assessed from the perspective of student engagement (in the sense of the widely-used international engagement surveys and benchmarks) and the extent to which MOOCs incorporate high impact activities is discussed. The paper is organised as follows. Section 2 presents a literature review relating to MOOC participation and attrition. Section 3 provides an introduction to the current landscape of student engagement in HE and maps some of the existing instruments and initiatives in this area. We then consider the issue of "engagement" within MOOCs, noting the divergence of terminology and limited assessment in the MOOC context. This leads to a discussion of the formats and pedagogies supported by the major MOOC platforms and the relationship of these to the widely used interpretation of "student engagement". Finally, we discuss the implications for MOOCs and their participants and propose an approach to evaluation which considers student engagement from a more active, high impact perspective.

# 2 Literature Review: Background and MOOC Participation

The term MOOC has come to be used for a very wide range of approaches. In terms of philosophy, "cMOOCs" or connectivist MOOCs focus on knowledge generation within a network of learners and emphasise the creation of digital artifacts as an inherent part of the learning process. In contrast, "xMOOCs" are more about knowledge dissemination and are often characterised by didactic, expert-led teaching (commonly via lecture videos). In terms of size, courses can range from just a few dozen participants to hundreds of thousands. Despite the name, not all MOOCs are free and the majority do not offer open in resources (in that they are not licensed for download and reuse). With respect to accreditation, many give course certificates as evidence of completion, with so far only a small minority offering transferable university level credits [36]. Several authors report the use of MOOCs for continuing professional development [12,31]. Considering mode of operation, many MOOCs are fully online courses intended to be used for individual development and interest. Those being offered for credit allow an alternative mode of learning to an existing fact to face course. There is also a growing number of blended learning or flipped-classroom approaches where the MOOC is not an externally accessible course but is an integrated part of a face to face programme [30]. A further approach seen in a number of computer programming MOOCs is that of providing scalable tutorial help allowing students to access expert help for their specific problems [31,35].

Although it is impossible to know an exact figure, the number of courses available and the size of registrations indicate that many millions of people have enrolled for one or more MOOCs. It is worth noting that although some MOOCs have a specific international reach, in practice it appears that MOOC participation has so far been predominantly from Europe and the US [5]. Although MOOCs have often been heralded as the way forward for education in developing countries, many communities are still reported to be inhibited by lack of awareness, technology difficulties, (e-)learning skills or a language barrier [20].

## 2.1 MOOC Completion

As the first reports on MOOCs emerged, so did the disquiet about low completion rates [10]. This has continued as a constant theme in MOOC literature [28,32]. A meta-analysis of published data conducted by Jordan [16] indicates completion rates ranging from 0.9 % to 36.1 % with an average of 6.5 %. The average rises to 9.8 % if only active students (those taking at least some part in the course) are included. Length of course is positively correlated with high drop-out rate.

It has been noted that drop-out rates may not be a useful measure of MOOC success since on average, half of those who enroll do not start the course [16]. Many may have personal reasons for not continuing and others may never have intended to complete the course but feel they have achieved their objectives in studying specific parts. These considerations have led some to question how attrition should be counted - and whether it really matters anyway. There are a number of reasons why it should be considered important [6]. Firstly, until we are sure that learners are leaving through choice and not because of lack of support there is an obligation to explore the issue. Secondly, it may indicate that courses are not providing enough information for learners to make an informed choice about suitability. Having to drop a course part way through may have an adverse effect on learners and damage confidence. From the course providers' perspective, time spent producing materials which are accessed relatively rarely may be better invested elsewhere.

### 2.2 Who Completes MOOCs?

Dropout rates are undoubtedly high, but within that there are further concerns that studying a MOOC to completion appears to be more achievable for certain groups of people. Some commentators have noted the great disruptive and transformative potential of MOOCs [7] and there are suggestions that MOOCs are ideally suited to students who have barriers to accessing education, for example, through geography, personal circumstances or lack of opportunity [14]. Others refer to MOOC learners whose lives have been transformed by MOOC study [11]. However, initial research points to the difficulties in practice imposed by technology, language, learning skills and digital skills [21]. Caution has been urged over "Western imperialism" in MOOC education [1] and indeed anecdotal evidence suggests that in many parts of the world MOOCs are still considered (if at all) as an irrelevance. Attempts to roll out MOOCs for remedial college courses in the US encountered difficulties with unacceptably high failure rates [11] although it appears that blended learning incorporating MOOCs may be having greater success.

Results of research conducted on MOOC participation and completion suggest that successful learners are predominantly established independent learners [3] who have a high level of academic or professional education and are used to learning in traditional ways [4]. For all the amount of effort expended on course development and discussion of there is as yet little evidence that MOOCs are really having significant impact in widening participation. Barriers to starting or progressing on these courses still seem to be significantly higher for the very groups they might be hoped to target. While this remains the case, MOOCs will find it difficult to move beyond being mainly leisure activities for those who already have a high level of education.

### 2.3 Using Learning Analytics

One benefit provided in abundance by MOOCs is data. Learning analytics are being used to discover more about the reasons for dropout and to predict when a participant is likely to leave from their pattern of behaviour [33,37]. Kizilcec et al. [17] identify four separate categories of MOOC user according to their engagement pattern (that is, how much they interact with different types of resource). Prediction of dropout is useful, but does not in itself provide a means of prevention. Neither does it necessarily give insight into why student behave in the manner observed. There is very little information on remedial initiatives in MOOCs to help support those at risk of dropping out. Perhaps it is already too late by the time the behaviour begins to be observed. Further, any planned remedial action has to work within the constraints of a MOOC. It is certainly necessary to investigate these issues further and to consider effective, adaptive action for those at risk. However, it may also be useful to view the problem from a different perspective and consider how far the methods and approaches of the basic course are likely to promote engagement and active learning.

## 3 Student Engagement in Higher Education

Over the past decade, there has been increasing emphasis on assessing the learning benefits to students of (traditional) HE courses. Learning gain is notoriously difficult to measure, and one model for gathering information is to focus on student experience which is easier to determine. Many surveys (such as the UK's National Student Survey) provide a national measure of student satisfaction and generate data which is made public to provide, for example, information for applicants. While helpful, such surveys do not give much insight on students' learning activities or on the educational strength of their course. There has thus been a move to assess student engagement. Surveys such as the widely used North American National Survey of Student Engagement (NSSE) [22] investigate how much time students spend on a variety of activities chosen as being "high impact" activities associated with high levels of learning, personal development and skills acquisition [19]. Some have question d the validity of the instruments used and the legitimacy of viewing the benchmark indicators as easy-to-implement proxies for learning gain [24]. However, a good deal of research indicates that they do correlate to learning gain [23] and they are now used in many countries including North America, Canada, Australia, New Zealand, China and the UK.

While the uses to which engagement survey data is put may be questioned, these surveys nevertheless come from a perspective which is entirely lacking in assessment of MOOCs. By considering the profile of learners across a particular course (or subject) they question what types of activities a course is in general encouraging participants to engage in. Do students spend all their time sitting in lectures or are they actively engaged in more replactive and analytic tasks associated with effective learning? These are questions which are currently not being asked of MOOCs.

NSSE is currently the most widely used student experience survey with 621 institutions participating in the 2013 survey [22]. The survey instrument and benchmark groupings have been adapted by other national surveys, but the intention is broadly similar. NSSE key indicators include:

- **academic challenge** assessed by 17 questions covering reflective learning, higher order learning and learning strategies;
- **learning with peers** assessed by 8 questions covering aspects of collaboration and diversity;

- **experiences with faculty** assessed by 9 questions relating to student-staff interaction;
- **campus environment** assessed by 13 questions relating to supportiveness of environment.

While some of the questions asked (such as opportunities for research activities with faculty) may not seem directly relevant to student learning they have been identified as being associated with high levels of learning gain [34]. Such measurements should not be taken uncritically and care must be taken in how they are interpreted. It is also likely that some aspects will not be applicable in online courses and MOOCs specifically. However, it is also likely that the approach of investigating student experience can offer some insights into MOOCs and suggest a way of providing a framework (or at least one aspect of a framework) for MOOC assessment. After all, if we want our on-campus students to be spending their time on high impact learning activities, surely that is also desirable for learners on a MOOC.

## 4 Student Engagement in MOOCs

In the growing MOOC literature student engagement is a recurring theme. However, the term has a different meaning to that of the engagement surveys.

### 4.1 What Is "Engagement" Taken to Mean?

Student engagement in MOOCs overwhelmingly refers to student actions such as videos watched, quizzes answered and posts made to forums. In some cases, this is a basic count, in others the time spent on the various activities and the scores obtained in assessments are used. This quantifies the level of activity with respect to the resources provided but does not question whether that activity is likely to lead to meaningful learning. Some studies use student engagement patterns to classify users in to different types, but the main way the data is employed is in predicting drop-out. Only one MOOC paper refered to student engagement in the sense used by the surveys [26] yet even in this work, the measures relate to counts of posting, viewing etc. and are intended to predict student survival on a course.

The position with connectivist MOOCs (cMOOCs) is a little different as there is more emphasis on active, user-centered engagement. This does not simply mean viewing resources but involves actively creating and communicating knowledge within a networked community. In this respect, and with their emphasis on creativity and connected learning, cMOOCs are much more likely to involve students in high-impact activities. However, cMOOCs have issues of their own and, while they have provided an inspirational experience for some participants, others have found them confusing and lacking in direction.

### 4.2 Frameworks for Assessing MOOCs

Student engagement surveys such as NSSE provide a framework against which to benchmark course provision, but there has been little of this nature so far for MOOCS. There has, however, been growing concern over MOOC quality,as evidenced by, for example, the EFQUEL MOOC quality project [9] in which contributors considered the issue from a variety of perspectives (for example, quality for different stakeholders; quality of information to learners and quality of peer interaction). Conole [7] approaches the issue from the perspective of quality of learner experience, linking this to quality enhancement through learning design. The "7Cs of Learning Design" suggested by Conole gives a fairly abstract check list of points for course developers to consider ("Conceptualize", "Capture","Communicate" and so on). The "Consider" aspect focuses attention on course design, content and activities but does not provide specific guidance on how to do this or what criteria should guide development of an evaluation rubric ("Consolidate").

The "OpenupEd" quality label is provided by the European OpenupEd MOOC portal as a benchmark for quality assurance in MOOCs [29]. These abstract considerations (such as openness, possibility of certification) cover a variety of aspects of student experience rather than the more specific and measurable engagement-related activities. A similar quality assurance approach using high level guidelines is taken by Read and Rodrigo [27]. Again, while learning design approaches are necessary they do not provide the specific relation to high impact activity associated with effective learning.

## 5 How Do MOOCs Fare on Engagement Measures?

Student engagement instruments elicit the extent to which students on a course are engaged in high impact activity. In this section we consider how this relates to what students on a MOOC might spend their time doing. Here, we are considering the more common "xMOOC" format and, of necessity, referring in generalities to the activities most commonly provided by major platforms.

### 5.1 What Are "High Impact Activities"?

NSSE, which has formed the basis for the other major engagement surveys, sets 10 benchmark areas: Higher Order Learning, Reflective Learning, Learning Strategies, Quantitative Reasoning, Collaborative Learning, Discussions with Diverse Others, Student-Faculty interaction, Effective Teaching Practice, Quality of Interactions and Supportive Environment. Each is evidenced by a group of questions which provide very specific measures contributing towards each benchmark area. The full NSSE survey instrument can be viewed at the NSSE website [22]. The following are examples of NSSE questions to indicate the structure and the level of data sought. Participants are asked to state how often they have done certain activities, with answers on a 5-point Likert scale ranging from Very Often to Never. Activities include:

- asked questions or contributed to course discussions;
- asked another student to help you understand course materials;
- connected your learning to societal problems or issues;
- examined the strengths and weaknesses of your own views on a topic or issue;
- connected ideas from your course to your prior experiences and knowledge;
- discussed your academic performance with a faculty member;
- summarised what you learned in class;
- worked with a faculty member on a research project.

Participants are also asked how much emphasis there is on a range of activities such as memorizing course material, applying facts and theories, evaluating information, doing assigned reading. Further questions illicit information on provision (such as giving feedback and support), and on knowledge, skills and personal development.

Other SE surveys differ in emphasis, in the specific questions asked and in the groupings into benchmarks. However, the intention of all is to investigate levels of activity promoted by the course which have been demonstrated to relate to high learning gain.

### 5.2 Typical MOOC Activities

Within many MOOCs, activity is centered around video presentations. These may be used to introduce a topic, and there may be additional reading which encourages learners to explore further. Forums are widely used to encourage active participation and to provide a means for discussion and support either from tutors or peers. Real time conversation is sometimes also supported by, for example Google Hangouts. Quick quiz assessment is a main form of assessment as this is automatically marked and therefore easy to scale. Peer assessment is also used to allow feedback and evaluation of more detailed assignments such as essays or programming tasks. The creation of digital artifacts such as a blog is also often employed as means of encouraging engagement and reflective learning.

In HE it has long been recognised that lectures are a very passive form of engagement and videos are even more so. Forums may in theory provide the opportunity for active, collaborative learning but in practice they are often used only by a minority and, in larger MOOCs, the proliferation of threads can become confusing and difficult to navigate. Virtual study groups and peer review are used to encourage social learning and to encourage skills of critical analysis and reflection (as well as being scalable). In practice, many learners have encountered serious difficulties with the operation of these methods which in themselves create barriers to learning rather than enhancing it.

### 5.3 Examples of Good Practice

While the activities mentioned in the previous section are typical of the majority of MOOCs, some developers are attempting to push the boundaries of the generic MOOC platforms. One good example is Edinburgh University's EDCMOOC

(E-learning and Digital Cultures). Public resources (videos and readings) were harnessed and linked by text and questions, with students being guided yet expected to find their own learning path [18]. In particular, EDCMOOC sought to improve the area (notably high impact) of interaction between students and staff which is often lacking in MOOCs. Teaching presence was maintained in the usual MOOC ways (forums responses, curation of materials etc.) but further supported by video discussion panels.

MOOCs which attempt to promote greater engagement and social learning have sometimes been referred to as "a bit cMOOC", but perhaps it is more that these courses are employing learner-focused pedagogy and emphasing high impact activities.

### 5.4 Learning in a MOOC

Instead of counting accesses to videos, a better indicator of MOOC student engagement may be to enquire what types of activity students devote their learning time to. Further, in assessing MOOC quality, it may be more beneficial to ask how far a course leads participants towards engaging with activities most associated with high levels of learning. Evaluation then relates to what types of learning activity (and learning) a MOOC promotes and engagement is about students' interaction with meaningful learning experiences.

It may be said that current xMOOCs provide the opportunity for high impact learning activity. For example, learners may be forming themselves into effective groups for peer collaboration and using the opportunity to benefit their learning through interaction with diverse others. Most are not. We need to be asking how much this is happening; to what extent MOOCs are leading students toward this type of activity and what opportunities there are to increase the levels of high impact activity within the MOOC format. The need to understand and support the "community" nature of MOOC learning may be a crucial aspect here as there is potential for a great diversity and richness of learning collaboration and peer interaction.

The need to provide more active learning has been recognised by some MOOC proponents. For example, Daphne Koller, co-founder of Coursera, promoted breaking videos into 10 min chunks interspersed with activities and using social media to encourage interactive study groups. However, there is still a long way to go in setting out an agenda for more active, higher impact MOOC learning.

It has long been recognised that transitional phases of learning (such as from school to university) present a critical phase for the learner which course providers need to manage and support. Certainly, the importance of transition to a new learning environment, greater learning independence and new ways of learning is seen as crucial for those starting university and dropout rates have been linked to the inabililty to make that step effectively. Similarly, the move from traditional learning to a MOOC learning environment necessitates a very different approach to learning. This points to the need to better understand the concept of learning in a MOOC and the associated learning strategies which will best equip learners to succeed.

## 6 Discussion

It appears (although there is currently no available data) that learners on many MOOCs are spending much of their learning time on activities which are not generally associated with high learning gain. When time is limited, it may well be the more time-consuming reflective and interactive activities that are skipped. It is certainly the case that most published measures of student "engagement" for MOOCs assess very narrow areas of participation some of which (notably watching videos) can be a very passive activity. This contrasts with the current perspective on student engagement in HE in general and the approach to assessment being widely adopted worldwide. While there are legitimate doubts about the interpretation of SE surveys, the aim of investigating the amount of "worthwhile" activity seems a very useful one. It has certainly attained a high level of respect in HE with aggregated results widely available and even in some cases the suggestion that university funding might be linked to such surveys.

While this level of response may be a little alarming, it highlights the difference between traditional courses and MOOCs. While we think of MOOCs as a leisure activity for the highly-educated this may not be an issue. But as soon as claims are made that MOOCs can, for example, solve participation problems in HE and experiments are undertaken to replace more traditional methods, the concerns become very real. We have learned that passive pedagogies are not the best way for students to learn - so what reason is there to think that this is acceptable in a MOOC? Research shows that some learning activities are more associated with high levels of learning than others. So why are we assessing traditional courses in this way but continue to count how many times MOOC learners watch videos?

There is an acknowledged lack of effective pedagogy in MOOCs. Measures that might be hoped to increase engagement and interaction (such as forums and peer review) have proved problematic in MOOCs and results on whether participation is associated with learning gain are mixed. One question that might be asked is whether it is possible even in theory for a MOOC format to support effective SE activity. Certainly, there are aspects which would be difficult to replicate. But in other areas (such as interaction with diverse others and opportunities for social learning) there is massive potential even if the way to harness it is as yet elusive. Current SE survey instruments are unlikely to be appropriate for MOOCs. However, investigating MOOCs from the SE perspective opens up the discussion on what high impact activities can be framed within this context.

Although it has not been possible here to present the full range of SE learning measures, there are other aspects which are relevant to MOOCs too. For example, such surveys investigate learner development and the acquisition of study skills and strategies. MOOCs need to be able to support participants in "learning to learn" and to find the appropriate balance between self-directed learning and learner autonomy. It is also the case that MOOCs should not raise unrealistic expectations as to what can be learned in a short amount of time. High impact learning activities are often time consuming. A lecture of 10 min may be the tip of the iceberg in terms of the effort needed on the part of the learner.

In terms of evaluation, quality and the hope of reducing drop out rates, it is imperative to consider what high impact activities MOOCs promote and what students on these courses are in practice spending their learning time doing.

## 7 Conclusions

There are many reasons why students drop out of MOOCs. Attrition rates are likely to be, in part, a symptom of malaise but because of the diversity of causes they are not in themselves a meaningful measure of what is going on in a MOOC. We need to consider further the nature of the courses and the activities they incorporate. One approach to this is to consider them (and participants' interaction with them) in terms of the level of high impact activity.

While we may have some scepticism about taking the use of NSSE-type surveys too far, this paper makes the case for the need to understand MOOCs from the student engagement perspective. Mass MOOCs are different to face to face courses or even to "traditional" online learning courses. Student engagement is likely to need a different interpretation but we can still ask the questions: to what extent is it possible to promote this in a MOOC? Are there different (possibly new) aspects that constitute appropriate high impact activities for MOOCs? Making progress on this agenda will lead to a clearer strategy for course evaluation.

Finally, we believe the questions raised in this paper are still open ones. That is, we have to be prepared for negative answers. If MOOCs on their own cannot provide a good learning experience for more than an exclusive few, it will be necessary to consider the implications. It may be that other ways of using MOOCs (such as for blended learning or flipped classrooms) can be harnessed to good learning effect, but if mass MOOCs appeared to have little prospect of achieving this there would be reason to question their rationale.

## References


1. Altbach, P.: MOOCs as neocolonialism: who controls knowledge? Int. High. Educ. **75**, 5–7 (2014)
2. Baron, P., Corbin, L.: Student engagement: rhetoric and reality. High. Educ. Res. Dev. **31**(6), 759–772 (2012)
3. Belanger, Y., Thornton, J.: Bioelectricity: a quantitative approach. Duke Universitys First MOOC. Technical report, Duke University (2013). Accessed 19 March 2013
4. Ben-Ari, M.M.: Moocs on introductory programming: a travelogue. ACM Inroads **4**(2), 58–61 (2013)
5. Christensen, G., Steinmetz, A., Alcorn, B., Bennett, A., Woods, D., Emanuel, E.: The MOOC phenomenon: who takes massive open online courses and why?
6. Clow, D.: MOOCs and the funnel of participation. In: Third Conference on Learning Analytics and Knowledge (2013)
7. Conole, G.: MOOCs as disruptive technologies: strategies for enhancing the learner experience and quality of MOOCs. Revista de Educación a Distancia **39**, 1–17 (2013)

8. Coursera. https://www.coursera.org/. Accessed 21 February 2015
9. Creelman, A., Ehlers, U., Ossiannilsson, E.: Perspectives on mooc quality-an account of the efquel mooc quality project. INNOQUAL-Int. J. Innov. Qual. Learn. **2**(3) (2014)
10. Daniel, J.: Making sense of moocs: musings in a maze of myth, paradox and possibility. J. Interact. Media Educ. **3** (2012)
11. Devlin, K.: MOOC Mania Meets the Sober Reality of Education. Huffington Post, 19 August 2013
12. Ecclestone, M.: MOOCs as a professional development tool for librarians. Can. J. Libr. Inf. Pract. Res. **8**(2) (2013)
13. edX. https://www.edx.org/. Accessed 21 February 2015
14. Escher, G., Noukakis, D., Aebischer, P.: Boosting higher education in africa through shared massive open online courses (MOOCs). In: Education, Learning, Training: Critical Issues for Development, p. 195 (2014)
15. Furedi, F., Attwood, R.: Satisfaction and its discontents. The Times Higher Education Supplement, 2040, March 2012
16. Jordan, K.: Initial trends in enrolment and completion of massive open online courses. Int. Rev. Res. Open Distrib. Learn. **15**(1), 133–160 (2014)
17. Kizilcec, R., Piech, C., Schneider, E.: Deconstructing disengagement: analyzing learner subpopulations in massive open online courses. In: Proceedings of the 3rd International Conference on Learning Analytics and Knowledge, pp. 170–179. ACM (2013)
18. Knox, J., Ross, J., Sinclair, C., Macleod, H., Bayne, S.: Mooc feedback: pleasing all the people? In: Invasion of the MOOCs, pp. 98–104. Parlor Press (2014)
19. Kuh, G.: The national survey of student engagement: conceptual framework and overview of psychometric properties, pp. 1–26. Indiana University Center for Postsecondary Research, Bloomington (2001)
20. Liyanagunawardena, T., Williams, S., Adams, A.: The impact and reach of moocs: a developing countries perspective. eLearning Papers (33) (2013)
21. Nanfito, M.: MOOCs: Opportunities, Impacts, and Challenges: Massive Open Online Courses in Colleges and Universities (2013)
22. NSSE: North American National Survey of Student Engagement. http://nsse.iub.edu. Accessed 10 March 2014
23. Pascarella, E., Seifert, T., Blaich, C.: How effective are the nsse benchmarks in predicting important educational outcomes? Change: Mag. High. Learn. **42**(1), 16–22 (2010)
24. Porter, S.: Do college student surveys have any validity? Rev. High. Educ. **35**(1), 45–76 (2011)
25. Quaye, S., Harper, S. (eds.): Student Engagement in Higher Education: Theoretical Perspectives and Practical Approaches for Diverse Populations, 2nd edn. Routledge, New York (2014)
26. Ramesh, A., Goldwasser, D., Huang, B., Daume III, H., Getoor, L.: Learning latent engagement patterns of students in online courses. In: Twenty-Eighth AAAI Conference on Artificial Intelligence (2014)
27. Read, T., Rodrigo, C.: Toward a quality model for uned moocs. eLearning Papers (37) (2014). http://www.openeducationeuropa.eu/en/elearning_papers
28. Rivard, R.: Measuring the MOOC dropout rate. Inside Higher Ed., 8 March 2013
29. Rosewell, J., Jansen, D.: The openuped quality label: benchmarks for moocs. INNOQUAL: Int. J. Innov. Qual. Learn. **2**(3), 88–100 (2014)
30. Sandeen, C.: Integrating MOOCS into traditional higher education: the emerging MOOC 3.0 era. Change: Mag. High. Learn. **45**(6), 34–39 (2013)

31. Sinclair, J., Boyatt, R., Foss, J., Rocks, C.: A tale of two modes: initial reflections on an innovative MOOC. In: Uden, L., Sinclair, J., Tao, Y.-H., Liberona, D. (eds.) LTEC 2014. CCIS, vol. 446, pp. 49–60. Springer, Heidelberg (2014)
32. Sinclair, J., Boyatt, R., Rocks, C., Joy, M.: Massive open online courses (MOOCs): a review of usage and evaluation. Int. J. Learn. Technol. (2015) (accepted for publication)
33. Sinha, T., Li, N., Jermann, P., Dillenbourg, P.: Capturing "attrition intensifying" structural traits from didactic interaction sequences of mooc learners. In: Proceedings of the Empirical Methods in Natural Language Processing Workshop (2014)
34. Umbach, P., Wawrzynski, M.: Faculty do matter: the role of college faculty in student learning and engagement. Res. High. Educ. **46**(2), 153–184 (2005)
35. Vihavainen, A., Luukkainen, M., Kurhila, J.: Multi-faceted Support for MOOC in Programming. In: SIGITE 2012 (2012)
36. Welsh, D.H., Dragusin, M.: The new generation of massive open online course (moocs) and entrepreneurship education. Small Bus. Inst.® J. **9**(1), 51–65 (2013)
37. Yang, D., Sinha, T., Adamson, D., Rose, C.: Turn on, tune in, drop out: anticipating student dropouts in massive open online courses. In: Proceedings of the 2013 NIPS Data-Driven Education Workshop, vol. 10, p. 13 (2013)

# Two-Dimensional Knowledge Model for Learning Control and Competence Mapping

Vello Kukk(✉), Kadri Umbleja, and Martin Jaanus

Department of Computer Control,
Tallinn University of Technology, Tallinn, Estonia
{vello.kukk,kadri.umbleja,martinj}@ttu.ee

**Abstract.** The paper presents two-dimensional model for knowledge representation with volume as one variable and ability as another one. This makes possible describing current state of learner's abilities and integration for higher level parameters e.g. grading related to course or other entities. Both values are related to atomized knowledge elements (competences) with volume interpreted as credit units and ability levels are formed during learning with application of forgetting. This model makes possible characterization (grading) of knowledge based on real abilities independently of predeclared courses and for 'drop-outs'. So, on that bases one can obtain grade for some course if proper knowledge has been obtained in different courses and schools even when courses had not passed. Also this model helps to build connections between courses as using courses in the role of prerequisites becomes less usable. Not wasting knowledge obtained in MOOCs is another example with high drop-out levels where classical passed-failed model does not work.

**Keywords:** Competence-based learning · Credit units · Abilities · Automatic processing of solutions

## 1 Introduction

The drop-out rate for MOOCs is very high and in recent years a lot of studies have been conducted to explain the reasons behind the phenomena. Despite dropping out, those students who quit, have learned at least something and the question rises – how to get some recognition out of the work done. The solution might be that if student knows that completing even part of the course is beneficial then this might be additional motivation for the learner not to stop early in the course.

For example [1] investigates four week long course with following weekly completion rates: 21.5 %, 13.80 %, 10.24 %, and finally 8.50 % of 680 registered students. Instead of classifying 13 % of students (21.5 % after one week the start minus 8.5 % who finished) as drop-outs (zero credits) they could obtain a quarter tom three quarters of credits (with details about their knowledge). This could also be applied to any regular course and even to full curricula. Another analysis of large number of courses [2] shows similar completion rates (6.5 %). Therefore, it could be assumed that the productivity within the course for the drop-outs might be similar (may be 10 % for 25 % volume).


L. Uden et al. (Eds.): LTEC 2015, CCIS 533, pp. 16–27, 2015.
DOI: 10.1007/978-3-319-22629-3_2

The idea of compiling credit units (or other information about learner's abilities) is becoming more acceptable. For example, IML [3] issues several types of qualifications. Collecting competences obtained in industry and education, including minor skills that might not be accompanied with certificate, into learning database is promising trend for life-long learning.

Two-dimensional model is in use but in a very limited manner: the first dimension – grading is measuring quality of learning and another one – credit units for evaluation of learning volume (time), for planning, and for calculating integrated measures (average grade). Unfortunately, both dimensions are not applied to learning control and serve as rather post-factum indicators. In this paper, we show how two-dimensional model can be used for learning control during whole learning cycle.

## 2 Competences

Key concept for this approach is low-level competence representing elementary unit that can be learned and usage of which can be measured.

There are many different definitions for the term 'competence'. Klarus has defined it as mix of skills, attitudes and knowledge that makes the employee or graduate successful in society and his/her profession [4]. Other definition states that by competence, we understand good performance in diverse, authentic contexts based on the integration and activation of knowledge, rules and standards, techniques, procedures, abilities and skills, attitudes and values [5]. We have defined competence-based learning as a knowledge based methodology which concentrates on measuring what a person can actually do as a result of learning [6]. In popular form, competence is explained as 'A competency, simply put, is something that a person or organization is competent in performing' [7] and 'Competence is the ability of an individual to do a job properly' [8]. All those (and other definitions) are very general, quite similar but do not help to implement learning environment directly.

Therefore, we prefer to use 'behavioural definition' stating that competency item must be usable in analysing outcomes of learner's activities so, that ability level related to every competence item can be measured (evaluated). Presumably, any of those items should appear in many actions combined with others. To avoid discussions concerning different definitions and interpretations of term 'competence', we shall use in this paper the word **'comp'**.

In other words, a comp is one item in learner's model which predicts reaction to specific action as input. Processes in feedback loops correct numerical data related to the comp (ability level, forgetting parameters). The model used is the following:

$$L(t) = L(t_0)f(\tau, p, t_0, t) \tag{1}$$

where $L$ is ability level, $\tau$ is time constant, $t$ is current time, $t_0$ is reference time, and $p$ is forgetting rate. Currently, the power law [15, 16] is used:

$$f(\tau, p, t_0, t) = \left(1 + \left(\frac{t - t_0}{\tau}\right)\right)^{-p}. \quad (2)$$

All three parameters $\tau, p, t_0$ are corrected after receiving learner's reactions.

## 3 Adaptive Control

Students tend to have very uneven background when they sign up for a courses in university, especially at higher levels of studies. Furthermore, during learning knowledge gaps may even increase because learning is a personal process. This will cause some students to pass courses really easy and on the other hand, some students are learning very slowly or dropping out. It is hard for the teacher to find suitable topics that would be manageable but still challenging for everyone in classic lecture format teaching. Therefore personal learning tracks become unavoidable to facilitate everyone's pace, state, and goals.

To facilitate personal learning and competence model, learner's state must be determined (measured) as precisely as possible. Number of levels in common grading systems (using 5 to 10 marks) is not sufficient to represent dynamics of learning. The learning environment we describe is functioning as follows. For every comp and for every student the following data referred in Eqs. (1) and (2) is recorded. Any action taken by the student that produces a recordable result is defined as task. All the results are analyzed automatically by the system evaluating which of the comps have been used when solving the task and how correct has been the usage [9]. Thereafter system modifies the state of corresponding comps. It is possible, in special case, that human (teacher) may be part of that process which usually causes time delays and less efficient operation of feedback loop.

There are several feedback loops in the system. Main difference from the classical closed-loop control is that the goal is not obtaining certain behavior of output signal but adjusting object to wanted behavior. The object (learner) is not simply reacting when input signals are applied but it is changing and our goal is to get wanted changes as efficiently as possible. In that sense, earning system is adaptive control (continuous identification) and model-based one as well. Ideas from both control theories are applicable but do not go into details in this paper.

In fact, two-dimensional model is used in education: abilities are measured by grades and volumes by credit units. However, those measures are applied to very large elements and credit unit has extremely high variation: usually, credit unit is related to average time but real personal time or amount of work differs at least 4–5 times for different students and courses. Our goals here is to introduce measurement units for both dimensions.

## 4 First Dimension – Ability

In order to model knowledge for personalized learning control, we use the ability as the first dimension of this model (ability comparable with that of Item Response Theory [10–12]).

To facilitate our detailed and desired granularity in the model, the assessment becomes complicated. For example, if the goal is to grade large object (e.g. the whole course) using very few available marks as formal education system expects is not proper for control. Better solution would be assess small parts of that large object independently where well-defined measures and rules could be used to achieve more precise feedback loops [13].

This model is simpler than for example IRT (Rasch model) which uses ability over scale of difficulty (probability of correct answer). In our model, only one numerical value is used which can be related to difficulty. IRT model parameters can be calculated form stored data but we are more interested in dynamics of learning and control.

Classical testing and also IRT assume that when knowledge is acquired it does not change with time. That, sadly, is not the case – if competence is not used over time, it starts to fade (forgetting). That should also be taken account in the model as otherwise, grading is simply snap-shot for certain time moment [14]. Using forgetting in the model enables learner to concentrate on relevant competences (new or forgotten) and avoid unnecessary efforts which do not improve knowledge.

The first dimension is produced in the system by processing learning action and expressing it with numeric value. It could be real number, for example in the range 0…1 (probabilities) or −1…+1 to emphasize true and false by signs etc. Binary values are quite common as they allow simple analysis. However, in certain cases dichotomy is not the best choice (for example, when presence of measurement errors are unavoidable).

This outcome of the analysis is used as input for evaluation of ability levels (and forgetting parameters). Ability levels can also be mapped into different scales. From practical point of view integers are preferred because of easy interpretation by humans and also simpler processing (e.g. table functions). In our model half byte is used (values from 0 to 127). That gives us good variety of marks to use and is large enough scale to avoid loss of details.

Example. Let us consider an ‘elementary’ Ohm’s law. In fact, application of this ‘primitive’ law assumes several knowledge elements/competences: Kirchhoff’s laws, understanding direction of current, that voltage is difference of potentials, measurement units, and prefixes. One can make mistake in every aspect of the task and learners do so. Misconceptions are common. Practice is needed and it might take weeks of work before competence is achieved. When analyzing such a small task where the answer is one number (or number with a unit), several different outcomes can be detected. Corresponding competence states have to be changed accordingly.

Ability level for a competence is a dynamic value which is changing in time caused by two factors – (1) learning actions/tasks (rehearsing) and (2) forgetting.

## 5 Second Dimension – Volume (Credits, Difficulty)

There are many different scales for measuring volume (time) for learning. In education systems, usually it is assumed that credit level for a course has direct connection to time needed. For example, course with higher credits has more contact hours, requires more hours of independent work etc. Here we use as synonyms the terms volume, difficulty, and credits emphasizing that they all represent the amount of work (in IRT the difficulty is comparable).

The role of this dimension is to close one feedback loop through integration (averaging) of abilities. One compulsory integrated value in formal education is official grade but even more important are such integrated values for motivating learners and control (selection) of actions. As this variable is used to calculation of integrated indicators, the most proper name would be 'weight'.

We need two types of weights:

- Difficulty levels assigned to learning actions/tasks which are solved by the learner during learning process
- Weights assigned to comps used.

Those two concepts are closely connected. For example, assume that the task $T_i$ is based on (using) comps $C_j$. Denote by $WT(T_i)$ measure of difficulty for task $T_i$ and by $WC(C_j)$ weight of competence $C_j$. Assume $WC(C_j)$ is assigned. Then we can assign difficulty $WT(T_i)$ to $T_i$ integrating weights of related comps. Different measures can be applied for integration as average, mean square, min, max etc.

Several methods have been considered to determine the weights:

(1) Predefined by the author who created the learning object. This may be based on obvious parameters, for example, on volume of work to be done (number of components of answer).
(2) Processing elapsed time obtained from real process – more time, higher difficulty (volume).
(3) Average result from log files; in case on dichotomic model it is equivalent to the probability of correct answer.
(4) Adjusting difficulty levels to obtain uniform distribution over set of tasks;
(5) Combination of algorithms 1–4

All described approaches above have been tested and modified over years in real learning environment. First, predefined difficulties were assigned based on teacher's assumptions about complexity of tasks. Then when real results were collected, corrections were made to match the'rule of positivness' (3 dB rule): average score of positive answers should be at the level of −3 dB or approximately 7 solutions from 10 should be correct. It was assumed that in such case learning process will be motivating and this rule proved to be effective as the number of corrections needed according to logs once or twice per year was decreasing. In other words, this −3 dB level appeared to be rather stable (and is still so).

Then, in 2010, when comps were attached to tasks, comps obtained weights which were assigned to comps manually on the basis of experience. When more results were collected, 3 dB rule was applied to correct weights. The same comp is used in more than one course but its focus or importance for the course may vary. That caused comps to be assigned different weights for different course to reflect their part in that specific module. For this purpose, a scaling factor was associated with course.

Let's comment the methods shortly.

*Method 1* – difficulty predefined by teacher (author of the tasks). This initial setting is needed to activate tasks at all. Analysis of log files showed that many assumptions (like 'smaller means simpler') were not correct. When analyzing records we have to keep in mind that recorded data are produced from closed-loop system and small task may appear more difficult as it appears when learner is just starting studying the topic. In real life, initial difficulty assignments had to be corrected sometimes substantially.

*Method 2* – using elapsed time may be useful; however, analysis showed that correlation between elapsed time and correctness of answers is very weak (almost 0).

*Method 3* – average results (averaging over all competences in all tasks). This method has proved to be rather stable to meet 3 dB law. As it has exhibited good stability, this method is considered as the most appropriate one.

*Method 4* – assigning levels to the tasks so that tasks are distributed evenly between difficulty levels.

Current solution (as of spring semester 2015) is as follows:

1. For new tasks 3 dB level is assigned and levels are reviewed when at least 5 solutions appear. In case when evaluation of amount of work is possible, deviations from 3 dB levels are accepted.
2. When revising task levels, two operations are used: grouping tasks on the basis of calculated average results and leveling task numbers per level. To simplify control (selecting tasks) in the latest implementation tasks are grouped into only 4 levels.

## 6 Weighing Comps

To control personalized learning process, the system should find proper task for learner depending on his/her current state. Action is initiated by learner who can point to specific comp he or she wants to learn or, in automatic mode, task selection is based on specific algorithm which determines the most suitable task for the learner.

Average result may be considered as probability of correct answer (when scale 0 … 1 is used), then we introduce the following measure. Denote by *w99* average number of attempts needed to reach 99 % confidence that at least one correct result is achieved. This means that if average result is *A* then probability of correct answer in *w99* attempts is $P = 1\text{-}(1\text{-}A)^{w99}$. From this we have $w99 = log\ (P)/log\ (1\text{-}A)$ where $P = 0.99$ and *w99* is a real number. For very small values of *A* the number of attempts *w99* is proportional to *1/A* and may obtain large values. For example for $A = 0.1$ we have $w99 = 43.7$ which means that there is practically no chance to give correct answer. To avoid unreasonable behavior for such unlucky comp an upper limit is to be set and if the situation does not change this comp should be removed from usage.

The value w99 has been turned into basic weight for comps. For higher level items (including courses) scaling factor is applied which converts w99 values to credit units. In reality, this factor appears to be in the range from 15 to 25 and is set when course is compiled.

## 7 Connection to Formal Credits

Usually formal credit systems are based on evaluation of time to be used by student to pass the course. This may be correct when learning means only physical participation in lectures/labs and could be appropriate before IT era. Nowadays most of classical assumptions about prerequisites and ways of learning are not valid. Globalization has brought us to the situation where students starting learning in a course may have extremely varying background. In many cases, learning is supported by technology and therefore there are no regular classes, students can be from very different time zones, having different cultural background etc.

This has become very clear in case of MOOCs which combine those aspects and contradiction between classical concepts of courses and reality. Drop-outs have become a serious problem for MOOCs. It could be explained by the 'winner takes all' principle: one has passed a course (curriculum) or not, what a student has really learned is not represented in certificate. The situation in real life is different – for employer real abilities are becoming more important than list of units passed by an employee. Note that working experience – very important for employers – can also be integrated into competence map.

Formal education systems are based on credit systems and credit transfer processes are used to combine different studies. This means that a transformation from difficulty/weights to credits must be implemented. This may be simple linear transformation which uses different scales in different courses. Two-dimensional maps discussed have one benefit: every comp is unique for any higher-level competence even if it has been considered in several courses.

## 8 Example

This example visualizes learning process of a student in one course during spring semester 2014 (Fig. 1). Higher (thin) line shows credits learned and the lower (thick) one shows confirmed credits. In order to "confirm" that he/she did the learning, students have to attend on-campus test when tasks are selected by system and during those tests, students have some restrictions. It is clearly seen that the process is not conventional 'collecting points' as the volume is not monotonic.

Figure 2 shows learning graph with sum of credit units on the horizontal axis and integrated ability level on the vertical axis. Grade zones are also shown and student's final decision is marked by a dot at V = 4.633 and L = 119 which is located in the zone 4 (equivalent to grade B). Final grade is 'picked up' by student when his/her state reaches grade zones and the grade satisfies the student. Final (formal) grade is produced from skew zones representing grades from 1 to 5 (from E to A).

We can see from the figures that the student could get information about her state in any phase of learning. Minimal information would be credits and ability level. For example, on April 21, 2014 she could ask for certificate stating credits = 2.727 ECU at level L = 120. Competences forming that result could be included in that certificate.

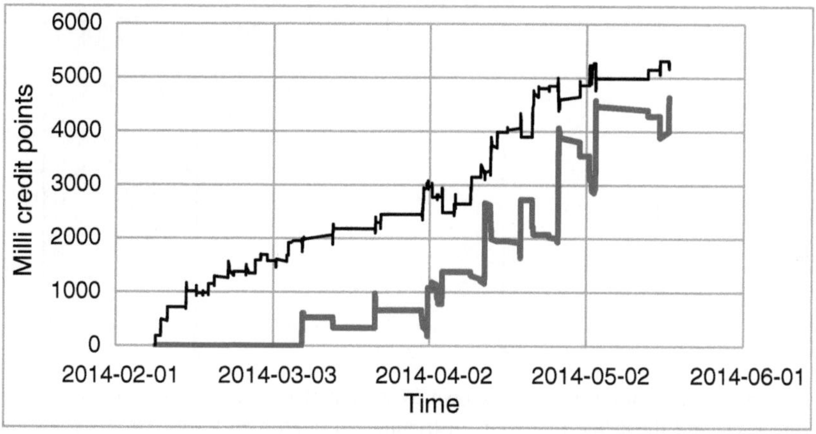


**Fig. 1.** Current credits and confirmed credits vs time. Credit units in mCU.

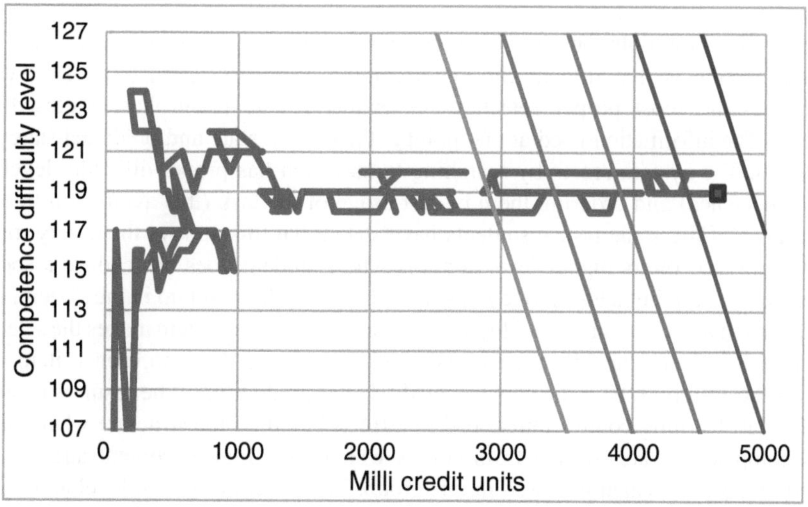


**Fig. 2.** Credits and corresponding competence levels at the final stage of learning the course. Final grade accepted by student is shown as a rectangular dot. It is in the zone of grade 4.

In electronic form, viewing tasks behind that certificate are possible and future states would be available. This particular student has lost very little in one year: on February 25, 2015 her credits had dropped from 4,633 to 4,589 and level from 119 to 118.

In Fig. 3 two tracks are shown: the narrow one represents everyday learning and the thick one represents confirmed units.

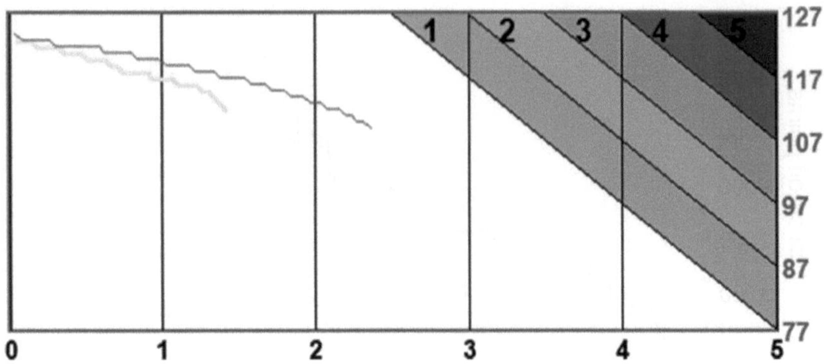


**Fig. 3.** Typical view of current state shown to student. Thin line is represents distribution of ordinary levels and thick line represents distribution of confirmed levels. On the right grading zones are seen.

## 9 Learning Control

System offers multiple options for personalized learning. The simplest (and quite popular) option is that student chooses a comp to activate (learn, test). The system determines the most proper selection for learner's state (controller in closed-loop system). The information used at that point is the current state and predicted state after 16 weeks. The system reacts by searching tasks which has proper difficulty level (for this competence) and ordering them by last usage of the task (this avoids too frequent appearance of the same task – students have stated that this annoys them very much).

System also offers higher level controls where student does not choose a specific lowest level comp but a group of comps from those which are set up in the system. Note that a comp may appear in several higher level items. Now the system makes the selection of a task based on learner's current state and contents of the competence item. This enables the system to be more sophisticated – better prediction of the result is possible.

The last learning control introduced in 2015 is based on the structure where higher level competences are formed from comps which have logical content and are supported by task set which is closed in this group. The structure is multilevel and regular course appears on the third level. Whole curriculum has not modelled so far but the fifth level could be the proper one. Such big joins are not appropriate to use in real learning but may be base for giving out certificates. A very important application is representing and analyzing relations between classical units like courses.

Graphical representation is based on using volume measures (from XXL to S) representing sum of *w99*-s involved in particular group (volume from more than 80 % to less than 20 %) and average ability levels shown in color code. In Fig. 4 second level competence from one course is shown and in Fig. 5 more deep case in another course where all 3 laws make separate competences is shown. It is nothing strange that even well-known laws of nature may have very different content depending upon what is included (deepness of knowledge). In these two cases substantial difference is in experimental base, i.e. which lab experiments are included.

**Fig. 4.** Representation of one competence with selection of volume L which has ability level 99 (from 127). Clicking on the selected area opens task for this level.

**Fig. 5.** Ohm's and Kirchhoff's laws as separate competences in another course. More low level abilities are covered here.

These diagrams can be used for learning (clicking causes activation of task) and examining (demonstration to somebody) when clicking shows which task could be proposed to the holder of that diagram. For example, in the examining mode clicking on different zones will pop-up the task from particular layer. Due to modelling forgetting, both levels and tasks which will be shown are changing in time.

Important note: this environment is never closed and a person can always activate any part for testing-learning. All parameters are changed as the result of actions. This is also true at course level: even when formal grade is assigned and transferred to formal system, the course as competence item will stay open forever.

## 10 Certificate

As well-known, the MOOCs have very high drop-out rate and unfortunately, only completed course results produce certificate. If the person has learned less, the work has not graded and formal result is zero. Now we demonstrate the possibility of certificate based on data for person whose learning process was shown on Fig. 2 (this is not real certificate).

| |
|---|
| **We confirm that on Feb 26, 2015 20:00** |
| the person identified as *Firstname Lastname* has the following competences: |
| *Ohm's law* – level 85% of maximum for volume XXL and 95% for volume L |
| *Norton and Thevenin circuits* – 80% for XL |
| *Using multimeters* – 90% for XXL and ... |
| ... |

## 11 Conclusions

Two-dimensional mapping for learning results has been introduced where one axis represents acquired knowledge difficulty and another one – quality (ability level). Current state can be represented by a dot on the map or by curve(s) which show distribution of ability levels over difficulties (volumes). Difficulties can be connected to credit units and formal grades by mapping functions.

There are three main functions of using two-dimensional maps:

(1) showing current state of learning to students;
(2) saving knowledge obtained in course that has not been passed;
(3) using as prerequisites (initial state) for learning.

Using forgetting model is vital part of the model as degradation is natural process and for starting state old data may be misleading. Power law model [16] has been widely used for modelling of forgetting and it has been shown that it gives proper results in similar situations [17].

## References

1. Gütl, C., Rizzardini, R.H., Chang, V., Morales, M.: Attrition in MOOC: lessons learned from drop-out students. In: Uden, L., Sinclair, J., Tao, Y.-H., Liberona, D. (eds.) LTEC 2014. CCIS, vol. 446, pp. 37–48. Springer, Heidelberg (2014)
2. Jordan, K.: Initial trends in enrolment and completion of massive open online courses. Int. Rev. Res. Open Distance Learn. **15**(1), 133–160 (2014)
3. ILM. https://www.i-l-m.com/Learning-and-Development/Our-approach/Units-credit-values. Accessed 27 February 2015
4. Rozeboom, H.: Competence based learning. Bull. Univ. Agric. Sci. Vet. Med. Cluj-Napoca **63**(1), 365–367 (2006)
5. Sánchez, A.V., Ruiz, M.P.: Competence Based Learning - A Proposal for the Assessment of Generic Competences, p. 29. University of Deusto, Bilbao (2008)
6. Jaanus, M.: The Interactive Learning Environment for Mobile Laboratories, p. 59. Tallinn University of Technology Press, Tallinn (2011)

7. http://www.ehow.com/info_8053775_competencies.html. Accessed 8 April 2015
8. http://en.wikipedia.org/wiki/Competence_(human_resources). Accessed 8 April 2015
9. Kukk, V.: Student's behavior in free learning environment and formal education System. In: Uden, L., Sinclair, J., Tao, Y.-H., Liberona, D. (eds.) LTEC 2014. CCIS, vol. 446, pp. 187–194. Springer, Heidelberg (2014)
10. Baker, F.B.: The Basics of item Response Theory: ERIC Clearinghouse on Assessment and Evaluation. University of Maryland, College Park (2001)
11. Muzzylane. http://muzzylane.com/files/Feedback_Loops_and_Learning.pdf. Accessed 28 February 2015
12. Al-A'Ali, M.: IRT-Item response theory assessment for an adaptive teaching assessment system. In: 10th WSEAS International Conference on Applied Mathematics, pp. 518–522, Dallas, USA (2006)
13. Umbleja, K.: Students' grading control and visualisation in competence-based learning approach. In: IEEE Educon 2015, pp. 294–303 (2015)
14. Wozniak, P.A.: Two components of long-term memory. Acta Neurobiol. Exp. **55**, 301–305 (1995)
15. IRT. http://www.creative-wisdom.com/computer/sas/IRT.pdf. Accessed 28 February 2015
16. Wixted, J.T., Carpenter, S.K.: The Wickelgren power law and the Ebbinghaus savings function. Psychol. Sci. **18**(2), 133–134 (2007)
17. Kukk, V., Umbleja, K.: Analysis of forgetting in a learning environment. In: 13th Biennial Baltic Electronics Conference, pp. 335–338, Tallinn, Estonia, 3–5 October 2012

# Learning, Knowledge and Competence in Global Online-Universities: How Terminology Shapes Thinking

## A Theoretical Approach to Innovation and Change in Academic Distance Education

Sabine Siemsen(✉)

Fernuniversität in Hagen, Universitätsstraße 33c, 58084 Hagen, Germany
sabine.siemsen@fernuni-hagen.de

**Abstract.** Learning, Knowledge and Competence are popular terms in scientific discourses on the conception and evaluation of academic education. With increasing frequency, those take place in online-settings. This leads to an increasing heterogeneity not only in age and educational background, but also in social-cultural aspects and roles. The traditional way of seeing heterogeneity as challenge to be overcome, has to be changed into recognizing its enormous potential for networked learning processes. To foster such a new learning culture, it is necessary to scrutinize the hidden influence and unconscious patterns behind terminology. To enable global learning communities to successful networked learning, we need to define a holistic key-competence, a tool to enable enhancement in heterogeneous contexts, and a change in methods and criteria to conceptualize and evaluate such learning-scenarios. This paper aims to gain epistemological perspectives for practical use in global online-courses through a fusion of the terms learning, knowledge and competence.

**Keywords:** Learning · Online-Learning · Knowledge · Competence · Online-University · New learning culture · Meta-Communication · Connectivism · Interactionism · Interaction · Learning networks · Learning theory · Paradigm shift · Disruptive innovation · Heterogeneity

## 1 Introduction

> *"Define something in terms of its relationships using contrast and context instead of isolating it with a name"* [1]

Lifelong learning, independent learning and permanent readiness for training and participating in a continuing education, but also »Digital Society« and »Globally available Knowledge Networks«, global access to knowledge and education through networked means of communications; all these are keywords that are characteristic of Western societies on their way to become, or to be, a »Knowledge Society«. Related to these are questions about how to measure learning and knowledge, respectively how to evaluate and analyze learning-scenarios. Or more provocative: Can one measure


L. Uden et al. (Eds.): LTEC 2015, CCIS 533, pp. 28–42, 2015.
DOI: 10.1007/978-3-319-22629-3_3

learning-processes and knowledge in global learning-Communities and global courses at all?

Most discourses seem to take clear-cut definitions for granted, about what is perceived as learning, as knowledge and as learning outcomes. But the number and variety of definitions and theories proves that there are no clear-cut definitions, but a deviating terminology. Looking at learning-processes and knowledge requires views from different angles, needs to include contexts (individual, cultural, linguistic, social) and first and foremost there has to be an awareness of these different contexts and their influence on definitions and expectations. This is (or should be) a crucial precondition for developing criteria to develop, change or evaluate learning-processes in »Knowledge Societies« that claim to be open, and globally available, and fostering democracy in learning-chances.

Another term which is increasingly used in an inflationary manner, and related to the above terminology, is »Competence«. Competence is often compared or set in contrast to terms like the German "Bildung", or Knowledge, and its definitions are as fuzzy and various as those mentioned above. Therefore models and criteria of competence also can only work in subject to contexts, and require a critical reflection of underlying aspects. This may be difficult, but manageable as long as it is possible to define a frame of competence for a specific job, similar to a skillset. But what about so called »key-competences« such as »social competence«; a Competence that should be transferable to totally different contexts and challenges?

One reason, why discourses on these topics are highly controversial can be found taking a closer look at the focus of the underlying questions. A common thread of nearly all of them is the question how to measure learning, knowledge or competences, how to set and define learning goals and how to deal with a growing heterogeneity in communities of learners and to enable all of them to reach specific learning goals. The answers given range between being different in particular aspects to being totally antithetic, particularly when talking about innovations in online-learning-scenarios in the context of digitalization and networking.

These have the potential to be disruptive (see also Sect. 4), and therefor threaten established and traditional models and institutions So the answer is likely to be looked for in didactic settings, in the design of learning-environments or platforms, and in various facilities, featured through technology, social media and Web 2.0. These »solutions« are associated with the illusion to be able to control, transfer or measure learning-processes, knowledge and competences and, that way, provide security against innovations that seem to threaten existing institutions, models and approaches.

The need to keep up this security leads to talking about preconditions (necessary to enable learners to use these didactically designed learning-scenarios efficiently) in a way that gives the impression of apparently homogeneous learning-communities which do not exist. They do not exist within western societies, and even more will not be found in global online courses. If education and educational settings really aim to close or at least narrow the knowledge-gap, they have to stop regarding heterogeneity as something to be overcome and start using it as resource and potential to foster a new culture of learning and »teaching«.

Such a new learning culture will have to go beyond theories and approaches focusing individual learning and learning-outcomes. It has to cover individual as well as social and cultural knowledge and learning-processes; ontogenetic as well as phylogenetic development. Both depend on each other and each of them has an influence and effect on the other. Social and cultural knowledge is basis for and result of individual learning-processes.

Neither standardized didactical design, nor propaedeutic courses (aiming to switch heterogeneity to a pretended homogeneity; to a common »level« enabling to participate in a subsequent program of study) will meet the affordances of such a new learning-culture. Just as traditional and standardized tools and methods cannot measure, compare or evaluate such innovative courses, they cannot prove that learning has been successful at the end of or at a fixed point in the course. A new learning culture requires reflection, change and enlargement of tools and methods, a fusion of terminology and theories which will be possible only by assuring and designing a new understanding of learning, knowledge, competence and heterogeneity.

The above contradictions regarding discourses on terms, definitions, and the question, of whether and to what extent new theories and paradigms are necessary (or already existing), can be followed up and analyzed particularly well by using the example of academic online-courses. Connectivism's attempt to offer a new »learning theory for the digital age« and the subsequent growing attempts to offer »academic education for all« through MOOCs (Massive Open Online Courses) startled scientists and educational institutions, as well as learners interested in academic education. Whether it is adequate to talk of a revolution or evolution, of a digital tsunami, or to negate their disruptive potential by calling these attempts »selling old wine in new bottles« (see also [11]), will remain a question this paper does not aim to find an answer to. But irrespective of one's position on this, there remain many points hardly controversial:

- In the context of higher education both, the heterogeneity of students attending courses and participating in learning scenarios, as well as of those, who actively provide and share information on the net, is permanently growing.
- Roles change, traditional boundaries between teachers/learners, experts/lay people or producer/user mix and merge, thereby new learning cultures emerge.
- New learning cultures create and require other, altered and enhanced learning processes.
- Academic education can no longer aim to transfer or manage static knowledge, but has to enable learners to generate fluid knowledge through and within new contexts.
- »Big Data« (here defined as the fact that an enormous amount and variety of data and information are both, distributed through different sources within networks, as well as being analyzed and used in a variety of contexts and with diverse intentions) requires altered and new competences in order to be able to use those in a responsible, critical and reflective way; as well on the part of students as on the part of teachers and researchers.

## 2 How to Define and Relate Learning, Knowledge and Competence in Global Learning-Communities?

Speaking about a new learning culture implies that there are criteria and aspects that define the recent or traditional, conventional learning culture that is – or has to be – about to change. George Siemens identifies "*the following as the key elements of a weltanschauung that define formal education*" [10]:

1. Learning Needs can be defined.
2. Learning (success) can be controlled.
3. Learning communities (students) are similar (age, grade, knowledge base …).
4. Learning processes are coherent and structured.

Even if these seem to fit to define such criteria and aspects of a former (or recent) learning-culture, and even focus on aspects, like definitions and heterogeneity (students **not** being similar); they still remain within the trap of a common terminology of learning and knowledge that has to be reflected (and re-thought) before basing a new learning culture (which is terminology itself) upon it.

**Knowledge** is expressed in codes. Language is such a code and terminology therefore includes, respectively is, a symbol for experiences. To be conscious about this means, to be conscious that the same terminology, or the translation of terms, can have a totally different meaning for others, than for oneself. But it also means, one has first of all to be conscious about hidden or underlying assumptions of one's own language and to recognize that the choice of words may affect the way others respond to communication.

The only way to a knowledge-based **learning** that does not aim to recite given content, but to generate knowledge, and to make sure to start learning in a learning group or learning community, without risking to affect one another in an unintended and hindering way, is through meta-communication (see Definition in Sect. 4.2).

In the New Zealand Curriculum "*using language, symbols, and texts*" and "*participating and contributing*" are listened as a key competences. It states that students being competent in this area also "*confidently use ICT (including, where appropriate, assistive technologies) to access and provide information and to communicate with others.*" [7]

This does not merely describe the ability to be an active part of a network, but also states that "*students who participate and contribute in communities have a sense of belonging and the confidence to participate within new contexts.*" The last comes up to Bateson's learning levels, including more and more contexts, while the first emphasizes the aspect that learning requires to recognize and to meet needs: Belonging and feeling confident. Both imply, not only being able to communicate and thereby 'participate and contribute', but also – respectively in forefront and as a precondition – to be conscious of, and to pick out as central theme, the importance and influence of contexts being different, and of context markers to be rethought and altered. Meta-Communication can be a perfect tool to enable this process and will be (re)defined in Sect. 4.2.

The relationships described above, seem to turn traditional relations between learning and knowledge bottom up. Those usually define »teaching« as a process where knowledge is transferred and imparted on students, and »learning« as a process of memorizing and adopting contents. In contrast to these definitions, the above description defines »learning« as a process where contents are critically reflected and transferred into other, wider contexts, and new knowledge is generated. In Gregory Bateson's [1] words: You have to change the way of thinking.

Another term used in the New Zealand Curriculum [7] quoted above is »competence«. The New Zealand Curriculum states that a competence (the competence to use language, symbols, and texts) results in trust or confidence (confidently use ICT).

Even if there are various and different competence models or competence profiles, they usually describe a set of skills, and knowledge, and abilities one is capable to use in different contexts and situations, that are visible as performance, and are results of a learning process. So »learning« leads to generating knowledge, and to gaining competence which in turn results in confident acting in various contexts.

The terms »Learning, Knowledge and Competence« therefore are inseparably related, but to use them as synonyms, or in a way that does not reflect on relations and interconnections, hinders to foster and come up to a new learning culture.

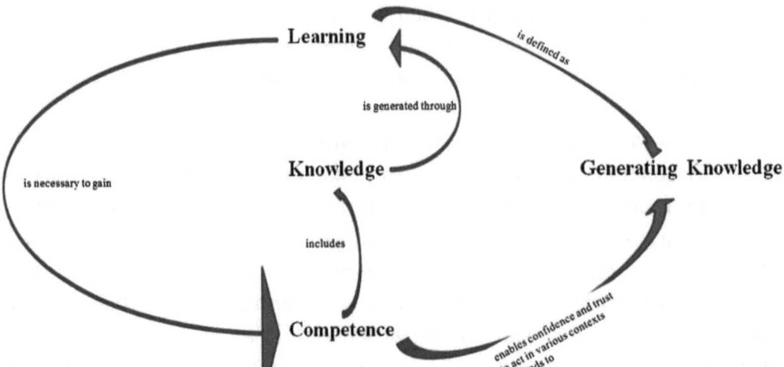


**Fig. 1.** Terminology in a new learning culture (Source: Authors' own compilation)

## 3 Heterogeneity as Constituting Element of a New Learning Culture

*"Relating to others is about interacting effectively with a diverse range of people in a variety of contexts. This competency includes the ability to listen actively, recognize different points of view, negotiate, and share ideas"* [7]

This quotation of the New Zealand Curriculum [7] shows that some countries and school curricula already have arrived at a point, where heterogeneity is not regarded as something to be overcome, and the own »symbol-system« (see Sect. 2) is not premise and condition, but has to be negotiated and (at least) to take different points of view in account. "*Relating to others*" is listed as key competence and defined as a competence that enables students to be "*open to new learning and able to take different roles in different situations*" – that's exactly what was described as new learning culture.

The described capability to be open to **new** learning is a need, that Gregory Batson [1] focused on, when he developed his model of different learning levels. And learning processes in a new learning culture, as it is defined in this paper, can no longer be described as »to learn to learn« (Bateson's Level II), as this does not imply "*to cope with a heterogeneity not only relating to different generations [...] but to formations of learning communities which bring together learners and teachers speaking different languages and having different cultural and social backgrounds [and therefore require] commonly found and shared* ***context markers*** *as pre-condition to reach a level of what Bateson defines as Learning III.*" [1]

So »Learning« isn't a clear cut process and the question of 'how to learn in the digital age' can clearly not be answered by finding a recipe or magic cure that then can cure all problems and answer all questions. But one can start with differentiating between two large dimensions or categories of learning:

- Learning as a process that enables to **remind** and to **reproduce** given content, like for instance vocabulary or mathematical formula.
- Learning as a process that enables constant **enhancement** by **reflecting** and »**rethinking** content«, whereas defining »content« as term that can include texts as well as any other explanations about »how things work«.

In-between and overlapping those two dimensions stands a definition of learning as »understanding«. In-between, because understanding can have the meaning of 'just' understanding formula or grammar, but also the meaning of beginning to reflect rules and explanations and to start thinking about other ways that might be easier, better or more adequate. Which – taking place in a heterogeneous learning-community – will (or at least has the potential to) lead to including and reflecting more and more different contexts and to become aware of one's own as well as of other's context-markers; which is, what was described above as a Learning Process of Bateson's Level III.

The following section focusses on (new) learning-processes, taking place within a »Learning-Landscape Global Online-University«. Here further dimensions of learning-processes come together:

- **Academic Learning** which usually is understood as formal learning that bases on at least a rough common level of basic knowledge that (should) enable(s) a deeper and more sophisticated way to deepen theoretical (and more and more also) practical knowledge within a specific study-field;

- **Online-Learning** as a process that is usually described as being demanding, both in regard to
  - being able to **self-control and self-motivate learning**-processes as well as to
  - a certain level of »**media-competence**«.

All of those will be taken in account and fused in the following sections, and operationalized for the further discourse as belonging to the category of learning processes that (should) go far beyond reminding and reproducing, but dwell deep on reflecting and rethinking »things«.

The term »Competence« will therefore be used (and finally – through the description of enhancement-competence – redefined) as a possibility, as well to distinguish academic learning from 'just' reciting (and believing) given static expert-knowledge, as well as to emphasize its potential to change the culture of learning into a culture that deserves to be spoken of as »new learning culture« for literally global learning-processes.

# 4 Learning Landscape Global Online-University

> *"In a world where students can learn anything from anyone anywhere online, why, he asked, would parents continue to pay exorbitant fees to send them to a campus somewhere for all of their schooling? Why not let them travel the world, experience different cultures, learn at home and in apprenticeships, and receive a high-quality education, for example that would be virtually free?"* [6]

Donaldson et al. [5] differentiate between innovations being sustaining, and innovations being disruptive. The first describes innovations that base on existing models or theories that are improved through the innovation. This category fits to most of the (first and recent) approaches of Online- and/or Blended Learning. Traditional institutions use technological tools, elements of Online or eLearning, to improve existing settings. They aim to reach more »customers« respectively potential learners; those who may not participate in »classical brick and mortal« learning scenarios because of various reasons and therefore profit from the flexibility of online-courses.

The second kind of innovations does not aim to improve traditional settings but to come into an existence as an innovating system of its own. Being disruptive describes innovations that – at least in the beginning – are just easier to handle, more cost-efficient, and often they are even of lower quality than established offers. But due to their usability and attractiveness they succeed very soon to improve and to reach a quality on a higher level than those of the systems being or becoming dispersed.

The greatest dangers those systems have to be afraid of are, not being able to reach a high quality fast enough or – a much more subtle danger – being »absorbed« by the traditional systems. Those may prevent the threat by hindering the innovation to become disruptive, by integrating it in the existing system, and therefore change a disruptive innovation into a sustaining one. [5]

The above descriptions of the necessity of new learning-processes for a new learning culture and the necessity to become conscious of the influence of terminology, shows that »just« the use and establishments of terms can lead to an attitude of hype or defense, depending on one's position within or outside established traditional institutions or sciences. A recent example was described on last year's LTEC in the paper »Connectivism and Interactionism Reloaded« [11] that focused on Connectivism and MOOCs as innovations whose potentials were (and are) controversially discussed by focusing on prefixes and acronyms instead of what stands behind those. Similar discussions can be found in discourses dealing with the term »Competence« which is, as mentioned in this paper's introduction, often compared or set in contrast to other terms like Vocational-Training, Knowledge, the German »Bildung« or Learning-Goals in academic courses.

### 4.1 The Perception of »Competence« in Higher Education

> *"Fueled by interest from hundreds of higher education institutions and the Department of Education, competency-based learning will gain steam. Coupled with online learning, as my colleague Michelle Weise has written, it will constitute a disruptive force in higher education unlike any we've seen."* [6]

The above quotation is one of "Five Predictions For Education In 2015" published by Forbes and written by Michal Horn, cofounder and Executive Director of Education at a "*nonprofit, nonpartisan think tank, dedicated to improving the world through disruptive innovation*". He is also co-author of a recently published book about »Using Disruptive Innovation to Improve Schools«. Being conscious that Forbes, a leading US Business Magazine, known for its lists and rankings, is not really a scientific resource for educational science, it nevertheless underlines the statement of the proposal of this paper, as it shows that

- innovations, having the potential to be disruptive, are threatening institutions;
- this fear is not really unsubstantiated;
- that the upcoming discussion about academic courses, having to become more competence-oriented, reinforce MOOCs or more general Global Online-Universities to become a disruptive innovation
- this innovation is reinforced through Technology, Digitalization and Social Media

As discussed above, the »question of competence« is a question that can only be answered considering very carefully contexts and objective target of learning scenarios it shall be applied to. So a shift to competence-based learning in higher education, especially in global online-courses, must consider not only which competences learners should be enabled to gain through the course, but also which competences are needed to participate in a course taking place in a virtual learning environment, being open to learners that are heterogeneous in various aspects and levels, and offering a maximum range of flexibility and freedom of learning (which is just the other side of challenging with a maximum need of not only self-organization but also self-motivation and orientation in different communities and platforms).

## 4.2 Competence in (or for?) Global Online-Courses

Talking of Competences in and for Online-Courses suggests to talk about media-competence. German (speaking) discourses use to base or build on Baackes four dimensions of media competence that are Media Critique, Media Knowledge, Media Use and Media Production. Manuela Pietrass (2007) concludes that "*Media critique is a competence which is not based on communication, such as producing and handling. Instead, it is what media competence allows man to be: a critical actor in regard to media communication.*" [8]. Following consequently the central theme of this paper, namely that learning, (generating) knowledge, and competence is a spiral process, within a system where each change in one component leads to changing the other components, shows that this conclusion leads into a trap of linear thinking. As competences presuppose learning, and as reaching further learning levels results from including other contexts, and (meta)communication being the »tool« that enables setting new context markers, a competence that "*allows man to be a critical actor in regard to media communication*" [8] cannot "*not base on communication*" [8]. Being a critical actor therefor has to include being critically aware of one's own and other's premises on and definitions of Knowledge and Learning. This has to base on communication, in order to lead to media communication that comes up to the expectations described.

This reveals another aspect of high relevance in regard to the interplay of (Meta-) Communication and the importance of the dimension of media critique, within a model of media competence: That of changed roles. If (Meta-)Communication is described as the tool, enabling learners to critically reflect on underlying premises, different understanding of what learning, teaching and knowledge is, one of the most important tasks teachers have to accomplish is, to help and enable learners to such a kind of communication (competence for global online-courses) in the forefront of trying to »teach« specific howsoever »competence-based« course-content (competence in global online-courses).

The following quotation will lead over to creating a new terminology, respectively a competence aiming to be holistic and general, as a key competence to learning and development on Bateson's Learning-Level III – individual as well as social-cultural.

Anja C. Wagner [14] asked in her weblog if and how »Collaboration« can be described or defined as competence. She finally preferred an answer that came from another weblog »Cisco« [4] asking: "*Collaboration: What does it really mean*?" and which came up with an own definition namely: "*Collaboration is highly diversified teams working together inside and outside a company with the purpose to create value by improving innovation, customer relationships and efficiency while leveraging technology for effective interactions in the virtual and physical space.*"

Transferred from the context of vocational workplace-learning to academic learning in Online Courses, this lead to the following adoption as Definition for Meta-Communication in Global Online-Courses:

»**Meta-Communication** is highly heterogeneous learner-communities cooperatively re-defining and putting in question definitions of **Learning** and **Knowledge**, in front of and while participating online-courses; with the purpose to set new commonly found context-markers, to create value by generating knowledge, while efficiently and consciously developing **Enhancement-Competence** in and for learning networks, including individual, social-cultural and digital-technological networks«.

### 4.3 A Shift in the Way of Thinking: From Heterogeneity as Challenge for Competence Based Development, to Enhancement-Competence Through Heterogeneity?

Learning within all contexts is enhancement, and includes for instance the development of cognition, social competences, communication-competence and technological competence; the latter not only meaning technological skills, but also the capability to include technological innovations into individual and social enhancement. Information-Competence includes media-competence, »traditional« as well as digital literacy; but also communication-competence. Meanwhile most institutions and provider of online-learning try to include at least some of this variations of competence in the conception and evaluation of their learning-settings. But nevertheless traditional and conventional learning settings have to regard heterogeneity as a challenge that has to be overcome, to fulfil key-element no.3 (Students respectively learning-groups are similar; see Sect. 2 [10]). Learning Goals, content, preconditions to and evaluation of such settings seek to transfer heterogeneity into homogeneity. In return, such an understanding inevitably leads to standardized didactical designs and propaedeutic courses (aiming to switch heterogeneity to a pretended homogeneity; to a common "level" enabling to participate in a subsequent program of study) as solutions to the »problem« of a rising heterogeneity.

A new learning culture will perceive heterogeneity as constituting element, as a resource of plenty contexts that enable learning-processes of Level III (see Sect. 3, first paragraph and [1]). But this is a statement that still does not give an answer to the question what exactly is the basis element, enabling such learning-processes? The mere existence of heterogeneity is necessary but not yet sufficient.

As described in Sect. 2 and above, the terminology of Learning, Knowledge and Competences is multifaceted, but nevertheless there can be shown general connections, influences and relationships by stepping back from a point of view restricted by specific scientific disciplines and methods, and being conscious of the aspect that terminology is both shaped by contexts (as goals, culture, language) and shaping contexts itself.

Figure 1 (Sect. 2) already visualized the relationship between learning, knowledge and competence on a general level. While Sects. 4.1 and 4.2 have broken down the term Competence to the specific field of Global Online Courses, this section steps back to a general level, and includes individual as well as social-cultural dimensions. It carves out their interplay, and finally comes to a new and more holistic definition and term: **Enhancement-Competence**. This terminology aims first of all to developing a deductive understanding of Enhancement-Competence, as a competence that enables a global understanding of heterogeneity as indispensable pre-condition for all processes of learning and enhancing learning processes.

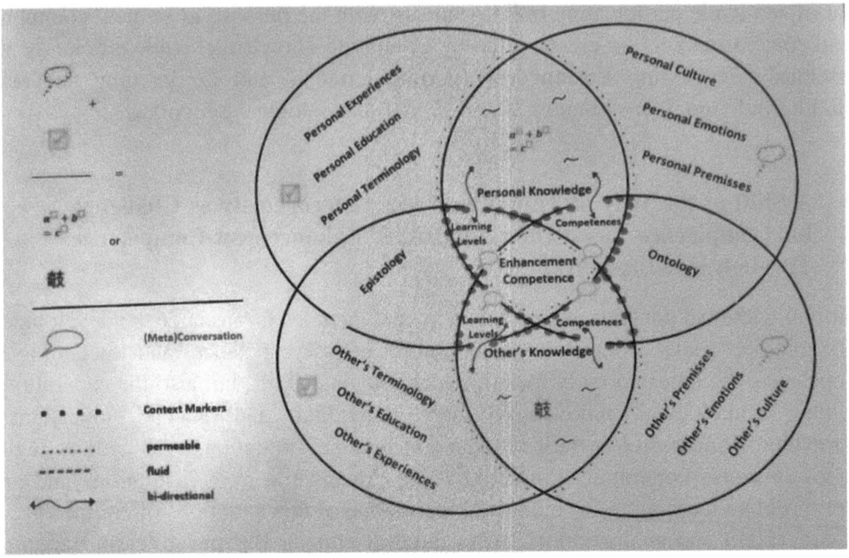


**Fig. 2.** Dimensions of enabling enhancement-competency (Source: Authors' own compilation)

Figure 2 shows four "key-dimensions" that influence the development of Enhancement Competence. The two circles right-hand are dimensions of the »sensual« world and show, read from the outward layer to the inward the influence and interdependency of culture, emotions and premises; the two circles left-hand are dimensions of experiences, education and thereof resulting terminology. Both of them exist on a social-cultural level (phylogenesis) as well as on an individual level (ontogenesis) and both base on and influence each other.

The circle and its different intersections give a model of a self-sustaining system with permeable frontiers and fluid peripheries – a change in one part of the system has influence on each other part of it. The intersections between the upper and lower circles (personal and social cultural) lead to different learning levels and different definitions and understandings of competence; individual ones and cultural ones whereas the intersections between the dimensions of the more »sensual« and the »experienced« world result in what can be described as knowledge. Therefor knowledge is permanently changed and (re)generated.

And where »Personal Knowledge« consequently has often proved to be helpful and therefor got familiar and easy to explain (which is symbolized by the formula); »Other's Knowledge« appears strange and difficult or impossible to comprehend (symbolized by the (from a Western point of view) cryptic characteristics. And as »personal« and »others« is always depending on the particular point of view and the »others« always exist in a superior number, the chance to learn through irritation, the need to reflect and to rearrange premises and terminology is the higher the bigger the heterogeneity in learning-communities is. Where brick and mortal universities bring together at the utmost different social and educational backgrounds and (recently also) generations, global learning online courses offer real heterogeneity in all kind of contexts, individual as well as social-cultural.

As symbolized by the speech bubble in the »windows« between the innermost intersections, it is not enough just to mix; only by communication and especially by meta communication about what is »brought by« from the outer circles it is possible to come to changing what Gregory Bateson calls "*context-markers*". [1]

And the permanent reflection of one's own and other's experiences, education, terminology (language!), culture, emotions and premises enables to enhancement-competence and generates new knowledge. And having reached enhancement competence enables to gaining all other »kinds of competences« by constantly reflecting and re-setting context-markers.

Defining Enhancement-Competence as a Key Competence that enables to learning-processes coming up to Bateson's Level III, and proclaiming Meta-Communication as a tool that leads to Enhancement-Competence, consequently leads to the question how to analyze this processes and how to conceptualize courses and learning-goals within such a New Learning Culture. So, such a changed system inevitable brings along and requires a shift in methods; methods of »measuring« efficiency, methods of evaluating courses, criteria for learning-goals and methods of exams and certification. Only if all of these components will come together, to change the system from within and holistically, only then there is a chance to improve and change learning cultures and learning landscapes in academic learning (for sure not only there, but this is the part of the puzzle this paper focusses on, and which – as shown above – will per se influence and therefor change all the other parts too).

## 5 Do Innovation and Change in Online-Education Require Innovation and Change in Methods?

> *"Exponentially developing knowledge and complexification of society requires nonlinear models of learning (process) and knowing (state). We cannot sustain ourselves as learning/knowing beings in the current climate with our current approaches. Networked (social, technological) approaches scale in line with changes, but require a redesign of how we teach, learn (and see learning), and come to know."* [9]

Reading and comparing literature and studies on competences leads to the impression that criteria shall be first of all measurable. The question, if the concept being evaluated, enables to develop competencies, questions about the »How« instead of »If or If not«, seem subordinate - if they are asked at all. Resulting data shall first and foremost enable to compare: Learning Societies, Learning Outcomes, and Learning-Economy. They foster competition and improvement - but in the sense of getting better results, and higher ranks than other countries, or institutions, instead of defining improvement as enhancement. The first being a question of economy, the latter a question of individual as well as social-cultural development in the sense of the above described new learning-culture.

As long as the success of learning is defined in this traditional way of measurable (homogenous) results that ignore, that "*there are too many factors that influence what grade a person earns in a course, things like developmental readiness, life circumstances, motivation, relationship with the instructor and classmates, physical well-being, the teaching methods and effectiveness of the instructor, distractions or lack thereof, and the classroom culture.*" [3] methods will be blind towards an individual (and, as described above, thereof resulting social-cultural) enhancement that results from courses, taking in account these aspects, by making them conscious, and including them in forefront of and going along with dealing with specific study-contents.

One of the most commonly used and found criticism on MOOCs is the low completion rate, especially compared to the high number of »participants«, respectively number of inscribers to such offers. Re-thinking effort as enhancement, and taking into account that each participant starts from an individual point of complex knowledge and learning patterns and expectation, within a specific and multifaceted learning-context, learning-success can no longer be fixed on a common point in time and knowledge, as for instance the completion rate does. Neither can standard tests; passed by all participants at the same time, and reflecting only a small variety of all the above listed factors (compare [3]).

Questioning those standard criteria and methods finally is a question of priority: Should evaluations and studies analyze concepts in regard to measurable (and comparable) data or in regard to underlying concepts enabling students to develop competences and to enhance?

So, when Tschofen et al. (2013) state that "*connectivism is viewed as a viable description of learning that incorporates emergent disciplinary and interdisciplinary understandings that may not yet have been tested in traditional forms*." [12] this should provoke posing the question, if this is possible at all? And would it still make sense to define learning in a way that could be "*tested in traditional forms*"?

> *"We can't see the way out yet because we are thinking within the existing structure. [...] Knowledge – and the affiliated concepts of learning and understanding – is a function of 'the network'"* [9]

## 6 Conclusion

The subsequent argumentation of this paper got behind and beyond terminology, to work out interdependencies and relationships, to follow up Gregory Bateson's advice to "*define something in terms of its relationships using contrast and context instead of isolating it with a name [... because] you cannot study one end of a relationship and make any sense. What you will make is disaster*" [2]

It aimed at showing that

- Needs, expectations, premises and communication influence individual as well as social-cultural learning-processes;
- Heterogeneity is the constituting element of a new learning culture that
  - comes up to a learning level enabling individual as well as social-cultural learning-processes and

  - leads to enhancement and to generating knowledge instead of consuming and preserving static "expert"-knowledge
- terminology is a mighty tool to shape thinking and acting,
- meta-communication is the "tool" enabling to make these aspects aware

because

- different definitions of learning, knowledge and competence not only lead to misunderstanding, but also are a danger to a new learning-culture,

as they can be used (and are used!) to

- reinforce and sustain conventional systems
- to turn heterogeneity into (assumed) homogeneity

and this way

- hinder learning processes to lead to enhancement
- hinder learning processes to generate new knowledge
- lead to individual and social-cultural remaining on what Bateson described as level 2 of learning (see Sect. 3 and [11])

A global online-university has an enormous potential to become a place where academic learning processes in real heterogeneity can lead to individual and social-cultural enhancement. First steps have already be taken and the question if Global Online Courses succeed being disruptive or 'just' lead to sustain traditional systems by adding some online-elements will remain an important task for further research. And it will depend on the openness, ability and willingness to become conscious of the impact of the use of terminology and resetting frames and contexts markers.

> "*It is necessary to rethink the foundational principles that can guide policy and practice for the future of learning in a changing world.*" [13]

## References

1. Bateson, G.: Steps to an Ecology of Mind: Collected Essays in Anthropology, Psychiatry, Evolution, and Epistemology. Chandler Publication Co., San Francisco (1972)
2. Bateson, N.: An Ecology of Mind: A Daughter's Portrait of Gregory Bateson. Remember the Future: Carl-Auer Verlag, DGSF, mindjazz, Alive (2010)
3. Bull, B.: Why do we have letter grades? http://etale.org/main/2013/07/15/is-the-letter-grade-system-an-outdated-educational-technology/
4. Dominguez, C.: Collaboration: What Does it really mean? (2011). http://blogs.cisco.com/news/collaboration-what-does-it-really-mean
5. Donaldson, J.: Massively open: How massive open online courses changed the world (2013)
6. Horn, M.B.: Unprecedented Opportunities: Online Learning Explosion Empowers GenDIY: Weblog-Post (2015). http://gettingsmart.com/2015/02/unprecedented-opportunities-online-learning-explosion-empowers-gendiy/
7. Ministry of Education: The New Zealand Curriculum: Key competencies. http://nzcurriculum.tki.org.nz/The-New-Zealand-Curriculum/Key-competencies

8. Pietrass, M.: Digital literacy research from an international and comparative point of view. Res. Comp. Int. Educ. **2**(1), 1–12 (2007)
9. Siemens, G.: Connectivism: Learning conceptualized through the lens of today's world (2007). http://www.elearnspace.org/presentations/connectivism_online_OCC2007.ppt
10. Siemens, G.: Technologically Externalized Knowledge and Learning (2009). http://www.connectivism.ca/?p=181
11. Siemsen, S., Jansen, R.: Connectivism and interactionism reloaded knowledge networks in the cloud. In: Uden, L., Sinclair, J., Tao, Y.-H., Liberona, D. (eds.) LTEC 2014. CCIS, vol. 446, pp. 1–12. Springer, Heidelberg (2014)
12. Tschofen, C., Mackness, J.: Connectivism and dimensions of individual experience. In: Paolucci, R. (ed.) Learning With MOOCs: Massive Open Online Courses, pp. 101–120. Interlearning Company LLC, East Norriton Pennsylvania (2013)
13. UNESCO. Rethinking Education (2009). http://www.unesco.org/new/en/education/themes/leading-the-international-agenda/rethinking-education/
14. Wagner, C.A.: Was bedeutet eigentlich Kollaboration als Kompetenz (2015). http://ununi.tv/de/acw/was-bedeutet-eigentlich-kollaboration-als-kompetenz

# MOOCs and the Integration of Social Media and Curation Tools in e-Learning

Jean-Eric Pelet[1(✉)], Marlene A. Pratt[2], and Stéphane Fauvy[3]

[1] KMCMS, LEMNA, IAE-IEMN – Nantes University, 33 rue Laurence Savart, 75020 Paris, France
je.pelet@gmail.com
[2] Griffith Business School, Griffith University, Gold Coast, Australia
m.pratt@griffith.edu.au
[3] ESSCA School of Management, LUNAM Université, Angers, France
s.fauvy@gmail.com

**Abstract.** MOOCs (Massive Open Online Courses) have gained popularity for e-learning purposes. Effectiveness depends on platform interface design and management, which should create student cohesiveness and optimize collaboration. A MOOC prototype was developed and e-learning applications were pilot-tested for one semester with a total of 160 students from graduate courses in a French business school. Students used a mobile supported e-learning environment and reported their experiences through the writing of a synthesis, the building of a CMS (Content Management System) and the elaboration of a content curation system.

**Keywords:** MOOC · Social media · Mobile learning · Knowledge management · Constructivist learning

## 1 Introduction

The "Learning For All" movement is currently stimulating active debates in the education space around the world. These debates combined with the emergence of new forms of blended learning as well as the arrival of Massive Open Online Courses (MOOCs) and other forms of open educational resources (OERs) have made e-learning front page news across all continents and societies.

Collaborative learning is one of the key instructional strategies that are being adopted worldwide. Collaborative learning has gained an increasing role in educational research and practices in recent years. Computer-supported collaborative learning (CSCL) is a pedagogical approach wherein learning takes place via social interaction using a computer or through the Internet [1]. This is possible thanks to the use of social media, enabling students to correspond, chat and comment on content related to a course. Many new technologies are emerging which offer new ways of teaching and learning, such as ubiquitous learning technologies, gesture-based computing, augmented reality technology, and learning analytics. Students who have grown up amidst new technologies are keen to use and adopt new devices, apps and various kinds of new ICT. Indeed,


L. Uden et al. (Eds.): LTEC 2015, CCIS 533, pp. 43–53, 2015.
DOI: 10.1007/978-3-319-22629-3_4

collaborative learning aims to promote students' individual cognition, group cognition and community cognition through the use of appealing, fun, easy-to-use and instantaneous tools. These tools enable students to communicate between each other, as well as sharing documents and ideas, as if they were in the same classroom or spaces. The new generation of students are experiential, interactive and social learners, multi-taskers, structured and relevant learners, and technology immersed learners [1].

The CSCL setting is characterized by the sharing and construction of knowledge among participants using technology as their primary means of communication or as a common resource [2]. The latter can be implemented online and in classroom learning environments, which can take place synchronously or asynchronously. The appropriate processes, assessment and interaction analysis methods can provide insight into effectiveness of collaborative learning in face-to-face and online contexts. Accompanying CSCL, ubiquitous e-learning is a notion that is becoming a pertinent factor in today's education [2] and [3]. Recent studies show increased rates of learning outcomes as a result of applying traditional and e-learning hybrid models [5]. Many universities are starting to experiment with hybrid educational models mixing digital technologies and social media with traditional teaching approaches. Universities are naturally migrating towards a more digitally coherent system of operation that is less expensive than the traditional model. Since the high cost of higher education is considered as one of the principal problems of today's educational system [5], a technological shift towards digital learning environments is a partial solution.

MOOCs may be a catalyst in the process of re-imagining higher education or re-enchanting e-learning, due to the powerful elements constituting the MOOC architecture. Whether MOOCs are part of a global open education initiative or a for-profit education model, today there is certainly growing R&D interest, as well as entrepreneurial attention to this form of learning. There is, however, substantial criticism and typical bystander skepticism about MOOCs. The negative appeal is largely a result of reports indicating low completion rates that many MOOCs encounter.

This article gives an overview of the development and application of MOOCs. It integrates social media and curation tools as a hot topic in e-learning and presents concrete ideas on how to enable and support learning in higher education with the use of electronic devices and free Internet tools. The paper focuses on learning as a collaborative process in which students developed their own functional knowledge management tools and actively participated in an expansive learning experience. Interaction between students and lecturers were formed by a self-regulated group of students, embracing one of the primary characteristics of MOOCs: collaborative development and constructivist learning situations.

## 2 Review of Literature

### 2.1 MOOCs

MOOCs can be defined as aggregate classes from multiple organizations, universities and schools, offered on a single digital platform. They are designed in a way enabling the delivery of specific courses to thousands of recipients simultaneously. There are many courses on a wide array of themes and topics available on MOOCs, most of them for free or at a very low cost. Gaebel [14] defined MOOCs as free, credit-less online courses where people can participate without limits on the amount of classes they can enroll in. A small proportion of MOOCs are financed by examination and diploma activities and new business models emerge regularly. De Waard [15] reinforced this definition by describing them as “time and cost efficient”. There are free tools available for building these courses, languages can be chosen and changed freely, tools can be tailored to the preferences of the participants and courses can be set up quickly. MOOCs can be beneficial to students as an informal means of supplementing their knowledge base and enhancing their productivity. Finally, they are cross-disciplinary and promote exchanges between the different fields of expertise [16].

The MOOC term connotes Open Access, which means that learners don’t need to be registered at any particular college, university or campus as a prerequisite to enrollment. One teacher can be responsible for hundreds or thousands of students. The large number of enrollees and courses allows MOOCs to offer two approaches to instructional design: (1) peer-review, group collaborations through “crowd sourcing” or (2) Automated feedback and self-assessments [17]. Often, MOOC students watch short videos (blended learning) which are graded either by computers or by other students. One of the problems encountered by students is the rather limited possibility of interacting with other students [18]. Additionally, [19] explain that learners may receive inferior educational experiences when receiving their education through MOOCs due to the lack of a teacher-student relationship. On the other hand, MOOCs make higher education more affordable and could benefit the global economy by helping students and workers become lifelong learners.

According to [20], the motivating factors fueling support for MOOCs include:

1. An altruistic initiative to increase access to higher education worldwide,
2. The desire to stay up-to-date with new pedagogical approaches without being forced into using online techniques, regardless if the emergent techniques takes a different form than MOOCs over time,
3. A desire to broadly increase their personal visibility in Academia.

Also, learners can make use of the wide range of technology-based multimedia activities in order to:

- Manage and reflect their learning process
- Create content for collaborating and communicating with others
- Grade their peers and receive peer evaluation
- Read and curate content and share it with their peers

### 2.2 e-Learning and Mobile Learning (m-Learning)

The design of an e-learning platform is of paramount importance for influencing learner interaction and behavior as well as the overall success of the learning experience.

Learners can benefit from the socialization of their platform which fosters the multiplication of social links, facilitating the curation of content to read, learn and share [21]. As pointed out by [22], with increased popular access to information and knowledge anywhere, anytime, the role of education is challenged and the relationships between education, society, and technology are now more dynamic than ever.

One of the most interesting aspects of m-learning is that users have the capacity to make documentations while they are in the field; thus bridging the gap between theoretical and practical knowledge [23, 24]. When we speak of m-learning, we refer to wireless hand-held devices such as personal digital assistants (PDAs), smartphones and tablets. Often these systems operate with wireless access protocols (WAPs) and wireless markup language (WML). The lightweight architecture of these protocols makes accessibility possible with a wide range of affordable devices. Although learning on mobile devices may never completely replace traditional in class teaching, it is widely accepted that if used correctly, this technology offers a significant complement to the learning environment [25]. Wireless handheld devices can be individualized to meet the needs and desires of its user, enhancing the collaborative process with automated information such as real-time course updates, deadlines and notifications. The learning sphere has become ubiquitous, centralized around the learner and increasingly oriented towards creating flexibility and optimizing content delivery [26]. Students enjoy using wireless handheld devices and appreciate the new age interactive and ubiquitous learning environment. These types of interactive social tools have broken the barrier between the academic and private spheres, and foster a sense of pleasure in taking part in the online *learning game* [4]. Learners are more successful and have higher retention rates when they enjoy the learning process. As wireless handheld devices become more affordable, the potential for integrating this technology into learning environments becomes more considerable [27].

## 2.3 Social Media and e-Learning

In 2013, 89 % of European Internet users ages 16 to 24 years old, participated in some form of social networking [7]. As a part of modernizing the traditional approach to education, many higher education institutions (and educators) find themselves in a situation where they must adapt to the heightened use of social media and create a link to educational engagement [28]. The majority of university students have mobile technology and use social media regularly; all the more reason why these elements should be integrated into tertiary level education [29]. As the technological framework is already in place, it is just a question of creating structured learning environments with the integration of these tools. Social networks such as Facebook have potentially positive benefits to teaching and learning, particularly with the development of educational micro-communities [30]. These micro-communities can be complemented with the use of other Web 2.0 applications that permit blogging, collaborative content sharing, podcasting and multimedia sharing. Structured learning environments can be created with simple collaborative features such as "Facebook groups" which can act as collaborative discussion boards in synchronous and asynchronous settings. Once the micro-community is established through the development of a group, other social media applications such as collaborative WIKIs can be integrated in order to add structural consistency.

Students are more likely to be connected simultaneously on their Facebook network than on any formal University Web portal and this enhances the potential for collaborative development between learning community members. Some universities have integrated micro-blogging on Twitter into the context of lecture hall discussions as students communicate synchronously with each other and the professor during the course. Certain studies show that the integration of micro-blogging into the educative experience successfully promoted active and continual feedback from the students [4]. Social media supports various innovations including: content creation, enhanced learner connectedness and collaboration [31]. Social media applications provide capacities which face-to-face instructions do not such as individualized tools permitting knowledge exchange and consultation without temporal or spatial barriers. In terms of education, social media is predominantly used by youth as a means of informal learning [32]. However, the gap between informal and formal learning can be filled with the implementation of structured learning spaces such as micro-communities and interactive videos that contain integrated quizzes.

## 3 Methodology

During an e-marketing course, 4 lectures were given to masters students in a Business School (BS) between September 2013 and January 2014. These 4 lectures included:

- Web 2.0 Strategy
- Fundamentals of e-business and e-marketing
- Communitarian and sensorial marketing
- New Marketing

Approximately 160 students from the BS used a main website (www.kmcms.net - Knowledge & Management System/Content Management System) to follow the course and prepare for their exam. This platform provided students with up-to-date lectures and theoretical content (books and articles). The platform also included roughly 1,700 posts ranging from one to several pages of content depending on the source. The platform was accessible to students, after registering and choosing the course they wanted to attend. Four "image links" were positioned on the homepage of www.kmcms.net redirecting students to 4 CMS (Content Management Systems). Websites on *e-business and e-marketing fundamentals* were available to the students. These 2 CMS used responsive templates enabling students to read, comment, grade, and write. They provided:

- Lectures on the two evoked topics
- Explanations regarding the content and revisions for the exam
- Explanations about their assessment during the course.

Two other curation platforms were available for the purpose of concatenating and curating content from the Web, such as blogs, organizational/business websites and management websites.[1] These curating sites were used in order to prepare topics on New Marketing as well as Communitarian and sensorial marketing.

Students are assuming an evolving role as the principal players in their educational endeavors. Within the course students were assigned a role as autonomous researchers and had the responsibility of curating content with a unique knowledge management tool, that they themselves created. Content curators are individuals who continually find, organize and share the best and most pertinent content related to specific issues on the Web. Although this was a strictly academic endeavor, students agreed that this newly acquired capacity for effectively managing massive amounts of information would benefit their professional futures. There are a few aspects about the term "content curator" that are worth being highlighted, such as the fact that content curators are people and not robots. Effective content curation cannot be performed solely with the use of an algorithm. In order to obtain high-quality information, its best to have a domain expert administering the curation in order to ensure finely tuned selectivity. This knowledge management process should be implemented continually and administrators should be consistently up-to-date with the domain that they are focusing on. Third, a curator is not simply regurgitating any content that they come across as they must be very discerning, discriminative, and selective in only sharing the "best and most relevant" content. Lastly, a curator focuses on "specific issues". They do not curate on all of the topics available. Instead, they specialize on specific topics and over time they may have the opportunity to become an authority and perhaps even a thought leader on those topics.

The landing page on our platform was linked to a Wordpress CMS platform. Landing pages are an essential element in online marketing. The first goal of the landing page is to convince the user to act. The same happens in an e-learning context. Students must be convinced and involved when studying, especially on a MOOC where nobody is there to instruct their actions. The landing page was made using a responsive web design. Responsive web design enhances accessibility by creating websites constructed to adapt to all screen sizes. In such cases, learners benefit with access to content on any device.

The Wordpress CMS platform is easy to manage once it is created. It also provides users with lots of widgets enabling curation, use of RSS, Search Engine Optimization tools and so on. The latter can be designed to mimic or resemble the landing page, in order to keep learners in a homogeneous online atmosphere. The landing page and the CMS represent an interesting combination for creating efficient online lectures and MOOCs adapted to ubiquitous learners.

Students were evaluated after the completion of 2 exercises:

- Creation of a website (Web 2.0 Strategy and Fundamentals of e-business and e-marketing)
- Preparation of a platform aimed at collecting RSS feeds and curating information on the Web (i.e. lectures on New Marketing as well as Communitarian and sensorial marketing)

---

[1] For an extensive review of curation platforms, compared according to their particular functions, please visit: http://socialcompare.com/fr/comparison/curation-platforms-amplify-knowledge-plaza-storify.

Students were also required to write a synthesis on the 4 lecture topics, using a Tumblr platform. This part of the course included peer-review and assessment and also counted as a part of the students participation grade. Students were also asked to complete a short online questionnaire in order to get feedback with regards to the methods used in teaching the course.

The main learning objectives of the course was to provide students with an experiential learning process using social media embedded on mobile devices. This process was designed to develop student proficiency with creating a landing page linked to a CMS and search engine optimization, as well as effective team interaction skills.

## 4 Results

The act of building a website proved to be very beneficial to students as they engaged in a hands-on approach to learning by doing which is one of the success factors of this pedagogy. The ability students have to write content on the Internet, whether on social media, UGC (User Generated Content) such as TripAdvisor, to give an opinion, mark a service or product, or comment another comment, seems to represent THE facilitator. This enabled students to express their opinion very easily and participate in the whole process of the course more instinctively, without the fear to be judged by peers. We present a synthesis of the most common responses given by the students:

- Students appreciated the facility of accessing information in a ubiquitous form. The websites had a very responsive character and offered an easy-to-read interface and facilitated mobile consultation.
- Students stated that the user interface facilitated the memorization of content, and the finding of information. Due to an ergonomic layout with good color contrast ratio, user-friendly graphical fonts, good font spacing and width of paragraphs also facilitated reading. These factors also facilitated the sharing of the information and knowledge management, particularly on mobile devices.
- The use of quick loading photography enhanced the quality of the information and facilitated understanding of the course content by reducing cognitive workload and providing graphic representations of information.

The ability of accessing content (e.g. websites, lectures, PowerPoint presentations, etc.) while students where constructing their own websites and RSS curating platforms, offered a form of ubiquitous mobile support. The term RSS is an abbreviation for Really Simple Syndication or Rich Site Summary as it provides a rich summary of a websites new content without the need to manually check the website. The fact that our CMSs were supported by mobile devices was a pertinent factor in the success of this educational initiative. It enabled students to ask questions and get responses easily, without temporal-spatial barriers.

Our post-course survey provided results on student's satisfaction and overall experience using the MOOC interface and its social media components. As shown in Table 1, students overall provided positive feedback to the course. The highest satisfaction was related to ease-of-use and learning compared to other courses. Results indicated that 58 % of the students who participated in this digital educational setting agreed or strongly agreed that it was an accessible form of pedagogy. Additionally, 58 % of the students who participated in these mobile e-learning courses agreed or strongly agreed that it was a satisfactory experience. Student productivity was also enhanced due to the flexible nature of the courses. Ease-of-use, flexibility and adequation to professional practices seem necessary when learning on this new form of support (mobile + social media).

**Table 1.** Questions/answers related to the student's satisfaction and overall experience using the MOOC interface and its social media components

| Student feedback | N | Mean* | Std. Dev | Min | Max |
|---|---|---|---|---|---|
| Did this form of teaching appear accessible for you | 19 | 3.7 | 0.7 | 3 | 5 |
| Documents submitted and teaching materials were satisfactory | 19 | 3.1 | 1.1 | 2 | 5 |
| The number of exercises and illustrative examples supporting the course was sufficient | 19 | 2.7 | 1.1 | 1 | 5 |
| Do you feel that the workload was reasonable | 19 | 3.7 | 0.9 | 2 | 5 |
| According to you, your level of involvement in this course (homework, participation…) was enough | 19 | 3.9 | 1.0 | 2 | 5 |
| Do you consider that your prerequisites were sufficient | 19 | 2.9 | 1.0 | 2 | 5 |
| Ease-of-use and learning compared to other courses | 19 | 4.0 | 0.9 | 2 | 5 |
| Was the course adequate in relation to professional practice | 19 | 3.9 | 0.6 | 3 | 5 |
| Was this form of learning accessible for you | 19 | 3.7 | 0.7 | 3 | 5 |
| In general, did you find this form of education satisfactory | 19 | 3.7 | 0.9 | 2 | 5 |

*1 = strongly disagree to 5 = strongly agree

## 5 Discussion and Conclusion

This paper presented an exploratory analysis around the use of a MOOC and m-learning with strong implementation of social media content creation tools in the context of university business school courses. The analysis allowed us to gain a better understanding of student perceptions on using MOOCs in m-learning situations, as well as their capacity to adapt to new learning environments strongly anchored in collaborative and constructivist learning. As social media usage increases, we find that it is in the best interests of students to integrate m-learning situations into traditional higher education. Our study shows that the use of a mobile supported MOOC facilitated mobile knowledge management, and created a flexible and effective learning environment.

Although the students rarely met with the professor, there was constant community support provided by other students as well as the content provided through the CMS. The digital learning setting provoked the active participation of students in a collaborative working architecture that one could easily refer to as "social learning". Students who were more fluent in the operation of the various development mechanisms provided support to the others as "technological stewards". The term "technology stewards" refers to technology savvy members of the learning community with excellent comprehension of the digital atmosphere. Although the teacher primarily assumes this role, learners who are highly fluent in the use of mobile and Internet ICT also acted as technology stewards. This type of leader oriented behavior is typical in the digital learning environment; it empowered students with a sense of gratification and motivation while fostering a sense of a united academic micro-community. Paradoxically, students developed autonomous working habits, as well as community oriented collaborative working skills. They successfully developed their own websites based on the themes provided by the instructor as well as a unique knowledge management tool with the function of curating RSS feeds on topics specified by the instructor. The RSS feeds, also called web feeds, are a type of content delivery vehicle used for syndicating news or other web content. The tools that the students created contributes to their individual lifelong learning processes and granted them new capacities as seen in the theory of expansive learning.

A new relationship between students and professors is developing characterized by collaboration and attributing new value to communication amongst students and with administrators. Social media and mobile Internet technologies reinforce the potential for effective communication between all of the participating parties. Computer supported constructivist learning is a hands-on approach that equips learners with fine tuned research skills and nurtures educational development in the lifelong learning continuum. The computer mediated setting facilitates the creation of visual representations of information, which reduces cognitive workload require by learners to understand knowledge in a more expedient manner. The implementation of digitized learning is reciprocally beneficial to teachers as evaluation processes become increasingly automated. Course administrators have detailed analytics that provide graphic representations of information which are much easier to understand than traditional grading methods. Having access to graphic visualization of student results also contributes to the individualization of learning in the digital environment as students and teachers alike are able to identify strengths and shortcomings much more easily than in a face-to-face educational setting. It's a win-win situation!

## 6 Future Research

MOOCs are still in their infancy and many uncertainties exist about their future role in traditional higher learning. Future research will help to shed light on the uncertainties surrounding MOOCs and embrace their potential to be a transformative educational innovation of the 21st century. Results from this exploratory study demonstrates that success can be achieved with the use of MOOCs in combination with social media constructivist tools (i.e. website development and content curation applications) in a mobile supported format. Additional research is to be conducted with the objective of identifying motivating factors behind student commitments and overall success in e-learning and m-learning environments. Future research will also strengthen the external validity of our preliminary results, which indicate a successful outcome with the use of social media constructivist tools for the purpose of knowledge management in a mobile supported MOOC scenario.

## References

1. Zheng, L., Junfeng, Y., Wei, C., Ronghuai, H.: Emerging approaches for supporting easy, engaged and effective collaborative learning. J. King Saud Univ. Comput. Inf. Sci. **26**, 11–16 (2014)
2. Stahl, G., Koschmann, T., Suthers, D.: Computer-supported collaborative learning: an historical perspective. In: Sawyer, R.K. (ed.) Cambridge Handbook of the Learning Sciences, pp. 409–426. Cambridge University Press, Cambridge (2006). http://GerryStahl.net/cscl/CSCL_English.pdf
3. Pelet, J.-É., Papadopoulou, P.: Handbook of Research on User Behavior in Ubiquitous Online Environments. IGI Global (2013). http://www.igi-global.com/publish/call-for-papers/call-details/841, http://www.kmcms.net/Doc/Call/Ucommerce/
4. Pelet, J.-É.: e-Learning 2.0 Technologies and Web Applications in Higher Education. IGI Global (2013). http://www.igi-global.com/publish/call-for-papers/call-details/798, http://www.kmcms.net/Doc/Call/Elearning/
5. Bowen, W.G.: The "cost disease" in higher education: Is technology the answer. The Tanner Lectures Stanford University (2012). http://edf.stanford.edu/sites/default/files/Bowen%20lectures%20SU%20102.pdf
6. Eurostat, Internet access and use in 2013. European Commision Eurostat, 18 December 2013. http://epp.eurostat.ec.europa.eu/cache/ITY_PUBLIC/4-18122013-BP/EN/4-18122013-BP-EN.PDF
7. Eurostat, Internet use statistics - individuals - Statistics Explained. European Commision Eurostat (2014). http://epp.eurostat.ec.europa.eu/statistics_explained/index.php/Internet_use_statistics_-_individuals. Accessed 22 February 2014
8. Allen, I.E., Seaman, J.: Changing Course: Ten Years of Tracking Online Education in the United States. ERIC (2013). http://files.eric.ed.gov/fulltext/ED541571.pdf
9. Collins, J., Doyon, D., McAuley, C., Quijada, A.I.: Reading, writing, and deconstructing: media literacy as part of the school curriculum. In: Wan, G., Gut, D.M. (eds.) Bringing Schools into the 21st Century, pp. 159–185. Springer, Heidelberg (2011). doi:10.1007/978-94-007-0268-4_8
10. Hargittai, E., Walejko, G.: The participation divide: content creation and sharing in the digital age1. Inf. Commun. Soc. **11**(2), 239–256 (2008). doi:10.1080/13691180801946150
11. Eurostat, Youth in Europe - Statistics Explained. European Commision Eurostat (2009). http://epp.eurostat.ec.europa.eu/statistics_explained/index.php/Youth_in_Europe. Accessed 22 February 2014
12. Eurostat, Internet access and use in 2012. European Commision Eurostat, 18 December 2012. http://epp.eurostat.ec.europa.eu/cache/ITY_PUBLIC/4-18122012-AP/EN/4-18122012-AP-EN.PDF
13. Jenkins, H.: Confronting the Challenges of Participatory Culture: Media Education for the 21st Century. The MIT Press, Cambridge (2009)
14. Gaebel, M.: MOOCs: Massive Open Online Courses. European University Association (2013). http://www.eua.be/Libraries/Publication/EUA_Occasional_papers_MOOCs.sflb.ashx
15. De Waard, I.: Explore a New Learning Frontier: MOOCs, Learning Solutions Magazine (2011). http://www.learningsolutionsmag.com/articles/721/. Accessed 1 June 2013
16. Bernhard, W., Bittel, N., Van Der Vlies, S., Bettoni, M., Roth, N.: The MOOCs business model. Soc. Behav. Sci. **106**, 2931–2937 (2013)

17. Kop, R.: The challenges to connectivist learning on open online networks: learning experiences during a massive open online course. Int. Rev. Res. Open Distance Learn. **12**(3), 19–38 (2011). Special Issue - Connectivism: Design and Delivery of Social Networked Learning
18. Rivard, R.: Coursera's contractual Elitism. Inside Higher Education (online edition) (2013)
19. Xu, D., Jaggers, S.S.: Adaptability to online learning: differences across types of students and academic subject areas, Community College Research Center, Teachers College, Columbia University, Working paper no. 54 (online publication) (2013)
20. Kolowich, S.: The professors who make the MOOCs, The chronicle of Higher Education (online edition) (2013)
21. Pelet, J.-E., Uden, L.: Mobile learning platforms to assist individual knowledge management. In: Uden, L., Oshee, D.F., Ting, I.-H., Liberona, D. (eds.) KMO 2014. LNBIP, vol. 185, pp. 267–278. Springer, Heidelberg (2014). doi:10.1007/978-3-319-08618-7_26
22. Traxler, J.: Defining, discussing and evaluating mobile learning: the moving finger writes and having writ. Int. Rev. Res. Open Distance Learn. **8**(2) (2007). http://www.irrodl.org/index.php/irrodl/article/view/346/875
23. Setaro, J.: If you build it, will they come? Distance learning through wireless devices. Unisys World, pp. 12–14 (2001)
24. Stone, A., Briggs, J., Smith, C.: SMS and interactivity-some results from the field, and its implications on effective uses of mobile technologies in education. In: Wireless and Mobile Technologies in Education 2002, pp. 147–151. IEEE Computer Society (2002). doi:10.1109/WMTE.2002.1039238
25. Chatti, M.A., Jarke, M., Frosch-Wilke, D.: The future of e-learning: a shift to knowledge networking and social software. Int. J. Knowl. Learn. **3**(4), 404–420 (2007)
26. Corbeil, J., Valdes-Corbeil, M.: Are you ready for mobile learning? Educase Q. **30**(2), 51–58 (2007). https://net.educause.edu/ir/library/pdf/EQM0726.pdf
27. Motiwalla, L.F.: Mobile learning: a framework and evaluation. Comput. Educ. **49**(3), 581–596 (2007). doi:10.1016/j.compedu.2005.10.011
28. Selwyn, N.: Social media in higher education. In: The Europa World of Learning 2012 (2012). http://sites.jmu.edu/flippEDout/files/2013/04/sample-essay-selwyn.pdf
29. Lewis, S., Pea, R., Rosen, J.: Beyond participation to co-creation of meaning: mobile social media in generative learning communities. Soc. Sci. Inf. **49**(3), 351–369 (2010). doi:10.1177/0539018410370726
30. Bosch, T.E.: Using online social networking for teaching and learning: Facebook use at the University of Cape Town. Communication **35**(2), 185–200 (2009). doi:10.1080/02500160903250648
31. Redecker, C., Ala-Mutka, K., Punie, Y.: Learning 2.0 - The impact of social media on learning in Europe. Policy Brief. JRC Scientific and Technical Report. EUR JRC56958 EN (2010). http://bit.Ly/cljlpq, http://www.ict-21.ch/com-ict/IMG/pdf/learning-2.0-EU-17pp.JRC56958.pdf. Accessed 6 February 2011
32. Ito, M., Horst, H., Boyd, D., Herr-Stephenson, B., Lange, P., Pascoe, C.J., Tripp, L.: Living and Learning with New Media: Summary of Findings from the Digital Youth Project. MIT Press, Cambridge (2009)

# The Role of Social Connections in Plagiarism Detection

Aljaž Zrnec(✉) and Dejan Lavbič

Faculty of Computer and Information Science, University of Ljubljana,
Večna pot 113, 1000 Ljubljana, Slovenia
{Aljaz.Zrnec,Dejan.Lavbic}@fri.uni-lj.si

**Abstract.** Plagiarism is considered as an unethical act. Over the past few years its rate has increased considerably due to a widespread access to electronic documents on the Web. Existing tools for plagiarism detection are not efficient enough and if we want to successfully prevent these kind of acts we must improve today's plagiarism detection approaches. The paper proposes a framework for improved detection of plagiarism, where we focus on integration of information from social networks, information from the Web and semantically enriched visualization of information about authors and plagiates. Visualization enables exploring data and seeking of advanced patterns of plagiarism. We also developed a special tool to support the proposed framework. The results of evaluation confirmed our hypothesis that employment of social network analysis and advanced visualization techniques improves plagiarism detection process.

**Keywords:** Integration · Social network anaylsis · Plagiarism detection process · Plagiarism visualisation

## 1 Introduction

Widespread availability of computers, mobile devices and contents on the Web change the approaches to teaching and learning processes. At the same time, we have to improve current plagiarism detection process, to be able to cope with increasing rate of plagiarism in the way of becoming more efficient.

Plagiarism is defined as unethical act of copying someone else's work [23]. Culwin and Lancester defined Four-Stage Plagiarism Detection Process (FSPDP) [6] used to systematically search for plagiarism in a given set of documents. FSPDP consists of four stages: collection, analysis, confirmation and investigation. Usually all stages were performed by human investigator, but with the development of different plagiarism detection methods supported by computers some stages in this process can be fully automated and some can be automated just in parts [13]. The effectiveness of the detection depends on the similarity engine [1, 9]. For a submission to become a plagiate, confirmation stage must be completed, where the submission is examined and verified by a human investigator. This stage can also be automated, but false positive and false negative results may occur. Any similarity from the second stage, which is concerned as positive, is further considered in the investigation stage.


L. Uden et al. (Eds.): LTEC 2015, CCIS 533, pp. 54–63, 2015.
DOI: 10.1007/978-3-319-22629-3_5

Most of the today's approaches [1] for detecting plagiarism are focused on the first two stages, leaving the investigator to perform latter two stages manually. That was a motivation for us to propose an approach where we focus on social aspects of potential plagiarists, by taking into account their social network connections and information on the Web to support investigator's work in the third stage of FSPDP. We believe that plagiarism detection process can be improved by reducing the number of manual examinations of potential plagiarised work. This could be achieved by employment of new visualization techniques that enable semantically enriched view of relationships among potential plagiarists. In this way, the confirmation or rejection of plagiarism can be more efficient.

The paper is organized as follows. In Sect. 2, we present related work and give the proposal for solution. Section 3 describes our Social Plagiarism Detection Framework and supportive software tool. In Sect. 4, we present the evaluation method for assessing our approach and discuss the obtained results. Section 5 concludes the paper discussing the possibilities for future work.

## 2 Related Work

### 2.1 Approaches and Tools

With the expansion of various types of plagiarism many different approaches for plagiarism detection have also emerged, especially with the proliferation of digital documents on the Web and the advent of social networks. Several successful studies have been applied to traditional approaches [15, 16, 20] focusing on program code or plain text.

According to [15], there are five different types of plagiarism varying from verbatim copying to advanced types of plagiarism [22] such as copying of ideas and plagiarism of translated text. The increasing use of computers and Web 2.0 tools have mainly positive effect on learning but also increase the possibility of using different types of plagiarism [21]. Early approaches to plagiarism detection heavily relied on methods that were based on string matching while modern methods include document parsing and using a synonym thesaurus. However neither of these methods perform well when faced with complex types of plagiarism [15] such as stealing of ideas or translation of the text.

Several approaches have been implemented in various types of software tools varying from autonomous applications to web services. Applications are run locally and scan for plagiarisms within a given corpus of documents. On the other hand web services allow us to search for plagiarisms among several sources on the Internet.

Software tools for detecting plagiarism are used to detect similarities in program code, text or both. Some of the most commonly used tools for detecting plagiarisms in source code are Sherlock [12, 16], JPlag [17] and Moss [19]. Their basic functionality is very simple. Selected submissions are run through similarity engine, which provides pair-wise results with potential plagiarisms. Modern software for plagiarism detection in source code is based not only on methods for string matching but also include methods for searching lexical and structural modifications in programming code [2, 3, 8, 10, 12]. On the other hand WCopyFind [4], Ephorus [7] and TurnItIn [5, 14, 18] are tools for detecting plagiarisms in free text. They are used to find the amount of text shared between two or more documents on the basis of fingerprinting [11, 15].

Despite many different approaches, researchers in [15] point out that currently available detection systems have numerous drawbacks which can be divided into two categories: (1) issues concerning the user friendliness of today' detection tools (implementation of the system) and (2) issues about limitations of the existing technologies for plagiarism detection.

### 2.2 Problem Definition and Proposal for Solution

The review of today's approaches pointed out that the research work is focused on the first two initial stages - collection (1st stage) and mainly analysis (2nd stage). Majority of existing approaches conclude the user support by providing pair-wise content similarity of documents and leaving the investigator to perform confirmation and investigation stage manually. In our approach we try to focus on social aspects of potential plagiarists, by taking into account their social network connections, activities and also information from the Web. This provides improved support for plagiarism detection in confirmation (3rd stage) and investigation (4th stage). We argue that our approach facilitates plagiarism detection by providing investigator better support. This results in the reduced number of potential plagiarised work that investigator has to examine manually and provision of new visualisation techniques that enable semantically enriched view of relationships. Therefore the confirmation or rejection of plagiarism can be more efficient. We also provide a tool to support the process that can visualize more corpora with additional information. That enables the investigator to have an overview of author's plagiarism in context of his previous work and work related to his colleagues not only by content similarity.

## 3 Social Plagarism Detection Framework

### 3.1 Descrition of the Proposed System

With introduction of Social Plagiarism Detection Framework (SPDF) we focus on latter stages of plagiarism detection process (confirmation and investigation) as depicted in Fig. 1.

Contributions of our approach are as follows: (1) **integration of social network information and information from the Web** that facilitates plagiarism detection process and (2) **advanced semantically enriched visualization** (semantic graph, co-occurrence matrix) of information about authors and documents that enables exploration of data in seeking of advanced patterns of plagiarism.

In confirmation stage, the system evaluates the content similarity report provided in analysis stage and performs additional evaluation of general search engine results and connectivity of authors on social networks. In case of ambiguity the investigator is provided with an option to review the social network analysis results. Based on all given information in the context (content similarity and user connections on social networks) he can confirm or reject pair-wise plagiarism. The main benefit of our approach is improved ranking of potential pair-wise plagiarisms where social information and also

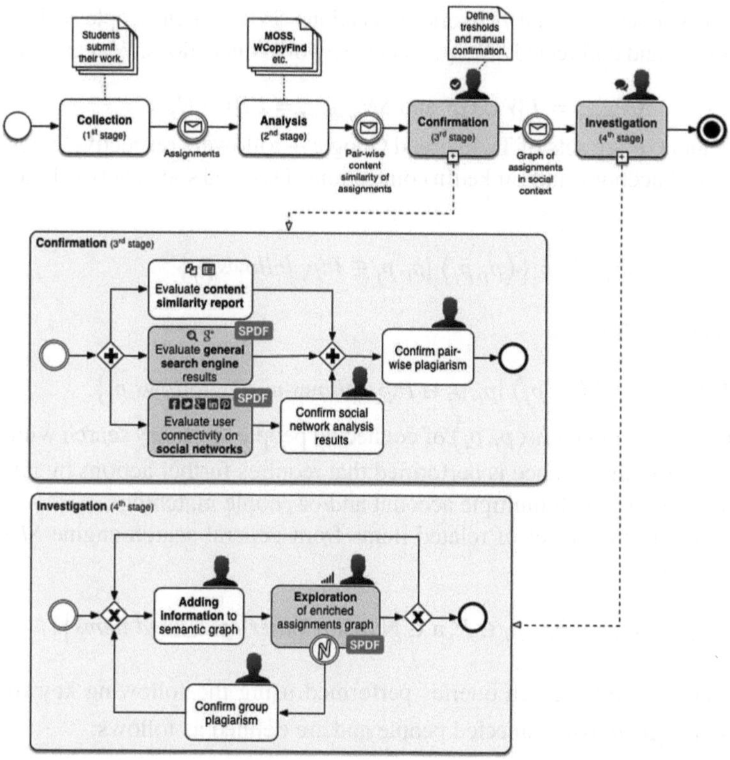


**Fig. 1.** Social Plagiarism Detection Framework (SPDF).

information from the Web is taken into account and therefore minimizing the effort required by investigator in confirmation stage. We argue and give comprehensive evaluation in Sect. 4 that impact of social information is statistically significant in performing plagiarism detection.

We can define $P$ and $D$ as non-empty sets of people and documents respectively,

$$P = \{p|p \text{ } is \text{ } a \text{ } person\},$$

$$D = \{d|d \text{ } is \text{ } a \text{ } document, \text{ } written \text{ } by \text{ } p \in P\},$$

where $W$ is a set of pairs $\langle p, d \rangle$ with $p$ as an author of a document $d$

$$W = \{\langle p, d \rangle \,|\exists p \in P \wedge d \in D{:}p \text{ } is \text{ } an \text{ } author \text{ } of \text{ } d\}.$$

We can further define content similarity

$$CS = \{\langle d_i, d_j, s_{ij} \rangle \,|\exists d_i, d_j \in D \wedge s_{ij} \in (0, 1]{:}s_{ij} \text{ } is \text{ } a \text{ } share \text{ } of \text{ } content \text{ } from \text{ } d_i \text{ } in \text{ } d_j\}$$

as a set of pairs of documents $d_i$ and $d_j$, with directed content similarity $s_{ij}$ between documents. With integration of social information to plagiarism detection we also introduce

$$SN = SN_{direct} \cup SN_{undirect},$$

which defines a set of social network connections $SN$ between people and consists of directed $SN_{direct}$ and undirected $SN_{undirect}$ social network connections. We can further define

$$SN_{direct} = TW \cup GP \text{ and } SN_{undirect} = FB \cup LN,$$

where $TW$ and $GP$ are sets of Twitter and Google + followers respectivelly and $FB$ and $LN$ are sets of Facebook and LinkedIn connections. Directed social networks are defined as

$$SN_{direct} = \{\langle p_i, p_j \rangle \mid p_i, p_j \in P{:}p_i \textit{ follows } p_j\}$$

and undirected as follows

$$SN_{undirect} = \{\langle p_i, p_j \rangle \mid p_i, p_j \in P{:}p_i \textit{ follows } p_j \wedge p_j \textit{ follows } p_i\}.$$

When determining pairs $\langle p_i, p_j \rangle$ of connected people the fuzzy search with employment of Levenshtein distance is performed that requires further actions by investigator in case of ambiguity with multiple account and/or people matching.

We also introduce a set of related items from general search engine $SE$ between person $p_i$ and $p_j$ as

$$SE = \{\langle p_i, p_j, n \rangle \mid \exists p_i, p_j \in P, n \in \mathbb{N}{:}n \textit{ is number of related items}\}.$$

There are multiple search queries performed using the following keywords $KW_{ij}$ between pairs $\langle p_i, p_j \rangle$ of connected people and are defined as follows:

$$KW_{ij} = KW_{p_i} \cup KW_{p_j} \cup KW_{assignment},$$

where $KW_{p_i}$ and $KW_{p_j}$ are keywords related to person information (e.g. name, surname etc.) and $KW_{assignment}$ is a set of assignment related keywords to narrow down the result set.

When performing plagiarism detection, the goal is to define the set of pairs of documents $DP$, where plagiarism has been confirmed:

$$DP = \{\langle d_i, d_j \rangle \mid \exists d_i, d_j \in D{:}d_i \textit{ is a plagiat of } d_j\}.$$

When using existing approaches, the investigator, who performs plagiarism detection, tries to find elements of $DP$, while considering $CS$ and some tacit knowledge $TK$ by investigation. The result of confirmation and investigation stage can be defined as a function $check_{woSocio}$, performed by the investigator

$$check_{woSocio}{:}CS \times TK \rightarrow DP.$$

When our approach is utilized, the following function $check_{wSocio}$ is defined

$$check_{wSocio}{:}CS \times TK \times SN \times SE \rightarrow DP$$

that takes into account social information of document authors. We furthermore argue that employment of $check_{wSocio}$ is more straightforward than $check_{woSocio}$ and enables investigator to perform the confirmation stage more efficiently. This results in total number of documents suspected of plagiarism that investigator has to manually review and confirm or reject plagiarism. For evaluation purposes the supporting tool has been developed to test and compare the aforementioned scenarios.

### 3.2 Plagiarism Detection Assistant

To support the proposed process, we developed the Plagiarism Detection Assistant (PDA) tool which supports the following functionalities: (1) creating and managing projects, (2) integration of existing plagiarism detection tools, (3) automatic acquisition of social network information and general search engine results, (4) confirming/rejecting assignments, (5) advanced visualization.

The initial action in the process is creating a project by an investigator and collecting the submissions. Then the following steps include preparation of data for confirmation stage: (1) **performing content analysis** by selected existing plagiarism detection tool, where pair-wise content similarity report is retrieved and (2) **acquisition of social network information** and general search engine results for investigated students.

After data is prepared, investigator enters the confirmation stage. The goal of this step is to assign one of the following status to the pair-wise assignments by two people that are considered to perform plagiarism: (1) "not checked" - assignments similarity has not been considered yet, (2) "rejected" - the assignments are not plagiarisms or (3) "confirmed" - the assignments are plagiarisms.

When making the decision the PDA tool assists investigator by providing extensive report of matches found on assignments submitted by different authors. There is a history of all assignments and their corresponding content similarity enriched with social component. The colours used depict the severity of warnings. When investigator reviews all provided information he can make a decision and confirms or rejects plagiarism. By performing these steps the confirmation stage of plagiarism detection is concluded (see Fig. 1) and investigation can start.

One of the views in PDA tool in investigation stage is depicted in Fig. 2 where the support for advanced visualization is provided. Investigator can interactively explore the semantic graph and co-occurrence matrix equipped with information about content similarity, connectivity on social networks and general search engine results. The data from social networks and the Web are collected by means of social network's public APIs and Web scrapping of publicly available data about authors. Because we do only pairwise analysis of data from the limited set of people, we don't have any problems with processing. By visualising the context of entire group (e.g. class at University) the investigator can perform plagiarism detection by exploring group plagiarism (Fig. 3).

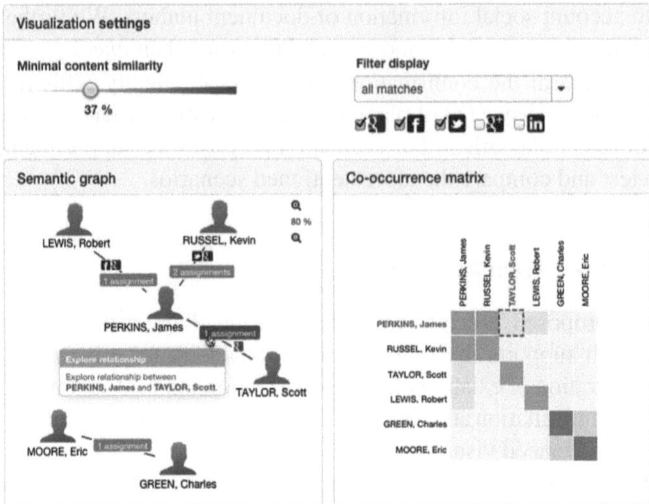


**Fig. 2.** Support for investigation in PDA tool.

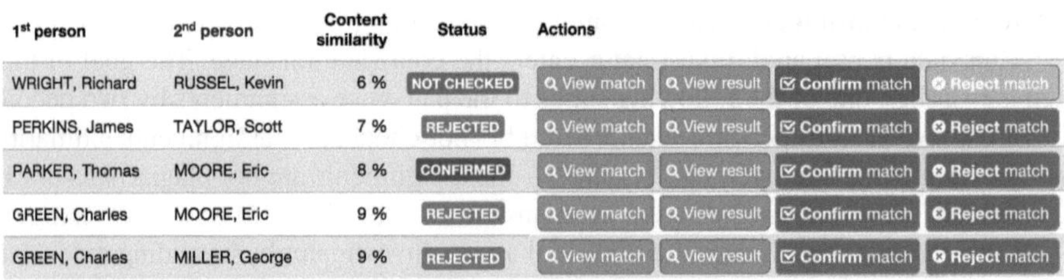

| 1st person | 2nd person | Content similarity | Status | Actions | | | |
|---|---|---|---|---|---|---|---|
| WRIGHT, Richard | RUSSEL, Kevin | 6 % | NOT CHECKED | View match | View result | Confirm match | Reject match |
| PERKINS, James | TAYLOR, Scott | 7 % | REJECTED | View match | View result | Confirm match | Reject match |
| PARKER, Thomas | MOORE, Eric | 8 % | CONFIRMED | View match | View result | Confirm match | Reject match |
| GREEN, Charles | MOORE, Eric | 9 % | REJECTED | View match | View result | Confirm match | Reject match |
| GREEN, Charles | MILLER, George | 9 % | REJECTED | View match | View result | Confirm match | Reject match |

**Fig. 3.** Pair-wise review.

# 4 Evaluation of the Approach

## 4.1 Method

Our approach was evaluated on a case study of 76 students taking one of the lectures from Computer Science at undergraduate level. Each student had to submit 5 programming homework assignments during the semester that were later checked for plagiarism. There were 2 experiments performed with 2 groups of evaluators that followed different approach on the same data set (76 student submitted 5 assignments, where 22 assignments were missing so in total 358 assignments). Both groups of evaluators had the common goal - to identify plagiarisms in student work. In the first approach $check_{woSocio}$ evaluators employed MOSS [19] and performed manual investigation on pair-wise content similarity, while in the second approach $check_{wSocio}$ our method with additional social network analysis results was used. The information from social networks employed in the second approach was extracted from public profiles of students. In our case study 54 students had publicly available information on Facebook and 43 students were active on Twitter. Students were informed about the use of all available public information in the process of plagiarism detection throughout the course.

The method used for evaluation of aforementioned approaches is generalized linear model with logistic regression where link function is defined as follows

$$g(Y) = log_e\left(\frac{n}{1-n}\right) = \beta_0 + \sum\nolimits_{j=1}^{p} \beta_j X_j.$$

The logistic regression is applied to a situation where the response variable $Y = cheat\_confirmed$ is dichotomous (0, 1). The model assumes that $Y$ follows a binomial distribution and it can be a fit to a linear model $g(Y)$. The conditional mean of $Y$ is the probability $\pi = \mu_Y$ that cheat is confirmed, given a set of $X$ values. The odds that cheat is confirmed are $\frac{n}{1-n}$ and $log\left(\frac{n}{1-n}\right)$ is the log odds or *logit*.

We've defined two models:

$$check_{woSocio}{:}cheat_{confirmed} \sim match\_cs \text{ and}$$

$$check_{wSocio}{:}cheat_{confirmed} \sim match_{cs} + match_{fb} + match_{tw} + se\_hits,$$

where $check_{woSocio}$ is nested model within $check_{wSocio}$ with the same response variable $Y = cheat\_confirmed$ and different predictors $X_{woSocio}$ and $X_{wSocio}$, where $X_{woSocio} \subseteq X_{wSocio}$. The predictor variables are as follows: *cheat_confirmed* is $\{true, false\}$ factor with information about confirmed plagiarism from investigator; *match_cs* is content similarity $s_{ij}$ between documents $d_i$ and $d_j$, where $\langle d_i, d_j, s_{ij}\rangle \in CS$; $match_{fb}$ is a S$\{true, false\}$ factor, based on existence of $\langle p_i, p_j\rangle \in SN_{direct}$; $match_{tw}$ is a $\{true, false\}$ factor, based on existance of $\langle p_i, p_j\rangle \in SN_{undirect}$ and *se_hits* is a number of search engine results $n$ between persons $p_i$ and $p_j$, where $\langle p_i, p_j, n\rangle \in SE$.

The employment of models $check_{woSocio}$ and $check_{wSocio}$ is not intended to predict plagiarism but rather for ranking of potential pair-wise plagiats that investigator can review and confirm in the latter stages of plagiarism detection.

In the conclusion of our experiment we performed a follow-through interviews with all of the students where they defended their work and evaluators determined if their submitted work is original. The evaluator's decisions were then used for $cheat_{confirmed}$ response variable to evaluate both models.

## 4.2 Results and Discussion

When building a model $check_{woSocio}$ the results show that the predictor variable *match_cs* is significant ($p \leq 9 \cdot 10^{-6}$) in predicting the response variable *cheat_confirmed*. Next step was to build another model $check_{wSocio}$ with integrated social information, where the results of this second model show that all predictor variables *match_cs* ($p \leq .0025$), *match_fb* ($p \leq .0289$), *match_tw* ($p \leq .0904$) and *se_hits* ($p \leq .0432$) are significant in predicting the response variable *cheat_confirmed*. Now we can compare both models, which consists of variables that all have significant impact on the prediction by performing ANOVA with Likelihood Ratios Test (LRT) on both models.

The measure used for comparison is deviance as a distance between two probabilistic models (in our case with generalized linear model it equals to two time log ratio of likelihoods between two nested models). Deviance can be regarded as a measure of lack of fit between model and data. We can conclude that the residual deviance in $check_{woSocio}$ (model 1) is significantly higher ($p \leq 6 \cdot 10^{-8}$) than in $check_{wSocio}$ (model 2). We can argue that the model 1 has poorer fit to the data and model 2 performs better.

To confirm that results are meaningful we have performed the test for overdispersion for both models that could lead to distort test standard errors and inaccurate test of significance. We have performed fitting of the model twice – once with binomial family and second with quasibinomial family and the results confirmed that overdispersion is not a problem (the non-central Chi-Squared test was not significant with $p_{woSocio} = .977$ and $p_{wSocio} = .990$). We have also assessed the model adequacy by checking for unusually high values in the hat values, studentized residuals and Cook's D statistics. The results of these tests also confirmed that the models are adequate.

## 5 Conclusion and Future Work

Plagiarism detection approaches mainly focus on the first two stages of FSPDP. However that is not sufficient to successfully reveal authors that are performing unethical acts relating to plagiarism, because we also have to deal with false positive and false negative results from the analysis stage.

To become more effective in the process of plagiarism detection we proposed approach and PDA software tool, that's able to successfully support the human work in confirmation and investigation stage. In confirmation stage we can efficiently narrow the set of potential plagiarists from previous stages and in investigation stage we can visualize the relationships among potential plagiarists with additional semantic information. The evaluation of two different models, on selected case study, demonstrates that the obtained results are significant. This proves that the inclusion of social network information of document's authors facilitates plagiarism detection process against the approach where these information from the social networks and the Web is not employed in manual decision making process of confirmation and investigation of plagiarism performed by human investigator.

Future work will focus on improving the framework by further analysis of social network connections between suspicious authors. The mutual communication will be analysed by using advanced methods for text analysis. We will also try to find the correlation between authors' mutual messages and plagiarism between their submitted documents.

## References

1. Ali, A.M.E.T., Abdulla, H.M.D., Snásel, V.: Overview and comparison of plagiarism detection tools. Paper presented at the DATESO 2011: Annual International Workshop on DAtabases, TExts, Specifications and Objects, Pisek, Czech Republic (2011)

2. Alzahrani, S.M., Salim, N., Abraham, A.: Understanding plagiarism linguistic patterns, textual features, and detection methods. IEEE Trans. Syst., Man, and Cybernetics **42**(2), 133–149 (2012)
3. Alzahrani, S., Palade, V., Salim, N., Abraham, A.: Using structural information and citation evidence to detect significant plagiarism cases in scientific publications. J. Am. Soc. Inform. Sci. Technol. **63**(2), 286–312 (2012)
4. Balaguer, E.V.: Putting ourselves in SME's shoes: automatic detection of plagiarism by the WCopyFind tool. Paper presented at the SEPLN 2009 Workshop on Uncovering Plagiarism, Authorship and Social Software Misuse (2009)
5. Buckley, E., Cowap, L.: An evaluation of the use of Turnitin for electronic submission and marking and as a formative feedback tool from an educator's perspective. Br. J. Edu. Tech. **44**(4), 562–570 (2013)
6. Culwin, F., Lancaster, T.: Visualising intra-corpal plagiarism. Paper presented at the 5th International Conference on Information Visualisation. London (2001)
7. Hanny, D.O., Van Wijk, C.: Plagiarism: Punish or prevent? Some experiences with academic copycatting in the Netherlands. Bus. Commun. Q. **74**(2), 196 (2011)
8. Đurić, Z., Gašević, D.: A source code similarity system for plagiarism detection. Comput. J. **56**(1), 70–86 (2013)
9. Hage, J., Rademaker, P., van Vugt, N.: A comparison of Plagiarism Detection Tools: Department of Information and Computing Sciences. Utrecht University, The Netherlands (2010)
10. Hein, J., Zobrist, R., Konrad, C., Schuepfer, G.: Scientific fraud in 20 falsified anesthesia papers: detection using financial auditing methods. Anaesthesist **61**(6), 543–549 (2012)
11. Introna, L.D., Hayes, N.: On sociomaterial imbrications: what plagiarism detection systems reveal and why it matters. Inf. Organ. **21**(2), 107–122 (2011)
12. Joy, M., Luck, M.: Plagiarism in programming assignments. IEEE Trans. Educ. **42**(2), 129–133 (1999)
13. Makuc, Ž.: Methods to Assist Plagiarism Detection. (Bachelor of Science), University of Ljubljana, Faculty of Computer and Information Science (2013)
14. Marsh, B.: Turnitin.com and the scriptural enterprise of plagiarism detection. Comput. Compos. **21**(4), 427–438 (2004)
15. Mozgovoy, M., Kakkonen, T., Cosma, G.: Automatic student plagiarism detection: future perspectives. J. Educ. Comput. Res. **43**(4), 511–531 (2010)
16. Mozgovoy, M., Fredriksson, K., White, D., Joy, M., Sutinen, E.: Fast plagiarism detection system. In: Consens, M.P., Navarro, G. (eds.) SPIRE 2005. LNCS, vol. 3772, pp. 267–270. Springer, Heidelberg (2005)
17. Prechelt, L., Malpohl, G., Philippsen, M.: Finding plagiarisms among a set of programs with JPlag. J. Univ. Comput. Sci. **8**(11), 1016–1038 (2002)
18. Rolfe, V.: Can Turnitin be used to provide instant formative feedback? Br. J. Educ. Tech. **42**(4), 701–710 (2011)
19. Schleimer, S., Wilkerson, D.S., Aiken, A.: Winnowing: local algorithms for document fingerprinting. Paper presented at the ACM SIGMOD International Conference on Management of data (2003)
20. Stein, B., Lipka, N., Prettenhofer, P.: Intrinsic plagiarism analysis. Lang. Resour. Eval. **45**(1), 63–82 (2011)
21. Underwood, J., Szabo, A.: Academic offences and e-Learning: individual propensities in cheating. Br. J. Educ. Tech. **34**(4), 467–477 (2003)
22. Witherspoon, M., Maldonado, N., Lacey, C.H.: Undergraduates and academic dishonesty. Int J. Bus. Soc. Sci. **3**(1), 76–86 (2012)
23. Youmans, R.J.: Does the adoption of plagiarism-detection software in higher education reduce plagiarism? Stud. High. Educ. **36**(7), 749–761 (2011)

# Cooperative Learning

# Eight R's – Case Study

Marja Naaranoja[1(✉)] and Lorna Uden[2]

[1] Vaasa University of Applied Sciences, Wolffintie 30, 65200 Vaasa, Finland
marja.naaranoja@vamk.fi
[2] Staffordshire University, The Octagon, Beaconside, Stafford ST18 0AD, UK
L.Uden@staffs.ac.uk

**Abstract.** Teaching engineering subjects is not trivial. Construction engineering is complex and involves many different topics and skills. Traditional approaches such as lecturing in a classroom are not effective. Students need practical skills in order to carry tasks that they meet in real life. It is important that we design the learning environment as authentic as possible. This paper describes the 8 R's that are used to illustrate how construction engineers are taught and what kind of needs are met for learning tools by this kind of learning.

**Keywords:** Learning · Problem based learning · Engineering · Learning tool

## 1 Introduction

Construction students need problem solving, communication, critical thinking and learning specific professional skills. However, many of the students fail to achieve these skills before graduation. One of the contributing factors to the inability to deliver the needed skills is that traditional engineering education doesn't have enough cross-disciplinary integration, or interfaces with real-life problems and usage of basic knowledge. Courses are often fragmented and they have often very little relationship with one another [14].

It is important for students to understand engineering concepts and go beyond the information level to higher levels of thinking. We need to help them apply, analyse and synthesize, create new knowledge and solve problems. Our duty as teachers is to support students learning by identifying efficient ways of teaching.

There are different ways to learn. People learn by seeing, hearing, memorizing, visualizing, acting, reasoning logically and intuitively, re-electing and drawing analogies and building mathematical models. Teaching methods also vary. Some use lectures, others demonstrate or discuss. Others focus on principles and some on applications. Many emphasize memory and others understanding. How much a student learns is governed partly by the student's inborn ability and prior preparation but also by the compatibility of his or her learning style, the instructor's teaching style and the online learning material (compare [7]).

It is typical that there is a mismatch between the teaching methods (including the online material and classroom behaviour) and the learning style of a student. This results in students becoming bored and inattentive in class or passive in online platforms.


L. Uden et al. (Eds.): LTEC 2015, CCIS 533, pp. 67–76, 2015.
DOI: 10.1007/978-3-319-22629-3_6

Students then do poorly on tests, get discouraged about the courses, the curriculum, and themselves, and in some cases change to other curricula or drop out of school. Society loses potentially excellent engineers. In order to overcome the problem, it is necessary that we move away from the teacher centred approach to a student learning approach. This means moving from behaviouristic learning to constructivist learning.

This paper describes the eight R's for teaching construction engineering students and what kind of technical tools are required when teaching using the 8 R's. The paper begins with a brief review of how to teach engineering. A case study describes the teaching of construction to students at Applied Science University and the evaluation of this approach.

## 2 Engineering Students' Learning

There are several important principles that need to be applied in order to teach engineering students effectively.

**Practical Examples.** Practical examples are used to increase effectivity [4]:

1. illustrate and explain the theoretical basis of the material. Practical examples help students to understand new concepts.
2. apply the course material in new situations. The goal is to show the students not only that the learned theories have practical applications, but more importantly, how to apply the principles in real life engineering problems.

Practical examples can be created by using (a) analogies, (b) observations, (c) demonstrations (experimental or mathematical), (d) sensing phenomena, and (e) observing secondary effects [4].

**Formulate and Publish Clear Instructional Objectives.** Instructional objectives are statements of what students should be able to do to demonstrate their mastery of course material and desired skills. The behaviour specified in an instructional objective must be directly observable by the instructor and should be as specific and unambiguous as possible. For this reason, verbs like know, learn, understand, and appreciate are unacceptable. These are critically important goals, but they are not directly observable [8].

Instructional objectives of the learning typically fall under a broad spectrum of complexity and difficulty. The taxonomy of educational objectives (Cognitive Domain) developed by Bloom and colleagues [1] define a hierarchy of six levels:

1. Knowledge—repeating memorized information.
2. Comprehension—paraphrasing text, explaining concepts in jargon-free terms.
3. Application—applying course material to solve straightforward problems.
4. Analysis—solving complex problems, developing process models and simulations, troubleshooting equipment and system problems.
5. Synthesis—designing experiments, devices, processes, and products.
6. Evaluation—choosing from among alternatives and justifying the choice, optimizing processes, making judgments about the environmental impact of engineering decisions, resolving ethical dilemmas.

Engineering course material may be categorized as being concrete (facts, observations, experimental data and applications) or abstract (concepts, theories, mathematical formulas and models).

**Learning Material in Context.** Teaching new materials is often done without putting it into context. In other words, the material should attempt to be related to things students already know from their own experience or from prior courses. Also there should be description of how the material will be needed to solve problems later in the curriculum or in professional practice. It is important to begin each new course and each new topic by describing the topics studied and the types of problems to be solved. If possible, there should be examples familiar to the students. Several realistic situations should be discussed.

Inductive teaching (wherein the information flow generally proceeds from specifics to generalities) can be very inspiring to students. Inductive methods utilise either discovery, inquiry, problem-based, just-in-time, or case study learning.

The goal is to get information and skills encoded in students' long-term memories. Cognitive research tells that people learn new material contextually; fitting it into existing cognitive structures [9]. New information that cannot be linked to existing knowledge is not likely to be retained. Moreover, once information is stored in long-term memory, cues are required for us to recall and use it. Linking the new material to familiar material provides a natural set of cues.

In teaching construction engineering, it is vital to provide context, establishing relevance, and teaching inductively [17]. Ramsden and Enwistle [13] argued that establishing relevance is one of the factors that induce students to adopt a "deep" (as opposed to superficial) approach to learning.

**Promote Active Learning.** According to the traditional approach in higher education, the students are supposed to passively absorb the material either presented online or taught in classrooms. Research indicates that this can only be effective for presenting factual information that can be memorized and recalled in short term memory. It would not work if the objective is to facilitate long-term remembering of information, or to help the students develop or improve their problem-solving or thinking skills or to stimulate their interest in a subject and motivate them to take a deeper approach to studying it. To promote these skills, students must be actively involved in learning. The challenge is to involve most or all of the students in productive activities without sacrificing important course content or losing control of the class. Active learning methods make learning much more enjoyable for both students and instructors.

Several authors have developed more formal active learning approaches. One is TAPPS (thinking-aloud pair problem solving), an activity in which pairs of students work their way through a problem [16]. People acquire knowledge and skills through practice and reflection, not by watching and listening to others telling them how to do something. Active learning is one of the seven, evidenced-based recommendations for improving learning [3].

**Cooperative Learning.** Cooperative learning involves students working in teams to accomplish a common goal, under conditions that include the following elements [10]:

1. Positive interdependence. Team members are obliged to rely on one another to achieve the goal. If any team members fail to do their part, everyone suffers consequences.
2. Individual accountability. All students in a group are held accountable for doing their share of the work and for mastery of all of the material to be learned.
3. Face-to-face promotes interaction. Although some of the group work may be parcelled out and done individually, some must be done interactively, with group members providing one another with feedback, challenging reasoning and conclusions, and perhaps most importantly, teaching and encouraging one another.
4. Appropriate use of collaborative skills. Students are encouraged and helped to develop and practice trust-building, leadership, decision-making, communication, and conflict management skills.
5. Group processing. Team members set group goals, periodically assess what they are doing well as a team, and identify changes they will make to function more effectively in the future.

Common tasks for cooperative learning groups in engineering are completing laboratory reports, design projects, and homework assignments.

**Models.** We concur with Urdarevik [15] that one of the biggest problems engineering students are facing is visualization. In fact, visualization skills have been found to correlate highly with successes in engineering, and mathematics in general. In order to help students to develop this skill and make teaching and learning more productive and interesting, a new teaching strategy based on using models has been developed. Experience in using the models shows that:

1. Students are able to learn the topic in most effective and easy way.
2. Students are fully engaged in the learning process.
3. Students can gain the knowledge and obtain the skills developed in this "hands on" approach in learning that affects students' ability to absorb knowledge in subsequent courses where good visualization skills are required.
4. Using the models makes students feel that engineering is an interesting field to study.

The benefits for teachers are:

(1) very little (or no) preparation time
(2) less lecture time
(3) easy to explain the topic
(4) test results are incomparable to teaching from a textbook.

## 3 The Eight R Model for Teaching Construction Engineering

This section describes the 8 R's by using a case study.

**Case Study.** The aim of the course is to learn how the property owners manage their facilities and a building project. The third year students have already learned the basics of construction projects and most of them have been working at least during summer time in a construction business. So they have some knowledge of the challenges of the construction process.

This case study illustrates how to use 8 R's when the students learn how the owner selects the agreement method. The students work in groups of three or four solving different problems.

The 8R's consists of the following process:

### 3.1 Relax

For students to learn effectively, it is important to provide them a relaxing environment where they can learn together. Brains in a state of relaxation are better able to remember new information.

A classroom environment can either support or prevent learning [2]. In order to create a relaxing environment, the students should be sitting around tables. This allows students to be able to face each other and a cooperative atmosphere is possible. The relaxing atmosphere is difficult to get in a normal classroom where the lecturer is in the front and the students sit at the back. To break the ice, students first express his or her interests and background related to the topic. This provides a supportive atmosphere for the students.

If the students are learning in distance mode they should also have a possibility to meet each other and get support from peers. Even then the students need a place to meet.

### 3.2 Recall of Prior Knowledge

The students are challenged to discuss what they know about agreements so far. The learning material should provide links to the previous courses in order to remember what has been learned earlier. This is needed to ensure that the taught new issues are not just fragmented new knowledge but are built on the already learned knowledge. It is accepted that both the acquisition of knowledge and the learning of skills is dependent upon entry behaviour (compare [12, 15]).

Beginning the session with a review of what has been learned before helps to activate prior knowledge. Presenting new information in its relationship to old not only helps students learn the new information but strengthens the remembering of old material. Introducing new concepts by contrasting them with some that have already been learned makes use of prior knowledge to aid in the learning of new. Better yet, having the students make those comparisons teaches them something about the way to approach the learning of new material and about the structure of the discipline. When new information to the student's prior knowledge is linked for them, it activates the student's interest and curiosity, and infuses instruction with a sense of purpose.

A simple strategy for tapping student prior knowledge is the use of Known and Unknown charts. At the beginning of the session, the new topic or concept is introduced to the class. Using documenting possibilities a chart with two columns is drawn. The first column should be labelled The Known and the second The Unknown. During this activity, instructor should check any student misperceptions.

During this step, students are asked to recap on what they have learned in the previous courses or real life situation and discuss in details. Each student is asked to contribute, making sure that no one is left out.

### 3.3 Resolve the Problem

Having retrieved what students have learned previously, it is important to refine the problem that they are trying to solve.

The aim of the learning task should be clarified at this point. In this case the students have to understand how the facility owners select the agreement method. The course-work is explained to the students so that they understand what they need to find out. For example one of the learning tasks is to find out what are the benefits and challenges of using public private partnership in building a hospital and whether the hospital should use this type of an agreement method.

The students need to have the fact explained to them, that the contracting type depends on the complexity of the project: what is good for a small project does not fit for a large complex project; and they should pay equal attention to the characteristics of the project and the agreement type. The characteristics of different types of projects are explained in order to give the students an understanding what might be relevant issues in each case. The different contracting characteristics are also explained. However, it is made clear that students have to find more information about everything.

### 3.4 Refine the Learning Issues or Objectives

After gaining understanding of the problem, the next stage is to refine the learning issues. Learning issues are the things that students must do when solving the problem.

At this stage, it would be useful to have a learning issues chart, as shown in Table 1. The lecturer and students define together what they know and what they need to know for the course.

**Table 1.** Example of the learning issues chart

| What I know already | What I do not know | What I need to know |
|---|---|---|
| Normal agreement method [link to the previous course] | How to select the agreement method [link to current learning material] | Benefits and challenges of other agreement methods (design built, public private partnership, quality evaluation) and their<br>Selection methods e.g. risk management methods<br>Who is actually selecting |
| I know how a normal block of flat project is designed and constructed. [link to the previous course material] | I don't know anything about complex projects [link to current learning material] | How a complex projects like hospital, police station, school renovation, or renovation project are designed and constructed |

## 3.5 Retrieve Information from Relevant Sources

Students now need to search for information that they do not know from the online material, Internet or books or any appropriate sources. It is important that students are trained to capture relevant information that they need to solve their problem.

Students typically start immediately to look for information. This should be discouraged. Students during this step should be reminded of the chart that they have produced. They should refer to the things that they have written down as not known and then use these to guide them in their search for information. After that students should be encouraged to use online material and many other resources such as books, journals and so on. They should also be warned to get reliable information and validate it before use. Some of the students may have access to company internal databases that can be also helpful.

## 3.6 Rehearse the Knowledge Learned

What the students have learned will be discussed by the group. This is to allow what each has learned to share his or her knowledge with the group. Each must present his or her learning and the knowledge learned must be articulated and agreed by the others in the group.

## 3.7 Realign the Learning

During this stage, the students should put all the learned knowledge together for the given problem. They should link up with knowledge that they have already known and integrate new knowledge to resolve their problem. Many students would have misconceptions regarding their work. It is important at this stage to challenge them by appropriate questions.

The groups should also have a possibility to check whether their work is on the right track. For this purpose the groups meet the instructor who will give them feedback. Often it is necessary to look for more details and thus realign the learning.

## 3.8 Retain the Learning

Students should reflect on their work in order to enable deep learning. Deep learning comes from a sequence of experience, reflection, abstraction, and actively testing the ideas (Compare [11]).

Zull [18] points out that learning is deepest when it engages the most parts of the brain. We learn from reflecting on experience. Teaching students to reflect on their work by noticing and correcting their own mistakes as well as which activities and behaviours allowed them to be successful is a vital part of the learning experience.

The students are motivated to analyse, reflect, relate, and question via these five prompts their coursework:

- Identify one important concept, research finding, theory, or idea or method … that you learned while completing this work
- Why do you believe that this concept, research finding, theory, or idea or method … is important?
- How can you apply this learning into your life?
- How do you improve on the concept, idea or method you have learned?
- Recap on what the problem you had is, how you arrived at the solution and why, and is there any way you can do better?

After the group work the student groups present the challenges and benefits of agreement methods case study. Especially the agreement methods that the students did not know beforehand are discussed in order to help the students to remember what they learned. This will help the group to remember what they have learned.

**Analysis.** The authentic problem that we have given to students provides them the opportunity to experience a real problem during the study. This is in line with the principle of constructivism. A relaxed round table room provides students with a place where they not only able to study, but in a place where they can relax socially. The environment also allows students to learn at their own pace, providing them s a structured approach to help them develop problem solving, critical thinking and communication skills.

By using the 8R's the students were able to learn how to learn effectively.

1. Relaxing helps the student to feel at ease with the learning.
2. Recalling of prior knowledge helps the student to remember what they already know about the subject and motivates them to learn more. In this case the students were asked what they know about agreement methods.
3. Resolving the problem means that the aim of the learning task is clarified in such a way that the challenge and the end results are crystal clear.
4. Refining the learning issues or objectives by reflecting on what they already know and what new issues they need to learn.
5. Retrieving information from many sources is important because students need to know what they have to find out.
6. Rehearsing the knowledge taught helps students to articulate their thoughts. Students also learn to share their knowledge with other members of the group.
7. Realigning the learning means students must learn how the solution they have produced actually arrived at a correct answer in line with the learning issues of the given problem. This helps students to develop metacognitive skills.
8. Retaining the learning is important because students should develop deep learning by integrating what they know with they learned, and be able to apply the knowledge to future problems.

Students found the learning stimulating and enjoyable because they were put in an environment that was not threatening in contact teaching. The relaxed atmosphere of an online course can also be created by a discussion forum where everybody introduces themselves and introduces prior-knowledge as well as the challenges of studying.

The 8R steps took them through what they have to do to learn. This promotes motivation among the students. Most students found the model beneficial and exciting. In the beginning students were not used to the approach because they were used to lecturing. However, as the learning progressed, students begun to see the benefits of the approach and actually enjoying the learning. The students started to understand that they need to first identify what they have to learn and then look for information to solve the problem. They not only have to get the information, but also need to make sure that the solution provided was correct through articulation and reflection. Reflection of their learning allows students to identify why some answers were not appropriate and why some were correct. This provides the chance to develop metacognition.

The learning method inspired the students to be present. 80 % of students were present and evaluated results were 3,75 (max 5) on average.

In another course the learning task was given by using only three of the 8 R's: In this second case, only 60 % of the students were present and the average evaluation of the learning task was 2.4 (max 5). Comparing these results we can say that the usage of 8R's motivates the students and learning results are better.

## 4 Conclusion

The 8Rs help the lecturers to plan how to create online learning material and to give learning tasks. In the case of contact teaching, it is possible this approach can be used to aid group-learning of students. The use of different perspectives –relax, recall of prior knowledge, resolve the problem, refine the learning issues or objectives, retrieve information, rehearse the knowledge learned, realign the learning, retain the learning –ensure the logical flow of learning both in contact teaching and online. If a student can learn in this way he/she does not only build on the previous knowledge but he/she can also remember what has been studied and hopefully also use it in other contexts. The first four R's help the students to start to find the information and the last four R's help the student to really learn what he/she has found.

Our sample of the empirical studies is very small, but we hope to extend the 8R's to as many classes as possible besides construction classes. It would be interesting to see the outcomes of the use of this internationally.

## References


1. Bloom, B.S., Krathwohl, D.R.: Taxonomy of Educational Objectives. Handbook 1: Cognitive Domain. Addison-Wesley, New York (1984)
2. Bucholz, J.L., Sheffler, J.L.: Creating a warm and inclusive classroom environment: planning for all children to feel welcome. Electron. J. Inclusive Educ. **2**(4) (2009)
3. Chickering, A.W., Gamson, Z.F.: Seven principles for good practice in undergraduate education. AAHE Bulletin, p. 3, March 1987
4. Courter, S., Balaraman, P., Lacey, J., Hochgraf, G. (eds): Strategies for Effective Teaching A Handbook for Teaching Assistants, College of Engineering, University of Wisconsin (1995)

5. Dochy, F.J.R.C., van Luyk, S.J.: Handboek Vaardigheidsonderwijs. Swets & Zeitlinger, Lisse (1987)
6. Felder, R.M.: Meet your students. III. Michelle, Rob, and Art. Chem. Eng. Educ. **24**(3), 130–131 (1990). http://www2.ncsu.edu/unity/lockers/users/f/felder/public/Columns/Objectives.html
7. Felder, R.M., Silverman, L.K.: Learning and teaching styles in engineering education. Eng. Educ. **78**(7), 674 (1998)
8. Felder, R.M., Woods, D.R., Stice, J.E., Rugarcia, A.: The future of engineering education II. Teaching methods that work. Chem. Eng. Educ. **34**(1), 26–39 (2000)
9. Haile, J.M.: Toward technical understanding, part 3. Advanced Levels. Chem. Engr. Educ. **32**(1), 30–39 (1998)
10. Johnson, D.W., Johnson, R.T., Stanne, M.E.: Cooperative Learning Methods: A Meta-Analysis. University of Minnesota, Cooperative Learning Center, Minneapolis (2000). http://www.cooperation.org/pages/cl-methods.html
11. Kolb, D.: Experiential Learning. Experience as the Source of Learning and Development. Prentice-Hall, Englewood Cliffs (1984)
12. Neisser, U.: Cognition and Reality. W.H. Freeman, San Francisco (1976)
13. Ramsden, P., Enwistle, N.J.: Effects of academic departments on students' approaches to studying. Br. J. Educ. Psychol. **51**, 368–383 (1981)
14. Uden, L., Beaumont, C.: Technology and Problem Based Learning. Idea Publisher, Hershey (2006)
15. Urdarevik, S.: Using models to teach and learn engineering. In: 2013 ASQ Advancing STEM Agenda Conference, Grand Valley State University - Grand Rapids, Michigan, 3–4 June, 2013. The Seymour and Esther Padnos College of Engineering and Computing (2013). http://rube.asq.org/edu/2013/05/best-practices/using-models-to-teach-and-learn-engineering.pdf
16. Whimbey, A.E., Lochhead, J.J.: Problem Solving and Comprehension: A Short Course in Analytical Reasoning. Franklin Institute Press, Philadelphia (1982)
17. Woods, D.R.: Three trends in teaching and learning. Chem. Engr. Educ. **32**(4), 296–301 (1998)
18. Zull, J.: The Art of Changing the Brain. Stylus Publishing, Sterling (2002)

# Designing a PBLJii Script in a CSCL Environment for Bolstering Collaboration and Communication Skills

Sofia Gkemisi, Fotini Paraskeva(✉), Aikaterini Alexiou, and Hara Bouta

Department of Digital Systems, University of Piraeus, Karaoli and Dimitriou Street 80, 185 34 Piraeus, Greece
s.gemissi@gmail.com, {fparaske,xmpouta}@unipi.gr, katialex@webmail.unipi.gr

**Abstract.** Teachers' training programs should focus on practical experiences and reflective practices through technology enhanced learning environments in order to foster their collaboration and communication skills. The aim of this research is the design and implementation of a collaboration PBLJii script (Problem-based learning & Jigsaw II Script), which is orchestrated along the principles of a Problem-based Learning model and the Jigsaw II collaborative strategy in a CSCL environment so as to bolster collaboration and communication skills among teachers. An experimental design research (one group only research) was conducted in a number of primary schools in Greece. The participants (in-service teachers) engaged in the training process through the PBLJii Script in History. There was both a quantitative and a qualitative analysis of the chat and forum messages exchanged by the in-service teachers in the CSCL environment and the results showed that they developed collaborative and communication skills to a great degree as a result of their participation in collaborative tasks.

**Keywords:** Problem Based Learning · Jigsaw II learning strategy · CSCL environment · Moodle · Communication skills · Collaborative skills

## 1 Introduction

Teachers' training programs should focus on practical experiences and reflective practices through technology enhanced learning environments in order to foster their collaboration and communication skills. In particular, they need to develop the ability to work in groups, to communicate effectively, to collectively assume responsibility for team work while at the same time valuing the individual contribution of each of the team members [17, 18].

Research has focused on designing technology enhanced learning environments (such as Computer Supported Collaborative Learning environments - CSCL), which orchestrate the learning process and structure online discourse in order to support learners to build knowledge and foster collaboration and communication skills. To this end, we propose the design of a collaboration script, which allocates roles and activities among


L. Uden et al. (Eds.): LTEC 2015, CCIS 533, pp. 77–92, 2015.
DOI: 10.1007/978-3-319-22629-3_7

learners and manages the progression between activities and role alteration in such a way as to maximize the learning benefits for the participants [8, 12, 14]. Our primary goal is to design a script with pedagogical foundations that triggers collaboration and communication so that the learners can co-produce solutions to authentic problems.

The current study is grounded on the idea of utilizing the principles of PBL [25–27] and Jigsaw II strategy [11, 28] in a script (PBLJii Script stands for PBL: Problem-based learning and Jii: Jigsaw II) in order to ensure the right conditions for communication and collaboration in a CSCL environment. The proposed PBLJii Script is embedded in a CSCL environment that aggregates the functionalities of a content management system (Moodle) and a set of interaction tools. This environment offers the possibility of creating and running e-lessons [9]. Participants interact, communicate and collaborate in groups within the environment and in doing so they construct mutual learning experiences with the others and thus acquire new knowledge. Bearing all these in mind, the aim of this research is the design and implementation of a collaboration script (PBLJii Script), which is orchestrated along the principles of a PBL model and Jigsaw II collaborative strategy in a CSCL environment so as to bolster collaboration and communication skills among teachers.

## 2 Theoretical Background

### 2.1 Problem Based Learning

Research has stressed the important role of Problem Based Learning (PBL) as an instructional learner-centered approach that requires learners to work together in small groups and to solve real-world problems. PBL allows learners to activate their prior knowledge, contribute to the discussion of the problem at hand and share their experiences in a small group. Learners work in groups trying to solve a series of problems which can either be independent or part of a larger one [15, 23–27]. Group discussions promote elaboration and understanding as learners state their ideas and argue about the meaning of the ideas [10]. The importance of group interaction in PBL is that leaners have to share information in trying to work out the solution to a problem and in this way they are indirectly forced on enhancing their communication skills. Learners develop their knowledge as well as transferable skills such as problem-solving, critical and creative thinking, communication, collaboration and leadership skills [2]. Many studies have found PBL beneficial for interpersonal, communication, and collaboration skills [13, 16]. The range of skills developed by PBL has been outlined by [10, 29]; these include critical thinking along with an ability to work out real-life problems; exploring, finding, evaluating and making use of relevant learning resources; working with others and making effective use of communication skills as well as using content knowledge and cognitive skills to further lifelong learning.

### 2.2 Jigsaw II

A PBL-based learning environment implies the collaboration of learners in teams so that they can solve a series of problems, which in turn forms parts of a larger task.

At the same time, Jigsaw II collaborative strategy [11, 28] encourages the interaction between individuals since it creates conditions conducive to collaboration through the various forms of groups that it employs (initial groups, expert groups, jigsaw groups). These groups meet in learning environments and engage in group tasks with common goals which foster the group spirit. Each participant becomes an 'expert' on a particular aspect and offers his/her knowledge to the other members of the group. Through carefully listening to each other the group members learn about the other sub-units – sub-tasks and they come to understand how each piece fits together and completes the whole puzzle. Jigsaw II is a variation of the Jigsaw strategy [11, 28].

### 2.3 Collaboration and Communication Skills in the 21st Century

Collaboration and communication skills occupy a prominent place among 21st century skills [17]. Teachers have to demonstrate their ability to collaborate and communicate within various teams flexibly and effectively. In particular, collaborative skills are associated with the development of the qualities below [17, 18].

(a) Team Spirit: This refers to collective activities and it focuses on the way in which individuals can work together [5].
(b) Collaborative Culture: This refers to the common expectations, respect and mutual concessions one often has to make, as well as to professional development, collaboration and learning [19, 21].
(c) Trusting Partnerships: This refers to the skills associated with notions of trust, respect and collective action [22].
(d) Collegial Consonance: This refers to the collective relationships which develop when in-service teachers collaborate, discuss and share ideas, knowledge and techniques [21].

Also, communication is a form of social interaction [3] and the quality of education in the various educational institutions is largely determined by the quality of communication. Teachers who develop their communication skills are more effective in all aspects of the educational process. They are capable of modeling, managing communication, making adjustments to interaction, retaining control of emerging social situations, as well as determining and adapting the aims of communication and discussion (see also the three strands of interaction involvement as described in [6]):

(a) Attentiveness: it relates to the way in which an individual interacts with another within a particular environment [3, 6, 20].
(b) Perceptiveness: this means listening, examining and perceiving what emerges as people interact with each other [3, 6, 20].
(c) Responsiveness: this means responding to various situations and having a sense of what needs to be said, when and how [3, 6, 20].

Education and the whole teaching process also rely on team work attitudes – the communication between the group members and the communication between groups [3]. On this basis, research has focused on the attitudes of group members as they communicate in order to complete a group project [1].

# 3 Method

## 3.1 Research Questions

The aim of this research is the design and implementation of a collaboration script (PBLJii Script), which is orchestrated along the principles of a PBL model and Jigsaw II collaborative strategy in a CSCL environment. Specifically, in the present study we tried to answer the following questions:

(a) Does the PBLJii Script promote collaboration skills?
(b) Does the PBLJii Script promote communication skills?

## 3.2 Participants

The participants in this study were 12 in-service teachers from various Primary schools in Athens. The study was conducted as part of an in-service training seminar in order to engage participants in the orchestrated process of PBLJii Script. Learners interacted so as to work out a solution to an ill-structured problem on 'The Golden Age of Pericles' unit of History.

# 4 Experimental Procedure

An experimental design research (one group only research) was conducted within various Primary schools in Athens. The subjects of the study (N = 12) participated voluntarily for reasons of professional development. The participants engaged in the training process through the PBLJii Script in order to enhance their collaboration and communication skills. In particular, the PBLJii Script was implemented through 6 Sessions (steps of the process). Each session comprised one on-line and one face-to-face encounters in order to solve the ill-structured problem set by the design of the PBLJii Script.

## 4.1 The PBLJii Script

Following the principles of the models "Maastricht 7-step: "seven jump" approach" by Maurer, and Neuhold, [17] and "Maastricht 7-step" by Savin-Baden [25–28] both based on the "Maastricht 7-step" and Jigsaw II strategy [14] we designed a collaboration script. The proposed PBLJii Script is embedded in a CSCL environment that aggregates the functionalities of a content management system (Moodle) and a set of interaction tools (Fig. 1). The PBLJii Script is carefully structured so that participants allocate roles and activities among learners and manage the progression between activities and role alteration in such a way as to maximize the learning benefits for the participants [15].

This means that the PBLJii Script consists of a number of steps characterized by five attributes: the type of task learners have to perform, how groups are formed, how

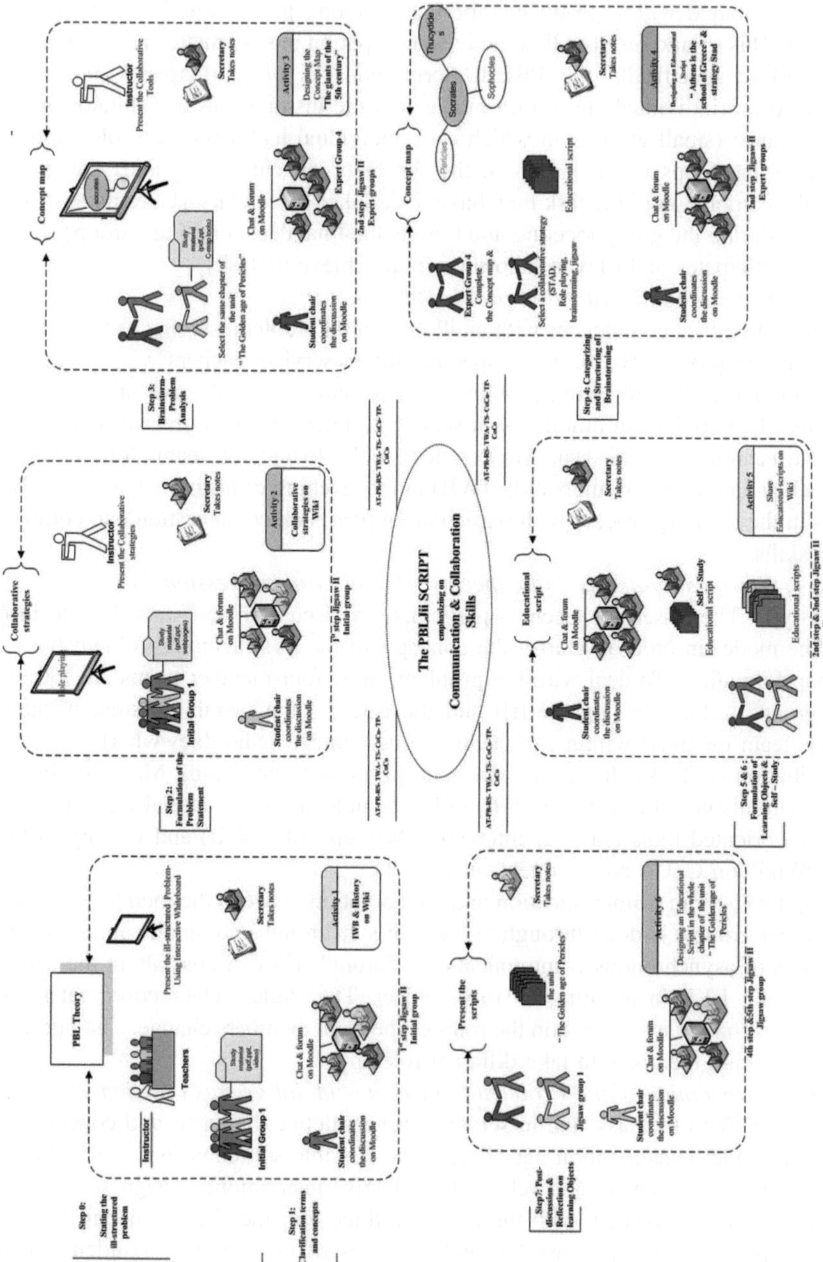


**Fig. 1.** Illustration of the PBLJii Script.

tasks are distributed within group members and among groups and how the groups interact [6]. This should result in their active participation in systematic and exploratory learning. More specifically the PBLJii Script consists of: participants (in-service teachers), roles: (individual and group modes and the instructor as a facilitator of the process), teams: (small groups- in which each individual had a selected role: student chair {leads the Steps of the group in the forum or on chat and guides the group towards the completion of the task they have undertaken}, secretary {takes notes of the discussions during the group meeting and reports the final decision of the group}, team member {participates and tries to help the group achieve its task}).

*Step 0: Stating the ill-structured problem (Session 0)*

The PBLJii Script commences with an ill-structured problem, serving as the vehicle for the learning process. To be more specific, the in-service teachers were invited to provide solution to the following problem. The scenario of the ill-structured problem introduces Mr. Pericles, an ambitious in-service teacher who is a great proponent of innovative technologies. This year, Mr. Pericles decided to integrate technology-oriented tools (such as Interactive Whiteboard - IWB) in the teaching of history so as to involve students in the learning process with particular emphasis on collaboration and communication skills.

*Step 1: Clarification terms and concepts - Initial Groups (Session 1)*

Task type: The in-service teachers participate in discussion activities (face-to face and online mode) in order to clarify the concepts of the ill-structured problem.

Group formation: To deal with the problem, three four-member teams are formed (initial groups – 1st step [Jigsaw II]) and the roles of the members (student chair, secretary, team member) within each team are determined (who does what).

Distribution of Tasks: In-service teachers go through the "Study Material" in the CSCL environment. Afterwards each team has to upload some material related to the technology-oriented tools (such as Interactive Whiteboard - IWB) and History in the team's "Wiki" on CSCL environment (activity 1).

Group interaction: Communication and collaboration between the members of each group (initial groups) is done through "spaces of synchronous communication – chat" and "spaces of asynchronous communication – forum". They discuss about the added value of using IWB in teaching History subject. The student chair coordinates the discussion on chat. In every session the roles of the team members change. The purpose is for all the team members to take different roles.

*Step 2: Formulation of the Problem Statement – Initial groups (Session 2)*

Task type: With this task, the in-service teachers define the terms and concepts of the problem under consideration and discuss the possible solutions. A set of collaborative strategies is presented as a vehicle for effective instructional design.

Group formation: To deal with the problem, three four-member teams are formed (initial groups – 1st step [Jigsaw II]) and the roles of the members (student chair, secretary, team member) within each team are determined (who does what).

Distribution of Tasks: Group members submit the materials about collaborative strategies in each team's collaborative Wiki in the CSCL environment (activity 2).

Group interaction: Each team (initial groups – 1st step [Jigsaw II]) get together in the forum and on chat in order to discuss the collaborative strategies and answer the questions. The student chair coordinates the discussion on chat.

*Step 3: Brainstorm- Problem Analysis – Expert groups (Session 3)*

Task type: The in-service teachers discuss about which collaborative strategy they will choose in order to propose suitable learning activities for the History subject using IWB. They use the brainstorming technique to activate their prior knowledge and create a concept map. The teachers share the concept map they have created online, so that each member can edit and shape it (activity 3).

Group formation: At this stage the group composition changes. The in-service teachers who choose the same chapter work together (expert groups of 3 members – 2nd step [Jigsaw II]). More specifically, they select a different unit of the chapter 'The Golden Age of Pericles' on which they are going to work: expert group1 - unit 1: "The Polity and Society of Athens in the time of Pericles", expert group 2 - unit 2: "The Golden Century of Art", expert group 3 - unit 3: "The daily life and education of the Athenians", expert group 4 - unit 4: "Athens is the school of Greece".

Distribution of Tasks: Each member of each expert team expresses their opinion about which collaborative strategy they will choose to create collaborative tasks on the IWB. The secretary of each expert team takes notes and records each member's opinion. Each expert team chooses a different strategy and the instructor of the process intervenes where necessary. Finally, they discuss on chat and decide about the theme of the concept map which they create based on the History unit each expert group has chosen.

Group interaction: Each team (expert groups – 1st step [Jigsaw II]) get together in the forum and on chat in order to discuss.

*Step 4: Categorizing and Structuring of Brainstorming – Expert groups (Session 4)*

Task type: The expert groups discuss on chat and in the forum about the structure of a well-designed educational scenario integrating collaborative strategies and communication techniques. Each group selects a collaborative strategy (STAD, Role playing, brainstorming, jigsaw) which corresponds to the different History units (1–4) that each expert group has selected (activity 4).

Group formation: The in-service teachers were divided into 4 groups according to the History chapters (expert group 1, 2, 3 and 4 - 2nd step [Jigsaw II]).

Distribution of Tasks: Group members decide on the allocation of the tasks which each member of each expert group will undertake to complete. The classification and organization of their ideas is done with the aid of concept maps.

Group interaction: Each team (expert groups – 2nd step [Jigsaw II]) get together in the forum and on chat in order to discuss.

*Steps 5 & 6: Formulation of Learning Objects & Self – Study - Jigsaw group (Session 5 & 6)*

Task type: Each teacher deepens his knowledge about collaborative strategies (self-study). As in-service teachers have been experts on the collaborative strategies (STAD, Role playing, brainstorming, jigsaw) (2nd step [Jigsaw II]) they discuss in order to deal with any queries they may have and ask for clarifications. They create the educational scenario with the collaborative strategy they have selected as well as the tasks that each member of the group has undertaken (5th session). Following this, they return to their initial groups in order to share their knowledge with the rest of the members of their initial group (session 6).

Group formation: With this knowledge transfer, the initial groups are now transformed into 'jigsaw groups' (3rd step [Jigsaw II]): expert group1 - unit 1: "The Polity and Society of Athens in the time of Pericles" & Brainstorming strategy, expert group 2 - unit 2: "The Gold Century of Art of the Athenians" & Jigsaw strategy, expert group 3 - unit 3: "The daily life and education of the Athenians" & Role playing strategy, expert group 4 - unit 4: "Athens is the school of Greece" & Stad strategy.

Distribution of Tasks: Firstly group member's self-study and afterwards one of them submits the scenario created in each team's wiki in the CSCL environment (activity 5).

Group interaction: In-service teachers become experts (2nd step [Jigsaw II]) and discuss and ask for clarifications in order to deal with any queries they may have.

*Step 7: Post-discussion & Reflection on learning Objects (Session 7)*

Task type: Members of each Jigsaw group study the educational scenarios, they collaborate and they create a new one arising out of a synthesis of the scenarios related to the chapter "The Golden Age of Pericles" (activity 6). Finally, they assess and evaluate the whole process which has led to their newly-acquired knowledge (4th and 5th step [Jigsaw II]).

Group formation: The members of each Jigsaw group (3 groups comprising 4 members each) study the educational scenarios.

Distribution of Tasks: Members of each group study the educational scenarios, collaborate and create a new one which the secretary uploads in the CSCL environment.

Group interaction: Group members discuss (both on chat and forum) about the experience of collaboration in the various shifting teams which they participated in during the seminar. They acknowledge and evaluate the value and contribution of the team in the solution arrived at.

## 5 Data Analysis

The data from the online discussions of the in-service teachers on chat and in the forum were analyzed qualitatively, while there was also a quantitative analysis of the various indices using the Wilcoxon non-parametric criterion (z). It is a mixed method of data analysis [4, 7] where we combine quantitative and qualitative data in order to bring together the strengths of both forms of research so as to validate results. In analyzing the context of the chat and forum log files, we focused on a number of qualitative criteria. In particular, we measured the number of times teachers: (a) "collaborated towards achieving the common goal and actively participated in the group activities" (Team Spirit/TS); (b) "cooperated respectfully in various teams, offering their help" (Collaborative Culture/CoCu); (c) "displayed trust for the diverging views of other group members" (Trusting Partnership/TP); (d) "took responsibility for the collective effort and participated in the group activities in an attempt to solve the group task" (Collegial Consonance/CoCo); (e) "communicated with the aim of informing, motivating or assigning work to others" (Attentiveness/AT); (f) "communicated having paid close attention to the views of the group members" (Perceptiveness/PR); (g) "expressed their views clearly and made positive and polite remarks" (Responsiveness/RS); and

(h) "managed difficulties with the aim of finding solutions to the common task" (Team Work Attitudes/TWA). The collaboration and communication indices which emerged from the analysis of the content of chat and the non-parametric Wilcoxon criterion (z) were used in order to see and compare the behavior of the same individuals through their various interactions in the CSCL environment (Table 1).

**Table 1.** Results of non-parametric analysis of variance (Wilcoxon z) related to the collaboration skills

| Collaboration skills | Criterion Wilcoxon (z) | | | | | | | |
|---|---|---|---|---|---|---|---|---|
| Criteria/ indexes | Step 1–2 | | Step 2–3 | | Step 3–4 | | Step4–(5,6) | |
| | Z | Mean Rank | Z | Mean Rank | Z | Mean Rank | Z | Mean Rank |
| Team Spirit/TS | −3.06** | 6.50 | −0.78* | 8.17 | −1.45* | 5.75 | −0.31 | 5.83 |
| Collaborative Culture/CoCu | −3.06** | 6.50 | −0.94* | 8.50 | −0.11* | 6.75 | −1.41* | 7.13 |
| Trusting Partnership/TP | −2.20* | 8.38 | −2.12* | 6.60 | −0.09 | 5.33 | −2.16* | 7.39 |
| Collegial Consonance/CoCo | −2.71 ** | 6.35 | −2.74** | 6.73 | −1.92* | 6.35 | −0.62 | 6.50 |

*p < 0.05, **p < 0.001

The index describing the development of skills relating to Team Spirit (TS) appears to be statistically significant. We notice that the index rises gradually from one step to the next, in particular compared to step 1 (Table 1). This means that the skills of the in-service teachers, which relate to collaboration, appear to be reinforced and developed from one step to the next as the seminar progresses. This probably has to do with the use of Jigsaw, through which in-service teachers collaborate in a range of groups (initial group, expert group, jigsaw group) and this ensures a range of conditions conducive to interaction. In addition, the PBL teaching approach used favors the involvement of participants in group tasks with common goals and attempts to promote a team spirit of collaboration.

It is only in Steps 4–5 that we notice that the TS index is not statistically significant. This is possibly due to the fact that the in-service teachers are required to work on an individual basis to a greater extent than in the other Steps. The values of the indices in the Table 1 confirm the results of our qualitative analysis. In the interactions recorded on chat and in the forum we notice the following dialogues which contribute to the development of the skills related to fostering team spirit in the groups. Here is an éxample of contributions from Expert group1 during Step 3 – related to the index showing that the teachers display flexibility and they collaborate towards achieving the common goal (TS1).

- Teacher 09: *It sounds really good... We could however use 'hegemony' as the central concept.*
- Teacher 01: *Why not have the concept of 'alliance' as the central axis and 'hegemony' as the secondary concept – what do you think?*
- Teacher 05: *No problems. So we continue on this basis.*

We can see in this exchange between the group members (expert group 1) that the in-service teachers display flexibility in trying to achieve their objective. They discuss together, they plan their course of work and they reach a decision collectively. They are flexible and they do not persist in their own view, but rather try to find a suitable solution in order to achieve the common goal.

In addition, we notice the development of Collaborative Culture skills (CoCu) as the work unfolds, particularly during the last Step. That is to say, the dialogues which took place in CSCL environment reflect the development of skills promoting a collaborative culture between the group members. This means that the in-service teachers develop common expectations, respect and make mutual concessions in order to do what is best for their group. This possibly has to do with the fact that in these steps teachers form groups in accordance with Jigsaw II and they prepare what they have to deliver collectively (i.e. the concept map, the educational script, etc.). Moreover, they develop a collaborative culture, since through the PBL they get involved in all the Steps of collaborative learning.

Finally, we notice the development of Trusting Partnership (TP) skills between the team members. This is understandable if we bear in mind that in these Steps the in-service teachers get to know the other members of the group as Jigsaw II requires them to work in groups. In particular, we notice that this index is noticeably statistically significant between the steps 1 and 2, 2 and 3, 4 and 5, 6. In these Steps, teachers get to know each other as they are called upon to work in groups (initial expert groups, jigsaw). Between Steps 3 and 4 the groups remain the same and as a result the mutual trust between the members is consolidated. At the same time, the learning conditions created by the PBL approach during Steps 1 and 2 get the in-service teachers to face the problem they need to solve and they need to clarify terms and concepts. This means they need to trust the others' views and respect their individual contributions, but they also need to recognize the value of the others' views so as to clarify the terms and concept of the problem under consideration. This can also be seen through a qualitative type of analysis of the content of the messages sent by the teachers (see the exchanges below – taken from Chat) reflecting the development of collaborative skills. Here is an example of contributions from Expert group 3 during Step 3 – the exchange relates to the index showing trust for the different views of the members of the group (TP3) and valuing the contribution of each individual of the team (TP1).

- Teacher 02: *About the concept map, I would suggest that we do not add any other concepts, so that we can analyze them in detail.*
- Teacher 10: *I agree that we should focus on these, but we could also add the role of women in the daily life of Ancient Athens... What do you think?*
- Teacher 02: *OK – that's a good idea... I will prepare a draft so you can check it out.*

- Teacher 06: *OK – Thank you very much! Student 2 – you are very methodical... well done!;-)*
- Teacher 02: *Thank you guys – it's just that I like working with you!*

In this exchange between the members of expert group 2 we can see the development of mutual trust and respect among the in-service teachers. The latter seem to acknowledge the value of the individual participation of the team members and they carefully consider the various opinions aired.

With regard to the Collegial Consonance (CoCo) skills, we notice a significant increase in most Steps as the in-service teachers get more involved in the collaboration process. This means that we notice a great development of the skills associated with taking collective responsibility and an interest in the completion of the group work. This index is particularly high during steps 1–3 where the in-service teachers have to take common decisions and undertake common responsibilities as they collaborate within the various groups (initial and expert groups – Jigsaw II). Exchanges recorded on chat like the one below are clearly related to the criterion of Collegial Consonance (CoCo) between the group members, an element which strengthens the level of collaboration between these members. Here is an example of contributions from Expert group 3 during step 4 showing members taking responsibility for the collective task (CoCo1) and an interest in the completion of the collective task at hand (CoCo5).

- Teacher 08: *Hi everyone!! I would like to propose the topic "Athens becomes the school of Greece" The giants of the 5th century...* Socrates, Pericles..
- Teacher 12: *Good... so we search around this topic.*
- Teacher 04: *It will be good... I would also recommend that we use the 'role playing' strategy. I think it suits our topic. Shall we allocate roles*?
- Teacher 08: *Yes... Full speed ahead!*
- Teacher 4*: I say we undertake the second step... If you would like any help, just let us know...*
- Teacher 12: *So, we get down to work and we'll be in touch again as soon as we have prepared something!*

As we can see from these exchanges, teachers decide together on the collaborative strategy they are going to choose with the aim of creating an educational script on a History unit. We find that the in-service teachers all share in the responsibility for the collective task and they proceed to the next step of allocating roles which each member undertakes to fulfill. They take an interest in the collective task and they make suggestions about its planning and completion. Also, the values of the communicative indices were extracted by analyzing the content of chat. The non-parametric Wilcoxon criterion (z) was employed so that we could look at and compare the behavior of the individuals as was manifested through the way they interacted with the others on CSCL environment (Table 2).

Our analysis shows that the development of skills corresponding to the Attentiveness index (AT) is statistically significant, particularly during steps 1–2. This may be due to the fact that during step 1, the in-service teachers are not involved in many tasks and as a result they have no incentive to communicate and to get involved in task-related discussions, something which does happen for instance in step 2.

**Table 2.** Results of non-parametric analysis of variance (Wilcoxon z) related to the communication skills.

| Communication skills | Criterion Wilcoxon (z) | | | | | | | |
|---|---|---|---|---|---|---|---|---|
| Criterion indexes | Step 1–2 | | Step 2–3 | | Step 3–4 | | Step 4–(5,6) | |
| | Z | Mean Rank | Z | Mean Rank | Z | Mean Rank | Z | Mean Rank |
| Attentiveness/AT | −3.06** | 6.50 | −0.66 | 5.25 | −0.90* | 6.31 | −0.71 | 5.00 |
| Perceptiveness/PR | −3.05** | 6.50 | −1.60* | 8.50 | −1.09* | 5.89 | −0.47 | 8.25 |
| Responsiveness/RS | −2.94* | 6.95 | −1.33* | 7.00 | −1.33* | 5.33 | −0.17 | 7.00 |
| Team Work Attitudes/TWA | −3.06** | 6.50 | −0.89* | 6.64 | −1.45* | 6.39 | −0.15 | 7.40 |

*p < 0.05, **p < 0.001

Assigning specific tasks and activities to the teams in accordance with the Jigsaw II strategy, as well as the gradual engagement in the completion of the process of solving the basic problem the participants address through the PBL, appears to contribute to the profile of the above-mentioned index.

Here for instance are some contributions from Initial groups during the 2$^{nd}$ step which show communication skills related to Attentiveness (AT2: this is an index which shows communication for a variety of reasons such as to inform, persuade, motivate or assign work to someone).

- Teacher 06: *I quite like the 'Brainstorming!*
- Teacher 08: *The first one, (Jigsaw) seems great but it's quite complicated at least for the first few times with the kids.*
- Teacher 07: *So – as of tomorrow we start implementing all the strategies!*
- Teacher 05: *Whatever can make the learning process more interesting is good.*

The in-service teachers interact with their team members and exchange their views about the various collaborative strategies presented during the seminar. In addition, some in-service teachers try to motivate the rest of the team to implement these same strategies.

With regard to the development of Perceptiveness-related skills (PR) we notice that with the exception of steps 1–2 where the interest in observing and listening to others increases rapidly, in the rest of the steps the discussion between the group members is smooth, without misunderstandings or communication problems. Here for instance are some contributions from Expert group 4 during step 3 which show how its members consider and understand the views and ideas of the other members (PR2).

- Teacher 08: *I would like us to work with the Stad strategy...*
- Teacher 12: *I too am interested in this strategy because I think it's a good idea to evaluate the students' knowledge both individually and collectively through the quiz.*
- Teacher 04: *I agree with my colleague! After the discussion we had in class, I think that the Stad collaborative strategy is suitable for children!*

From the above exchanges between the in-service teachers, we notice that the latter receive and decode the messages they get from the other members of their team (PR1) as they communicate to complete the group task. We also note that the discussion between the group members proceeds smoothly, without misunderstandings or communication problems. As a result, both indices of this criterion which relate to the comprehension of the views of the other members (PR2) and the active listening of their opinions (listening first and then only then responding) (PR3) show an upward trend as mentioned above.

The development of skills associated with Responsiveness (RS) also appear to be positive as can be seen from the participation of group members in the discussions. They have to collectively plan their course of action and to decide on the allocation of duties among the group members. Quite apart from the fact that this forces them to communicate in writing, all this involvement actually promotes a certain degree of familiarity which manifests itself through non-verbal language. In particular, in Step 4–5 we notice that the values of some indexes are not statistically significant. This is possibly due to the fact that the in-service teachers are required to work on an individual basis to a greater extent than in the other Steps.

Finally, with regard to the Team Work Attitudes index (TWA), the in-service teachers appear to communicate and express their attitudes towards the group work they have to undertake at each step. In particular, from the second step onwards, where the in-service teachers are involved in more activities, they appear to be consistently positive about their participation in them (T4). What is more, they adopt attitudes indicative of directness and a desire for trouble-free interactions without tensions (T1). This is also reinforced by their positive attitude in managing disagreements (T2) or any difficulties which come up (T3). The in-service teachers share their ideas in the forum as to the strategy they are called upon to choose in order to create their educational script. We can see that the in-service teachers are positive towards group work and their views converge.

In the 7$^{th}$ step there are no activities for the development of the indices mentioned above as the in-service teachers did not participate in any team activity. The purpose of this step was to enable the in-service teachers to evaluate their views on the level of collaboration within the teams. To this end, an intra-peer assessment rubric was given to team members. This was then analysed quantitatively. In addition, in-service teachers were given a seminar-evaluation questionnaire. This was also analysed quantitatively so the seminar could be evaluated. A qualitative analysis of the forums was also carried out and this confirms the above-mentioned results. In this paper we have analysed and presented the results of the chat messages on CSCL environment through Steps 1 to 5, 6.

## 6 Discussion – Suggestions for Further Research

This study has examined the design and implementation of a collaboration script (PBLJii Script), which is orchestrated along the principles of a PBL model and Jigsaw II collaborative strategy in a CSCL environment so as to bolster collaboration and communication skills among teachers. There was both a quantitative and a qualitative analysis of the chat and forum messages exchanged by the in-service teachers in the CSCL environment and the results showed that they developed collaborative and communication skills to a great degree as a result of their participation in collaborative tasks.

In particular, the in-service teachers develop Team Spirit skills while collaborating and they demonstrate a tendency to participate more and more actively in the discussions of the various teams they belong to. In addition, as they involve themselves in collaborative activities, we notice that they develop Collaborative Culture skills, something that can be explained by the fact that in-service teachers get to know the other members as they are called upon to work together in teams through Jigsaw II. As regards the development of mutual trust between the team members, we notice that through their discussions the in-service teachers work with the other members of their team showing trust in their views and respect in the way they work. Furthermore, the in-service teachers developed Collegial Consonance skills as they worked through the various teams they were involved in reaching mutual decisions and taking on common responsibilities. Also, our analysis showed that the in-service teachers developed attention/focusing skills as they communicated with the members of the groups they belonged to, and their involvement in collaborative activities motivated them to communicate in order to be informed and to inform others, to persuade or to motivate the other members of the team in order to carry out the tasks assigned to them during the various phases of PBL. Also, assigning various tasks and activities to the various groups in accordance to the Jigsaw II strategy and the gradual involvement in the completion of the Steps for the solution of the basic problem dealt with through the PBL appears to contribute to the development of perceptiveness and responsiveness in in-service teachers. Finally, the in-service teachers communicate and express their attitudes towards the group work they are called upon to complete at each step and they appear to be positive throughout the whole process. In addition, they adopt a particular attitude reflecting directness and a penchant for smooth communication without tensions. This is also reinforced by the positive attitude they display in the effective management of disagreements or difficulties which come up between the team members.

Numerous researchers have called for further research both in the field of PBL and in that of 21$^{st}$ century skills development, and the current study is meant to partly meet this perceived need. The innovative feature of the current study focuses on supporting the development of collaboration and communication skills through a technologically supported learning environment utilizing PBL and the collaborative strategy Jigsaw II. As a follow up, we would recommend utilizing different collaborative strategies together with PBL in the design of a CSCL Script. We would also recommend applying this teaching model to the teaching of other subjects.

**Acknowledgements.** This work was supported by the University of Piraeus Research Centre (UPRC). We acknowledge the UPRC contribution to this research paper.

## References


1. Adler, R.B., Elmhorst, J.M.: Communicating at Work – Principles and Practices, 4th edn. Allyn & Bacon, London (2004)
2. Barrows, H.S., Tamblyn, R.: Problem-Based Learning: An Approach to Medical Education. Springer, New York (1980)
3. Bjekić, D., Zlatić, L.: Effects of professional activities on the teachers' communication competences development. In: Brejc, M. (ed.) Cooperative Partnerships in Teacher Education, Proceedings of the 31st Annual ATEE Conference, pp. 163–172. National School for Leadership in Education, Ljubljana (2006)
4. Bouta, H., Retalis, S., Paraskeva, F.: Utilizing a collaborative macro-script to enhance student engagement: a mixed method study in a 3D virtual environment. J. Comput. Educ. **58**(1), 501–517 (2012)
5. Bryant, S., Timmins, A.: Portfolio Assessment: An Instructional Guide. Department of Curriculum & Instruction HKIEd, Hong Kong (2001)
6. Cegala, D.J., Savage, G.T., Brunner, C.C., Conrad, A.B.: An elaboration of the meaning of interaction involvement: toward the development of a theoretical concept. Commun. Monogr. **49**, 229–248 (1982)
7. Creswell, J.W., Plano Clark, V.L., Gutmann, M.L., Hanson, W.E.: Advanced mixed methods research designs. In: Tashakkori, A., Teddlie, C. (eds.) Handbook of Mixed Methods in Social and Behavioral Research, pp. 209–240. Sage, Thousand Oaks (2003)
8. Dillenbourg, P.: Over-scripting CSCL: the risks of blending collaborative learning with instructional design. In: Kirschner, P.A. (ed.) Three Worlds of CSCL. Can We Support CSCL, pp. 61–91, Open Universiteit Nederland, Heerlen (2002)
9. Dougiamas, M., Taylor, P.C.: Interpretive Analysis of an Internet-Based Course Constructed Using a New Courseware Tool Called Moodle. Curtin University of Technology, Australia (2002)
10. Hoidn, S., Kärkkäinen, K.: Promoting Skills for Innovation in Higher Education: A Literature Review on the Effectiveness of Problem-based Learning and Teaching Behaviours, OECD Education Working Papers, No. 100 OECD Publing (2014). http://dx.doi.org/10.1787/5k3tsj671226-en
11. Kagan, S.: Cooperative Learning. Charlesbridge, Boston (1995)
12. King, A.: Scripting collaborative learning processes: a cognitive perspective. In: Fisher, F., Kollar, I., Mandl, H., Haake, J.M. (eds.) Scripting Computer-Supported Collaborative Learning: Cognitive, Computational, and Educational Perspectives, pp. 13–37. Springer, New York (2007)
13. Koh, G.C., Khoo, H.E., Wong, M.L., Koh, D.: The effects of problem-based learning during medical school on physician competency: a systematic review. CMAJ **178**(1), 34–41 (2008)
14. Kollar, I., Fischer, F., Hesse, F.W.: Collaboration scripts—a conceptual analysis. Educ. Psychol. Rev. **18**, 159–185 (2006)
15. Maurer, H., Neuhold, C.: Problems everywhere? Strengths and challenges of a problem-based learning approach in European studies. In: Teaching and Learning Conference 2012 of the American Political Science Association (APSA), Washington, DC, pp. 17–19, February 2012
16. Nandi, P.L., Chan, J.N.F., Chan, C.P.K., Chan, P., Chan, L.P.K.: Undergraduate medical education: comparison of problem–based learning and conventional teaching. Hong Kong Med. J. **6**(3), 301–306 (2000)
17. Pacific Policy Research Center, 21st Century skills for Students and Teachers. Kamehameha Schools, Research & Division, Honoloulou (2010)

18. Partnership for 21st Century Skills: http://www.21stcenturyskills.org/
19. Peterson, K., Deal, T.: Shaping School Culture: The Heart of Leadership. Jossey, San Francisco (1999)
20. Reardon, K.K.: Interpersonal communication: Where Minds Meet (Cin Croation: Interpersonalna Kommunikacija: Gdje se misli susrecu) Alinea, Zagreb (1998)
21. Rosenholtz, S.J.: Teachers' Workplace: The Social Organization of Schools. Longman, New York (1989)
22. Royal, M.A., Rossi, R.J.: Schools as Communities. ERIC Clearinghouse on Educational Management, Eugene (1997)
23. Savin-Baden, M.: Problem-Based Learning in Higher Education: Untold Stories. Society for Research in Higher Education and Open University Press, Buckingham (2000)
24. Savin-Baden, M.: Understanding the impact of assessment on students in problem-based learning. Innov. Educ. Teach. Int. **41**(2), 223–233 (2004)
25. Savin-Baden, M.: A Practical Guide to Problem-Based Learning Online. Routledge, London (2007a)
26. Savin-Baden, M.: Learning Spaces. SRHE/Open University Press, Maidenhead (2007b)
27. Savin-Baden, M.: Challenging models and perspectives of problem-based learning. In: de Graaff, E., Kolmos, A. (eds.) Management of Change: Implementation of Problem-Based and Project-Based Learning in Engineering, pp. 9–29. Sense Publishers, Rotterdam/Taipei (2007c)
28. Slavin, R.E.: Cooperative Learning: Theory, Research and Practice, 2nd edn. Allyn and Bacon, Boston (1995)
29. Uden, L., Beaumont, C.: Technology and Problem-Based Learning. Information Science Publishing (2005). ISBN: 1591407443

# Applying Adult Cooperative Learning Underpinning Principles to Learning with Social Media

## An Overview and Implications for Research

Jonathan Kaplan[1,2,3](✉)

[1] Institute of Sciences and Practices of Education and Training (ISPEF), Lumière University Lyon 2, Lyon, France
[2] Education, Cultures & Policies (EA 4571) Research Unit, Lyon, France
[3] CHArt-UPON (EA 4004) Research Unit, Paris, France
kaplan@kaplan-consultants.org

**Abstract.** Borrowing from Cooperative Learning (CL) elements as well as from principles used in Study Circles (SC) to define Adult Cooperative Learning (ACL), this paper proceeds to examine the applicability of principles to learning with social media. Following the appraisal of the principles in the context of learning with social media, conclusions are drawn on areas worthy of research to provide for conditions favourable to learning cooperatively in the realm of internet technologies and social media networks.

**Keywords:** Adult Cooperative Learning · Study Circles · e-Learning · Social media

## 1 Introduction

Adult Cooperative Learning [16] designates processes taking place in adult learning communities in which members are concerned with the learning of their peers. Being concerned with the learning of one's peers implies that one's own learning is supported by the entire community one is taking part in. By following some principles, one may contend, a learning environment that is more enabling and supportive can be designed. Principles to be followed in such learning communities may lay the foundation for creating an environment that upholds interest, engagement, volition and agency. This paper begins with a description of Cooperative Learning elements [13] and Study Circle principles [24]. Study Circles are advocated in Sweden where the practice is culturally embedded as a format for adult learning. The Study Circle format used in Nordic countries has also inspired a re-appropriation of this timeless practice in other parts of the world. Study Circle or Learning Circle principles provide the basis for a model of Adult Cooperative Learning [14–17]. In this paper these principles are examined in light of their applicability to learning through the use of social media.


L. Uden et al. (Eds.): LTEC 2015, CCIS 533, pp. 93–103, 2015.
DOI: 10.1007/978-3-319-22629-3_8

## 2 Cooperative Learning Elements

Cooperative Learning (CL) is a field of practice and research in education that has attracted much attention. Application of CL to the classroom began in the early 1970s [35]. Many methods of CL have been researched,[1] though it is what is in common that establishes the approach. CL methods are intended as instructional designs in which students learn with each other in a cooperative manner to enhance learning. Cooperating to enhance learning is based on the premise that each learner is a member of a collective effort who is concerned by the learning of his or her peers and will therefore benefit from the learning effort his or her peers put into his or her own learning. In such a configuration interactions that are taking place among learners are directed at helping each other in the process of learning, rather than selfishly dealing with solely one's own learning objectives. This, and the idea of sharing members' resources, combining effort and enjoying being part of a group that shares a common goal characterises positive interdependence [13]. Learning with concern with only oneself is often the result of learning in competitive environments. When one is concerned with the learning of one's peers, one can most probably rely on the goodwill of peers to help in accomplishing one's own learning goals and benefit from the rewards of sharing. The conditions for such co-learning efforts can be promoted by appealing to principles that enable cooperation and establish a basis for benevolence.

Promoting positive interdependence is one of five elements of CL referred to in the work of David Johnson et al. [13]. Their "learning together" model of CL is intended to also be used in higher education and can therefore be considered in light of its applicability to other contexts of learning in adulthood. Cooperative Learning elements comprise of: (1) positive interdependence, (2) face-to-face promotive interaction, (3) individual accountability and personal responsibility, (4) social skills, (5) group processing. According to these authors, positive interdependence leads to promotive interaction. For promotive interaction, social skills are needed as well as being skilled at evaluating and adjusting the group process.

There is one element that could be set aside – Individual Accountability and Personal Responsibility. This element can be understood by a need for instructors to ensure that individual effort is contributing to group learning. It can be explained by the constraint in educational contexts to grade students; a practice that promotes competitive attitudes and produces counter-beneficial behaviours to CL aims. This institutionally required practice of grading can be seen as defying benevolence, a trait that can hardly be expected to arise as a result of external prompting i.e., by the instructor. Hence, Individual Accountability and Personal Responsibility can be interpreted as a constraining element. It coerces students to act appropriately and in conformity with CL's expectations. Unfortunately, this supposes that benevolence cannot emerge of its own. As a result, it substitutes it with controlled motivation [8,26,29,30,32] to act in a manner favourable to the emergence and the sustaining of interactions that pro-

[1] More than 600 studies over 90 years of research were claimed in 1991 by Johnson et al. [13].

mote learning for all group members, that bring about appropriate social skills and that support reflective and evaluative action to regulate and improve group processing. Individual Accountability and Personal Responsibility is perhaps a legacy of the early use of CL methods in primary and secondary education where CL was first applied. It is not perhaps as appropriate to adult learning where motivation is far more autonomous.

## 3 A Brief Overview of the Study Circle Format

A Study Circle (SC) is a small group of adult learners who get together on a regular basis to gain knowledge and develop new understandings, approaches, and sometimes newly thought solutions to a problem, on a specific topic. Learning Circles are ideally composed of five to eight participants [7] but SCs can practically be organised with up to 12 participants. Study Circles are organised usually around one or two weekly sessions, each lasting two to three hours. Learning can range all domains and can lead to further action once the SC ends if its participants so decide. Ultimately, participants determine their learning objectives and the means to attain them. One of the SC's participants acts as facilitator (sometimes referred to as the Leader). Study Circles are known though to vary in practice [1]. It therefore makes sense to define SCs on the premise of their guiding principles. These principals will be discussed in Sect. 4.

Study Circles organised by educational bodies usually have a facilitator appointed; or preferably, *proposed* by the organiser. But, SCs can also exist informally. In informal SCs i.e., SCs that are initiated by the participants themselves without registering the activity with an educational organisation, naturally no facilitator is appointed to the group; rather, a facilitator may be chosen among the group members. This can be paralleled to informal learning communities that use the Internet to get together. In other online communities a moderator is present. The moderator's role may be assimilated in some cases to that of a SC facilitator. Then again, some online communities include members who are recognised as specialists in the domain. This is also the case in e-learning. It may be paralleled to SCs in which the facilitator is recognised as a specialist in the field of study.

Although descriptions of SC principles and merits do exist [2–4,24,25,36], little research has sought to observe practice. Known research on SC practice was conducted in Sweden by Bystrm [6] and in Norway by Brattset [5]. More recently, quasi-experimental research in France [15,17] has explored strategies used by SC participants to regulate their learning. Study Circles have gained momentum around the world since the mid-1980s. A quick detour to provide some background is therefore worthwhile.

In the Nordic countries, particularly in Sweden where SCs are culturally embedded as a popular format for learning, they have also attracted attention concerning their presumed role in shaping a democratic society and in fostering active citizenry [9,19,20]. In many English-speaking countries though, where SCs are sometimes referred to as Learning Circles, attention has been mostly directed to the opportunities they offer in bridging gaps between people from different ethnic background. Reference is made to the inclusiveness of SCs; not only of people as such, but of differing outlooks, understandings, and epistemologies. In these countries, educators are using them to foster community-wide action.

Several authors have explored non-Western epistemologies where differences in "ways of knowing" [22] serve as a basis for learning and development in multicultural societies. This is reinforced by the ethical consideration that the majority should no longer impose its worldview on minorities, be they related to lifestyle choices or to cultural background. Parallel to these tendencies and complementarily, a steady shift away from a focus on education as an individualistic and competitive means, to a social and cooperative means to a better life, is gaining terrain. Study Circles are invoked as providing for these too.

One may wonder about the suitability of the SC format for developing knowledge in distinct disciplines. Accounts of the use of the format however do not point to it being ill-suited for studying certain disciplines, such as engineering for example. The SC format can be apprehended as a framework within which learners are able to choose suitable techniques and methods for the study they are engaged in. The SC is dynamically shaped in accordance with study objectives and other factors that can be taken into account. Assessment of knowledge developed in SCs can be approached in numerous ways too. Again, learners should be associated in deciding appropriate means under prevailing circumstances. By following SC principles, an enabling learning environment can be cultivated; one in which learners shape the environment in accordance with their requirements.

## 4 Study Circle Principles

Eight SC principals are proclaimed by ABF (Worker's Educational Association, the largest organiser of SCs in Sweden) and are invoked in part or fully in different sources [15,17,24]. They are: (1) equality and democracy, (2) liberation of potential, (3) cooperation and companionship, (4) freedom and self-determination, (5) continuity and planning, (6) active participation, (7) use of printed study materials, (8) change and action.

Based on the research in France, in which collective processes of regulation of the learning were observed as predominant [15,17], one may regard SC principles as sustaining collective direction by means of cooperation. Drawing on that research, a brief review of the principles will serve to highlight how they may underpin cooperation: Equality and democracy (1) support horizontal interaction among participants through dialogue as a means for all to express their points of view and understandings gained through their life experiences. Liberation of potential (2) pertains to valuing and using these life experiences to promote learning for all participants. This requires that recognition and sharing give everyone an equal opportunity to express their ideas and opinions. Empathy sustains cooperation and companionship (3). Freedom (4) to choose the study topic, plus objectives and means to attain them, promotes autonomous self-regulation [8,32]. The research pointed to the collective dimension in the process of regulation. This included support for continuity and planning (5) that were sustained individually and collectively. Active participation (6) was evidenced in the interviews that were conducted for the research. Printed materials (7), designed into the research, were used systematically as well as other learning resources that were chosen by participants. Change and action (8) pertain to continued action after the SC ends. This is a key principal in relation to the potential power SCs hold for social change. This principle was not an object of the research, as an inquiry into the internal processes was considered a prerequisite to the inquiry into the role that SCs play in shaping encompassing communities, or possibly society.

## 5 Adult Cooperative Learning

Adult Cooperative Learning (ACL) [15–17] needs to take into account characteristics of learning in adulthood [23]. For example, motivation can be reckoned to be autonomous and cooperation can be expected to be the outcome of relatedness [31, 34] and connectedness [27, 28], contributing to well-being. Well-being can sustain volition in various ways, though coercing learners to cooperate through rewards could jeopardize these advantages.

Study Circle principles are intended to promote an environment that is enabling for SC participants to bring into play their innate resourcefulness in learning from and with each other. These principles are not intended as a blueprint for a method. Study Circle principles can be acknowledged as reminders for setting the frame of mind of the community of learners. The frame of mind is not one to which participants are estranged. One may even dauntingly advance the idea that these principles simply echo customary ways of learning that were immutably present in small human communities that people grew up in and lived most of their lives with. These communities differ from many of today's communities which are made up of people beforehand strangers to one another.

Which of the SC principles can be useful to reestablishing the sense of community that was once part and parcel of living in a world not yet a "global village" [21]? Examining the principles one by one may help to answer this question.

Equality and democracy, the first of the principles, establishes the equal power that participants share as a foundational element of democratic learning. By establishing the equality of all members, one is preventing any one person from taking over power and dominating when choices are being made by the group. This intrinsically democratic value is meant to enable individual members and the group as a whole to be self-determining. Self-determination is foundational to autonomous motivation.

Liberation of potential, the second principal, is closely related to autonomous motivation, as one cannot expect people to express their full potential in contributing to the group's learning if it is not through free will that they do so.

Cooperation and companionship, the third principle, buttresses the idea of helping each other. Obviously, cooperation cannot be enforced and companionship can only result from empathy toward one's peers. Cooperation and companionship follow from dialogue between group members.

Freedom and self-determination, the forth principle, is here to remind participants that it is them and not someone exterior to their group who determine and decide what the topics are that they will be working on and how they shall go about it. This principle links the previous favourable condition-establishing principles with the learning tasks.

The fifth principle is one which distinguishes the SC from other types of groups that use dialogue: a SC is a group set out to pursue learning goals. Continuity and planning require that members plan to meet on a regular basis and plan what topic they will be studying during each session. According to choices group members make, some may wish to design learning activities for one or several sessions. As different techniques and methods can be used by the group, one should not refer to the SC as to a method; rather, the SC is a model that is used to inaugurate and maintain enabling [33] learning conditions suitable to adult learners.

The sixth principle, active participation, can be understood as a reminder for participants to watch for signs of fatigue or loss of interest. After all, learning is an activity that requires cognitive effort.

Use of printed study materials, the seventh principle, dates back to times when printed media was predominant. The principle evokes the necessity to build on knowledge that others have come to accept as valid, as well as to acquire knowledge of diverse points of view on the topic being studied. Having access to differing points of view is essential to initiate dialogue among participants. It enables to consider different ways of understanding and explaining the topic that participants can discuss and use to put their own experiences into perspective. From a constructivist epistemological standpoint, having several understandings of a topic is what stimulates cognitive activity and reflexivity. In present times, obviously all media that enable conveying the expression of others can be used.

Change and action is the eighth principle. It bears on the aim of the SC to provide a means for change. Looking back at the model's emergence at the start of the 20th century can help grasp the importance this principle had in the context of popular movements and workers developing their skills in order to fend for their rights and improve their conditions. In particular, the fact of thinking at the end of a SC about what further action can be taken on the basis of the new knowledge just developed, links the study undertaken by the participants to their personal, social and work-life contexts. Deliberately linking one's experiences and prior knowledge at the beginning of the learning process and again contextualising the new knowledge at the end, give knowledge meaning. Learning as adults enables using knowledge gained through past experience as a resource for further learning. Learning is goal-oriented action. Thinking about how the newly developed knowledge can open up opportunities for future action reinforces implication and agency.

Adult cooperative learning may be described as learning that takes place within a community of adult learners in which the relationships between learners are based on caring for each other's learning. This perhaps overly narrow definition is nevertheless sufficient in that it recognises the social and affective dimensions of learning. Caring for each other's learning can only be sustained if one acknowledges that each person with her or his life experience through which she or he *knows*, and each one's way of knowing, are unique. The acceptance of the diversity of ways of knowing and of knowledge is the cornerstone for dialogue as defined by Isaacs [10–12]. Hence the mutual respect that leads to a horizontal social organisation of the learning, as opposed to a hierarchical one. Exchanges between learners through dialogue establish a process of collective meaning-making.

Based on the elements used by the cooperative learning method developed by Johnson et al. [13] and on the principles promoted by ABF [15,17,24], what principles can be used to guide ACL as a practice in the age of social networks using Cloud computing technologies? Before looking at the applicability of these elements and principles, the next section briefly examines what the use of these technologies changes in the ways learners interact.

## 6 Learner Interactions in Social Media

One of the main differences between face-to-face and online communities is that in the latter, members have probably never met in person. Members acquire knowledge of each other through the mediating technologies they use to discuss and interact. Can this difference imply less strong bonding between participants or bonding of a different kind? If bonding is affected, are empathic feelings between participants weaker? The ability to understand and share feelings using dialogue is essential for cooperation to emerge. Cooperation and companionship can be expected to emerge if conditions enable bonding. They will in turn lead to promotive interaction between members pursuing learning goals in a joint effort.

The kind of bonding that occurs through social media is perhaps more utility oriented. If this were the case, should CL elements guide instructors or online tutors to coerce students to cooperate? The problem, as stated earlier, is that in situations where learner motivation is controlled, regulation of the learning will be expected by the students to occur in a controlled manner too. Under these circumstances, learners will not be as autonomous.

Networks of learners using social media are vast, they often enable thousands of people to engage in interaction. The success of social media has affected the design of e-learning applications. As a result, learning management systems are in the process of shifting to mobile learning (m-learning). Responsive Web-based applications are being backed up with applications devised specifically for m-learning that offer functionality similar to social media applications. Furthermore, the current trend for some higher education establishments to offer Massive Open Online Courses (MOOCs) requires of learners to be autonomous in managing and conducting their learning with the support of their peers. This is particularly the case in MOOC designs that rely on peer interaction [18]. Can interactions take place on the basis of empathy bonding students in small groups that form within these vast networks? If this were the case, learners would be more autonomous in regulating their learning. These are questions that need researching. As a first step, the next section suggests focusing on the applicability of ACL principles to learning with social media.

## 7 Applying Principles to Learning with Social Media

Examining the principles that could be used to guide ACL should assist in reflecting on their applicability to instructional designs that make use of social media.

Equality and democracy are perhaps more easily enacted by learners interacting online. This may be due to ethics of respect that have developed over the Internet. It is customary if not essential to be nonjudgmental as one is only acquainted in a limited manner with the person with whom one is interacting through channels of communication at a distance.

Social media also liberate potential as online media are perceived as spaces of free expression where one can safely publish opinions and thoughts. It is therefore worth stressing the need to remind learners using social media that they can and should feel free to use their online means of communication to express themselves without constraint. This freedom is required in order to seek better understanding of the topics at hand through dialogue that enables examining areas of interest from different perspectives.

If dialogue is free and co-occurs with empathy then cooperation and companionship should follow.

Perceiving oneself as being free and hence unshackling self-determination depends on the content and form of instructions that are given by teachers, tutors and facilitators. Factors that can affect perceptions of liberty include the way instructions are communicated to learners. Are these instructions commanding? Conversely, do they enable making choices within designated limits? The answers to these questions may help apprehend perceptions of freedom that learners have. The degree of liberty designed into applications used for online learning and instructional design will potentially similarly affect perceptions. Choice is central to the perception of liberty.

Continuity and planning are generally built into learning environments through instructional design, learning programmes and deadlines for learning tasks. Freedom for learners to organise small team work can also be built into course designs including freedom to self-manage activities.

Active participation can be expected in situations where learners are enjoying the learning activities and enjoy carrying out their assigned tasks. Working in small groups can also affect effort to participate as groups can co-regulate task efforts when they are organised through cooperative interaction [18].

Concerning the use of study materials, as it is inherent to most educational provision at a distance it does not pose any significant challenge to learning through the use of social media.

Finally, change and action, as mentioned earlier, are reminders of the need to relate learning to previous experience and to seek continuity in the use or the application of the newly developed knowledge to further future endeavours. Linking experience and future prospects can be stimulated no matter the mediating technologies being used in educational settings.

## 8 Discussion and Conclusions

Dialogue and empathy are two areas that require further investigation. Is learning how to be dialogic needed for students using social media? If so how does one go about enabling to learn to listen and accept differing opinions than one's own? Letting each peer express herself or himself is in fact easier when using the written word; each expressing alternately their thoughts and ideas in a forum for instance. Empathy, which entails feelings, cannot be taught. Empathy requires social bonding to occur first. What favours bonding over social media channels remains to be explored. Another aspect still to be explored concerns group sizes that enable forming communities in which participants feel close to one another and responsible for each other's learning. These are communities in which learners are confident that their peers share similar feelings; in turn helpful for one's own learning through peer efforts to help in building one's knowledge.

Borrowing from CL elements and the SC model, ACL as a framework opens avenues for exploring conditions for learners to form cooperative learning communities over social media channels. The relationships between social bonding, social belonging, dialogue, empathy and cooperation are some directions suggested for research to take.

## References

1. Andersson, E., Laginder, A.M., Larsson, S., Sundgren, G.: Cirkelsamhället, Studiecirklars, betydelse för individ och lokalsamhälle. Utbildningsdepartmentet (1996)
2. Bjerkaker, S.: The study circle - a method for learning, a tool for democracy. In: FACE (Forum for the Advancement of Continuing Education) Annual Conference (2003)
3. Bjerkaker, S.: Learning to be democrats. Adults Learn. **15**(8), 20–21 (2004)
4. Bjerkaker, S.: The study circle - for learning and democracy. Convergence **39**(2/3), 49–60 (2006)
5. Brattset, H.: Adult learning - the study circle as a method. IACE Research Seminar, Kungälv, Sweden, June 24–27, p. 13 (1979)
6. Byström, J.: Alla Ŝtudiecirklarb̈lirinte Studiecirklar (All Study Circles are not Study Circles). Report of the Institute of Pedagogy of Stockholm University, Stockholm (1977)
7. Collay, M., Dunlap, D., Enloe, W., Gagnon, G.W.: Learning Circles: Creating Conditions for Professional Development. Corwin Press, Thousand Oaks (1998)
8. Deci, E.L., Ryan, R.M.: Intrinsic Motivation and Self-Determination in Human Behavior. Perspectives in Social Psychology. Plenum, New York (1985)
9. Gougoulakis, P., Bogataj, N.: Study circles in Sweden and Slovenia - learning for civic particiaption. In: Frane, A. (ed.) Social Capital and Governance - Old and New Members of the EU in Comparison, pp. 203–235. Lit Verlag, Berlin (2007)
10. Isaacs, W.: Dialogue. In: Senge, P., Kleiner, A., Roberts, C. (eds.) The Fifth Discipline Fieldbook: Strategies and Tools for Building a Learning Organization, pp. 357–364. Currency, New York (1994)
11. Isaacs, W.: Dialogue and the Art of Thinking Together: A Pioneering Approach to Communicating in Business and in Life. Currency, New York (1999)

12. Isaacs, W., Smith, B.: Designing a dialogue session. In: Senge, P., Kleiner, A., Roberts, C. (eds.) The Fifth Discipline Fieldbook: Strategies and Tools for Building a Learning Organization, pp. 374–385. Currency, New York (1994)
13. Johnson, D.W., Johnson, R.T., Smith, K.A.: Cooperative learning: increasing college faculty instructional productivity. ASHE-ERIC High. Educ. Rep. **20**(4), 157 (1991)
14. Kaplan, J.: Vers la construction d'un modèle d'évaluation dans les apprentissages coopératifs autodirigés. Master's thesis, Aix-Marseille 1 University, Lambesc (2006)
15. Kaplan, J.: Self-direction in cooperative learning - the case of study circles. Ph.D. thesis, Paris 10 University, Nanterre (2009)
16. Kaplan, J.: From self-direction to co-direction in adult cooperative learning. In: Brigham, S.M., Plumb, D. (eds.) Connected Understanding: Linkages Between Theory and Practice in Adult Education, pp. 176–180. Adult Education - Congresses, Montreal (2010)
17. Kaplan, J.: L'autodirection dans les apprentissages coopératifs: Le cas des Cercles d'Étude. Éditions Universitaires Européennes, Sarrebrücken (2010)
18. Kaplan, J.: Co-regulation in technology enhanced learning environments. In: Uden, L., Sinclair, J., Tao, Y.-H., Liberona, D. (eds.) LTEC 2014. CCIS, vol. 446, pp. 72–81. Springer, Heidelberg (2014)
19. Kaplan, J., Carré, P.: Self-direction in study circles - a hypothesis in support of active citizenship in 21st century Europe. In: Lucio-Villegas, E., del Carmen Martinez, M. (eds.) 5th ESREA European Research Conference. Adult Leaning and the Challenges of Social and Cultural Diversity: Diverse Lives, Cultures, Learnings and Literacies, vol. 2, pp. 80–87. Diálogos, Seville (2007)
20. Larsson, S.: Seven aspects of democracy as related to study circles. Int. J. Lifelong Educ. **20**(3), 199–217 (2001)
21. McLuhan, M.: Understanding Media - The Extensions of Man. Routledge, London, New York (1964)
22. Merriam, S.B. (ed.): Non-Western Perspectives on Learning and Knowing. Krieger Pub. Co, Malabar (2007)
23. Merriam, S.B., Caffarella, R.S., Baumgartner, L.: Learning in Adulthood: A Comprehensive Guide. The Jossey-Bass Higher and Adult Education Series. Jossey-Bass, San Francisco (2007)
24. Oliver, L.P.: Study Circles: Coming Together for Personal Growth and Social Change. Seven Locks Press, Cabin John (1987)
25. Oliver, L.P.: Building community through study circles. In: Medel-Anonuevo, C. (ed.) Integrating Lifelong Learning Perspectives, pp. 226–243. UNESCO, Hamburg (2002)
26. Reeve, J., Ryan, R.M., Deci, E.L., Jang, H.: Understanding and promoting autonomous self-regulation: a self-determination theory perspective. In: Schunk, D.H., Zimmerman, B.J. (eds.) Motivation and Self-Regulated Learning : Theory, Research, and Applications, pp. 223–244. Lawrence Erlbaum Associates, New York (2008)
27. Rovai, A.P.: Development of an instrument to measure classroom community. Internet High. Educ. **5**(3), 197–211 (2002)
28. Rovai, A.P.: Sense of community, perceived cognitive learning, and persistence in asynchronous learning networks. Internet High. Educ. **5**(4), 319–332 (2002)
29. Ryan, R., Deci, E.L.: Intrinsic and extrinsic motivations: classic définitions and new directions. Contemp. Educ. Psychol. **25**, 54–67 (2000)
30. Ryan, R.M., Deci, E.L.: Self-determination theory and the facilitation of intrinsic motivation, social development, and well-being. Am. Psychol. **55**(1), 68–78 (2000)

31. Ryan, R.M., Deci, E.L.: The darker and brighter sides of human existence: basic psychological needs as a unifying concept. Psychol. Inquiry **11**(4), 319–338 (2000)
32. Ryan, R.M., Deci, E.L.: Overview of self-determination theory: an organismic dialectical perspective. In: Deci, E.L., Ryan, R.M. (eds.) Handbook of Self-Determination Research, pp. 3–33. University of Rochester Press, Rochester (2002)
33. Sen, A.: The Idea of Justice. Penguin Books, London (2010)
34. Sheldon, K.M., Filak, V.: Manipulating autonomy, competence, and relatedness support in a game-learning context: new evidence that all three needs matter. Br. J. Soc. Psychol. **47**(2), 267–283 (2008)
35. Slavin, R.E.: Cooperative Learning: Theory, Research and Practice. Allyn & Bacon, Needham Heights (1995)
36. Suda, L.: Learning circles: democratic pools of knowledge. ARIS Resour. Bull. **12**(3), 1–4 (2001)

# Social Tagging for e-Learning: An Approach Based on the Triplet of Learners, Learning Objects and Tags

Luciana A.M. Zaina[1(✉)], José F. Rodrigues Júnior[2], and Anderson R. do Amaral[1,3]

[1] Federal University of São Carlos, Rdv João L. Santos, Km110, Sorocaba, SP, Brazil
lzaina@ufscar.br, anderson.amaral@etec.sp.gov.br
[2] University of São Paulo, Av. Trabalhador São Carlense, 400, São Carlos, SP, Brazil
junio@icmc.usp.br
[3] ETEC FernandoPrestes, R. Natal, 340, Sorocaba, SP, Brazil

**Abstract.** The emerging of the Web 2.0 has allowed users more interactivity with Web applications. Social tagging has been recognized as an important solution to the description of resources available on the Web. In the context of e-learning it may be used as an auxiliary mechanism to the composition of learning object metadata. This paper presents an approach based on the triplet of learners, learning objects and tags for providing the social tagging for e-learning. We performed an experiment with 336 technician students that marked 218 electronic learning objects for about 4,985 times. Although our results have shown that social tagging is a promising practice for e-learning some challenges on how to implement it has to be overcome.

**Keywords:** Folksonomy · Social tagging · Learning objects · Web 2.0

## 1 Introduction

The term Web 2.0 has been created to refer to a new generation of Web applications mainly characterized by providing support for collaboration and sharing of user-generated content [13]. Usually, companies developing applications for Web 2.0 use the Web as a platform to create collaborative and community-based websites, such as social networks, blogs, wikis, and others. The idea is to make the online environment more dynamic, where users can play a more active role and work together for producing and organizing the content, unlike the traditional Web (Web 1.0) where users were mostly readers of information.

The use of Social Web applications for different purposes increase since the emerging of Web 2.0. Specially, applications that promote the interrelationship of people and of knowledge through the Web have gained popularity. The social networks have been seen as an e-learning environment [22]. Accordingly, academic and commercial e-learning systems have adapted to the characteristics of these applications, becoming more appealing to students [5].


L. Uden et al. (Eds.): LTEC 2015, CCIS 533, pp. 104–115, 2015.
DOI: 10.1007/978-3-319-22629-3_9

In the social Web, a remarkable feature is the possibility of tagging online content, what allows the users to create vocabularies that categorize the resources - or learning objects [9] - they interact with. From the freedom of marking the objects arise the concept of folksonomy (folk, as for people; sonomy, as for taxonomy), which can be defined as a classification system outlined by people, without rules for terms' creation [3]. In the folksonomy the users freely choose keywords (also called tags) to identify, describe and classify the resources [19]. The folksonomy manifests in the form of social tagging systems [21]. In the practice of social tagging, users collaboratively use tags to annotate and make sense of content, a valuable source of information that has the potential of bringing order (indexing and classification, or cataloguing) to vast volumes of information [1].

Social tagging systems assume that users will express their impressions by means of tags that they use to classify the content they use [11]. Social tagging fulfills the impracticable classification that would be performed by specialists [7], its main features include: flexibility, as the users use their everyday dynamic vocabulary; pattern identification, as the users spontaneously choose the words that best describe the content; and collaboration, as predicted by Social Web applications.

Within the context of electronic learning (e-learning), the tagging systems may provide a process for indexing the resources based on the tags attributed from the user (teacher or student). The educational resorces usually are called learning objects (LOs). Formally, learning objects refer to entities used in the teaching-learning process; videos, images, simulator software, and text, among other possibilities. In the electronic-learning domain, it is desirable that learning objects be reusable for different learning objectives, or be combined to build up more complex objects [10]. To this end, the objects must carry metadata that contextualize and describe their use in a standard manner [20]. The main standard for learning objects is the IEEE LOM (Learning Object Metadata) [20]. Each category has a specific purpose, such as describing general attributes of objects, and educational objectives.

The possibility of tagging system is converging as a new model for cataloging learning objects based on the tags provided either by students or by professors. In the case of students, the tagging process concerns a reflection experience in which students tag the objects based on their own experience [2, 15]. Then, the repositories of tagged learning objects can be searched by the very students or by other people in the course of learning [4]. For achieving a cataloging that effectively describes the learning objects is mandatory to follow a tagging process that fulfill learning purposes. In e-learning area the vocabulary of tags must be suitably heterogeneous in order to extensively describe the objects.

The goal of this work is to present an approach based on the triplet of learners, learning objects and tags aiming to provide the social tagging for e-learning. To empirically examine the proposal, we performed an experiment with 336 technician students who have tagged 218 learning objects marked 4,985 times. In our experiment, we did not use a particular pedagogical learning model. But we believe that our proposal can be extended to different pedagogical theories. The focus is the cataloging of learning objects which facilitates the access to such objects.

The remainder of this paper is organized as follows: Sect. 2 presents the related work; the proposed model is presented in Sect. 3; Sect. 4 outlines the experiment results; finally, Sect. 5 remarks the main conclusions.

## 2 Related Works

Social tagging systems grew in popularity in the last years due to their simplicity to categorize and retrieve content based on tags. The increase in the number of users that provide information to such mechanisms caused the emergence of systems that assume the users express their preferences by means of the tags they create and use [11].

The main features of social tagging are: communication and immediate feedback, fast adaptation to vocabulary alterations, single or collective organization of objects, potential of cataloging, and assistance in the recommendation of content, among others. The tags entered in the system allow users to freely explore objects and other users' profiles without having to follow a rigid predefined hierarchy of concepts [14].

A collaborative model for construction of learning object repository is proposed by Monge et al. [12] which pointed out that the educational materials should be available in an open and multidisciplinary environment. They consider that technique of social tagging adds a rich-semantic for the description of a material that can improve the social dynamics of learning repositories, building - teachers, students and research institutes - a large network of knowledge. The approach proposes by Sierra and Valmayor [16] aim at the creation and extension of metadata of learning objects using the social tagging to pinpoint the attributes of the metadata. We consider the idea of cataloging the learning objects using the tags an opportunity to create large repositories that reflect the perception of the users.

Bateman et al. [2] analyze social tagging applied to e-learning by using tags collected from the interaction of students and professors with learning objects. In their study, they observe that the professors use a more specialized terminology than the students, and that an initial set of tags (a seed) must be provided during the earlier stages of the system. We follow their advice providing our students with such a set during the experiments; differently, we further discuss the behavior of the students, and the resulting vocabularies of tags, tracing some relevant hypotheses.

In a recent work, Zervas and Sampson [23] evaluate how the motivation affects the enlargement of tagged learning repositories. Although they discuss some interesting issues about the influence of the profiles of the students, they do not put conclusive considerations about this interesting topic. In our research, we follow a similar investigation to settle, as much as possible, revealing remarks about how social tagging occurs in the educational domain.

Sinclair and Cardew-Hall [17] claimed that a tag cloud reflects the folksonomy's vocabulary in a social navigation tool, reducing the cognitive effort on the understanding of a tag and promoting the relationship of tag to learning objects. In a review of social tagging, Gupta et al. [7] suggest that in the representation of the tag cloud can be used font sizes and colors to draw a distinguish on the frequency of the use of tags. In our work we adopted the visualization through tag clouds where the font size increases according the use of the tag.

## 3 e-Learning Social Tagging Approach

Based on the presented concepts and related works, we have defined a model to conceive the tagging system as a triplet made of students, tags, and learning objects that, together, interact to form a descriptive vocabulary (Fig. 1). The descriptive vocabulary represents the students' understanding about the topics of the learning object adding to the repository the feature of social dynamics as proposed by Sierra and Valmayor [16].

The proposed model introduces an evolutive cycle that allows the learners the creation and the reuse of tags. The cycle starts from the search by t and retrieval of learning objects (1); proceeds to the creation and reuse of tags (2); and evolves through the refinement achieved by the association of tags to the objects (3). These three steps cycle for some indefinite time, during which a repository of tags is built. The repository is organized as two sets: "my tags" - the tags created by a specific user who is logged in the system; "global tags" - the universe of all the distinct tags created by all users for a specific learning object. Along time, some tags are recurrently used for describing the learning objects. The convergence of the tags to a stable descriptive set defines a vocabulary (4).

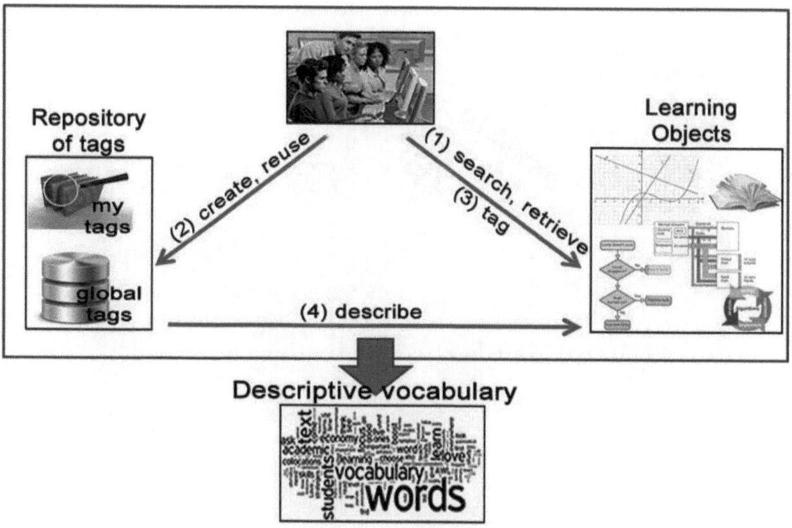


**Fig. 1.** e-Learning social tagging model.

In the model proposed the student becomes an active agent in the process of learning objects description, contributing to the maintenance and organization of objects. The repository of tags can be seen as a "living" dictionary, constantly updated by the users. The use of tags as descriptors of objects favors the indexing, navigation and recommendation of different learning objects.

After we drew the cycle, we seek for tools that matched to our model and could support our experiment. We noticed that previous works did not offer an adequate (open source and accessible) environment for experimentation according to our model. For this reason, our research group designed and developed the TagLink tool [18], which is able to (1) retrieve learning objects, (2) create/reuse tags, (3) support the tagging of objects, (4) manage a descriptive vocabulary of tags, and (5) display the tag in a tag cloud.

TagLink was designed following the scheme presented in Fig. 1. It allows students to search and retrieve learning objects from the Web using Google's Custom Search API [6]. To do so, the students provide search terms and TagLink returns the objects and their corresponding links. Each link is processed as a learning object to which students can associate tags.

TagLink tool is configured with a set of relevant repositories of learning objects. The repositories are registered in TagLink together with a priority indicator that specifies in which order they are to be searched. The step for tagging the learning objects is showed in Fig. 2. First the student search the keyword (A) and the results returned by TagLink correspond, each, to one learning object; the student select the object that it (B) can be tagged with a new (E) or with an existing tag (C) and (D). The field "tags of the object" (C) shows all the tags that were attributed to the object, regardless of who did; and the field "my tags" (D) reports the tags that the student has been used in any object. These attributes encourages the vocabulary construction collaboratively.

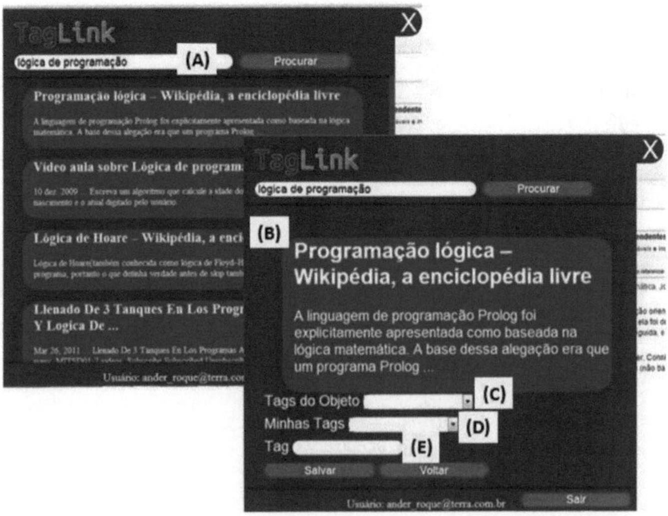


**Fig. 2.** TagLink tool – search and tagging view.

The students can search the learning objects that are stored in the repository through the tag cloud (Fig. 3). The words represented by a larger font, are the tags that were attributed to more than one object. How much larger the font of the tag is the meaning is that more objects were assigned to it. When a tag is selected (A) in the cloud TagLink displays the list of the objects that were marked by this tag (B). The student can then click on it to access it.

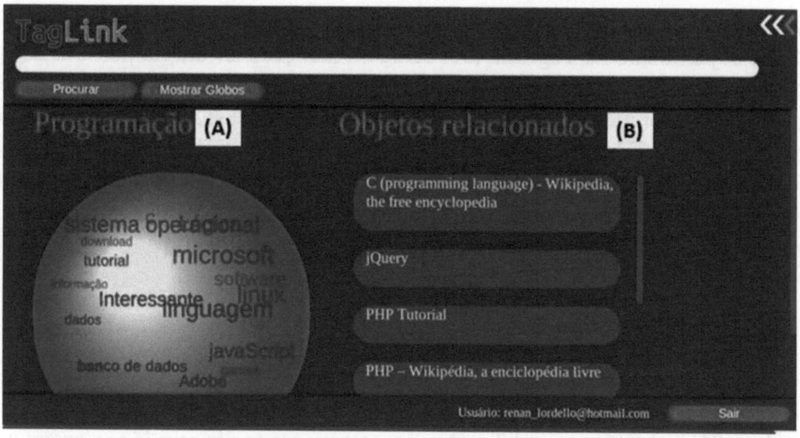


**Fig. 3.** TagLink tool – tag cloud view.

In TagLink, it is possible to register users and to organize them in groups - classes, or workgroups, for instance - so that it becomes possible to observe the behavior of specific sets of students. It also supports the retrieval of data about the tags: creation date, how many times it was used, who created it, corresponding objects, and so on; and the retrieval of data about the learning objects: which tags, times of use, origin, and so on.

# 4 e-Learning Social Tagging Approach in Action

We carried out an experiment with 336 students from the vocational education level (information technology technicians) at a country side school in São Paulo, Brazil. The students were instructed to search and retrieve learning objects related to their current courses and to tag these objects through TagLink tool. The activity of the students was recorded for analysis.

A preliminary poll revealed that most of the students were regular users of social networks; and that they were familiar with tagging, but they had never used such functionality for educational purposes. Based on this, we decided to provide the students with an initial training before using the system.

## 4.1 Planning the Experiment

We chose to split the student in two groups: Group A (GA) consisting of the older students, and Group B (GB) consisting of the younger students. We also defined two sets of search terms - both with 5 terms each - according to the students course. These sets answer for the initial seed necessary at earlier stages of tagging systems as suggests Bateman et al. [2] and we reported in Sect. 2:

- Ta: contained generic terms for information technology, like logic, C#, Databases, Windows, and Linux; and
- Tb: contained web programing terms, like JQuery, PHP, XNA, Android and Flash.

The experiment should have 2 phases. In the Phase1, the students would be told to search the object from the TagLink tool using all the terms of the set that was assigned to him/her. They should also select at least one learning object from each search result, and to create three or more tags for this object. In Phase 2, the students would be allowed to use existing tags, either of their own (my tags) or of other students (tags of the object), or to create more tags. The goal will be to have the students build a vocabulary of tags. Prior to the experiment we had an introductory period when the students learned about how to use TagLink and about the importance of the experiment.

### 4.2 Experiment in Action

We conducted the two phases of the experiment during 2 months, switching the sets of search terms to the groups: first, GA has used set Ta and GB has used Tb; and after GA has used set Tb and GB has used Ta. Our intention were to observe if one group would use the tag of other group, showing us the evolution and the estabilization of the vocabulary. At the end we had 2,019 distinct tags for 218 learning objects selected by 336 students.

### 4.3 Analysing the Outcomes

Aiming to verify the potencial of use of social tagging to catalog learning objects, we analyze two aspects: the number of times and of students that created new tags; and the number of times and of students that reused existing tags. The two aspects can show us the involvement of the students with the process of tagging learning objects. We verified that 1.279 out of 2.019 tags (63.34 %) were used just once, when they were created; the other 740 tags (36.65 %) were reused. Table 1 summarizes how the students used the system in relation to the creation and to the reuse of tags. It is important to highlight that the summarization does not consider only tags used just once, reflecting the students activities in the system.

**Table 1.** The relevant terms according to the responses of students.

| Group | Phase1 | | Phase2 | | Total | |
|---|---|---|---|---|---|---|
| | Created | Reused | Created | Reused | Created | Reused |
| A | 1,126 | 648 | 144 | 303 | 1,270 | 951 |
| B | 1,329 | 933 | 139 | 363 | 1,468 | 1,296 |
| Total | 2,455 | 1,581 | 283 | 666 | 2,738 | 2,247 |

In Fig. 4, we can verify one first concentration in the data defining a nearly Gaussian-peaked distribution around 2 tags per student; and one main second concentration defining a nearly Gaussian-smooth distribution center around 12 tags per student. The first concentration is expected; since the participation in the experiment was optional, a significant fraction of the students created no more than 3 tags. The second main concentration revealed that 4 times as much students took part of the experiment creating from 4 up to 18 tags each. The participants of the second main concentration created 2,420 tags - not necessarily distinct - or nearly 11 tag creations per learning object.

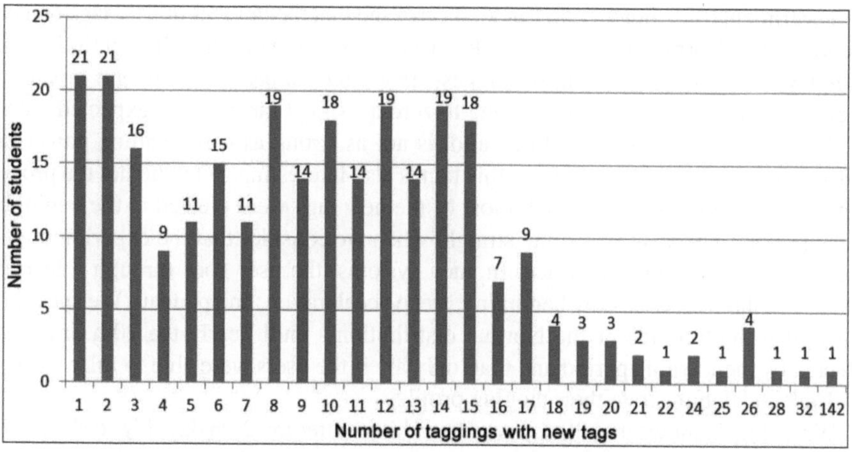


**Fig. 4.** Distribution of the number of students per number of tags created.

In Fig. 5, we can verify two peaks, one around 5 reused tags per student, and another one around 15 reused tags per student. The distribution now is shifted if compared to the distribution of new tags per student - Fig. 5. In the place where there was a peak, now there is a valley; the events indicate that there was an increase in the participation of the students who did not create tags before - more to the left in the distribution. Meanwhile, a smaller set of students engaged even more in the experiment and increased the expected value - more to the right in the distribution. This is a curious observation, it shows three behaviors for the students, as derived from Table 1: a set with students

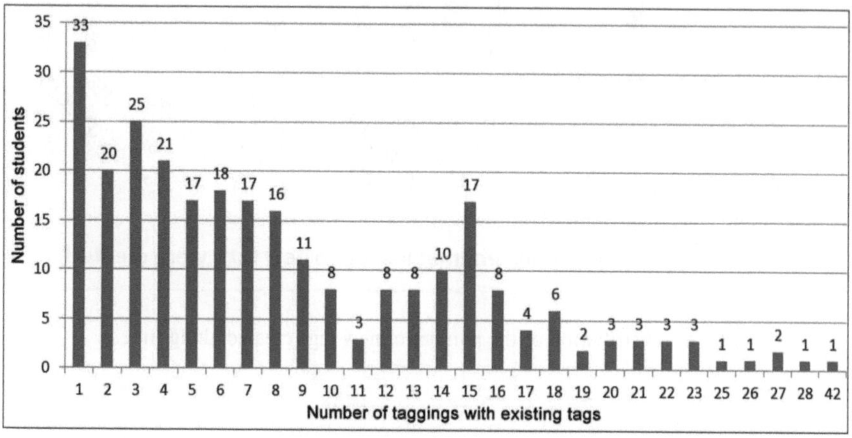


**Fig. 5.** Distribution of the number of students per number of tags reused.

that only created new tags (11.3 %), a set with students that only reused tags (8.9 %), and a set of students that did both things (79.7 %).

Observing the aspect of convergence to a well-defined descriptive vocabulary of tags, we had to analyze the number of new tags created in the system along the time of the experiment (two months). In Fig. 6, we can see that the number of new tags behaves according to a Normal distribution with a peak close to the middle of the period - in the 28th day. The Normal distribution suggests that after the peak, the students create just a few more new tags, a number tending to zero as we get far from the expected value.

The Normal distribution, while valid, is not as strong as a descending power-law distribution would be; nevertheless, this fact is also interesting. Why did not the process behave like a power-law in which most of the new tags were created at the beginning of the period? The answer is quite straight when we consider that the experiment goes over a human-computer interface. In such systems, the user goes through a learning curve with three phases: slow beginning, steep acceleration, and plateau. We speculate, hence, that the left side of the Normal distribution - until nearly the 20th day - was affected by the learning period and that, only after, the users were able to fully work on TagLink and demonstrate their tagging profiles.

While Fig. 7 shows that the tags are to stabilize after the 28th day, Fig. 6 shows that a small subset of tags dominates the usage in the system. More precisely, there were 2,019 different tags; among them, 1,972 of them were used less that 17 times - not shown in the figure; and only 47 were used 17 times or more - shown in the figure. These characteristics describe a long heavy-tailed distribution indicating a strong imbalance as the students concentrate on a very small subset. Table 2 complements our view about the tags used by the groups (GA and GB) in each phase.

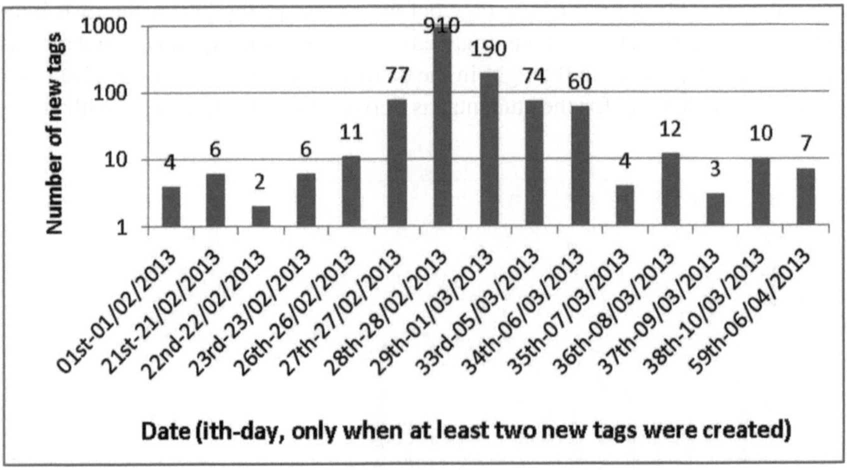


**Fig. 6.** Distribution of the number of new tags created along time.

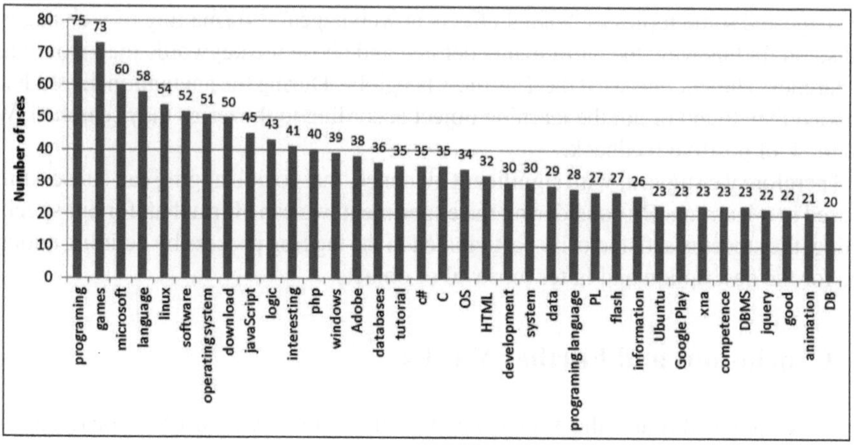


**Fig. 7.** Distribution of the number of times each tag was used.

By comparing this dominant set of terms with the set of seed terms provided in the beginning of the experiment (Ta and Tb) it is possible to observe a great intersection. This fact indicates that the seed of terms strongly influenced the vocabulary and that, possibly, this seed accelerated the process as suggested in other works. Therefore, based on the evidences of Figs. 6 and 7, we argue that social tagging is supposed to converge to a well-defined set of tags. We also argue that an appropriate set of seed terms may provide some control over this process, influencing the definition of the set of most frequent tags and, consequently, influencing how descriptive they will be.

**Table 2.** Tags used by groups in each phase.

| Tag x Group x Phase | | | | | |
|---|---|---|---|---|---|
| | Phase 1 | | Phase 2 | | |
| tag | Grup A | Grup B | Grup A | Grup B | Total |
| programming | 30 | 7 | 6 | 11 | 54 |
| Microsoft | 20 | 17 | 6 | 8 | 51 |
| Linux | 23 | 13 | 2 | 2 | 40 |
| logic | 27 | 0 | 1 | 5 | 33 |
| software | 13 | 10 | 7 | 10 | 40 |
| language | 16 | 19 | 3 | 9 | 47 |
| operating system | 14 | 10 | 7 | 10 | 41 |
| JavaScript | 0 | 28 | 9 | 0 | 37 |
| SO | 10 | 3 | 2 | 9 | 24 |
| interesting | 1 | 19 | 3 | 0 | 23 |
| Total | 154 | 126 | 46 | 64 | 390 |

Aiming to enrich our conclusions, after the experiment we asked to other students' group (200 students of 3 different course) to elaborate a study evolving the terms described on Ta and Tb (see Sect. 4.1). However, instead of inform exactly the terms we suggested some topics as "visual effects in web pages", "formatting of web pages", and so on. In this way, the participants defined and chose the keywords they would use in searches. The students used the Taglink's tag globe. During the navigation the students reported they found or not the learning object according to the terms they searched. We had 98 % of positive feedback.

Therefore we suggest, with significant evidence, that social tagging can successfully be used in e-learning. By considering the experiment, we can affirm that, for our specific setting, the students satisfactorily participated in the tagging process by defining enough tags for the description and latter retrieval of objects.

## 5 Conclusions and Further Works

The folksonomy through the social tagging allows the creation of a vocabulary of learning objects collaboratively. This possibility brings the student to a more active role in the process of organization and maintenance of learning objects.

Considering this opportunity, this paper presented an approach based on the triplet of learners, learning objects and tags for providing social tagging is the e-learning. The proposal could be achieved by the construction of the TagLink tool which address the proposed approach and supported us in our evalutation phase.

In a real setting with 336 students we found that: (1) the use of social tagging is viable in the sense that students are inclined to build extensive catalogs over the learning objects; (2) despite their colloquial experience with tagging content in social networks, students will tag learning objects using descriptive (formal and general) terms that aid the posterior use of objects catalogs; and (3) the vocabulary of terms converges to a "rich" subset of terms that answers for over 95 % of the tags crated and/or reused by the students, indicating that guidance (an initial set of terms) can lead to a faster convergence and to an improved control over the process.

In any case, our experience brings insights that could be used as first assumptions in motivating the construction of social tagging learning systems. Looking at the lessons learned in the experiment, we observed that the reuse of tags can also be seen as a suggestion process of tags. This encourages us to study the possibility to include a tag recommendation cycle on our approach, improving the tagging process.

**Acknowledgments.** We thank the the students of Fernando Prestes school for participanting of our experiment.

## References

1. Ahn, L., Dabbish, L.: Labeling images with a computer game. In: CHI 2004 Proceedings of the SIGCHI Conference on Human Factors in Computing Systems, pp. 319–326 (2004)
2. Bateman, S., Brooks, C., Mccalla, G.: Applying collaborative tagging to e-learning. In: Proceedings of ACM WWW (2007)
3. Dahl, D., Vossen, G.: Evolution of learning folksonomies: social tagging in e-learning repositories. Int. J. Technol. Enhanced Learn. **1**, 35–46 (2008)

4. Garcia-Penalvo, F.J., Morales, E., Barron, A.: Learning objects for e-activities in social web. WSEAS Trans. Syst. **6**(3), 507–513 (2007)
5. Glavinić, V., Granić, A.: HCI research for e-Learning: adaptability and adaptivity to support better user interaction. In: Holzinger, A. (ed.) USAB 2008. LNCS, vol. 5298, pp. 359–376. Springer, Heidelberg (2008)
6. Google's Custom Search API. https://developers.google.com/custom-search/?hl=en. Accessed October 2014
7. Gupta, M., Li, R., Yin, Z., Han, J.: Survey on social tagging techniques. Newsl. ACM SIGKDD Explor. **12**(1), 58–72 (2010)
8. IEEE LOM, Draft standard for learning object metadata. http://ltsc.ieee.org/wg12. Accessed December 2014
9. Jäschke, R., Hotho, A., Mitzlaff, F., Stumme, G.: Challenges in tag recommendations for collaborative tagging systems. In: Pazos Arias, J.J., Fernández Vilas, A., Díaz Redondo, R.P. (eds.) Recommender Systems for the Social Web. ISRL, vol. 32, pp. 65–87. Springer, Heidelberg (2012)
10. McGreal, R.: Learning objects: a practical definition. Int. J. Inst. Technol. Distance Learn. **1**(9), 21–31 (2004)
11. Milicevic, A.K., Nanopoulos, A., Ivanovic, M.: Social tagging in recommender systems: a survey of the state-of-the-art and possible extensions. Artif. Intell. Rev. **33**(3), 187–209 (2010)
12. Monge, S., Ovelar, R., Azpeitia, I.: Repository 2.0: social dynamics to support community building in learning object repositories. Interdisc. J. E-Learn. Learn. Objects **4**, 191 (2008). Informing Science Institute
13. O'Reilly, T.: What is Web 2.0: Design Patterns and Business Models for the Next Generation of Software (2005). http://oreilly.com/web2/archive/what-is-web-20.html
14. Shepitsen, A., Gemmell, J., Mobasher, B., Burke, R.: Personalized recommendation in social tagging systems using hierarchical clustering. In: Proceedings of the 2008 ACM Conference on Recommender Systems (2008)
15. Shih, W., Tseng, S.: Folksonomy-based indexing for retrieving tutoring resources. In: 2012 Seventh IEEE International Conference on Wireless, Mobile and Ubiquitous Technology in Education, pp. 97–101 (2012)
16. Sierra, J.L., Valmayor, A.F.: Tagging learning objects with evolving metadata schemas. In: Eighth IEEE International Conference on Advanced Learning Technologies, ICALT 2008, Santander, Spain (2008)
17. Sinclair, J., Cardew-Hall, M.: The folksonomy tag cloud: when is it useful? J. Inf. Sci. Feb. **34**(1), 15–29 (2008)
18. TagLink tool. http://200.133.238.112/tag/
19. Trant, J.: Studying social tagging and folksonomy a review and framework. J. Digit. Inf. **10**(1), 1–42 (2009)
20. Vazquez, A.R., Ostrovskaya, Y.A.: Analysis of open technological standards for learning objects. In: Proceedings of 4th LA-Web, Puebla Cholula, Mexico, pp. 105–108 (2006)
21. Wal, T.V.: Explaining and showing broad and narrow folksonomies. Off the Top [blog] (2005). http://www.vanderwal.net/random/entrysel.php?blog=1635, Accessed 13 December 2013
22. Zaina, L.A.M., Almeida, T.A., Torres, G.M.: Can the online social networks be used as a learning tool? A case study in Twitter. Commun. Comput. Inf. Sci. (Print) **446**, 114–123 (2014)
23. Zervas, P., Sampson, D.G.: The effect of users' tagging motivation on the enlargement of digital educational resources metadata. Comput. Hum. Behav. **32**, 292–300 (2014)

# Learning Engineering

# Learning Analytic and Evaluation in Malleable Learning Environments

Manel BenSassi(✉), Mona Laroussi, and Henda BenGhezala

RIADI Laboratory, ENSI, Manouba University, Manouba, Tunisia
bensassi.manel@gnet.tn

**Abstract.** Education has evolved from the traditional classroom of blackboard and chalk to multimedia software teaching, online teaching, hybrid education and so on. Learning objects and scenario are growing in scale and functionality. Because of this increase in complexity, the likelihood of subtle errors is much greater. One-way to achieving this proposed goal is by pre-evaluation of these environments. Many companies and departments have their own evaluation criteria and requirements, but the relative and subjective are too much, so they can not meet the general evaluation. For this reason, we propose a framework able to analyse the learning scenario functionalities and aspects and gives an early evaluation of the designed scenario. The evaluation framework is based on contextual elements: Times, Actors, network, user location and correlation between activities. Then we propose to evaluate learning scenario through formal methods which are mathematically based languages, techniques and tools for specifying and verifying. Use the formal methods does not a priori guarantee correctness and successful. However, they can greatly increase our understanding of the learner's behaviour with the existing scenario by revealing inconsistencies, ambiguities and incompleteness that might otherwise go undetected.

## 1 Introduction

The "learning engineering" is an iterative process that has got different objectives: the development, evaluation and elaboration of educational materials. This process leads to predictable and repeatable improvement of learning environments and creates conditions that enable robust learning and effective instruction.

Advances in computer technology, intelligent environments, context modelling applications and recent developments in the field of wireless and pervasive communications, have created a wide array of new possibilities for technology users. When these technologies started to be used in education, a new learning paradigm, malleable learning, emerged. Thus, many new issues emerge and need to be explored. In this paper we are interested, in particular, on evaluating in malleable learning. First, it's our research field. Second, while evaluation in e-learning systems has attracted much attention, malleable learning is still struggling with basic technological and pedagogical problems. In fact, learning in pervasive and mobile settings introduces certainly new methods of evaluation. So, the relevant questions which need to be answered are:


L. Uden et al. (Eds.): LTEC 2015, CCIS 533, pp. 119–133, 2015.
DOI: 10.1007/978-3-319-22629-3_10

- *Did methods of evaluation in e-learning remain relevant in malleable learning?*
- *What to evaluate in malleable learning systems, when and how?*

In fact, the higher cost of the implementation of malleable learning scenarios (mobile, pervasive, hybrid, social..) and the complexity of their context and functionalities emphasizes the need to understand the designed scenario. Besides, learning scenario evaluation are performed a posteriori. On the contrary, we claim that a priori evaluation malleable scenario can be useful. It can help designers to anticipate several problems that can arise before starting the implementation and the deployment and thus return on the phase of scenario design to add missing elements, retraining in this way development cost.

It is for this reason that we propose a formal approach based on a framework incorporating the relevant components to evaluate educational scenario at early stage. After these components and their interactions are described, the use of the framework will be discussed.

The rest of paper is organized as follows: Firstly, we define the malleable learning scenario and its challenges. In the following section, we present current evaluation methods of learning scenarios. Section 4 focus on our evaluation methodology for early evaluation based on the timed automata modelling and formal verification properties while an experiment of our work through pervasive learning scenario is included in Sect. 5. Section 6 concludes the paper and outlines future research directions.

## 2 Malleable Learning Scenario: Definition and Challenges

Malleability is traditionally described as a feature of interactive software that allows the change of certain aspects of the software in order to meet different users profiles and business requirements.

It's widely agreed that the design of malleable system is an important future challenges [1]. Since malleable systems support the structured recognition of complexity and dynamics of tasks and organisations as ell as of inter- and intra-individual differences between end users.

Malleable activities can be performed at different system components, requiring knowledge and understanding of the users carrying out these activities [2].

Certainly, advances in computer technology, intelligent environments, context modelling applications and recent developments in the field of wireless and pervasive communications, have created a wide array of new possibilities for technology users. When these technologies started to be used in education, a new learning paradigm, *malleable learning*, emerged.

It's flexible, context-aware, co-adaptive, extensible and technology-enhanced learning [3]. It takes advantage of different types of learning: conventional learning, e-learning, M-learning, P-learning and U-learning (Fig. 1). This malleable learning merges indoor and outdoor activities and enables students to learn through factual cases and to experiment various learning scenarios using smart technologies.

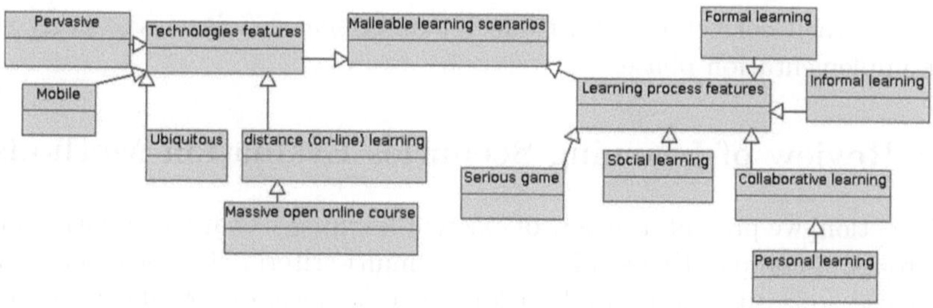


**Fig. 1.** Malleable learning environment features

As a consequence, malleable Learning scenarios enable learners to adapt learning process, to particular needs. As a matter of fact, this new learning philosophy ensures learners' autonomy, motivation and challenge. Additionally, it helps to improve formal and informal learning through collaborative and challenging educational activities taking place in different locations and various stages.

### 2.1 Properties and Challenges

The hierarchical activities' correlation leads to a coherent and collective scenario, that we call here "*Malleable learning scenario*". Malleable scenarios aim at ensuring learner's autonomy, motivation and challenge by experimenting various learning scenarios.

The malleable learning scenario model may be used and reused by other educational scenarios and the composition of them may be exposed as a new malleable scenario. As a consequence, malleable learning environment have many properties and the most important are:

**Co-evolution.** All sub-environments exist within their own environment and they are also part of that environment. Therefore, as the context of execution changes, the learning environment needs to change to ensure best fit.

**Co-adaptivity.** Co-adaptivity models all possible interactions between context and learning activity because context and learning activities influence each others in learning processes. Indeed, it defines two classes of "adaptivity": adaptivity of context to activity and activity to context. Such a bijective adaptation aims to facilitate the students learning and to create an adequate environment which helps him/her to concentrate better on her/his learning tasks [3].

**Requisite Variety.** The greater the variety within the system the stronger it is. In fact, the variety of tool and the multiple strategies of learning abound in learning in malleable learning environments which use these possibilities to create adaptive environment to co-evolve with their environment.

When developers target towards the construction of learning scenarios providing that kind of flexibility, complexity and various adaptive functionalities they need to evaluate their correctness and to detect functional deficiencies at early stage before implementation phase.

## 3 A Review of Learning Scenarios Evaluation Methods

In this section, we present a review of existent learning scenario evaluation methods through a comparative study based on multi-criteria classification. In fact, we propose a classification based on four criteria (level of stratification, degree of formalism, user implication and stage of the evaluation) [12]:

- **Level of Stratification:** We define a stratified evaluation (a hierarchical evaluation) as a layered structure formed by ranked criteria. The criteria composition allow designer to analyse educational scenario from different point of views. Two types of evaluation are possible: Mono-level evaluation and multi-level Evaluation.
- **Degree of Formalism:** This criteria describes the nature of the evaluation method: formal or informal.
- **User Implication:** This criteria shows whether the learning scenarios related actors (designers, teachers, learners or coaches) are explicitly or implicitly implied in the evaluation process.
- **Stage of Evaluation:** Laurillard [4] states the evaluation process as an iterative one and should take place at every stage in the design, implementation and deployment of the educational scenario.

Several evaluation methods are generally used to evaluate educational scenarios. But most of it fall into one of the three following categories:

- Analytical methods (such as questionnaires, observations, check-list, interviews,...) request analytical staff to write the evaluation dimensions and criteria and then to draw the whole evaluation report and outcomes. These methods observe the entire learning process and record students response and then let them fill out pre-designed questionnaires and conduct interviews to obtain their point of views about the realized scenario [5].
- Evaluation system based on tracks analysis requests both analytical and technical staff. The first group is responsible for defining scores for various features of the e learning scenario according to a specific set of evaluation coefficients. This team also specify the quality of the learning scenario. The technical staff develops the system or specify the evaluation framework to the mentioned scores [6].
- Teaching test methods are based on an appropriate testing program that is suitable to different goals and characteristics of the teaching style. These methods implement the pre-test, the post-test of the learning scenario, and other steps to test the knowledge of students and their skills and finally determine the effectiveness of teaching scenario [5].

The following Table 1 summarizes our comparative study. The review of learning scenarios evaluation methods, shows that:

**Table 1.** A comparative study of evaluation's techniques

| Methods | Stage of evaluation according to the deployment and the implementation | Degree of formalism | Student implication | Level of stratification |
|---|---|---|---|---|
| Analytical methods | After | Informal | Explicit | Multilevel |
| Index system based on tracks analysis | After | formal or semi formal | Implicit | Multilevel |
| Teaching test methods | Before and after | Informal | Explicit | Multilevel |

- Most of it could be applied **only after the deployment and the execution of the educational scenario** so designer couldn't anticipate and predict learners' difficulties.
- These methods are **not formal** and mathematically based for describing the evaluation process. Then, it doesn't provide frameworks within which designers can specify, develop and verify designed scenarios in a systematic, rather than adhoc manner.
- None of it supports mobile and pervasive learning scenario evaluation, because designers find difficulties in getting proper information about the students and their learning behaviour (ethical problems, track's collect problems, ...).

Several research have pointed out that the engineering of malleable environment lack development procedures, frameworks and effective support since designers have to take into account several problems which classical methodologies do not address.

For that reason, we propose methodological and conceptual framework to evaluate the usability of malleable learning environment. In doing so, malleability is related to contextual functionalities.

# 4 Formative Pre-Evaluation Methodology for the Re-Engineering of Malleable Learning Environment

## 4.1 Specification of Evaluation Dimensions

*Stages of the Evaluation Methodology.* The iterative engineering presents our straightforward view of the system development of the learning scenario's life cycle, which includes five stages: conception, contextualisation, pre-evaluation, deployment and finally retaining and post-evaluation.

Basically, the stages of the traditional life cycle remain [7,8]. We add a pre-evaluation stage stressing the aspect of the re-engineering process which could be happen at early stage (before deployment).

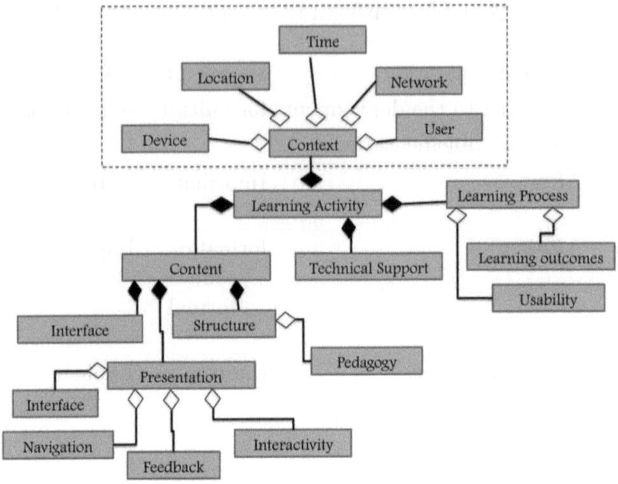


**Fig. 2.** Different features that could be evaluate in the learning scenario

Our evaluation methodology can be applied to contextualisation and retaining stages.

During the contextualisation stage, the malleable learning scenario functions/prototype and designs could be formally modelled and checked before implementation.

We can also apply the evaluation model to the retaining stage. We analyse learners' tracks and we re-model it into a formal model that reflects different activities done by the student. This feature is particularly useful because it will be possible de check each learner's automata with different properties extracted from the intentional scenario model. Thus the evaluation results can indicate a clear refinement direction for pedagogical designer to let the designed scenario accommodate to the learner's requirement.

*Contextual Evaluation: What to Evaluate in Malleable Learning Scenario?* According to [9], we can evaluate these following dimensions in a learning scenario: content, technical support, learning process (see Fig. 2). Each dimension includes a number of sub categories and criteria that could be considered in the evaluation process. All these aspects are equally important, as the learning activity has to be simultaneously pedagogically and technically sound.

However, we propose that the learning activity's context should also be considered for evaluation. The context is a set of evolutive elements appropriate to the interaction between learner and learning application including the learner and the learning environment themselves. Figure 2 presents in a diagram the different aspects that we can combine and include in the evaluation framework.

- The device dimension: we consider that it is important capabilities of user's device, especially hardware attributes, for mobile learning due to the fact they have a big impact on learning scenario execution.
- The network and connectivity dimension: nowadays mobile device might be connected to the "Net" via many technologies: GPRS, UMTS, WiFi, 3G-telecommunication, etc. Mobile devices often have periods of disconnection that had to be considered in evaluation of the usability of the learning scenario. The connectivity quality depends on user's location and mobility.

We believe that the proposed framework provides an insight into the design of each activity and phase of the learning process and thus facilitating the improvement of conceived learning scenarios. The decomposition of the learning scenario into layers contributes to the reuse of each learning components.

### 4.2 Evaluation Techniques: Formal Specification and Trace's Analysis

Using automata theory as a method of specification, it is possible to use the formal verification techniques to demonstrate that a system design is correct with respect to its specification. The main objective of formal specification and verification is to minimize the creation of functional errors and limits. By creating a formal specification of the educational scenario, the designers are forced to make and to define a detailed scenario analysis at early stage before its deployment into the TEL system. This analysis will usually reveal errors or consistencies through simulation.

In our context, formal specification methods can solve many problems (track's collecting, monitoring problems, behaviour study of learners...), guaranteeing non-ambiguity and supporting powerful analysis capabilities.

We believe that automata formalism can be used to structure and describe learning activities. Moreover, automata formalism can support the evaluation of educational scenario in different ways (Fig. 3):

- When the design process requires to define an educational scenario or multiple scenarios (which might illustrate single step of learning or the whole process). Each scenario could be formalized through an automata formalism. Then, this formalism could help to identify coaching requirements and then support re-engineering decision.
- We use this formalism to support evaluation of learners' performance. We analyse learners' tracks and we remodel it into an automata model that reflects different activities done by the student. This feature is particularly useful because it will be possible to check each learners automata with different properties extracted from the intentional scenario model.

## 5 Conceptual Architecture of ReStart-Me

In this section, we present our proposed framework with a brief description of each of its components and how they interact. Formal evaluation of educational scenario is based essentially on these components (shown in Fig. 4):

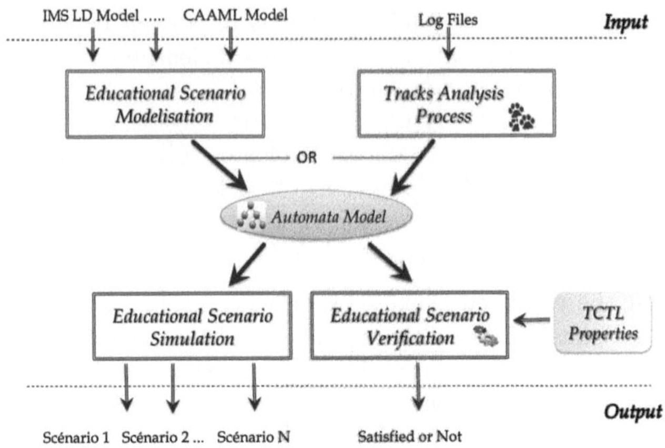


**Fig. 3.** Overview of our approach workflow

1. *The role of Educational scenario design.* Instructor introduces the content in term of activities, their sequencing, their description and their explanation. To ensure the clarity of the scenario's description, it should be specified with the Learning Design standard or the Unified Modelling Language. The instructor should also draw his constraints of deployment and monitoring requirements.
2. *The role of the learning process.* The educational scenario is deployed and launched by the learning environment. Each learning units is observed and tracked by the TEL system.
3. *The role Formal Modelling of Educational Scenario.* The description of educational scenario is translated in Automata Model based on transformation rules described in [10]. We extend the obtained automaton with global and local clocks. We also define constraints and correlation between different activities. By creating a formal specification of the educational scenario, the designers are forced to make and to define a detailed scenario analysis at early stage before its deployment into the TEL system.
4. *The role of evaluation process: Simulation and interpretation.* Using automata theory as a method of specification, it is possible to use the formal verification techniques to demonstrate that a system design is correct with respect to its specification. This analysis will usually reveal errors or consistencies through simulations.
5. *The Role of the Re-engineering process.* The re-engineering process aims to build a remedial scenario.

## 6 Case Study: Evaluation of a Malleable Learning Scenario

We want to show that automata formalism can describe the different learning activities and all the paths to follow in order to evaluate and to monitor the educational scenario through simulation and tests generation. In fact, our automata model is composed of three sub classes:

- **The nominative automata:** describes the basic path that learner is expected to do it. It englobes the nominative sequence of events generally defined by the designer.
- **The alternate automata:** Each tested rule may produce an alternative path that the learner may realize it, with an alternative set of steps that run in parallel with the basic path.
- **The failure automata:** describes the result of a step in the basic path that fails to produce a successful result.

To test our proposed Evaluation method, we used pervasive learning scenario models generated by the authoring tool *ContAct-Me* [3].
The objective of this study reported in this section is twofold:

- to check practicality of the proposed framework when building an actual mobile scenario
- and to evaluate qualitatively the benefits of such methodology.

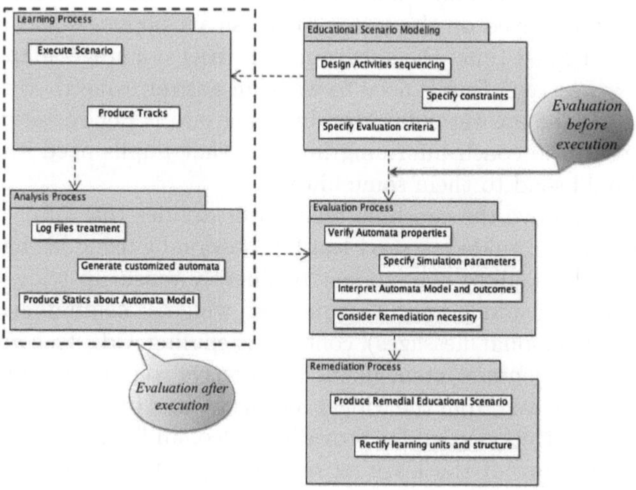


**Fig. 4.** Full evaluation framework

A team of researchers composed mainly by of five designers has prepared a textual description of the mobile learning scenario.

**Learning Scenario Description.** The conceptual designers' meetings have produced a scenario design document that describes the sequencing of different activities and rules of the pervasive learning scenario. To summarize, the learning scenario can be described as follows:

A high school decides to organize an excursion to apply different rules discussed in the Natural Science course. This trial enables pupils to learn through factual cases and to experiment various scenarios using social media and networks, pervasive and mobile technologies.

The physical setting of this trial is the scientific campus where an ubiquitous learning environment is developed for guiding pupils in their tours. This campus offers different learning activities in various disciplines: mathematical, ecological and historical activities.

In order to boost intra-group competition, students were divided in groups under the supervision of their coach and each group consisted of two pupils. The ultimate goal behind this clustering is to reinforce teamwork and collaboration within the individual subgroups and to make it a collaborative and challenging game that takes place in different locations.

Each subgroup is equipped with a smart phone with a wireless internet connection.

At the beginning of the first stage, the outdoor subgroup is localized by a localization sensor and a notification is sent to ask students to identify and take a photo of the QR-code stuck to the plant. Instantly, a text adapted to the pupils' level and pictures that visualize and describe the activities to accomplish in the current stage is displayed on the screen of the smart phone.

After a pre-defined time, the subgroup will receive a stage-adapted quiz via automatic text message. Pupils need to write an answer using their smart phone and submit it. If the answer submitted by the group is not correct, the system sends an alert to the coach informing him/her that pupils need some support. The coach should send to them some hints.

In order to improve the coaching task, tutor decides that after three wrong attempts, the pupil is guided to start learning session by using his mobile device. The e-learning client allow the student to directly mash up widgets to create lesson structure and add powerful online test widgets, communication widget (chat, forum and personal messages), content scheduling widgets, communication tracking, announcements, content flows, cooperative content building widgets.

The pupil could drag from the widget repository and drops into the e-learning client UI all the widgets needed for providing video, audio and other multimedia content. The duration of the learning session depends on the intensity of the signal as we show in Fig. 5.

Else, if the answer is correct the indoor subgroups will receive the list of activities of the second stage and will get joined by their corresponding outdoor subgroups that will hand over the picked plant samples.

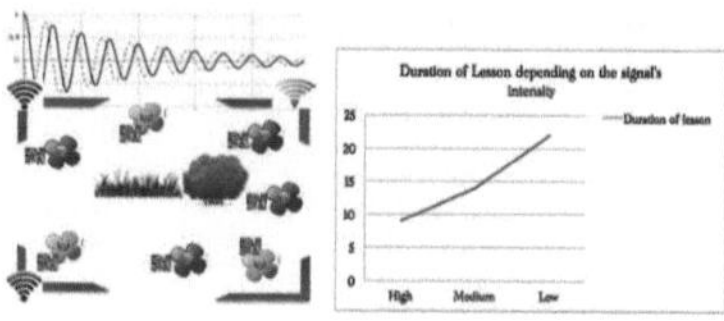


**Fig. 5.** Overview of the signal's quality in the ecological zone

### 6.1 Modelisation and Evaluation

**Formal Modelisation.** Figures 6 and 7 provide an overview of different automata modelled for the planned learning activities (outdoor activities, quiz, and lesson) and corresponding to student. We define a global variable "clock" named *Time* that gives idea about the duration of each activity. The timing constraints associated with locations are invariants. It gives a bound on how long these locations can be active. We also define other integer global variable *Power* to calculate the energy of battery of the smart-phone.

In order to facilitate the learning scenario analysis, we model each activity separately. The idea is to define templates for activities that are instantiated to have a simulation of the whole scenario. The motivation for the use of templates is that the understanding, the share and the reuse of different components of the learning scenario become easier.

The whole scenario is modelled as a parallel composition of timed automata. An automaton may perform a transition separately or synchronise with another automaton (channel synchronisation) or it can be activated after a period of time through flags.

Figure 7 shows a timed automaton modelling the behaviour of the Smart-phone. This device has several locations (or states):

1. *idle*: This state is activated when the smart-phone is switched on.
2. *InQuiz*: The learner is responding to the quiz's questions.
3. *Localisation*: This state is activated when the learner has to do his lesson. The smart-phone had to be connected to the gived wireless network.
4. *LessonHigh*, *LessonMedium* and *LessonLow*: One of these three states is activated. The learner drags and drops into the elearning client UI all the widgets needed for providing video, audio and other multimedia content. We should note that *LessonLow* is undesirable state because technical studies demonstrate that in this zone, student couldn't download correctly the lesson.
5. *FinLesson*: The student has finished the lesson successfully.
6. *BatteryOver*: This undesirable State is activated when the smartphone is switched off because the battery state is over.

The usability of the learning scenario heavily depends on several contextual contraints, especially the quality of the network connection and the energy provided by the mobile phone's battery. In fact, a smartphone is, in general, limited and for sure not keeping pace as the mobile devices are crammed up with new functionalities [11]. For this reason, designers elaborate this technical study.

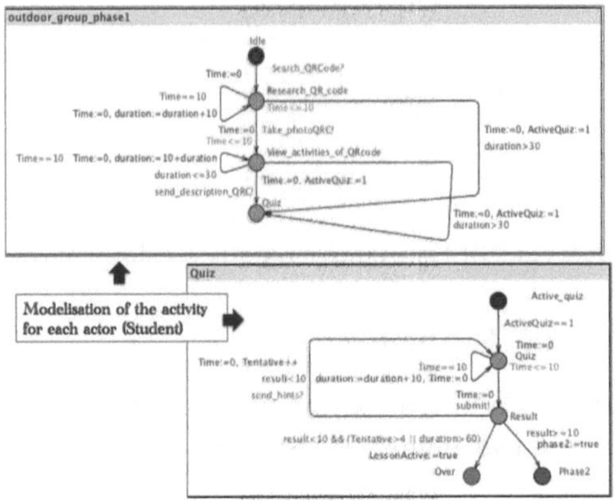


**Fig. 6.** The automata model of different activities for one actor (student)

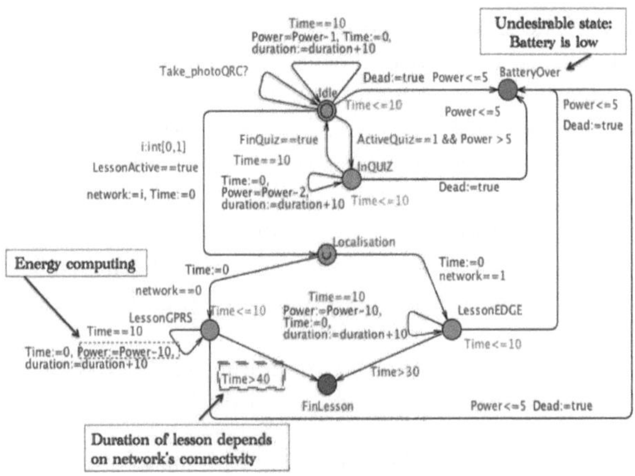


**Fig. 7.** The automaton model of the smartphone

Figure 8 summarizes this study and shows values of power consumption of different activities that learners had to realize in the learning session. The power consumption is quite higher when student download lesson, and drop into the elearning client all widgets needed for providing video, son and representation.

**Simulation and Formal Verification.** Based on automata presented above, tracks simulations are generated visualizing all possible interactions between different actors. A screen dump of the simulation of the designed educational scenario is below (see Fig. 9). In order to help designers to improve their educational scenario and to obtain better outcomes, through the generated simulations, we try to localise design errors, to answer and to verify the following questions:

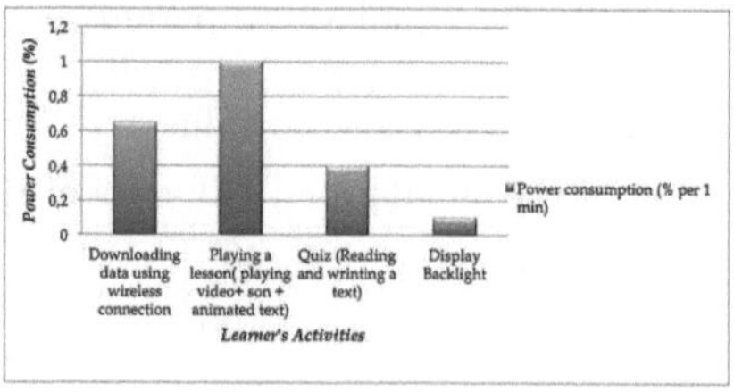


**Fig. 8.** Energy consumption on a smartphone when switched on

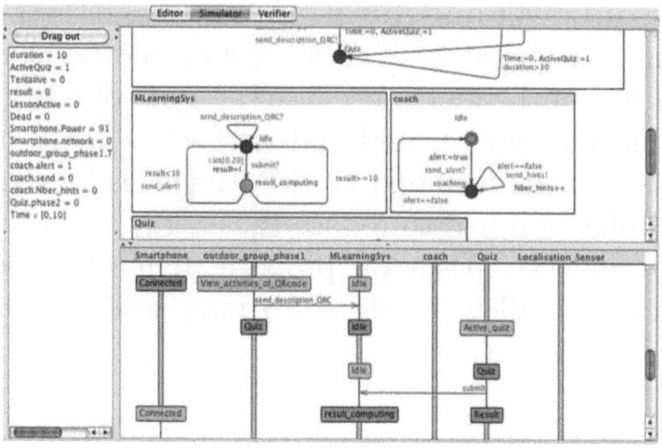


**Fig. 9.** Simulation of the modelled learning scenario

- *Does the description of the learning scenario clearly define time constraints for each activity and the whole scenario?*
- *Is there any situation of deadlocks, liveness or starvation?*

We fixed different parameters of the learning scenario's simulation as shown in Table 2. A first possible situation of deadlock is detected within tracks simulation of the whole scenario; In fact, students could have a period of inactivity especially when they begin their lesson in the lower quality zone where the network connectivity is lower and smart-phone' energy is limited. To check this property, we are based on reachability property that is considered as the simplest form of properties. We ask whether a given state formula, possibly can be satisfied by any reachable state. Another way of stating this is: **Does there exist a path starting at the initial state, such that "*the battery state*" is eventually over along that path?**

We traduce this property in temporal logic formula: "**E** <> **Smartphone. BatteryOver and duration** < 240" and this property is verified.

A second possible situation of deadlock could happen when student starts lesson in the Lower zone. To check this property, we are again, based on reachability property: **Does there exist a path starting at the initial state, such that "student couldn't finish the learning scenario successfully?"**

**Table 2.** The simulation's parameters

| Parameter | Value |
|---|---|
| Duration of the simulation | 240 units of time |
| Number of learners | 40 |
| Phone's energy | 100 % |

We traduce this property in temporal logic formula: "**E <> Smartphone.LessonLower and duration** > 240" and this property is verified.

This experiment shows that 37 % of students could be blocked at this stage. They couldn't progress in the lesson because the state of energy is low. Then, we conclude that usability is not assured and we had to adapt mobile application to the learning environment's context (if the student is located in *Lower quality zone*, the mobile application had to reduce the energy's consumption by loading only the necessary widgets. Also, we propose to notify student whether the quality of signal doesn't allow to start learning session. Then, he should to move on.

## 7 Conclusion

ReStart-Me (Re-engineering of the Educational Scenario based on Timed Automata and Tracks Treatment for Malleable Learning Environments) is a formal pre-evaluation method for malleable learning scenarios. It aims at supporting pedagogical designers and teachers to validate their scenarios at an early stage through automata modelling, Tracks simulations and properties verification. The proposed evaluation provides an inexpensive mean of errors and fault detection before starting implementation (thus returning on the learning scenario design phase to add missing elements and restraining development cost).

Finally, we will attempt in future works to deepen our proposal on learning scenario re-engineering process in such a way that a comparative report concerning different iterations of evaluation can be generated automatically.

## References

1. Stiemerling, O., Cremers, A.B.: Tailorable component architectures for cscw-systems. In: Proceedings of the Sixth Euromicro Workshop on Parallel and Distributed Processing (PDP 1998), pp. 302–308. IEEE (1998)
2. MacLean, A., Carter, K., Lövstrand, L., Moran, T.: User-tailorable systems: pressing the issues with buttons. In: Proceedings of the SIGCHI Conference on Human Factors in Computing Systems, pp. 175–182. ACM (1990)
3. Malek, J., Laroussi, M.: A model-driven approach for modelling and simulating new malleable learning scenarios for digital native generations. Int. J. Learn. Technol. **6**(3), 288–319 (2011)

4. Laurillard, D.: Rethinking University Teaching: A Framework for the Effective Use of Learning Technologies. Routledge, London (2002)
5. Jia, Z., Han, X.: Construction of evaluation system on multimedia educational software (2013)
6. Zorrilla, M., Álvarez, E.: Matep: monitoring and analysis tool for e-learning platforms. In: Eighth IEEE International Conference on Advanced Learning Technologies (ICALT 2008), pp. 611–613. IEEE (2008)
7. Strijker, A.: Reuse of learning objects in context: human and technical aspects. University of Twente (2004)
8. Pernin, J.P., Lejeune, A.: Dispositifs d'apprentissage instrumentes par les technologies : vers une ingnierie centre sur les scnarios. In: Actes en ligne du colloque TICE Mditrrane, p. 48, Novembre 2004
9. Elissavet, G., Economides, A.A.: An evaluation instrument for hypermedia courseware. Educ. Technol. Soc. **6**(2), 31–44 (2003)
10. Knapp, A., Wuttke, J.: Model checking of UML 2.0 interactions. In: Kühne, T. (ed.) MoDELS 2006. LNCS, vol. 4364, pp. 42–51. Springer, Heidelberg (2007)
11. Perrucci, G.P., Fitzek, F.H., Widmer, J.: Survey on energy consumption entities on the smartphone platform. In: IEEE 73rd Vehicular Technology Conference (VTC Spring), pp. 1–6. IEEE (2011)
12. BenSassi, M., Laroussi, M.: Formal Evaluation Methodology of Educational Scenario in Distance Learning. In: Wang, J.-F., Lau, R. (eds.) ICWL 2013. LNCS, vol. 8167, pp. 61–70. Springer, Heidelberg (2013)

# Knowledge-Management by »Social Writing«

## The Launch and Establishment of an Online-Writing Lab Using the Example of Citavi-Online-Tutorials at the Faculty of Cultural and Social Sciences of the Distance-University in Hagen Germany

Sabine Siemsen(✉)

Fernuniversität in Hagen, Universitätsstraße 33c, 58084 Hagen, Germany
sabine.siemsen@fernuni-hagen.de

**Abstract.** This paper presents the conception and first evaluations of an Online-Writing Lab at the Faculty of Cultural and Social Sciences of the Distance-University in Hagen. Academic Writing includes being able to find resources, to do research on the state of art and to critically reflect on recent discourses. Research tools that make this part of academic work easier exist, but require additional (media) competences. These competencies are more or less taken as granted; enabling students to gain them is not really an integral part of study-modules. At the same time the student's heterogeneity not only in regard to previous knowledge and prerequisites rises, and collaborative and cooperative learning and the necessity to communicate on it becomes an important factor for success and motivation in learning-processes. The conception of the Writing-Lab is an approach to provide students with tools for collaborative learning processes that enable them to gain those competencies.

**Keywords:** Social writing · Academic writing · Collaborative learning · Cooperative learning · Research tools · Citavi · Propaedeutic courses · Communication · Heterogeneity · Adobe connect · Virtual classroom · Moodle

## 1 Introduction

Successfully completing academic studies requests not only gaining knowledge on specific issues and being able to transfer it into diverse contexts. Students have to be able to do research on the scientific state of art of a topic and to prove that they are able to find, combine, transfer and re-generate knowledge. In the field of social and cultural studies this often takes places by the task to write an academic paper or thesis at the end of a term. This requests skills and competencies belonging to the field of knowledge-management which could be improved through peer-assessment and an (individual and cooperative) use of research-tools that facilitate the research and management of resources and discourses.

Web 2.0, eLearning or Online-Learning, and Social Software have become common in discourses on educational offers in Germany. One can find various and different


L. Uden et al. (Eds.): LTEC 2015, CCIS 533, pp. 134–147, 2015.
DOI: 10.1007/978-3-319-22629-3_11

definitions for those terms and taking them literally would lead to a paradox, since neither can the complex process of learning be electronically, nor can software be »social«. What it is about, is cooperative and collaborative learning, respectively the process of networked »knowledge management« that can be supported by means of technology (compare also [10]).

A closer look makes clear that behind the above terms there is a wide range of learning theories and different educational models, learning scenarios and learning environments. Evaluations on the success of e-learning or online-learning often differ and focus on explicit aspects within the spectrum of eLearning or online-learning. Accordingly, there are plenty of prefixes that are combined with and specifying the term learning: "*e-, m-, online, ubiquitous, life-long-lifewide-, personalised-virtual*" (compare [17]). All of them do not only reflect hypes and trends, but base on needs resulting from social-development. A result of this is a change to a new learning culture.

Instructional design and learning-scenarios should therefore not be limited to isolated aspects or approaches and methodologies, or even worse, regard those as incompatible. Instead they should see them as complementary »tool-kits« that use technology to combine, and enhance online learning scenarios by providing tools and approaches which can be extended. Goeth and Schwabe [12] concluded that a conscious and reflected position to the question of didactic requires re-thinking existing traditional pedagogical paradigms. Learning objective should not focus on a mere transfer of knowledge and understanding; instead of this they should focus on skills like »Apply, Analyze, Synthesize and Evaluate«. First approaches could be found, but "*still there is a lot of yet unused potential*". »Knowledge Management« in this context becomes an important competence for both, teachers and learners.

Just as there is a wide variety of definitions and approaches to e-learning terminology, there is to evaluation and »quality« of e-learning activities. Behind and beyond terminology is the question of the extent, to which media, or the use of it, can influence effectiveness and efficiency of learning. And, resulting from this, consequently the question of how can quality and outcomes be measured.

This paper depicts the complexity and plurality of the above mentioned aspect by means of an eLearning course at the University of Hagen. The Moodle online course »Writing Lab« is presented, with focus on objectives, design and implementation of the workshop »Citavi[1] - From the Management of Resources and Literature to Writing a Study-Thesis« (Sect. 2). Section 3 discusses theoretical and conceptual questions regarding requirements for its evaluation and quality assurance, presents the resultant methods and concepts to evaluate the workshop and – exemplary - first results of surveys that took place at the FernUniversität in Hagen as first parts of the evaluation of the »Writing Lab«. Section 4, as a conclusion, summarizes the findings of the work and shows prospects for media-educational perspectives.

[1] www.citavi.com/en/ A Swiss research tool to research, collect, organize, and cite textes; similar to Zotero (www.zotero.org).

## 2 The Open Moodle Course "Writing Lab" as an Study-Accompanying Course for Academic Writing

The Moodle course »Writing Lab« was first offered in the summer term 2011, as an open learning environment that should help students - mainly studying the courses Education Science (BA) and eEducation (MA) - to gain academic writing-skills while working with study material, and additional literature.

Not only freshmen, but also students of advanced study phases, each semester have to face the challenge of a complex Knowledge Management: They must work with study-materials and additional literature, and have to research resources. At the end of each term the must have worked out relevant content, either in preparation for an exam or for writing a homework that comes up to academic writing standards. Among other things, they are expected to be familiar with rules of citation and copyright, and - in regard to writing theses - aspects such as an »appealing« formatting, clear structure, and intelligibility. Online research-tools and programs exist and can be helpful but many of the students never worked with research tools before, or do even know such exist. Others have already installed and tested some tools, but only a small part of those really takes advantage of the full potential such programs offer (Fig. 1).

Also with regard to further skills like working with word processing programs, or knowing about and using different techniques of writing or reading, one finds very heterogeneous profiles in competences; but the expectations and requirements in regard to learning objective like a »successful exam« or »academically written thesis« are the same for all of them. So regarding to an equality of chances to succeed, the beneath cartoon gets to the point of the problem. The translation below the picture says (translated from German [24]) "*To make a fair selection we have the same task for all of you: Climb the tree.*"

Abbildung 12: Karikatur „Zum Ziele einer gerechten Auslese lautet die Prüfungsaufgabe für Sie alle gleich: Klettern Sie auf den Baum!" (Cartoon von Hans Traxler 1999:36/37)

**Fig. 1.** Justice of learning objectives. Source: ([19, 24])

To come up to all these expectations requires a high degree of self-organization and self-learning skills, to successfully complete the study modules beyond their content. "*In this way, learning becomes an active process which is constructed independently by the learners, who can become responsible for at least a part of their learning-contents*" (Translated from [18]). But neither from the potentials that are provided through digital media, nor from the need to learn self-organized, one should draw the conclusion this would result in teachers becoming obsolete. Self-organized learning requires skills that do not arise just because of the availability of new technological opportunities. The offer "*does not automatically turn students into being enthusiastic self-directed learners*" (translated from [4]). It still (or more than ever?) remains the teacher's task to help learners identify and practice ways to acquire these skills and to support them by means of didactic analysis and prearrangement of content. The statement that a good teacher can make up for poor technique, but never technique could save poor teaching is certainly more relevant than ever (see [1], with respect to [3]). Kerres et al. [16] compare the new role of a teacher with that of a "*gate keeper*", whose motivation and competence become a key element to anchor new forms of teaching and learning, and to establish an innovative learning culture (ibid).

The »Writing lab« hence was developed aiming to provide students with a wide spectrum of tools and techniques as well as with competencies to efficiently use those in order to improve their academic working skills. The latter includes the competence of cooperative and collaborative learning, as for example by giving peer-assessment, peer-support and sharing knowledge. At the time of the first evaluations, the workshop »Citavi- from the Management of Resources and Literature to Writing a Study-Thesis« was running for three terms and two additional courses (»Citavi for Working with study materials and preparing for exams« and »Academic Writing«) were intended to be launched during the next two terms. Later, a course on the efficient use of word processing programs shall follow. The long-term planning of the writing lab was therefore not designed as a loose chaining of various tutorials, but pursued a holistic approach: To offer of an open course that

- is not limited to terms, specific courses of studies, or course content,
- enables to acquire and exercise academic working;
- takes place in the secure and familiar learning-environment of the University Moodle
- combines the support of tutors and tutorials with a social community, peer support and collaboration and therefor
- uses a broad spectrum of digital media.

It integrates elements of both, computer-based and web-based training: Flexible location and time of learning, elements that can also be used offline, multimedia, discussion forums, synchronous and asynchronous tools and a virtual classroom,[2] where learners and teachers can see and hear each other and use text-based elements such as presentations and chats complementary, so that even participants who do not have headsets and/or camera, can participate (Compare also [20]).

## 2.1 Moodle as a Communication and Learning Platform in eLearning Courses

To implement new forms of teaching and learning in online-education means above all, to use the potential of Web 2.0 and social software to change learning-platforms from isolated learning management systems (focus on content) into gateways to the Web. Kerres (translated from [15]) compared the first with "*islands of material in the ocean*

[2] Adobe Connect.

*of the Internet*", whereas the latter would change the role of teachers to "*gatekeepers who engage as a guide, provide micro content, and enable learners to find their way to self-directed learning*" (translated from [9]). But again: Even a technologically perfectly designed learning environment, a supply with plenty and multifaceted hints to further information, and the most elaborate content have little effect, as long as it is not possible to depict the benefits of this »digital learning environments« to learners. One will have to motivate and support them to improve learning strategies and to integrate offers and »places« into an individually and situationally appropriate Personal Learning Environment. The writing lab therefore consistently attempts to provide cross-references and links to both, the module environments (moodle-courses), as well as to further information and quotes on the topics in the Web. It motivates students to self-expand this offer, for example by collecting links in wikis, by participating in discussion forums and supporting each other.

Moodle as an open source software has great potential for the implementation of such a concept. Bader [2] denotes Moodle in an article dealing with the integration of web-based learning environments in higher education as space, "*where students have a great chance to transfer and imply social demands on communication [...] into a web-environment.*" (ibid)

Daft and Lengel [7], Daft and Wiginton [8], Rice [22], Valacich et al. [25] and Sproull [23] (quoted from [5]) state that each medium can be described using five characteristics, which are *Immediacy of Feedback*, *Variety of Symbols*, *Parallelism*, *Reversibility*, and *Reusability*. Moodle is a learning environment, where technologies of the Web 2.0 and social software can easily be integrated and adapted to individual and social needs. It has high potential in all of the above characteristics: it supports interactions in many different ways (Immediacy of Feedback), offers efficient and diverse channels for communication (Variety of Symbols), allows simultaneous communications using different channels (Parallelism), students can correct their posts (Reversibility) and the messages and statements that resulted from and through this communication may be followed up and re-used in form of a kind of FAQ (Reusability). The latter makes it possible to use the tutorials and forums not only as a workshop, but also as a sustainable work of reference.

## 2.2 The Citavi Tutorials: Design and Didactic Concept

As the platform Moodle has already been established at the Distance University in Hagen and thus was installed and usable, the decision on the software yet had to be made at a content level (which research tool and which word processing tool) as well as in regard to the production of vodcasts. The vodcasts were produced with Camtasia Studio 7 and the examples that relate to an interaction between Citavi and word-processing program were created using Microsoft Word.[3] Also the technological equipment and pre-competences of the students were taken into account (see Sect. 3). The thereof resulting discussions (Citavi not being compatible with Apple and Linux, alternatively using other research tools such as EndNote or Zotero; word processing tools being open source

[3] Citavi has an integrated interface to Microsoft Word.

products, such as OpenOffice or latex) will not be discussed in this paper. Nevertheless this paper wants to point out explicitly that a discussion on compatibility and the use of open-source products in »the age of Web 2.0«, and with regard to the social dimension of learning environments, is highly important and should and will be focused in further research and evaluations on the topic.

The conception of the instructional design decided on a modular structure for the workshop »Citavi- from the Management of Resources and Literature to Writing a Study-Thesis«. The workshop took place over a period of six weeks and had weekly units. Each unit included 2 vodcasts, an integrated task, and had a forum of the week where the task could be discussed. In addition there was a forum called »Plauderecke« (a German term describing a place to have a chat) where the students had the possibility to discuss topics connected to the writing lab and the workshop, and a »news forum« where teacher announced news and introduced and led over to upcoming units.

This setting aimed to enabling and motivating students to learn content and skills through cooperation, collaboration and communication; attended and supported by the course instructor. The course instructor gave motivation for example by thanking the students for weeks with high interactions or commenting on peer-feedbacks that were especially helpful or supportive. This made clear that active participation was evidently registered and appreciated. As the course "Writing Workshop" is neither mandatory nor relevant to the exam, motivational aspects played a particularly important role.

Teachers participate and give support in the week-forums, taking into account the methods of scaffolding and fading[4] (see [13]). Support does not (only) mean to answer in the form of solutions, but also includes giving hints to how and where to find solutions and therewith fosters self-organized learning. Depending on tasks and problems this can just be hints to other forums on the question, or screenshots, or giving examples that illustrate the solution. Instructors also have to find a balance between answering close in time and waiting long enough, to enable peers to give peer support. Scaffolding here can be used as a mean to foster interaction between the students.

The Writing Workshop offers a variety of communication channels that allow interaction between teachers and students, in-between students and between students and the medium »Moodle as a learning environment«. Moodle allows to integrate "*Study materials*" and "*Activities*", which enables to use a broad variety of media. Those should not only be regarded as being technical components, but also as contributions to enable interaction becoming realistic and authentic. They are important means of communication that convey participants in virtual scenarios a sense of reality (Compare [5]).

A theory with particularly good fit for an inclusion of the social environment into processes of communication is the concept of teaching presence [5, 11]. It defines Teaching Presence as "*the design and preparation, the support of the teaching/learning discourse and the support of cognitive and social processes valuable to learning outcomes*". So the process of Teaching Presence starts with the question and decision which kind of visual or auditory or textual components could be most helpful to foster

[4] Scaffolding und Fading are terms from the model of Cognitive Apprenticeship (compare [21]). Teachers adopt and reduce their support in regard to the tasks and rising self-learning-competences of the students.

Teaching Presence and when and where to integrate those into the didactical design. The decision to offer tutorials that combine videos, exercises and discussion-forums with meetings in the virtual classroom, took into account that visual and auditory media convey a higher degree of social presence as (only) text-based communication.

The course content is split into small units that present examples and suggestions how to use Citavi efficiently. They cover the most commonly used tools of the software and encourage to try further possibilities and individual variants. Thus, the aim is to promote self-learning skills and to enable to transfer the presented examples onto individual needs. The approach of »small steps and small portions« is particular important as participants join this course optional and in addition to their regular and examinable modules. So motivation and enthusiasm could easily fade, if there was an »informational overload«.

## 3 Evaluation of the Tutorials and the Additional Benefit Through the Integration of the Virtual Classroom

The evaluation of and research on a project like the above described Writing-Lab aims at

- Consideration of the participant's being heterogeneous in regard to requirements, experience, skills and expectations
- Enabling cooperation, collaboration and communication
- Fostering Peer-Support
- Helping to gain competences and practice in academic working
- Support of improving self-organized learning, motivation and knowledge-management

As described in Sect. 2, the Writing Lab aims to offer several workshops and courses that are related to each other and to the process of academic work. Thus, depending on the stage of the lab's development and the existing courses, there have been and there are different interests of research and evaluation. They were and are taken into account by performing intern accompanying formative evaluations as well as summative evaluations (for instance after the completion of specific offers, such as final meetings in the virtual classroom or at the end of an overseen workshop). Thus they base on different levels and objects: The project »Writing Lab«, the use of a product (Research tool, on the example of Citavi), and the efficiency of (a combination of) peer- and tutor-support. This shall improve the offer and the conception of further courses within the Writing Lab.

The following sections will present hitherto existing evaluations of the Writing Lab, its objectives, methods, and first results. Consequently those help to derive suggestions and take decisions on the future of the Writing Lab (compare [20]).

### 3.1 Evaluations in the Framework of the Project »Writing Lab«

First of all it was important to have information about preconditions of the participants in regard to knowledge, software- and technological equipment; as didactics can only foster learning if they take into account the participants requirements. For this purpose,

Moodle's voting-Tool was used which can also ask questions by using options. The questions were about how the students decide on relevance of contents (from course material), their use of additional literature, their prior experience with software as research tool, which word processing program is used and if different media are used for reading. The Voting-Tool remained permanently active and so offered to keep track of the inquired aspects. Results have served and serve for the further development of the workshop and were also presented during the meetings in the virtual classroom and shared with the participants by presenting them within the course-environment.

After the workshop had run twice and had been available as a reference book in the time between the tutorials, a Survey[5] was conducted in conjunction with a complementary meeting in the virtual classroom. It targeted to conducting students experiences with and expectations to the implementation of a Virtual Classroom into a Moodle course. We wanted to know which aspects of such a combinations are regarded as most important additional benefits (Efficiency? The »social factor«? Motivation and Satisfaction?), and which are regarded as barriers and inhibition thresholds (Technology? Time-Consume? Fear of embarrassing oneself by interaction synchronously and using Camera and Microphone?). The questionnaire consisted of 10 closed questions (offering the possibility to give additions) and one open question. It focused on the factors »Communication« and »Completing Asynchronous Learning Environments by the Implementation of Synchronous Events«. The closed questions were analyzed quantitatively using Excel, the open question and supplemental free answers qualitatively using MAXqda,[6] a Qualitative Data Analysis Software. First results and findings from this survey were presented at the University of Hagen as part of an Adobe Connect User Day[7] (Social Writing – the use of the virtual classroom as part of the Moodle Course Writing Lab) and provided to the participants as podcast in the Moodle environment of the course.

Another evaluation set a different focus and did not – or less – object on the student's experiences with the tutorials and the writing lab as such, but asked about »successful learning«; regarding aspects like the influence of participating in such courses on structure, efficiency, grading and comments of student assignments, written homework and seminar papers. Again a survey was conducted which target audience were not only participants of the Writing Lab (as in the survey described before) but all students that had already passed at least one seminar paper or written homework.

This questionnaire contained mainly open-ended questions (13 of 18), as hypotheses and findings should be developed inductively from the responses of the participants and not deductively via predetermined response options. The five closed questions were used to distinguish the samples of the target audience (users/non-users of Citavi/other research tools than Citavi; participants/non-participants in the workshop, number of already absolved written homework or seminar papers; Structure of the Use of the Software). In addition Forums contributions in regard to the aspect »successful learning« of the participants were qualitatively analyzed using MAXqda. This analysis was limited to the Forum »Plauderecke« (see Sect. 2.2), as this forum expressed the greatest variety

[5] Research Tool used: LimeSurvey https://www.limesurvey.org/en/.
[6] http://www.maxqda.com/.
[7] http://www.fernuni-hagen.de/videostreaming/zmi/201204/.

and heterogeneity of questions, feedback forms and factors/dimensions that influence learning-processes.

### 3.2 Method

Regarding the scenarios described in the introduction of the writing workshop as an open and independent module Moodle course, one can speak of a »small-scale research project« which can be critically examined and analyzed for its validity. The following descriptions of the methodology are based on Cropleys [6] definition of qualitative research.

The above described and up to now conducted evaluations of the Citavi tutorials and workshops analyzed elements in both, qualitative and quantitative, terms; the design is non-experimental, they are not experimental, as they took place in »real« life (even if the learning environment is a virtual one …), data had been deducted through a voting-tool in Moodle, via questionnaires/surveys (containing standardized closed-ended and open questions) and through an analyses of the participants-adoption and usage-patterns in a course forum. They contain numeric and descriptive values, that provide statistical analysis and values oriented on meaning. Hypotheses were developed, not tested (inductive approach). According to Cropley [6] they thus range on the first two of three possible levels of a qualitative-study-design on quasi-qualitative and phenomenological studies. A rather high validity of data can be presumed, since the tutorial was not limited to explicit modules or study-courses and no »socially desirable« answers are to be expected as the participation is optional and does not aim on certifications or grades (compare [6]).

To transfer results from Lime Survey to MAXQDA these were first exported as table (Excel), than two groups were build (users of research tools/non-users) by recoding »yes/no answers«. An additional column was added (numbering all questionnaires that have been completed), Questions were paraphrased into precise short phrases or key-words, which helped (pre) encoding the texts in MAX QDA (this part deductively from hypotheses that were basis for the creation of the questions). These codes were further differentiated through MAXQDA and used to the (here inductive) generation of further codes and sub-codes.

In order to get findings on the success of learning processes in writing homework and seminar papers, participants were asked whether errors in quotations had resulted in comments or worse grades on homework and papers and whether these have improved after passing the workshops.

Other level that enable findings on success or learning are "*strategic knowledge on self-regulation and the competence to develop strategies*" [19] and the "*Sustainability*" of gained competences. For the first level mentioned, both, the student's posts in the forum, as well as their answers to the question of how they structure their preparation of homework and papers, were therefor coded into appropriate categories. For findings on *Sustainability*, answers that for instance stated that results of structuring a paper and working with a research tools enables to re-use the results in further papers, were coded with the category »sustainability«.

According to Kerres [14] it is important to also include subjective factors, such as "*emotional reactions*", motivation, acceptance and satisfaction with one's learning-patterns. To make these factors measurable, forum-post were coded into appropriate categories.

Quantitative statements were gained by analyzing the results of the Moodle Voting-Tool using Excel. The answers to the closed questions that enable quantitative evaluation were obtained from the questionnaires (yes/no answers; frequency in responses on options, frequency of the occurrence of certain codes and categories) and through recoding variables from MAXQDA using data matrices and cross tables.

To depict findings concern the aspects of »social learning«, respectively »social writing« presented on the Adobe Connect User Day, data on these aspects were isolated and presented using charts and graphs, some of them will be added below (Sect. 3.3).

### 3.3 Results

As the extend of this paper does not allow the enclosure of the complete and detailed data and results, subsequently exemplary results are presented in a condensed form. An appendix with a detailed presentation and analysis can be requested from the author.

**Pre-competences and Technical Equipment.** About 70 % of respondents (n = 129) said they were afraid to use a research tool. Of the remaining 30 % (n = 37) about 86 % already use some of the functions of Citavi, the rest had already tried EndNote (1) and Zotero (1).

As word processing program 67 % of respondents (n = 121) used a current version of Microsoft Word (2007 and 2010). Of the remaining 33 % (n = 41) almost 30 % used an earlier version of Microsoft Word (12), 56 % (23) used OpenOffice and 14 % (6) another word processing program.

When asked about structuring the formulation of study material, almost 65 % of respondents (n = 158) stated to use a combination of reading, marking, writing excerpts

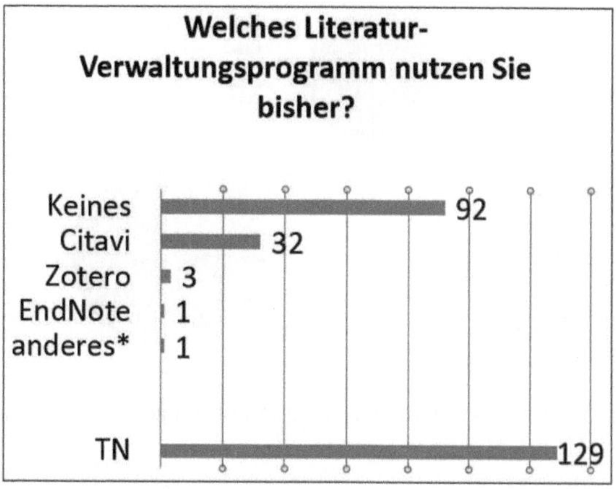


**Fig. 2.** Graph on the use of research tools by the course-participants

and flashcards, about 20 % just learn with markings in the study material and 12 % only learn with the help of flashcards and/or excerpts.

Using additional literature 16 % of respondents (n = 131) answered they hardly see a need of using additional literature so far (21), 22 % »just read« through the literature (29) and the rest uses combinations of marking and summaries. Only 4.5 % (6) capture literature regularly using a bibliographic manager.

As a reading medium 65 % (n = 125) use a combination of paper and screen (82), 27 % read only printed material (34) and 7 % (9) use an eBook reader (Fig. 2).

**Cooperation, Collaboration and Communication.** Statements about cooperation, collaboration and communication were obtained both in the survey on the use of the Virtual Classroom (VC) within the Moodle course, and in the survey on »successful learning«.

About 75 % of respondents (n = 29) indicated that the integration of audio and video elements (compared to a mere text elements both for communication and for presenting content) was regarded as a very important or important supplement. More than 90 % would like to make use of such offers several times within the workshop, and according to thematic blocks. Regarding the VC very similar proportions were desired: online lectures (79 %) online seminars (69 %), online consulting hours (79 %) and online learning-communities with peers (62 %).

Most benefit arguments were coded to be related with social issues and needs (60 %), 40 % were related to questions of content and no argument was related to a benefits through the use of technology (Fig. 3).

This was different asking for barriers: 52 % of them were found on the social level, of which 64 % were at the level of (lacking) self-confidence and 36 % were on a »time-level« (a lack of spare time, flexibility, obligatory courses regarded as too time-consuming) but 48 % on a technological-level, whereas here no aspects with regard to contents have been named (Fig. 4).

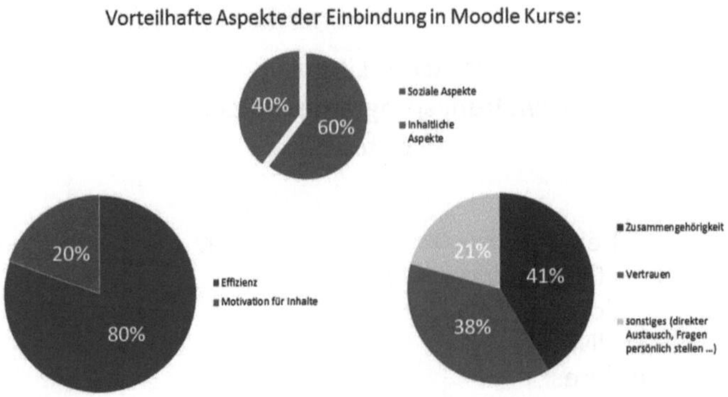


**Fig. 3.** Aspects regarded as most important additional benefits

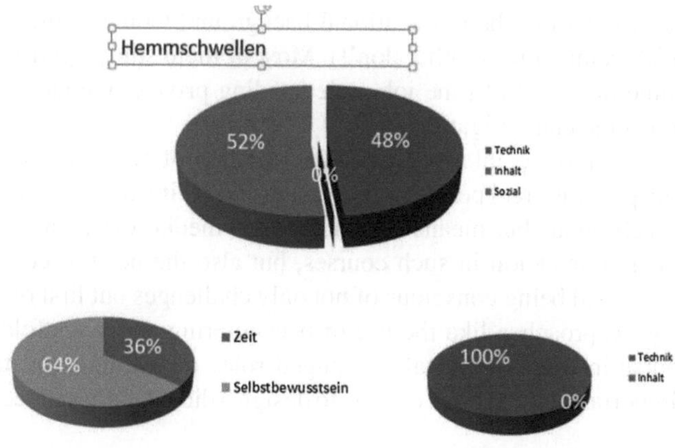


**Fig. 4.** Aspects regarded as barriers and inhibition thresholds

**Dimensions of Knowledge and Learning-Success.** The results of this survey have not yet been evaluated. The questionnaire and the list of (yet still provisional) variables and coding (MAXQDA) can be requested from the author.

## 4 Conclusion and Prospects

The high demand for a Moodle course which is optional and does not (directly) lead to grades or certificates and the analyses of the discourses and evaluation proves both; the need for courses on competencies for academic work and research, and the highly different preconditions of the students. After opening the Writing Lab, the Moodle course had about 80 participants at the end of the first term (summer term 2011). Recently (end of the winter-term 2014/2015) 2.519 participants have enrolled. Also the (unexpected and unusual) high level of participation in the last survey, which even took place at a time when students were involved in preparing their exams and writing their homework, shows a high intrinsic interest in and acceptation of such offers.

Especially the survey on the Virtual Classroom being implemented into Moodle courses has revealed that fostering media-competence is indeed important but by far not sufficient to compensate a lack in social presence. Social skills that enable to cooperative and collaborative learning, to give and accept peer account, are equally important. And as already mentioned above, a technologically perfectly designed learning environment, a supply with plenty and multifaceted hints to further information, and the most elaborate content do not compensate for a lack in enabling learners to communicate and interact in a way that makes them become conscious of the potential of using different and various tools and approaches to generate and manage learning. And this potential does not only apply to the use of different tools. Presumably an important aspect leading to the findings of this paper is the highly heterogeneous constitution of the students at the FernUniversity in Hagen.

They are not only heterogeneous in regard to preconditions like competences and knowledge (which is a »challenge« brick-and-mortal universities face all the same) but also in age and in regard to their educational background (some of them having final secondary-school examinations, other don't). Most of them study »part-time« in addition to a part-time or even full-time job, a demanding private live having children of their own, and other social obligations.

As the findings show, social aspects and the question of needs like self-confidence and experiencing peers as »real persons« by hearing and seeing them, by communicating not only by asynchronous but means of synchronous media reveals not only the high importance of communication in such courses, but also the need to communicate by taking into account and being conscious of not only challenges but first of all potentials of heterogeneity. Approaches like the use of peer-tutoring and a scaffolding of interventions of course-instructors, but also changed roles of learning and teaching will become more important as questions on how to design a didactically and technologically perfect course.

## References

1. Arnold, R.: Ziele und Strategien zur Förderung von Selbstorganisiertem Lernen von Erwachsenen im interaktiven Web. In: Hornung-Prähauser, V. (ed.) Selbstorganisiertes Lernen im Internet: Einblick in die Landschaft der webbasierten Bildungsinnovationen; Sammlung von ausgewählten Fach- und Praxisbeiträgen zu interaktiven Lehr- und Lernszenarien aus den EduMedia-Konferenzen, pp. 59–67. Studien-Verl, Innsbruck, Wien, Bozen (2008)
2. Bader, R.: Orientierung im virtuellen Raum: Mentale Modelle internetgestützter Lernumgebungen im Studium der Sozialen Arbeit. In: Hugger, K.-U. (ed.) Digitale Lernwelten: Konzepte, Beispiele und Perspektiven, 1st edn. pp. 157–174. VS, Verl. für Sozialwiss, Wiesbaden (2010)
3. Bates, A.W.: Technology, open learning and distance education. Routledge, New York (1995 / 1999)
4. Böhner, M., Mersch, A.: Selbststudium und Web 2.0. In: Hugger, K.-U. (ed.) Digitale Lernwelten: Konzepte, Beispiele und Perspektiven (1st edn.), pp. 229–244. VS, Verl. für Sozialwiss, Wiesbaden (2010)
5. Boos, M.: Wissenskommunikation in virtuellen (Lern-)Gemeinschaften, p. (Kursnr. 33058). FernUniversität in Hagen, Hagen (2011)
6. Cropley, A.J.: Qualitative Forschungsmethoden: Eine praxisnahe Einführung, 4th edn. Klotz, Magdeburg (2011)
7. Daft, R., Lengel, R.H.: Organizational information requirements, media richness and structural design. Manage. Sci. **32**(5), 554–571 (1986)
8. Daft, R., Wiginton, J.: Language and organization. Acad. Manag. Rev. **42**, 179–191 (1979)
9. Ehlers, U.-D.: Qualität für digitale Lernwelten: Von der Kontrolle zur Partizipation und Reflexion. In: Hugger, K.-U. (ed.) Digitale Lernwelten: Konzepte, Beispiele und Perspektiven, 1st edn. pp. 60–73. VS, Verl. für Sozialwiss, Wiesbaden (2010)
10. Ehlers, U.-D.: Qualitätsentwicklung im E-Learning: Grundlagen, Lernorientierung und notwendige Kompetenzen: Studienbrief der FernUniversität in Hagen - Kursnummer 33085. Hagen (2011)
11. Garrison, D., Anderson, R.T., Archer, W.: Critical inquiry in a textbased environment. computer conferencing in higher education. Internet High. Educ. **2**(2), 87–105 (2000)

12. Göth, C., Schwabe, G.: Mobiles Lernen. In: Haake, J., Schwabe, G., Wessner, M. (eds.) CSCL-Kompendium: Lehr- und Handbuch zum computerunterstützten kooperativen Lernen, 2nd edn. pp. 283–293. Oldenbourg, R., München (2011)
13. Höbarth, U.: Konstruktivistisches Lernen mit Moodle: Praktische Einsatzmöglichkeiten in Bildungsinstitutionen. Verlag Werner Hülsbusch, Boizenburg (2007)
14. Kerres, M.: Multimediale und telemediale Lernumgebungen: Konzeption und Entwicklung, 2nd edn. Oldenbourg Verlag, München (2001)
15. Kerres, M.: Potenziale Von Web 2.0 Nutzen. In: Hohenstein, A., Wilbers (Hrsg.), K. (ed.) Handbuch E-Learning. München: DWD (2006)
16. Kerres, M., Stratmann, J., Ojstersek, N., Preußler, A.: Digitale Lernwelten in der Hochschule. In: Hugger, K.-U. (ed.) Digitale Lernwelten: Konzepte, Beispiele und Perspektiven, 1st edn., pp. 141–156. VS, Verl. für Sozialwiss, Wiesbaden (2010)
17. Kress, G., Pachler, N.: Thinking about dhe 'm' in m-learning. In: Pachler, N. (ed.) Mobile Learning: Towards a Research Agenda, vol. 2007, pp. 7–32. Institute of Education University London, London (2007)
18. Preußler, A.: Neue Medien und erziehungswissenschaftliche Innovationsprozesse in Schulen: Empirische Befunde der zweiten Koordinatorenbefragung, Schulen ans Netz. Diplomarbeit im Fachbereich Erziehungswissenschaften und Soziologie der Universität Dortmund (2002)
19. Preußler, A.: Anwendungsbezogene Bildungsforschung Teil 1: Die Messung von theoretischen Konstrukten in Lernprozessen - Studienbrief der FernUniversität in Hagen - Kursnummer 33086, Hagen (2011)
20. Preußler, A.: Anwendungsbezogene Bildungsforschung Teil 2: Bewertung von Online-Lernen in der Praxis - Studienbrief der FernUniversität in Hagen - Kursummer 33087, Hagen (2011)
21. Reinmann, G.: Didaktisches Design: Von der Lerntheorie zur Gestaltungstheorie (2010)
22. Rice, R.E.: Computer-mediated communication and organizational innovation. J. Commun. **37**, 65–94 (1987)
23. Sproull, R.F.: A lesson in electronic mail. In: Sproull, R.F., Kiesler, K. (eds.) Connections: New Ways of Working in the Networked Organization, pp. 177–184. MIT Press, Cambridge, MA (1991)
24. Traxler, H.: Alles von mir. Frankfurt a. Main (1999)
25. Valacich, J.S., Paranka, D., George, J.F., Nunamaker Jr., J.F.: Communication parallelism and the new media: a new dimension for media richness. Commun. Res. **20**(2), 249–276 (1993)

# The Design of Personal Learning Environments (PLE) with Scope on Information Literacy in High School

Sabine Seufert[1], Katarina Stanoevska-Slabeva[2], Severina Müller[2], and Nina Scheffler[1](✉)

[1] Institute of Business Education and Educational Management, University of St.Gallen, St. Gallen, Switzerland
{sabine.seufert,nina.scheffler}@unisg.ch
[2] Institute for Media and Communications Management, University of St.Gallen, St. Gallen, Switzerland
{katarina.stanoevska,severina.mueller}@unisg.ch

**Abstract.** Information literacy is considered a key competence for the networked 21st century. Despite of its importance it has not been anchored in educational technology research and practice in sufficient manner yet. The paper at hand contributes to this research gap by providing a concept for design of personal learning environments with scope on information literacy. Personal learning environments (PLE) can be defined as conceptual and technological frameworks that help learners take control of and manage their own learning. This includes providing support for learners to: set their own learning goals and manage their learning in terms of both learning outcomes (content) and process. By applying the design science approach, a framework for PLE is proposed that combines subject-oriented learning objectives with goals to build and foster information literacy. The focus of the research lies in the initial theoretical phase of the design cycle. Based on a systematic literature review first a model for measuring information literacy is developed. The developed model is than embedded in a generic PLE framework that supports building and measuring information literacy in addition to other subject-specific learning goals. Therefore, the paper outlines a framework to conceptualize PLE focusing on information literacy by pursuing the design-based research paradigm.

**Keywords:** Information literacy · Personal learning environment (PLE) · Design-based research

## 1 Introduction and Motivation

Life-long and personal learning as well as information literacy are considered to be key competences for the networked society. The networked society provides us more and more with digital information and knowledge that can be the source for life-long and personal learning. However, the usage of digital media requires a high level of information literacy, i.e. competences to deal with information. In general, information literacy is defined as the ability to recognize problem-driven information needs, to


L. Uden et al. (Eds.): LTEC 2015, CCIS 533, pp. 148–163, 2015.
DOI: 10.1007/978-3-319-22629-3_12

select information sources, to access, evaluate and use information, and to reflect the information process as well as the information results [7, 16]. It is considered a key competence that facilitates participation in society, a self-determined life as well as lifelong learning [16]. Even though the inter-relationship of personal learning and information literacy has been mentioned in research (see for example [7, 16]), these two phenomena have been subject of research in different disciplines and have not been considered in an integrated manner in research and education yet.

Personal learning environments (PLE) are considered in educational design research and can be defined as systems that help learners take control of and manage their own learning. This includes providing support for learners to set their own learning goals as well as to manage their learning process and learning outcomes [5]. PLE are not an application or a software system but rather a new approach to the use of digital technologies for learning. PLEs provide learners with their own spaces that are under their own control and support the development and sharing of their ideas [17]. Moreover, PLEs can provide a more holistic learning environment, bringing together sources and contexts for learning. PLEs can bridge the "walled gardens of the educational institutions with the worlds outside" [5]. Based on the PLE concept learners can develop the judgements and skills or literacy necessary for using new technologies in a rapidly changing society.

Information literacy was initially a research field embedded in the library science. In 1989, the American Library Association (ALA) Presidential Committee on Information Literacy provided a useful pedagogical context for information literacy. Subsequently, alternative definitions have been developed by educational institutions, professional organizations and scholars and the information literacy phenomenon has been picked-up by other research disciplines as information science, educational science as well as media and communication science within the last decade. Besides of its growing importance, information literacy has been considered only sporadically in educational research for example as a separate necessary competence. In practice, in order to enable development of competences to deal with information early in life, the development of information literacy is considered an important goal of schools. However, empirical evidence demonstrates that this goal has not been achieved yet. Various studies show that adolescents easily adopt search engines and various information sources, but partially deal naively with online information (see for example [22]). This tendency can be explained by the insufficient integration of information literacy as a learning objective in the existing curriculum and learning environments. One reason for this is the lack of a scientifically sound and proven model to operationalize, gather, and measure information literacy. Another reason is the lack of learning environments that consider, support and foster building of information literacy and its measurement.

The paper at hand contributes to this research gap, by combining the learning objective "Information literacy" with the concept of PLE. By applying the design science approach a framework is developed following the main research question: "How to design internet-based PLEs that develop and measure information literacy in high school, exemplary for the subject "economics and law"? In order to answer the research question, first existing research related to definition, conceptualization and measurement of information literacy is synthesized. Based on a systematic literature review on information literacy the following sub-research questions are addressed: *"Which terms exist associated with information literacy and how is it defined in the literature? What are salient conceptualizations and measurement models of information literacy? Which methods are applied in order to examine information literacy?"*

By applying the design science approach, a framework for PLE is proposed that combines subject-oriented learning objectives with goals to build and foster information literacy. Design research emerged mainly in the last years as an approach to develop innovative educational solutions. Design research is conducted as a collaboration of researchers and practitioners in a real-world setting and comprises the following iterative phases: 1. Analysis/Exploration, 2. Design/Construction and 3. Evaluation/Reflection. This paper focuses on the first phase of the design cycle "Analysis/Exploration" and on theory building regarding a model for the measurement of information literacy and its inclusion in PLE.

The paper is structured as follows: Section 2 explains the methodology applied. Section 3 provides an overview of the achieved results. Section 4 concludes the paper by providing recommendations for developing and measuring information literacy by the use of PLE and for future research.

# 2 Methodology

## 2.1 Design-Based Research Paradigm

The goal of the research presented in this paper is the development of a framework for PLE that focuses on the objective to embed information literacy as an additional competence into subject-oriented PLEs. The exploration of innovative design possibilities in an iterative development cycle in cooperation among research and practice seems to be a promising research approach in order to achieve this research objective [13, p. 353]. Design research lends itself as a suitable approach, in particular as it is necessary to combine new technological innovations with new pedagogical goals. Thus, instead of focusing on the technology-oriented research question "What are the potentials of PLE for business- and law courses in high school?", a design research approach was selected that involves pedagogical methods for developing the problem solution and is guided by the following research question: *"How to design internet-based PLE that develop and measure information literacy in high school, exemplary for the subject "economics and law"?*

Table 1 illustrates the design research cycle applied in this paper. It is based on the generic design research cycle for cooperative research and design among representatives from research and practice as proposed by ([27], p. 127, based on [20]) and adjusted to the specific research question of this paper. Each phase of the design cycle is characterized by specific goals and encompasses complementary research and design tasks for involved representatives from research and practice. The design cycle starts with the "Analysis/Exploration" phase, which is dedicated to the definition and clarification of the research questions as well as to the identification and setting up of the theoretical and methodological framework for the design process. The second phase of the design cycle - "Design/Construction" - builds upon the results of the first phase and is devoted to the development and testing of design solutions. The evaluation of the proposed designs is subject of the third design phase – "Evaluation/Reflection".

**Table 1.** Design research: iterative cycle based on the cooperation between research and practice [27, p. 127], based on [20]

<table>
<tr><th colspan="2">Phase: Analysis / Exploration</th></tr>
<tr><td colspan="2">Goal of the phase: 1) Clarification of research problem and goals; 2) Clarification of partners' expectation for the research cooperation.<br>Expected Results: Defined research goals and related (at this point of time still preliminary) research and design questions concerning the clarification of information competences as well as PLE</td></tr>
<tr><td>Role Researcher</td><td>Role Practitioner</td></tr>
<tr><td>- To explain the scientific relevance of the expected solution and its rate of innovation.<br>- To determine the application range and the generalizability of the expected solution (Can the target solution and its relevance be generalized beyond an individual case?)</td><td>- To determine the practical relevance of the expected solution.<br>- To estimate the practical applicability of the solution with given time, personnel and material resources</td></tr>
<tr><td colspan="2">Theory Building: Analysis and evaluation of existing literature and prevailing practical experiences<br>Goal and Result: Theoretical foundation of the target design with preliminary descriptions of potential measurements to achieve the target goals.<br>Example: Development of a preliminary model for the operationalization of information literacy as well as a theory driven conceptualization of the subject-specific PLE (for instance digital case studies of GAFA (Google, Apple, Facebook, and Amazon) enterprises. Development of Internet exercises, provision of a tool for problem solving as part of the PLE, accompanying and integrated blog, design of gamification elements for collection of experience points.</td></tr>
<tr><td>Role Researcher</td><td>Role Practitioner</td></tr>
<tr><td>- Identification of a range of relevant research results;<br>- Integration of scientific and practical theories as well as knowledge;<br>- Identification of open research and</td><td>- Activation of hidden tacit knowledge of stakeholders and practical experts</td></tr>
</table>

*(Continued)*

**Table 1.** (*Continued*)

| | |
|---|---|
| design questions. | |
| **Phase: Design / Construction** | |
| **Goal and expected result of the phase:** 1) Development and testing of the design solution; 2) Development of *prototypes of* potential approaches for the development and measurement of information competences (based on the theoretical foundation) and their inclusion in subject-specific PLE.<br>This phase requires several (3-5) development cycles for design and testing. | |
| *Role Researcher* | *Role Practitioner* |
| - Validation of the relevance of the designs;<br>- Specification of designs based on relevant characteristics and attributes that can be observed and evaluated within mini- and macro-design cycles.<br>- Documentation of evaluation results for the various designs. | - Validation of practical applicability of the designs.<br>- Readiness to test developed designs (3-4 times) until a „saturated design solution" is reached. |
| **Phase: Evaluation / Reflection** | |
| **Goal and expected results of the phase:** 1) Development of a concept for evaluation of the developed designs; 2) Analysis of the data collected from evaluation; 3) Discussion of the implications of the evaluation results. | |
| *Role Researcher* | *Role Practitioner* |
| - Balancing of focus and openness of the evaluation;<br>- Enabling of diverse evaluation perspectives in the team;<br>- Focus of the data analysis on core aspects;<br>- Determination of relevant quality standards;<br>- Documentation of the design cycles. | - Capture of the applicability of the various designs in practice;<br>- Evaluation of the designs;<br>- Communication of results (trial results), i.e. participant narratives among colleagues. |
| *Role Researcher* | *Role Practitioner* |
| - Extraction of commonalities of different specific designs (interventions or cases);<br>- Methodology based approach for extraction of generic design principles and reflection on the scientific contribution of the research results. | - Evaluation of the transferability of the design principles to other domains (problems);<br>- Comprehensive feedback to the documentation of the results. |
| **Result**: Design principles for the development and evaluation of information competences and their inclusion in PLE in secondary schools as well as empirically tested designs for PLE. | |

### 2.2 Literature Review Approach

In order to systemize the perspectives on information literacy, a structured literature review was conducted. The main focus was thereby on the research questions of how competences related to information literacy can be achieved, enhanced, and measured in the educational context. The literature analysis followed the approach proposed by Webster and Watson [31]. First a set of relevant search keywords was identified. The keywords were then used to search relevant databases and information sources. This broad search resulted in a high number of articles related to information literacy. An analysis of the abstracts of the first selection of articles under the perspective of the research question allowed a final focused selection of 48 research papers that were analyzed in depth.

The keywords "Information literacy", "Internet", and "Education" have been used to search two databases: EBSCO and Science Direct. These two databases cover almost all of the relevant journals and conferences were research on information literacy is published. Thus, these databases were considered comprehensive enough to gain a set of literature that represents the current status of information literacy research.

The three keywords have been applied in combination in both information sources: (EBSCO: Information literacy AND Internet AND Education, limiters: Full Text (Online), language: English, subject: Information literacy; Science Direct: Information literacy AND Internet, limiters: Open Access, topic: Information literacy). In a second step, in order to consider related terms as well, the keyword "Information literacy" has been replaced by the keywords "Information competence", "Media literacy", and "Media competence". Finally, in a third step, all considered keywords and combinations were translated into German and applied to search for German publications within the EBSCO and Science Direct databases.

The resulting body of literature was analyzed with respect to three dimensions: definition of information literacy, conceptualizations/measurement models of information literacy, and applied research methodology for assessment of information literacy. With regard to the definition, we assigned a code for each definition given in a paper. Overall, this led to 28 codes describing a wide range of definitions associated with information literacy and related constructs. In order to provide insight into the utilized theoretical frameworks, published conceptualizations and measurement models developed or/and applied in the literature were analyzed and aggregated. With reference to the research method, we assigned a code for each research method applied in a paper which resulted in six different codes. As the case study design was one frequently method, we added six additional codes to make a further differentiation of the approaches used for evaluating the information literacy assignments.

## 3 Results

### 3.1 Literature Review: Conceptualizations and Measurement Models

After a thorough and systematic selection, 48 papers were subject to an in-depth literature analysis. Out of the selected body of literature about information literacy, 21 articles were identified as conceptual papers. The theoretical/conceptual contributions were particularly prevalent in the social media context and propose extensions of information literacy to social media. In this context, only few empirical studies have been conducted so far. The literature reveals that research is still engaged with the transformation of informational literacy conceptualizations and measurement models from Web 1.0 to Web 2.0 and social media. Thus, the conceptual papers reveal future research directions and questions, but do not provide a basis for identification of suitable models for measuring information literacy.

Table 2 summarizes the results of the systematic literature review of the remaining body of literature along the three dimensions considered in the analysis: definition of information literacy, conceptualizations/measurement models of information literacy, and applied research methodology for assessment of information literacy.

The literature analysis revealed a plethora of various approaches to conceptualize and measure information literacy. There is a lack of suitable standardized measurement methods to capture information literacy holistically and transfer it to viable learning concepts and environments. Most of the proposed approaches provide merely insight into partial aspects of information literacy [7].

A clear lack of consensus in prevailing research with respect to conceptualization and measurement of information literacy becomes evident in Shenton's [29] study. Shenton compares two different conceptualizations of information literacy that describe the stages of information literacy. According to the concept of Eisenberg and Berkowitz [15], the stages of information literacy contain the following components: define task, formulate information-seeking strategies, locate and access information, use information, synthesize work, evaluate effectiveness and efficiency. On the other hand, according to SCONUL's Seven Pillars Model [26], the stages of information literacy consist of the following components: recognize information need, distinguish ways of addressing gap, construct strategies for locating, locate and access, compare and evaluate, organize, apply and communicate, synthesize and create. Although the two concepts describe the same stages on the whole, the specific terms differ widely.

A similar conceptualization is found in the work of Argelagos and Pifarré [3]. Based on the current state of research, the authors summarize five difficulties in developing different cognitive skills involved in solving an information problem: defining the problem, searching for, scanning, processing, organizing and presenting information.

A different description but again similar content has the definition of the American Library Association's (ALA) Presidential Committee on Information Literacy used as a measurement model in Mackey's (2005) study. The ALA was one of the first institutions that responded to the information age in 1989. The committee called for an active learning process that involves students in: knowing when they have a need for information, identifying information needed to address a given problem or issue, finding needed information and evaluating the information, organizing the information, using the information effectively to address the problem or issue at hand.

Pinto and Sales [24] enhanced the ALA information literacy standards by taking into account their own expertise. Based on these sources they developed a conceptual model of information skills, containing the following stages: understanding information, identifying and defining information needs, locating and retrieving information,

**Table 2.** Overview of definitions, conceptualizations, and methods of information literacy

| Authors | Definition | Conceptualization | Method |
|---|---|---|---|
| Ali et al. (2010) | ALA | Concept identification | Case study |
| | | Search strategy | Questionnaire |
| | | Document types | Citation analysis |
| | | Search tools | |
| | | Use of results | |
| Thirion and Pochet [30] | ALA | Concept identification | Quantitative survey |
| | | Search strategy | |
| | | Document types | |
| | | Search tools | |
| | | Use of results | |
| Mackey (2005) | ALA | Knowing | Case study |
| | | Identifying | Questionnaire |
| | | Finding | |
| | | Organizing | |
| | | Using | |
| Marshall [19] | ALA | Identify a topic | Instrument development and quantitative survey |
| | | Determine source requirements | |
| | | Know how to search for needed information | |
| | | How to locate and retrieve the information | |
| | | Evaluate the information | |
| | | Synthesize and organize the information | |
| | | Understand ethical, legal and socio-political issues of the information | |
| | | Appropriately use mass media for information | |
| | | Present the information | |
| | | Learn from feedback and apply to other projects | |
| Miller and Barlett [21] | ALA | Net-savviness | Quantitative survey |
| | | Critical evaluate techniques | |
| | | Diversity | |
| Pinto and Sales [24] | ALA | Understand the information | Theoretical/conceptual |
| | | Detect and define the information needs | |
| | | Know the methods and techniques | |
| | | Evaluate and filter the information | |
| | | Incorporate the information | |

(*Continued*)

**Table 2.** (*Continued*)

| Authors | Definition | Conceptualization | Method |
|---|---|---|---|
| | | Share knowledge | |
| | | Generate information | |
| Klein et al. [18] | ACRL | Detect information | Quantitative survey |
| | | Locate effectively and efficiently | |
| | | Evaluate and manage critically | |
| | | Obtain new findings | |
| | | Understand and recognize implications | |
| Wittich and Jasiewicz [32] | ACRL | Identify information | Theoretical/ conceptual |
| | | Detect | |
| | | Obtain | |
| | | Evaluate | |
| | | Use effectively | |
| Shankar et al. [28] | Doyle (1992) | Starting | Case study |
| | | Chaining | Software program |
| | | Browsing | |
| | | Differentiating | |
| | | Monitoring | |
| | | Extracting | |
| Balceris [7] | ALA Chaka [12]; Rader [25] | Information needs | Instrument development and quantitative survey |
| | | Information source selection | |
| | | Information access | |
| | | Information evaluation | |
| | | Information use | |
| | | Reflection of the information process and findings | |
| Shenton [29] | No explicit definition | Define task | Theoretical/conceptual |
| | | Formulate information-seeking strategies | |
| | | Locate and access information | |
| | | Use information | |
| | | Synthesize work | |
| | | Learn from feedback and apply to other projects | |
| | | Recognize information need | |
| | | Distinguish ways of addressing gap | |
| | | Construct strategies for locating | |
| | | Locate and access | |
| | | Compare and evaluate | |
| | | Organize, apply and communicate | |
| | | Synthesize and create | |

analyzing and evaluating information, integrating, synthesizing and using information, sharing information, and generating information while respecting intellectual property.

Two studies [1, 30] applied the Information Literacy Competency Standards for Higher Education published by the Association of College and Research Libraries (ACRL) and the International Federation of Library Associations guidelines on information literacy. According to the association, information research skills are grouped into the following five themes: concept identification, search strategy, document types, search tools, and use of results. Based on these five themes, a questionnaire containing 20 questions to measure information literacy was developed by the Conference of Rectors and Principals of Quebec Universities for a Quebec survey [23]. In 2009, Thirion and Pochet [30] used this questionnaire for their study aiming at objectively describing the initial level of information literacy in higher education institutions in the French Speaking Community of Belgium. In 2010, Ali et al. utilized the same questionnaire for their study on information skills in a Malaysian college.

The work of Wittich and Jasiewicz [32] and Klein et al. [18] also address the ACRL Information Literacy Competency Standards for Higher Education. The standards of the Association of College and Research Libraries differ from other conceptualizations in their additional focus on the understanding and implications of information. According to ACRL standards, students should be able to determine the extent of information needed, access the needed information effectively and efficiently, evaluate information and its sources critically, incorporate selected information into one's knowledge base, use information effectively to accomplish a specific purpose, understand the economic, legal, and social issues surrounding the use of information, and access and use information ethically and legally.

The overview of the various definitions and conceptualizations of information literacy presented in Table 2 reveals that information literacy is considered to be a complex phenomenon that consists of several components or competences. The definitions and conceptualizations of information literacy proposed in the literature vary in overall scope and the number and granularity of information literacy components contained in them. Another source of differences in the proposed definition is the different naming of the various components of information literacy. After a process of comparison, systematization and matching of both the different definitions for information literacy and their components, the following generic definition of information literacy was extracted: *Information literacy is defined as the ability to recognize problem-driven information needs, to select information sources, to access, evaluate and use information, and to reflect the information process as well as the information results* (see also [7, 16]). This definition serves as basis for further research presented in this paper, for the extraction of a measurement model for information literacy and for its inclusion into subject-specific PLE. It furthermore provided the basis for evaluation of the completeness of published models for measurement of information literacy.

With regard to the applied research methods to measure information literacy, the analyzed body of literature revealed a mixed picture: three studies used qualitative methods (data collection and data analysis), 10 studies quantitative methods, and 16 studies were based on case studies out of which 11 case studies used either qualitative or quantitative methods and the remaining five case studies used a mixed method approach (combination of qualitative and quantitative methods). The case studies involved different assignments for the participants. For analyzing the participants' assignment results and by that also their level of information literacy, a variety of quantitative and qualitative approaches has been applied. Quantitative assessments involved surveys after the assignments (applied in eight of the 16 case studies) and test evaluations (used in four of the 16 case studies). The qualitative assignment analysis involved various qualitative methods such as content analysis of homework, essays, project work, or papers (applied in six of the 16 case studies), analysis of the Internet search strategy recorded by a software program that captures the screen (applied in five of the 16 case studies), participant observation (used twice), and focus groups (also used twice).

Overall only two authors proposed measurement models for information literacy that cover all components of information literacy as required by the extracted definition and that have been empirically tested. These are: the Information Competency Assessment Instrument (ICAI) proposed by Marshal [19] and the measurement model proposed by Balceris [7]. Marshal [19] developed ICAI based on a broad literature review and the consideration of various information literacy standards. The ICAI is based on self-assessment and involves ten aspects that Marshal considered of common importance for an individual to be information literate: (1) identify a topic, (2) determine source requirements, (3) know how to search for needed information, (4) how to locate and retrieve information, (5) evaluate the information, (6) synthesize and organize the information, (7) understand ethical, legal and socio-political issues of the information, (8) appropriately use mass media for information, (9) present the information, and (10) learn from feedback and apply to other projects. Beyond the solely conceptualization, Marshall [19] tested ICAI empirically with two different populations at two different times. The two tests revealed good reliability and validity of the ICAI as approach for measuring information literacy from a self-assessment perspective. Another attempt to measure information literacy in a comprehensive and empirical way was made by Balceris [7]. In his work, he also conflated a wide range of definitions, concepts, and standards including those from the ALA, ACRL, ANZILL, including Chaka [12] and Rader [25]. After a comprehensive evaluation of the literature, Balceris developed and tested a measurement instrument containing six stages: information source selection, information access, information evaluation, information use, and reflection of the information process and findings.

The instruments developed by Marshall [19] and Balceris [7] merge crucial aspects of frameworks and conceptualizations of information literacy presented in literature. Thus, it can be concluded that Marshall's and Balceris' work closed a gap in research by conflating different approaches to two measurement instruments that assess information literacy from two complementary perspectives: the ICAI model of Marshal from the perspective of self-assessment and Balceris's model based on information literacy tasks for each of the relevant information literacy competences identified in his model. These two models served as foundation for development of a new model for measurement of information literacy that is based on a combination of them.

### 3.2 Framework for the Design of Personal Learning Environments with Focus on Information Literacy

The qualitative studies found in the literature research are of great interest and provide insights into the topic. However, they do not offer a valid measurement model in the scope of information literacy at high schools and the results cannot be generalized. In contrast, the quantitative studies acquire a higher relevancy as they enable comparability and generalizability. Yet, our research has shown that there is no consensus among the studies and only little verification. Although many studies carry out a conceptualization, only a few of them verify information literacy empirically. We therefore hold that information literacy research requires one generic measurement model that establishes itself and is generally valid. Of the evaluated literature, it can be concluded that the conceptualizations of Marshall [19] and Balceris [7] are both suitable as they merged crucial aspects of various frameworks and subsequently developed and tested a measurement instrument. The underlying similarities in the concepts of Balceris [7] and Marshall [19] are readily apparent. The presentation of the elements within the two models, side by side, reveals the extent to which the two models of different characteristics share fundamental concepts. Common features among the two different models can be recognized: Although Marshall's model is with its ten stages more comprehensive than Balceris' six stages model, each stage of one model can be assigned to a stage of the other model. What is particularly noticeable is that Marshall subdivides the component describing the use of information into four specific components, while Balceris works with only one component. Hence, for Marshall the question rises whether the instrument can be reduced in order to make it more comprehensible. Overall, we believe that neither Marshall's nor Balceris' instrument are generic models yet as they both have not been applied in many studies and contexts and need to be verified. Thus, both instruments have not been established in research and practice so far. Nevertheless, they build a starting point and appear suitable for a foundation for a valid measurement model.

Based on these findings and a combination of the two measurement models proposed by Marshal and Balceris, the 7i model for systematical measurement of information literacy in High School was developed. The 7i model is presented in Table 3. It comprises 7 components of information literacy and combines in each component self-assessment and tasks-based, i.e. competency based dimensions. Table 3 illustrates also the inclusion of information literacy and its support by PLE.

Competencies are activity-based and consist of knowledge, beliefs/attitudes, and skills. Learning outcomes can be regarded as developments in these activity fields. Thus, student learning can be defined as an active process in which learners engage in activities that lead to changes in knowledge, beliefs and/or teaching practices (skills). In research studies it is common to categorize learning outcomes according to this threefold distinction. Bakkenes et al. [6] define categories of learning outcomes for example as follows: changes in practice, and changes in knowledge and beliefs (including emotions). Therefore, the 7imodel consists of seven phases including knowledge, skills, and attitudes relevant for building information literacy and is supported by the personal learning environment (PLE).

**Table 3.** PLE framework with the focus on information literacy

**Information Literacy Model**

Information-based Problem Solving as pattern to design teaching & learning in high school

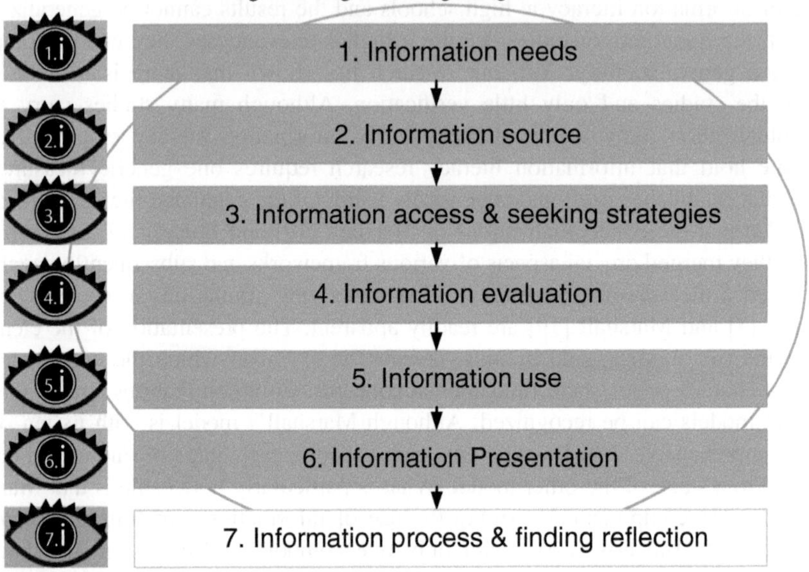


| **Knowledge – knowing Know what?** | **Skills – doing Know how?** | **Attitudes – Being Know why?** |
|---|---|---|
| Designing learning material, curating internet resources | Designing learning tasks and strategies | Designing motivational factors and reflection process |
| *Examples:*<br>- Material, instructional video about information literacy and the model<br>- Knowledge about tools (e.g., mindmap, delicious, wiki, blog) and use strategies<br>- Knowledge about the subject matter, starting points for the internet research | *Examples:*<br>- Introduction to the problem, the cases to solve giving an overview<br>- Explaining the learning task for each phase<br>- Coaching (by peers, by lecturers) to use appropriate strategies and tools in each phase<br>- Demonstrating good practice examples | *Examples:*<br>- Motivational factors: designing expert groups for each internet company (google, apple, facebook, amazon)<br>- Gaming elements, e.g. experience points as rewards<br>- Reflection process by using a blog |

**PLE = Personal Learning Environment**

School wide Learning management system (Educanet) as the main communication platform providing links and access to appropriate tools for each phase

Many institutions develop campus-specific solutions for PLEs such as customizable portals or dashboards that help students organize their research and resources and post their reflections. Yet, as much institutional involvement conflicts with the philosophy of a PLE, many educators prefer to use free applications like iGoogle and MyYahoo!, which offer adequate platforms for learner-centric PLEs. In this context, the PLE represents a shift away from the model in which learners consume information through independent channels such as the library, a textbook, or a courseware, moving instead to a model where students draw connections from a growing amount of resources that they select and organize. A PLE puts students in charge of their own learning processes, challenging them to reflect on the tools and resources that help them learn best. By design, a PLE is created from self-direction, and therefore the responsibility for organization rests with the learner. However, despite their ability to quickly learn new online tools and computer applications, many learners at high schools lack the necessary information literacy. Therefore, we suggest in our framework a balanced model between complete openness and access of resources and tools as well as providing helpful guidance and orientation along the necessary phases of information literacy.

## 4 Conclusion and Recommendation for Future Research

This paper provides two major results: a systematic overview of the available body of knowledge about information literacy and a framework for a PLE focusing on information literacy. With these results, the paper provides a significant scientific and practical contribution.

Information literacy as newly required competencies in the digital age is a challenge for high schools to integrate in their curriculum. Competencies can be defined in categories of learning outcomes such as changes in practice, and changes in knowledge and beliefs (including emotions). Based on the findings of our literature review, we elaborated the 7i model to foster and measure information literacy as a process- and competency-oriented approach. Therefore, the technology-enhanced personal learning environment should support the seven phases of the information literacy model to help learners manage their learning, both outcomes (content, e.g. by using wikis, etc.) and process (in particular by reflecting in blogs).

Guided by the research goal to inter-relate information literacy into PLE in schools a first framework for inclusion of information literacy in PLE was developed. The framework is based on a theoretical model for the development and measurement of information literacy developed from the results of a broad and systematic literature review. The achieved results cover the first two phases of the design process. Next steps in the research are the evaluation and validation of the framework in practice. Several evaluation cycles in different settings will be necessary in order to validate the proposed model.

While the proposed framework is defined on a generic level, different learning subjects might require specific adjustments of the generic model. Thus, further research is necessary to evaluate the generic framework and to develop specific solutions for specific subjects.

## References


1. Ali, R., Abu-Hassan, N.: Information literacy skills of engineering. Int. J. Res. Rev. Appl. Sci. **5**(3), 264–270 (2010)
2. American Library Association: Presidential Committee on Information Literacy. Final Report. American Library Association, Chicago (1989)
3. Argelagós, E., Pifarré, M.: Improving information problem solving skills in secondary education through embedded instruction. Comput. Hum. Behav. **28**, 515–526 (2012)
4. Association of College and Research Libraries (ACRL): Information literacy competency standards for higher education (2000). http://www.ala.org/acrl/sites/ala.org.acrl/files/content/standards/standards.pdf. Accessed 27 Nov 2014
5. Attwell, G.: The personal learning environments - the future of eLearning? eLearning Pap. **2** (1), 1–7 (2007)
6. Bakkenes, I., Vermunt, J.D., Wubbels, T.: Teacher learning in the context of educational innovation: learning activities and learning outcomes of experienced teachers. Learn. Instr. **xx**, 1–16 (2009)
7. Balceris, M.: Medien- und Informationskompetenz - Modellierung und Messung von Informationskompetenz bei Schülern. Dissertation, Freie Universität Berlin (2011)
8. Basefsky, S.: Six questions and a strategy for campus-wide information competence. Working paper, Cornell University ILR School (2009). http://digitalcommons.ilr.cornell.edu/cgi/viewcontent.cgi?article=1172&context=workingpapers. Accessed 26 Nov 2014
9. Bassellier, G., Reich, B.H., Benbasat, I.: Information technology competence of business managers: a definition and research model. J. Manag. Inf. Syst. **17**(4), 159–182 (2001)
10. Brasley, S., Beile, P., Katz, I.R.: Assessing information competence of students using iSkills™: a commercially-available, standardized instrument. In: Proceedings of the Library Assessment Conference: Building Effective, Sustainable, Practical Assessment 2008, Seattle (2008)
11. Burke, M.: Overcoming challenges of the technological age by teaching information literacy skills. Community Junior Coll. Libr. **16**(4), 247–259 (2012)
12. Chaka, C.: The changing faces of literacies. information and media literacy in the context of higher education. In: Leaning, M. (ed.) Education, Practice and Pedagogy, pp. 31–50. Informing Science Press, Santa Rosa (2009)
13. Clarke, J., Dede, C.: Design for scalability: a case study of the river city curriculum. J. Sci. Educ. Technol. **4**(18), 353–365 (2009)
14. Design-Based Research Collective: Design-based research: an emerging paradigm for educational inquiry. Educ. Res. **1**(32), 5–8 (2003)
15. Eisenberg, M.B., Berkowitz, R.E.: The six study habits of highly effective students: using the Big Six to link parents, students, and homework. Sch. Libr. J. **41**(8), 22–25 (1995)
16. Gapski, H., Tekster, T.: Informationskompetenz in Deutschland - Überblick zum Stand der Fachdiskussion und Zusammenstellung von Literaturangaben, Projekten und Materialien zu einzelnen Zielgruppen. LfM, Düsseldorf (2009)
17. Jafari, A., McGee, P., Carmean, C.: Managing courses, defining learning: what faculty, students, and administrators want. EDUCAUSE Rev. **41**(4), 50–71 (2006)
18. Klein, R.N., Beutelspacher, L., Hauk, K., Terp, C., Anuschewski, D., Zensen, C., Trkulja, V., Weller, K.: Informationskompetenz in Zeiten des Web 2.0: Chancen und Herausforderungen im Umgang mit Social Software. Inf. Wiss. Prax. **60**(3), 129–142 (2009)
19. Marshall, R.K.: An instrument to measure information competency. J. Literacy Technol. **6** (1), 1–27 (2006)

20. McKenney, S., Reeves, T.: Conducting Educational Design Research. Routledge, New York (2012)
21. Miller, C., Bartlett, J.: 'Digital fluency': towards young people's critical use of the internet. J. Inf. Literacy **6**(2), 35–55 (2012)
22. Miller, D.: Lernstrategien und neue Medien (Entwurf SNF Projekt). UZH, Zürich (2013)
23. Mittermeyer, D., Quirion, D.: Information literacy: study of incoming first-year undergraduates in Quebec. In: Quebec, Conference of Rectors and Principals of Quebec Universities (2003)
24. Pinto, M., Sales, D.: Infolitrans: a model for the development of information competence for translators. J. Doc. **64**(3), 413–437 (2008)
25. Rader, H.: Information literacy – a global perspective. In: Martin, A., Rader, H. (eds.) Information and IT Literacy: Enabling Learning in the 21st Century, pp. 24–42. Facet Publishing, London (2003)
26. SCONUL Advisory Committee on Information Literacy: Information skills in higher education: a SCONUL position paper (1999). http://www.sconul.ac.uk/sites/default/files/documents/Seven_pillars2.pdf. Accessed 25 Nov 2014
27. Seufert, S.: Design Research für die Implementation von eLearning: ein vielversprechendes Paradigma für die Zusammenarbeit von Wissenschaft und Praxis? HMD Praxis der Wirtschaftsinformatik **1**(52), 120–131 (2015)
28. Shankar, S., Kumar, M., Natarajan, U.: A profile of digital information literacy competencies of high school students. Inf. Sci. Inf. Technol. **2**, 355–368 (2005)
29. Shenton, A.K.: Information Literacy and scholarly investigation: a British perspective. J. Int. Fed. Libr. Assoc. Inst. **35**(3), 226–231 (2009)
30. Thirion, P., Pochet, B.: Information literacy in students entering higher education in the French speaking community of Belgium: lessons learned from an evaluation. J. Int. Fed. Libr. Assoc. Inst. **35**(2), 152–170 (2009)
31. Webster, J., Watson, R.: Analyzing the past to prepare for the future: writing a literature review. MIS Q. **26**(2), xiii–xxiii (2002)
32. Wittich, A., Jasiewicz, J.: Orientierungsrahmen zur Vermittlung von Informationskompetenz in der Schule. Inf. Wiss. Prax. **62**(4), 167–172 (2011)

# Effectiveness of Blended Learning Approaches in Engaging Non-law Students to Study Law

Kanchana Chandran[1(✉)], Sanath Sukumaran[2], and Kalpana Chandran[3]

[1] Sunway University, No. 5, JalanUniversiti, Bandar Sunway, 46150 Petaling Jaya, Selangor, Malaysia
kanchanac@sunway.edu.my
[2] School of Computing and IT, Taylor's University, 1, Jalan Taylor's, 47500 Subang Jaya, Malaysia
sanath.sukumaran@taylors.edu.my
[3] Hogan Lovells International LLP, Atlantic House, Holborn Viaduct, London, UK
kalpana.chandran@hoganlovells.com

**Abstract.** This paper focuses on the blended learning measures used in engaging non-law students to study law. The challenge of teaching law to non-law students is that they come with a preconceived notion that law is difficult. It is therefore important for educators to have a more realistic expectation on non-law students compared with law students. The aim of this study is therefore to ensure that lessons are appropriately targeted for the non-law students along with increasing their level of participation in class. The paper employs a method involving THREE (3) broad stages of experiments, observations and surveys stretching over 14 weeks. This paper concludes with the finding that the activities built in during the lesson clearly exhibited a lot of student engagement and interest as shown from the results of the surveys conducted. The study also found that the participants were ready to embrace new methods in teaching and learning with the use of online tools thus enabling student-centered learning.

**Keywords:** Blended learning · Student engagement · Student-centred learning

## 1 Introduction

The general trend of non-law students when asked about studying law is that they come with a preconceived notion that law is difficult to study as it requires memorization. It is not surprising that the participants in this research too share the same view, much influenced by their seniors. Educators must have realistic expectations with regards to non-law students studying law compared to typical law student who are on the route to becoming lawyers.

This research encompasses the module on Business and Hospitality Law for the participants progressing to degrees in the field of Culinary Management and International Hospitality Management. The primary focus of this module is to introduce the participants to selected areas of law that are fundamental to the hospitality industry, and


L. Uden et al. (Eds.): LTEC 2015, CCIS 533, pp. 164–173, 2015.
DOI: 10.1007/978-3-319-22629-3_13

give the participants an appreciation of how the law and legal principles relate to the hospitality industry.

The participants consist of approximately 23 hospitality students, studying law for the first time. The participants include a number of international students. Despite the diversity, the international nature of the hospitality education is such that the basic standards and practices are much the same in many countries.

The objectives of the research are as follows:

- To evaluate whether the lessons were appropriately targeted for the students;
- To evaluate whether the researcher had sufficiently engaged the participants throughout the lessons.

## 2 Literature Review

**Keeping the objectives in mind**, a holistic outlook of how people learn ought to be examined. Hence, the works of Brookfield is a worthy mention. Brookfield espoused a series of self-reflection to assess one's own teaching and learning through four lenses as follows [4]:

(i) Self lens – the need to reflect on our past experiences as learners and teachers.
(ii) Student lens – the need to communicate or reflect upon how our students are experiencing the learning process in terms of what is supporting or hindering their learning, which may well include, our own approach to teaching that we may need to change.
(iii) Peer lens – the need for mutuality of support where our colleagues can assist in improving teaching and learning. Lave and Wenger summarized this as Communities of Practice (COP) where "groups of people share a concern or a passion for something they do and learn how to do it better as they interact regularly" [6].
(iv) Scholarly lens – the need for literature to shed light on issues that we are facing and offer a host of options that would best suit our context.

These lenses are crucial inputs in what can be termed as holistic teaching. It is imperative that from the feedback that we get through these lenses, we make changes to our teaching styles and move forward taking a student-centred approach.

Since the study is focused on "Business and Hospitality Law", the required skill set in learning law is necessary, as with all other disciplines. Walker and Hobson emphasised that learning law involves a different skill set from other disciplines. It requires both knowledge and skills in problem identification [8]. The skills needed for law include the ability to understand legal terms and legal duties coupled with the ability to apply this knowledge to actual situations. Walker and Hobson offered the analogy that, if learners are neither given the essential knowledge nor the basic skills to apply the knowledge, it is comparable to an Ikea furniture with no instruction booklet. Likewise, the approach in teaching law cannot be a 'one-size fits all'. One needs to show the learners a step by step procedure on how to achieve the end result. The old adage "practice makes perfect" applies to any kind of learning.

In developing the specific skill set required for law, the lessons will have to be appropriately targeted for the students, which brings us to the first objective of this research. Under this objective, it is perhaps necessary to relook at the very system set out to teach young adults today. Prensky commented that "Today's students are no longer the people our educational system was designed to teach. Our Digital Immigrant instructors, who speak an outdated language (that of the pre-digital age), are struggling to teach a population that speaks an entirely new language" [7]. He stressed that this is a critical issue in today's education as our Digital Immigrant teachers take for granted that today's learners are no different from the learners of yesteryears and that the same approaches that were suitable for them as students would also be suitable for their own students. As put by Prensky, "Should the Digital Native students learn the old ways, or should their Digital Immigrant educators learn the new?" [7].

Therefore, educators today must start encroaching into the very domain young learners are familiar with. As illustrated in Fig. 1 below, Barkley described that student engagement is created as a result of motivation and active learning [1].

Motivation, was defined by Brophy as "the level of enthusiasm and the degree to which students invest attention and effort in learning" [5], while Bonwell and Eison, defined active learning as "doing what we think and thinking about what we are doing" [3].

Likewise, in today's digital world, students have grown up with technology, where information is just a click away. Therefore, using online tools like Edmodo, todaysmeet.com and a host of other contemporary Android and iOS apps using mobile phones, is essential in paving the way towards a heightened level of student engagement. Zepke summed up well by saying that "students need to believe that all strengths they bring into the classroom are appreciated" [9]. Therefore, educators in turn must be open enough to facilitate such a transition to take place.

Hence, having a fusion of approaches, commonly referred to as blended learning will go a long way in ensuring that diverse learning styles are adopted to cater for the different needs of learners.

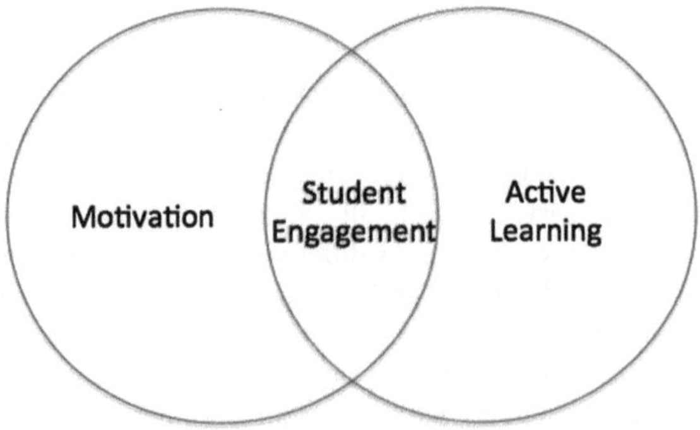


**Fig. 1.** Venn diagram model of student engagement. Adapted from Barkley [1]

## 3 Methodology

The overview of the research methodology is shown in Fig. 2 below;

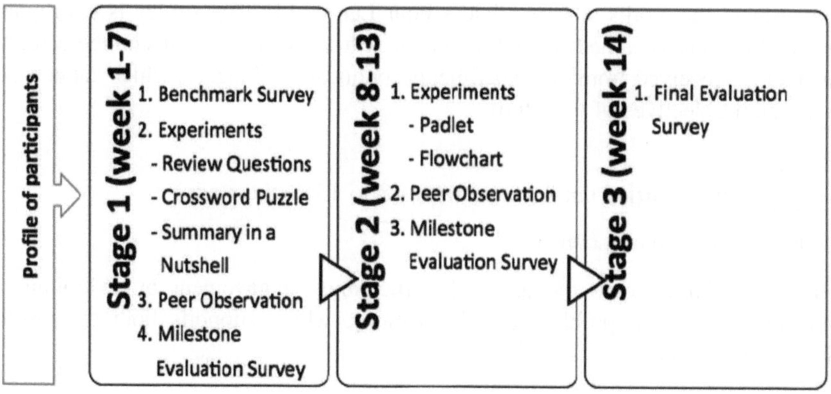


**Fig. 2.** Methodology employed in the research

The research methodology primarily involved THREE (3) broad stages (1, 2 and 3) with one stage leading to another progressively, over a span of a typical semester of 14 weeks.

Profile of participants (obtained prior to Stage 1).

The purpose was to find out the demographic information and cognitive abilities of the participants in line with the research objectives of this study.

**Stage 1**

Benchmark Survey (carried out during week 1 of the study)

Purpose: To document the participants' preferred learning styles, which supports both the research objectives of this study.

Experiments (carried out during weeks 1 to 7 of the study)

(i) Review Questions

Purpose: To ascertain if this periodic formative evaluation has any effect on the participants understanding of the lesson, which supports both the research objectives of this study.

(ii) Crossword Puzzles

Purpose: To ascertain if this periodic formative evaluation has the desired effect of improving the participants' understanding of the salient key concepts of the law, which supports both the research objectives of this study.

(iii) Summary in a Nutshell

Purpose: To allow participants to replace legal jargons with plain English, which supports both the research objectives of this study.

Peer Observation (carried out in week 3 of the study)

Purpose: (i) to minimise research bias; (ii) to objectively validate the outcome of the findings of the experiments carried out in Stage 1; and (iii) mutuality of support i.e. to elicit critical and constructive feedback as part of an ongoing continuous learning process, which support both the research objectives of this study.

Milestone Evaluation Survey (carried out in week 7 of the study)

Purpose: To improve on the researcher's own teaching. The survey instrument was adapted from the works of Brookfield's Four Lenses [4]. The survey is both quantitative and qualitative aimed at eliciting feedback from the participants on the perceived benefits they received from the experiments conducted in Stage 1, which support both the research objectives of this study.

**Stage 2**

Experiments (carried out between weeks 8 to 13 of the study)

(i) Padlet (http://padlet.com/)

Purpose: To increase the level of participants' engagement by exhibiting the application of law to problem based questions, which supports both the research objective of this study.

(ii) Flowcharts

Purpose: To ascertain if the participants were able to conceptualise their thought processes through constructive alignment by being able to connect the keywords in a lesson to create the 'big picture' [2]. This supports both of the objective of this study.

Peer Observation (carried out in week 11 of the study)

Purpose: (i) to minimise research bias (ii) to objectively validate the outcome of the findings of the experiments carried out in Stage 2 (iii) mutuality of support i.e. to elicit critical and constructive feedback as part of an ongoing continuous learning process, which support both the research objectives of this study.

Milestone Evaluation Survey (carried out in week 13 of the study)

Purpose: To improve on the researcher's own teaching, the survey instrument was adapted from the works of Brookfield's Four Lenses [4]. The survey is both quantitative and qualitative aimed at eliciting feedback from participants on the perceived benefits they received from the experiments conducted in Stage 2, which support both the research objectives of this study.

**Stage 3**

Final Evaluation Survey (carried out in week 14 of the study)

Purpose: To evaluate the final outcome of Stages 1 and 2 of the study and to determine if the research objectives have been met in its entirety. The survey was both quantitative and qualitative, which supports both the research objectives of this study.

## 4 Analysis of Findings

Profile of Participants (carried our prior to week 1 of the study)

The profile of participants informed that a majority of the participants were between weak to average students with a cumulative average (CAVG) of 51.23 %.

**Stage 1**

Benchmark Survey (carried out during week 1 of the study)

17 out of 23 participants responded to the survey. Generally, the participants expected their lecturers: (i) To give good examples related to the subject; (ii) To have in-class activities to engage students; and (iii) To guide students on how to answer questions. Some of the most preferred teaching styles indicated by the students were: (i) Lecture with lots of examples; (ii) Lectures with some quizzes to enhance understanding; (iii) Learning together with friends; and (iv) In class exercises. 76 % of the students felt that their lecturers in the past were interesting. Some of the suggestions put forward by the students to improve teaching and learning were: (i) To be more engaging and enthusiastic; (ii) To pay attention to each student; (iii) To give more examples for students to understand better; (iv) To use key points or abbreviations to make the subject easier; (v) To teach slowly; and (vi) To conduct a revision class.

Experiments (carried out during weeks 1 to 7 of the study)

(i) Review Questions (refer to the Peer Observation comments below for the outcome of the experiment).
(ii) *Crossword Puzzles (*refer to the Milestone Evaluation Survey findings below for the outcome of the experiment).
(iii) *Summary in a Nutshell (refer to* the Peer Observation comments below for the outcome of the experiment.

Peer Observation (carried out in week 3 of the study)

(i) Review Questions

The peer observer (from outside the researcher's department) found the questioning techniques used throughout the lesson to assess the participants' level of understanding very effective. The frequent checks by asking probing questions and also asking if the participants understood the lesson provided a way for the researcher to assess whether the participants understanding of the lesson was sound. In getting the participants to respond to the questions posed, the Peer Observer had suggested to call on specific participants to answer the question. The researcher had adopted this suggestion in subsequent lessons and found that this helped the researcher to check on the understanding of the participants who were generally quiet.

(iii) Summary in a Nutshell

The peer observer found that the strategy in asking participants to summarize the key features of the relevant piece of legislation in simple words helped the participants to verbalise their understanding. It also encouraged the participants to think further, reflect and apply their own interpretation to the relevant piece of legislation. The peer observer was able to ascertain this by observing what the students were doing and could see that the students were at ease in expressing themselves which is a vital skill to have for aspiring law students.

Generally, from the post observation discussion, the peer observer commented that the Benchmark Survey carried out during week 1 of the study had significantly and positively contributed to the researcher adapting teaching strategies to suit the participants' learning needs and achieving the intended learning outcomes.

Milestone Evaluation Survey (carried out in week 7 of the study)

18 out of 23 participants responded to the survey. 100 % of the respondents indicated they understood the objectives of the lesson; 94 % of the respondents indicated they were given the opportunity to ask questions; 89 % of the respondents indicated they were given the opportunity to share their thoughts; 72 % of the respondents indicated they were given the opportunity to apply what they had learnt during the lesson; 83 % of the respondents indicated that the lesson was engaging (interesting); 89 % of the respondents could follow the lesson well; 72 % of the respondents felt the classroom environment supported their learning; 78 % of the respondents felt their concerns were addressed during the lesson; 67 % of the respondents felt they could complete the activities given; and 83 % of the respondents indicated they were not scared to ask questions.

The participants' found the lesson engaging for the following reasons: (i) The lesson was kept simple, straightforward and relative; (ii) They were given the opportunity to express their thoughts and share their views; (iii) The explanations were clear and the examples were interesting; (iv) They were able to interact with the lecturer; (v) They saw how relevant the lesson was, as it was made easy; and (vi) The lesson had a practical element that the participants could relate to.

**Stage 2**

**Experiments** (carried out between weeks 8 to 13 of the study)

(i) Padlet (refer to the Milestone Evaluation Survey findings below for the outcome of the experiment).
(ii) Flowcharts (refer to the Final Evaluation Survey findings below for the outcome of the experiment).

Peer Observation (carried out in week 11 of the study)

The peer observer (from within the researcher's department) observed that the researcher guided the participants to adopt a specific structure in addressing issues in law and solving legal problems. This methodical approach helped the participants to understand the subject better. The use of pictures in the slides was also good as it helped the participants visualise their study of law.

Generally, the post observation discussion was fruitful in that the peer observer shared that it is important that eventually the students themselves should learn how to develop the flowchart or mind map as it will help them see where the law is and how it is applied within the bigger picture.

Milestone Evaluation Survey (carried out in week 13 of the study)

16 out of 23 participants responded to the survey. 100 % of the respondents indicated they understood the objectives of the lesson; 94 % of the respondents indicated they were given the opportunity to ask questions; 88 % of the respondents indicated they were given the opportunity to share their thoughts; 100 % of the respondents indicated they were given the opportunity to apply what they had learnt during the lesson; 100 % of the respondents indicated that the lesson was engaging (interesting); 94 % of the respondents could follow the lesson well; 88 % of the respondents felt the classroom environment supported their learning; 100 % of the respondents felt their concerns were addressed during the lesson; 88 % of the

respondents felt they could complete the activities given; and 100 % of the respondents indicated they were not scared to ask questions.

The participants' found the lesson engaging for the following reasons: (i) they found the lesson far more interactive and interesting with the use of padlet; (ii) there was a clear direction and goal; (iii) the lesson was explained well with relevant examples; (iv) everyone could participate in the discussion; and (v) they found the lesson applicable to real life situations.

**Stage 3**

Final Evaluation Survey (carried out in week 14 of the study)

The end-of-term evaluation survey showed the following overall ratings by the participants. 90 % of the participants felt that they had a clear understanding of the subject; 91 % of the participants felt that the subject was well structured; 86 % of the participants felt that the subject enabled them to achieve the learning outcomes; 89 % of the participants felt that the subject was intellectually stimulating, i.e. that it made them think; 86 % of the participants felt that the subject developed their problem solving skills; 89 % of the participants felt that the learning resources assisted them in learning this subject; 87 % of the participants felt that they received helpful feedback on their progress in the subject; 90 % of the participants felt that overall they were satisfied with the quality of the subject; 90 % of the participants felt that the lecturer was well organized; 91 % of the participants felt that the lecturer's explanations helped their understanding; 89 % of the participants felt that the lecturer inspired them to learn; 91 % of the participants felt that the lecturer encouraged them to be involved in their learning; and 89 % of the participants felt that the lecturer encouraged them to participate.

## 5 Conclusion

The researcher's formative experiences as a learner had in many ways consciously influenced the way the researcher had approached teaching. Memorization was never an option to learn law. Law has to be understood and the more one becomes familiar with the subject through practice, the easier it becomes. The researcher's working experiences have also been just as influential. It is through practice that one becomes better in the field and learning becomes more meaningful in the process. The researcher is well aware that the context in which the participants are working in is different from the professional environment in which the researcher was in. Nevertheless, it is hoped that what the researcher experienced and what the participants are experiencing will eventually be a valuable source of understanding as to what is involved in law and how one needs to think in law.

In this research paper, the lecture materials and the blended learning activities built in during the lessons clearly exhibited a lot of student engagement and interest as shown from the results of the surveys conducted. The researcher, however, had to endure hours of relentless effort to prepare and effectively plan for the learning activities and engagement to take place within the lesson. The desired outcomes had to be carefully crafted to suit the learners' needs, expected learning outcomes and the nature of the session (lecture or tutorial). The research had to also ensure that the materials were not voluminous and could be completed well within the stipulated duration whilst injecting elements of fun and curiosity. The researcher had to grapple with other challenges including insufficient lesson time which hampered stimulation of meaningful discussions taking place which would have otherwise been a source of rich input to the teaching and learning process.

The researcher found that the participants were ready to embrace new methods in teaching and learning. In the use of flowcharts, for example, the researcher clearly applied student centred learning by getting the participants to come up with the flowcharts during the revision session. This was presented by the participants in groups and shared with all before the final exam. The blended learning measures introduced in the study showed a marked increase as far as the students' level of engagement and interest were concerned. Non-law students particularly found the use of blended learning approaches non-intimidating in as far as expressing themselves as opposed to traditional ways of teaching and learning. The fear which typically surrounded non-law students studying law was almost non-existent. They were ready to embrace concepts of law introduced to them with little resistance. This led to the students taking charge of their learning and becoming active learners.

## 6 Opportunities for Further Research

The research methodology employed in the study was on the whole qualitative in nature and addressed concerns of validity. However, there is still room for improvement for further scholarly work.

One such area for further improvement is on peer evaluation conducted at the end of Stages 1 and 2. Peer evaluation for instance could be conducted using the Delphi approach, which in effect validates the view of the observations conducted and consequently nullifies aspects of biasness.

Another area for further research is to be able to embark on more online tools in addressing the second research objective for improving student engagement. Taking advantage of the pervasiveness of mobile devices and smartphones proliferating academics and students alike, it would not be far-fetched to expect that the use of mobile apps, which are platform independent, will surely take centre-stage. Hence, it would be an interesting observation to see how the fusion of such apps in mobile devices improve student engagement in particular and learning in general.

Finally, it would be interesting if the study can be extended to examine if the initiatives taken by the researcher in the study has any bearing towards the participants' results in their final examination. It would be a phenomenal piece of revelation if a benchmark can be made with the previous cohort and the current cohort in terms of the final examination performance of the participants.

## References

1. Barkley, E.F.: Student Engagement Techniques. Wiley, Jossey-Bass, San Francisco (2010). ISBN 978-0-470-28191-8

2. Biggs, J.: What The Student Does: Teaching For Quality Learning At University. Open University Press, Buckingham (1999)
3. Bonwell, C.C., Eison, J.A.: Active Learning: Creating Excitement in the classroom. School of Education and Human Development, George Washington University, Washington, DC (1991)
4. Brookfield, S.: Becoming a Critically Reflective Teacher. Jossey-Bass, San-Francisco (1995)
5. Brophy, J.E.: Motivating Students To Learn. Erlbaum, Mahwah, NJ (2004)
6. Lave, J., Wenger, E.: Communities of practice. Acessed on 9 June 2008
7. Prensky, M.: Digital natives, digital immigrants part 1. Horiz. **9**(5), 1–6 (2001)
8. Walker, S., Hobson, J.: Interventions in teaching first-year law: feeding forward to improve learning outcomes. Assess. Eval. High. Educ. **39**(3), 326–338 (2014)
9. Zepke, N.: Student engagement: a complex business supporting the first year experience in tertiary education. Int. J. First Year High. Educ. **4**(2), 1–14 (2013). doi:10.5204/intjfyhe.v4i1.183

# Learning Tools & Environments

# The Information Society, a Challenge for Business Students?

Viktorija Florjančič(✉)

Faculty of Management, University of Primorska,
Cankarjeva 5, SI-6000 Koper, Slovenia
viktorija.florjancic@fm-kp.si

**Abstract.** We welcome digital natives to our university assuming they are competent computer and internet users. However, testing their computer skills at the beginning of the course revealed that they are not as highly skilled as was initially expected. The majority of students had surprisingly never heard of the massive open online courses that have been challenging higher education in recent years. Moreover, a lot of students do not use freely accessible learning resources on the web. Collecting data from Eurostat statistics raises an interesting issue – more and more EU households are getting broadband internet access and internet penetration is not only following users that have accessed the internet once in the last 3 months, but users that access the internet daily. It would be expected that individuals, especially those aged under 30, are highly computer and internet literate, but the data analysis revealed otherwise. Not only students included in the research presented in the empirical part of this paper, but also an average young internet user of one of the 28 EU countries. Using Facebook and the first Google search result is not enough anymore.

**Keywords:** ICT literacy · Information society · Open education

## 1 Introduction

People born in the last 15 years of the previous century, were born in the so-called digital era [8]. It is common for this generation to be described as "digital natives", compared to the older generation for whom the metaphor "digital immigrant" is used [7, 8]. It is thought that "digital natives" take information-communication technology (ICT) for granted and have no problem using it. However, after working with students we became aware that they are not as ICT literate as would be expected. Their digital competencies are often limited to using Facebook and to accepting the first Google search result. Our observations are not isolated. The International Computer and Information Literacy Study [5] reports that being born in a digital era, does not mean sufficient use of ICT critically and creatively. The research shows that 25 % of surveyed


L. Uden et al. (Eds.): LTEC 2015, CCIS 533, pp. 177–187, 2015.
DOI: 10.1007/978-3-319-22629-3_14

students,[1] except Czech and Danish, demonstrate low levels of ICT literacy. ICT literacy is a set of key skills to acquire relevant information to build knowledge and to actively participate in the information society. Deficiency in these digital skills caused the digital divide, which is still present even in so-called modern countries. The digital competence, that involves basic ICT skills, was declared as one of the eight key competences for lifelong learning, by EC back in 2006.[2] After almost 10 years, this issue is still relevant. Not only the e-business trends, but also the trends in education, anticipate digitally literate participants. The Opening Up Education initiative, launched by EC in 2013 [4], stresses the importance of re-shaping the EU education in the sense of actively using ICT in the education process and to open access to education and open learning resources. Using all the potential benefits of the digital revolution in education requires ICT literate participants – not only students but teachers too.

Taking into consideration all these facts, we try to use ICT intensively in our course; not only for our lesson preparation, which is still very widespread in the educational field, but to motivate students to use ICT actively and in a creative way. Years ago, we expected "digital natives" to come to university highly skilled in ICT and thus we stopped teaching them how to use it. However, we then became aware that they are not as skilled as we thought and we started to implement more technology in the course, using the learning-by-doing approach. To adapt the course content to their knowledge, each year we asked students to complete a survey at the beginning of the course. The anonymous e-survey was prepared using the LimeSurvey[3] application and was launched through an e-mail invitation. The questions used in the e-survey were mostly closed. Students' opinions or their attitudes where expressed (estimated) on a 5-degree Likert's scale, where grade 1 represents the lower grade (do not agree at all, never, non-skilled user) and 5 is used to present the highest grade – (completely agree, always, well-skilled user). The data was analysed using the SPSS programme[4] (ver. 21).

## 2 Information Society

### 2.1 ICT Usage and e-Skills

The information age, the computer age or the digital age, synonyms for the intensive use of ICT in contemporary society which is known itself as the information society. ICT has become a part of our everyday lives. We are ordering goods and services online, communicating with each other, acquiring information and knowledge through the internet etc. Businesses are changing from purely physical organisation (bricks-and-mortar organisations) throughout partial e-business organisation (clicks-and-mortar

---

[1] ICILS covers EU countries: Croatia, Czech Republic, Denmark, Germany, Lithuania, Netherlands, Poland, Slovak Republic, Slovenia and non-EU countries: Australia, Chile, Hong Kong, SAR, Republic of Korea, Norway, Russian federation, Switzerland and Turkey [5].

[2] http://eur-lex.europa.eu/legal-content/EN/ALL/?uri=CELEX:32006H0962.

[3] https://www.limesurvey.org/en/.

[4] http://www-01.ibm.com/software/analytics/spss/.

organisations) to virtual organisation, where the whole process is done digitally [10]. Not only businesses, but education and public administration are also moving their activities online. Not being able to use these services means that all those who are not able to adapt to these changes will be excluded from the (information) society. A digital divide, that is usually defined as a "have's" and "have's not" divide, dividing people who have access to ICT from those who do not have it [8], is not only a problem in the "third world". Working with students and following different reports about ICT literacy, challenges us to a wider dimension of contemporary digital divide – a divide between those who are able to acquire relevant information, to evaluate it and to be able to use it. We need to emphasise that only data that has meaning and value for the user is defined as information [10]. Living online, participating in different social networks, following different news track, open a divide between those who are able to use information critically and effectively. ICT skills are becoming one of the most important skills in the information society.

Based on Eurostat statistics for 2014 [6], 79 % of households in the 28 EU member states (EU 28) have broadband access to the internet. Slovenia (SI) broadband connection penetration is 77 %. Households in Denmark, the Netherlands, Finland, Sweden and the United Kingdom are top of the list with 90 % and more. If years ago we were talking about "internet connection", nowadays "broadband connection" is a term used to present internet penetration. Individuals can access the internet from different places – at home, work, school and other places. The most common internet access point, in 2013, was home computer – 72 % of individuals in the EU 28 used Internet at home (70 % Slovenian users). One third of individuals (32 % in the EU 28, 34 % in Slovenia) accessed the internet at their place of work and 10 % of the EU 28 accessed the internet at the educational institute (SI 11 %). Obviously individuals can access the Internet from different locations. Eurostat collects data on how frequently users access the internet. Years ago, a regular internet user was defined as a person who uses internet (or computer) at least once in the past 3 months. Nowadays, daily internet usage is presented among 65 % of EU 28 individuals (SI 58 %). Scandinavian users are on the top with more than 80 %. And 75 % of all EU 28 citizens access the Internet at least once a week.

Based on Eurostat data [6] 43 % of individuals access the internet using a mobile device (laptop or desktop computer, mobile or smart phone or any other handheld device). The mobile internet access via mobile phone network or wireless connection, seems to have become a substitute for the traditional wired internet access. Internet services usage is not limited to home or place of work/school anymore. Web content is available at any time and from anywhere. The use of mobile devices is particularly widespread among people aged between 16 and 24, 63 % of individuals in the EU 28 used this device in 2012. There are still some differences between the usage of men compared to women – men were more likely to use mobile devices than women.

Broadband and mobile access to the Internet give EU citizens the prerequisite to use the internet from anywhere and at any time. Besides data on internet access, the Eurostat collects data on other indicators that measure the adoption of ICT and its usage in EU countries; among them the percentage of individuals with low/medium/high computer and internet skills. Based on the Eurostat data about how many computer or internet activities[5] individuals are able to do (in the group of all individuals and in the group aged between 16 and 24 years), we calculated the average number of activities in two different years, as followed by Eurostat – for computer activities in 2014 and 2011 and for internet activities in 2013 and 2011. The means comparison is presented in Table 1.

**Table 1.** Computer and internet skills

| | Computer skills (2014/2011) | | Internet skills (2013/2011) | |
|---|---|---|---|---|
| | All | 16–24 | All | 16–24 |
| EU 28 | 0.99 | 0.99 | 1.02 | 1.02 |
| Slovenia | 1.01 | 0.98 | 0.96 | 0.97 |

While the average number of internet activities in EU 28 slightly increased ($M_{11} = 2.96$, $M_{13} = 3.03$),[6] the average of computer activities decreased ($M_{11} = 3.90$, $M_{14} = 3.88$), which could be explained by the transfer of user activity into the cloud – computer skills are becoming less important than internet skills. In Slovenia, the situation is slightly to the contrary, computers skills have increased and internet skills decreased. The decline in the group of younger people is a bit worrying. The younger generation should be more skilled than an average user in the population, those aged between 16 and 24 spend more years in schools, and the educational attainment is rising.

## 2.2 Higher Education in the Digital Age

Different issues have arisen over the recent years. The most worrying are the facts and evidence that our schools are not able to offer a creative environment for children to develop their natural talents and creativity (Sir Robinson,[7] Alphabet by Erwin Wagenhofer[8]). We are facing a rapid growth of ICT and new teaching paradigm and it is therefore understandable that this might happen. Maybe we are not aware that schools are not the only place knowledge can be found [12] and we do not take this as a challenge. Nowadays, knowledge can be found anywhere, mostly on the web. The Massive Online Open Courses (MOOC) are the most evident consequence of this movement. The first MOOC came to light in 2008 [9], but only since 2012 are we witnessing an abundance of MOOC, offered by Udacity, Coursera and edX [1]. Well-known and recognised institutions stand behind all these suppliers: Stanford, Harvard and the MIT

---

[5] E-skills are measured on three levels – low level at which individuals ticked 1 or 2 computer/internet activities, medium level with 3 or 4 computer/internet activities and high level with 5 or 6 computer/internet activities.

[6] $M_{11}$ – an average number of activities for 2011, $M_{13}$ – an average number of activities for 2014.

[7] http://www.ted.com/talks/sir_ken_robinson_bring_on_the_revolution?language=en.

[8] http://www.alphabet-film.com/.

institute. But MOOC development does not stop at these three suppliers. Each year, new suppliers enter the market – not only offering MOOCs in English (Harvard, MIT, Stanford, Yale, Duke, UC Berkley etc.), but in other languages as well. A student can attend MOOCs in Spanish,[9] French,[10] Chinese,[11] and Arabic[12] etc. Since 2013, MOOCs in Slovenian[13] have also been available on the market.

Based on MOOC Infographic data [2], 5 million students all around the world (34.0 % from USA, 7.3 % from India, 4.4 % from Brazil, 3.9 % from UK, 3.4 % from Canada, 2.7 % from Spain etc.) are participating in MOOCs. Half of them participating only for curiosity, but 43.9 % of them like to acquire specific skills that enable them to perform their job better. Only 13.2 % of them were enrolled in MOOCs to acquire knowledge they needed to complete their degree. It is more than obvious that the presage that the MOOC will kill the traditional higher education degree is not serious, as was also explained by The Economist [13].

40 % of the MOOC participants are younger than 30, but 10 % of them are older than 60. It is interesting that 88 % of them are male and more than a half (62 %) are employed. MOOC really supports lifelong learners and there is no doubt that it will substitute on-campus education [11].

When considering the upcoming expansion of MOOCs needs to take into account some facts [3] – not all MOOCs are "open" (some of them are payable or participants need to meet some requirements), not all MOOCs are "massive", some of them gather lower number of participants (i.e. BOOC – Big Open Online Course or SPOC – Small Private Online Course) and not all MOOCs are "courses", meaning the content is not delivered in a course manner (learning outcomes are not defined, no assessment is included etc.).

Opening Up Education, not only by MOOCs, is an initiative launched by the European Commission, in September 2013. It was launched with the aim of stimulating "high-quality, innovative ways of learning and teaching through new technologies and digital content" [4]. The Opening Up Education initiative will contribute to the Europe 2020 goals, especially reducing early school leaving and increasing the portion of the population with tertiary education. The initiative declares that EU education is failing in keeping pace with the digital society (ibidem), as we exposed in the previous chapter.

## 3 Research Among 1st Year Business Students

The survey was carried out among first year Management students. Students can study Management at the 1st Bologna cycle in a university degree program (UDP) or in a

9 https://www.miriadax.net/.
10 http://www.france-universite-numerique.fr/.
11 https://www.xuetangx.com/.
12 http://www.rwaq.org/.
13 Slovenia has only 2 mio of citizens. The Academic Research Network – ARNES (www.arnes.si) is offering the MOOC about Secure Internet usage.

professional degree program (PDP).[14] The UDP is implemented only at the Faculty's headquarters, whilst the PDP is also implemented at two additional locations. This research was carried out among students that are studying at the Faculty's headquarters, meaning that the entire population of 1st year UDP students and 43.1 % of the 1st year PDP students are included in this research.

In the 2014/2015 academic year there were 106 students enrolled in the 1st year of the PDP and 37 in the UDP. Not all of the enrolled students were willing to participate in the course of Business informatics in the 2nd quarter,[15] some of them were enrolled just to obtain "student" status, which offers them social security and other benefits, or they left their study after the first unsuccessful exam attempts.

The students were invited to the e-survey via an e-mail invitation at the beginning of the course. Their response is presented in Table 2.

**Table 2.** Student response.

| Program | No. of students | Full filled surveys | % of response |
|---|---|---|---|
| PDP | 106 | 71 | 67.0 % |
| UDP | 37 | 27 | 73.0 % |
| **1st year students** | **143** | **98** | **68.5 %** |

Legend: PDP – professional degree program, UDP – university degree program

Among the surveyed PDP students 47.8 % of students are not from the local area. At the UDP the portion is higher – 70.4 % are not from the local area, which is not surprising as students are only able to study this programme at the Faculty's headquarters. More than half of the surveyed students are female (58.2 %) which is comparative to the gender structure of all undergraduate students at our Faculty. The average student is 20.1 years old.

Students use desktop computers and other mobile devices to access the internet. They use the equipment more or less regularly. They estimate the regularity on a 5-degree scale. Mobile devices become more and more popular among young people – 71.4 % of surveyed students used their smart phones (M = 4.5) to access the internet regularly. One fifth of them (19.4 %) do not use desktop computers (M = 2.9) to access the internet at all. The tablet computers are not as widespread as one would probably expect. More than half of them (57.1 %) never use a tablet computer (M = 1.9) to access the Internet at all. Laptop computers (M = 4.2) are frequently used as well (53.1 % of the surveyed students used them always).

[14] A student that accomplished general upper-secondary education can be enrolled in PDP and in UDP. Students that come from technical or vocational upper-secondary schools can be enrolled only in PDP. If these students passed an additional exam of one of the external examination (Matura) subjects they can be enrolled in the UDP too.

[15] The pedagogical process in the undergraduate programmes is organised in quarters – students attend 2–3 courses in each quarter. After the quarter they have the quarter's exams. In the 1st year all courses are compulsory.

Students access the internet from different places. They estimate the frequency of particular place usage on a 5-degree scale. Even though students from who use of library facilities would be expected, 39.8 % of them never use the school library to access the internet and 35.7 % of them use it rarely. Homes are the most common used places for Internet access (M = 4.5), but wireless connection has become popular (M = 3.5) too. Students were asked to estimate the frequencies of cyber cafe usage (M = 3.0) and school usage (M = 2.7) too.

Windows (version 7 or 8) is the most used operating system on desktop and laptop computers. There are only 2 students that use Mac OSX and 1 Linux user between surveyed students. Three quarters (75.5 %) of the surveyed students use smart phones, with the Android operating system (82.4 %) and iOS (17.6 %).

Students were asked how often they used some of the most known applications. The estimation was made on a 5-degree scale. Students estimated how frequently they use two groups of software – commercial (MS Office: Word, Excel and PowerPoint, Adobe Photoshop, InDesign and Corel Draw) and open source alternatives (OpenOffice.org – OO or Libre Office – LO package components: Writer, Calc and Impress, Gimp, Inkscape, Blender and Audicity). Even if students are not able to buy expensive license software they used it more frequently than open source alternatives because they are thought to have used them in pre-university schooling (Fig. 1). Copyright is an issue on the business informatics curriculum therefore only open source software is used in the pedagogical process. But, as can be seen from Fig. 1, students enter into the course with almost no experience of working with open source software. Writer is the only exception – 23.4 % of surveyed students use it frequently or always. There are no statistical significant differences between PDP and UDP students found.

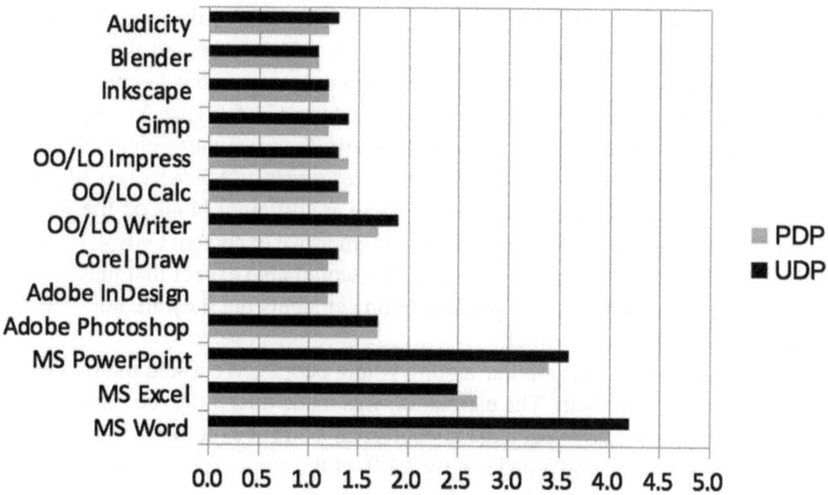


**Fig. 1.** Means for the frequency of software usage

For searching and using web content, students mostly use Chrome (87.8 %) and/or Firefox (41.8 %).

In the information society, e-communication is very important. Students can use different applications, more or less frequently. The frequency was estimated on a 5-degree scale (Fig. 2).

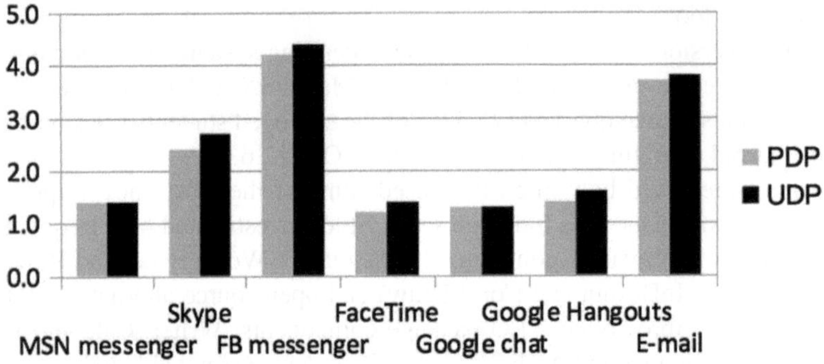


**Fig. 2.** Communication channels

Facebook messenger (FB messenger) is the most used communication channel among surveyed students (Fig. 2). Students use e-mail communication frequently, while other communication channels are not so popular among 1st year students. There are no significant differences between the two degree programmes.

Nowadays, internet users are no longer passive users. They can create web content, share it and/or share and comment on other's work. We would like to find out how our students are using the Web 2.0 services (Table 3). It was expected that the younger generation would use this possibility to create web content more but, as can be seen from Table 3, it is not so. Only one third of surveyed students (31.6 %) use YouTube or other similar channels to upload their videos, but mostly they use these channels to watch other's work. Students like to use Wikipedia resources (74.5 %) even though this resource is not acceptable in the academia. There are different blogs on the web, from different fields, but our students do not follow them as we expected. Only 4.1 % of them contribute to blogs or write their own blogs. We would also expect that massive multi-player online games (MMOG) are present among students but they are not – 36.7 % of them have never played them at all.

Social networks are very popular among young people. We asked them to estimate how frequently they use them. The estimation was made on a 5-degree scale. The most used social networks are, as expected, Facebook and YouTube (both M = 4.6). Facebook is not used by only 5.1 % and YouTube by 3.1 % of the surveyed students. Other social networks (LinkedIn, Pinterest, Twitter, Google+, MySpace, Instagram, Flickr, Ask.fm) are used never or rarely (all averages are under 2).

**Table 3.** Using Web 2.0 services

| | I don't know | Know, but do not use | Use & not contribute | Use & contribute |
|---|---|---|---|---|
| Tools for photo exchange (e.g. Flicker) | 12.2 % | 38.8 % | 41.9 % | 7.1 % |
| Tools for video exchange (e.g. YouTube) | 2.0 % | 5.1 % | 61.3 % | 31.6 % |
| Blogs | 10.2 % | 75.5 % | 10.2 % | 4.1 % |
| Wikipedia | 1.0 % | 10.2 % | 74.5 % | 14.3 % |
| Massive multiplayer online games (MMOG) | 36.7 % | 50.0 % | 6.2 % | 7.1 % |

Living in an information society means using the internet for other daily activities; ordering goods and services, following the news, reading books, watching online TV programmes, dealing with public administration etc. The students were asked to estimate the frequency of which they do activities on the internet on a 5-degree scale. It is interesting that a lot of students never order books on the internet (67.7 % of them never order physical books and 85.9 % e-books). The most frequent e-business activity is following the news on the web (M = 3.6 for local language news and M = 3.5 for foreign language news). An average of 3.4 used e-services to find a student job. All other e-business activities were estimated under an average of 3 (watching online TV 2.9, ordering clothes and shoes 2.7, buying movie tickets 2.5, e-tourism services 2.4 etc.).

In the previous century, students needed to go to school if they wanted to acquire knowledge. Nowadays more knowledge, in different formats at different levels, is available on the web. It is interesting that almost one third of the surveyed students (30.3 %) never use videos as a learning resource, and only of 3.0 % always use them (M = 2.3). Three quarters of the surveyed students (76.8 %) have never attended a MOOC (M = 1.4). During the teaching process,[16] we later discover that a lot of them do not know what a MOOC is. Acquiring knowledge online is not yet common among the surveyed students. This is one of the reasons why the course of Business informatics is partly performed online. We would like students through "learning by doing" to become able to work in an online environment.

But working and studying online demand computer and internet literacy (ICT literacy). Therefore, we would like to investigate how well they are able to do basic computer and internet tasks. The research was performed in two paths. Firstly, the students estimated their general skills of using a computer and internet on a 5-degree scale. After the general estimation they were asked to check several tasks they are able to do in word processor (35 tasks), spreadsheet (31 tasks), presentation application (16 tasks) and using web data/information (13 tasks). Tasks that were offered to them are

[16] The survey was launched at the beginning of the course.

all part of the ECDL certificate.[17] For the purpose of analysis, the number of tasks checked was recalculated on a 5-degree scale. It is interesting that students estimated almost all their general skills higher than we calculated them from the checked tasks. It is surprising that the calculated value regarding Excel skills was higher than the general value (Fig. 3). Using correlation analysis showed that there is a negative, statistically significant, correlation between the general estimation of computer skills and skills that are calculated based on tasks they are able to do. Students who estimated their skills higher are actually able to do fewer tasks.

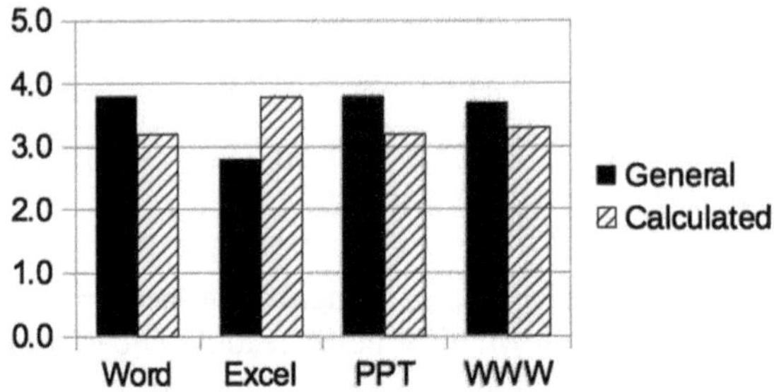


**Fig. 3.** General estimated and calculated ICT skills

The main goal of our research was to find out if our students are able to participate in the information society. They enter university not as skilled as we thought that digital natives need to be. Even if the MOOC is widely presented in education, a lot of our students do not know this term. They do not use open resources, like video guides, to acquire new knowledge. Based on the correlation analysis we found that MOOC is known and used by students who are more active on the web – communicate using different instant messaging programmes (not only that incorporated in Facebook), video-conferencing programmes, like Google Hangouts, social networks like Flickr, MySpace, Google+ and Twitter. Students who are inclined to use MOOCs are also more likely to blog. In contrast to those students who are not MOOC fans, the MOOCs are accepted by students who more actively use e-business services. All these correlations are statistically significant.

## 4 Conclusion

ICT infrastructure in EU countries offers a broadband connection to the internet to more than 70, in Scandinavia, more than 80 %, EU 28 households. The so-called digital natives that were born in the middle of 80s and in the 90s of previous century, are becoming adults and it would be expected that all individuals in the group aged 16–24 have sufficient ICT skills and have no problem using e-services and participating in the information society. However, data reported by documents presented in this paper and data collected among 1st year business students show that the effective infrastructure and

[17] ECDL – European Computer Driving License (http://www.ecdl.com/).

being born in the digital age is not enough to survive in a data overloaded information society. It is concerned that an average EU 28 individual aged between 16 and 24 is only a middle e-skilled person. The situation among business students is not much different. The stimulation of innovative ways of learning and teaching, supported by ICT, as is defined by the Opening Up Education initiative, is much more than welcome. We need to work on redefining learning and teaching, not only to focus on building the infrastructure but more to educate and train teachers how to use ICT effectively and efficiently to resolve everyday problems and how to stimulate innovative ways of thinking and doing. We need to take a leaf out of the business world's book – the implementation of ICT into business, forced the business process renovation. It seems that implementing contemporary ICT in education often only supports the traditional learning and teaching processes and does not stimulate an innovative way of using it.

## References

1. Baggaley, J.: Reflection MOOC rampant. Distance Educ. **34**(3), 368–378 (2013)
2. Blake, D.: The Rising Power of MOOCs [Infographic] (2014). http://moocs.com/index.php/the-rising-power-of-moocs-infographic/. Accessed 23 February 2015
3. Cusack, A.: MOOC INFOGRAPHICS. MOOCs – Think Massively (2014). http://moocs.com/index.php/category/mooc-infographics/. Accessed 8 February 2014
4. EC – European Commission: Opening up Education: Innovative teaching and learning for all through new Technologies and Open Education Resources (2013). http://eur-lex.europa.eu/legal-content/EN/TXT/?uri=celex:52013DC0654. Accessed 22 February 2015
5. EC – European Commission: The International Computer and Information Literacy Study (ICILS) – Main findings and implications for education policies in Europe. European Commission, Brussels (2014). http://ec.europa.eu/education/library/study/2014/ec-icils_en.pdf. Accessed 22 February 2015
6. Eurostat: Information society statistics – households and individuals, Statistics Explained, April 2014. http://ec.europa.eu/eurostat/statistics-explained/. Accessed 9 February 2015
7. Fee, K.: Delivering E-learning: A Complete Strategy for Design Application and Assessment. Kogan Page, London (2009)
8. Haag, S., Cummings, M.: Management Information Systems for the Information Age, 8th edn. McGraw-Hill/Irwin, New York (2009)
9. Kolowich, S.: George Siemens Get Connected. The Chronicle of Higher Education – Technology (2014). http://chronicle.com/article/George-Siemens-Gets-Connected/143959/. Accessed 3 July 2014
10. Rainer, R.K., Turban, E., Potter, R.E.: Introduction to Information Systems: Supporting and Transforming Business, 1st edn. Wiley, Chichester (2006)
11. Self-Driving Education: The Huffington Post (2015). http://www.huffingtonpost.com/sebastian-thrun/selfdriving-education_b_4676484.html. Accessed 24 February 2015
12. Solomon, G., Schrum, L.: Web 2.0: New Tools, New Schools. ISTE, Washington, D.C. (2007)
13. The Economist: Will MOOCs Kill University Degrees? 1 October 2013. http://www.economist.com/blogs/economist-explains/2013/10/economist-explains. Accessed 22 February 2014

# System Support for Social Learning in Computer Science at a Distance University – The University of Hagen

Birgit Feldmann(✉)

Department of Computer Science,
University of Hagen (FernUniversität in Hagen),
Hagen, Germany
birgit.feldmann@fernuni-hagen.de

**Abstract.** Students working collaboratively are more successful than students working alone, these fact was shown by research on technology-supported learning and teaching have clearly confirmed the general understanding that. Therefore, it should be a logical consequence to integrate communication and collaboration as a key factor into a distance study environment. However, this is not a trivial task from various points of view. For instance, for public universities in Germany studies have to be free of charge – which then raises the question, how to finance highly interactive small classes? Another problem is the professional restrictions of working distance students: their time budget is very limited. The consequence is that students typically have very limited contact to their peers and their tutors until the final examinations. The drop-out rates are extremely high. E-learning improved the situation substantially (even though poorly used by the teachers in many environments), but by far not enough. Former research showed, that students' want more social learning application. This paper shows how social learning could be integrated in an existing technical and organizational infrastructure and so open up new possibilities to approach these challenges, and how it can be used to improve the situation substantially.

**Keywords:** E-learning · Social learning · Distance education · Learning management system · Personal learning environment

## 1 Introduction

Distance study systems face fundamental problems like isolation of students and finding a compromise between requirements of private and professional life and studying [7]. To improve the situation the University of Hagen (FernUniversität), the only public distance teaching university in Germany with about 75,000 students, started to develop a Virtual University (VU) in 1996 [1]. The new form of teaching and learning through the Virtual University eased the situation of the distance students remarkably, but there remained a lack of social interaction and group-awareness. Various research projects as well as our own experience clearly show that being part of a group and having suitable


L. Uden et al. (Eds.): LTEC 2015, CCIS 533, pp. 188–196, 2015.
DOI: 10.1007/978-3-319-22629-3_15

communication partners lead to higher and more consistent motivation and therefore to more successful and faster studies [1, 3, 7, 8, 14, 17, 20]. An additional effect is that organizational support by the university gets less critical as students can easily and very directly assist each other. This, in turn, reduces overhead at the university. A survey at our university also showed that most students are convinced that contact to fellow students, especially through different types of groups, is of utmost importance for successful learning [1, 3]. They are not satisfied with the existing system and call for new and better communication and group support [1, 3] and social learning.

The obvious conclusion of these observations is that a new learning environment with strong emphasis on social learning is necessary. The kernel concept of the vision developed here is to start out from the students' view and research results as described above – which is completely different from the classical approach to deliver content and to have group elements and communication as an add-on. To build this platform the integration of Web 2.0 technologies is essential. To provide such a new and community oriented environment we have to look closer into the various fields of groups and their mechanisms with the goal to support these groups with the necessary technical and organizational features. The necessary first step has been to investigate the different group types and their meaning in a distance teaching setting. The paper exemplifies two possible technological solutions to support social learning for the group types already existing University of Hagen. These group concepts, their properties, the way they are used by students, their overall potential have been main topic of another paper, therefore only the conclusion is citrated in this one. A detailed discussion of a complete e-learning system centered on social and community aspects cannot be given here due to space-limitations; further research is going on about how to build this kind of system.

The paper is structured as follows: Sect. 2 contains the state of the art, Sect. 3 describes the current situation and developments for group support at the University of Hagen. The following Sect. 4 investigates alternatives for a technological solution of the integration of social learning. The paper concludes with a short summary of the findings and an outline for further necessary research.

## 2 State of the Art

Schulmeister [19] not only evaluated 23 existing studies about learning management systems but also undertook his own research about more than 62 learning management systems. He concludes that existing learning management systems typically focus on delivering content; they do not support building and establishing long-lasting student groups, or – if at all – they do it very poorly [19]. This correlates with our own results as only 19 % of our students use the integrated communication features and only 2 % the groupware functionalities [1, 3]. If group oriented features are available, they are provided only for advanced students in the context of the provided content. These results are confirmed by research of Kerres [9].

Today, the importance of collaborative learning and working is without controversy in the research community [1–11, 17, 19, 20]. But the group processes and the various categories of group types in a more general meaning are still not well understood as will be investigated in chapter four of this paper, [6, 15, 16, 17]. Some valuable insights can be found in the field of community oriented learning [5, 8–10, 12–14, 18]. However, the community types discussed in this field, like learning community or community of practice, do not sufficiently cover the needs of distance learning students as they are either too strictly structured (e.g. restricted to an exactly defined group of students like in classes) or just the opposite, they have no structure at all. Some essential group types are not considered.

Many different definitions of "group" exist in different disciplines (computer science, psychology, sociology etc.), but none of them clearly describes the different existing group types in distance education from a practical point of view [6, 8, 11, 15, 17].

Therefore, we undertook our own definition of group types at our university and found the following different types (Table 1):

**Table 1.** Group types at the University of Hagen [4]

| | Member | Institutionalization | Content oriented | Duration | Intention | Liability |
|---|---|---|---|---|---|---|
| A | Varying, no limitation of members<br>Students of different universities and of different faculties. | None | No | Unlimited | Motivation, interdisciplinary communication, networking, questions of every day life | Low |
| B | Varying, usually not more than class size.<br>Students of one university and the same faculty. | Low | Yes | Starts out of a specific learning event, lasts until credits are achieved or until degree; one term or longer | Collaborative learning, preparation of exams, motivation, support in organizational matters | High |
| C | Fixed, 2 to max. 5 students.<br>Students of one university and usually the same faculty. | High | Yes | As long as the teaching event itself, usually one term.<br>Sometimes alter to B. | Working together at a given or chosen topic, outcome is i.e. a piece of software or a written contribution | Medium |

A: Study group, B: Learning team, C: Working team

More detailed information about the group types could be found in [4].
In our own study [1, 2] we found out the current need of our students (Table 2):

**Table 2.** Group types at the University of Hagen [2]

1. Easy access, intuitive to use
2. Professional information management
3. Awareness-function
4. Integrated communication and interaction possibilities like:
   a. Interdisciplinary communication and interaction, e.g., by integrating popular social networking sites like Facebook
   b. Infrastructural support to set up and to support different group types
   c. An Alumni network
   d. Private rooms without access for teaching staff.
5. High security measures
6. Integrated linkage to existing Web 2.0 tools (Messaging tools, Social Networking Sites, blogs, social bookmarks etc) for instance via the Open Social API
7. Personalized information learning and knowledge management
8. Intelligent search engine

## 3 The Hagen Situation

As very shortly described in Sect. 2, we do have different types of existing social and learning groups at our university. Also, we do have a wide variety of very different existing learning technology. And we do have pressing needs of our students to fulfill. Besides the didactical possibilities a new technological infrastructure has to be installed, as the current situation could not be run for long in an economically reasonable way. The current technological situation is, that we run two different learning management systems, three different collaborating system and many small solutions at the faculties (Table 3):

**Table 3.** e-Learning software at the University of Hagen

| Learning-management-systems | Groupware | Assignments | Conferencing | Communication / Information | Student support |
|---|---|---|---|---|---|
| Moodle Lernraum Virtuelle Universität (LVU)<br>Mahara | CURE<br>BSCW | Lotse<br>WebAssign | Adobe Connect<br>IRC | Email<br>Newsgroup<br>Blogs | Self-manage-menttool (SMT) |

To decide, which solution will be suitable, we developed a reference model on the basis of Gross and Koch [8]. In this model all social entities, social interactions, system support paths and the different tool classes are described. A detailed description could be found in the author's doctoral thesis (to be published) (Fig. 1).

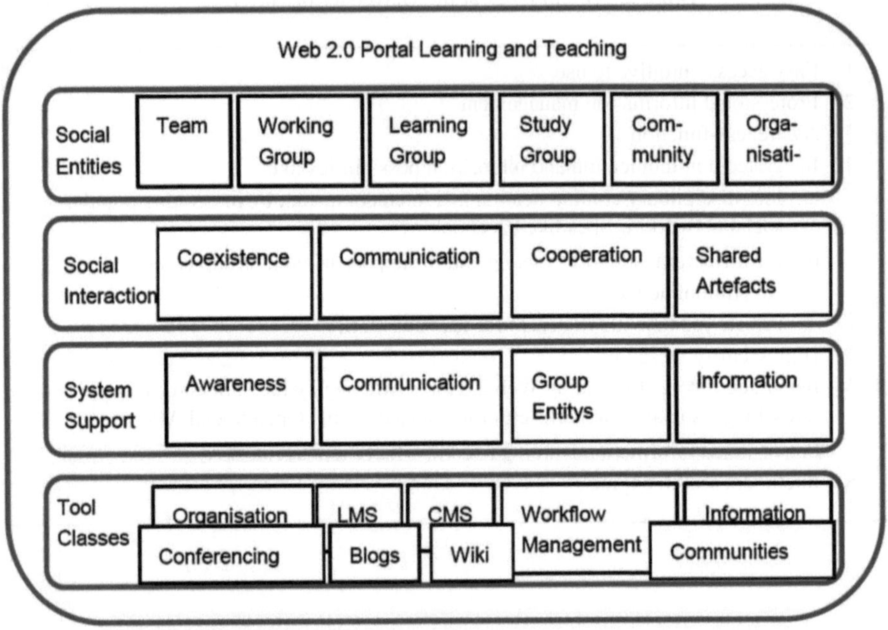


**Fig. 1.** Reference model for social learning in distance education [8]

## 4 Possible Solutions

As possible solutions we examined different systems like portal software, community software, and groupware, different types of learning management systems, campus management systems and personal learning environments (PLE). Currently, we found out, that the PLE is the solution that matches the most needs of our students. The ongoing discussion now is, to decide which one is the best to fit in the existing architecture and will a complete change be better than a step-for-step replacement? As a researcher, I understood, that some of these questions are not only didactical and technological, but also political in an organization like an university. Therefore, we focused on two possible infrastructure solutions:

**Solution 1 – Complete change.** In this scenario, we will replace all old learning connected systems by suitable new ones:

The advantage of this solution is the manageability, as the whole system architecture will be in future less complex and therefore easier to administrate. On the other hand, some of the features our teachers and students are used too, will be a lot more different and/or also new, this could cause less acceptance of the system (Fig. 2).

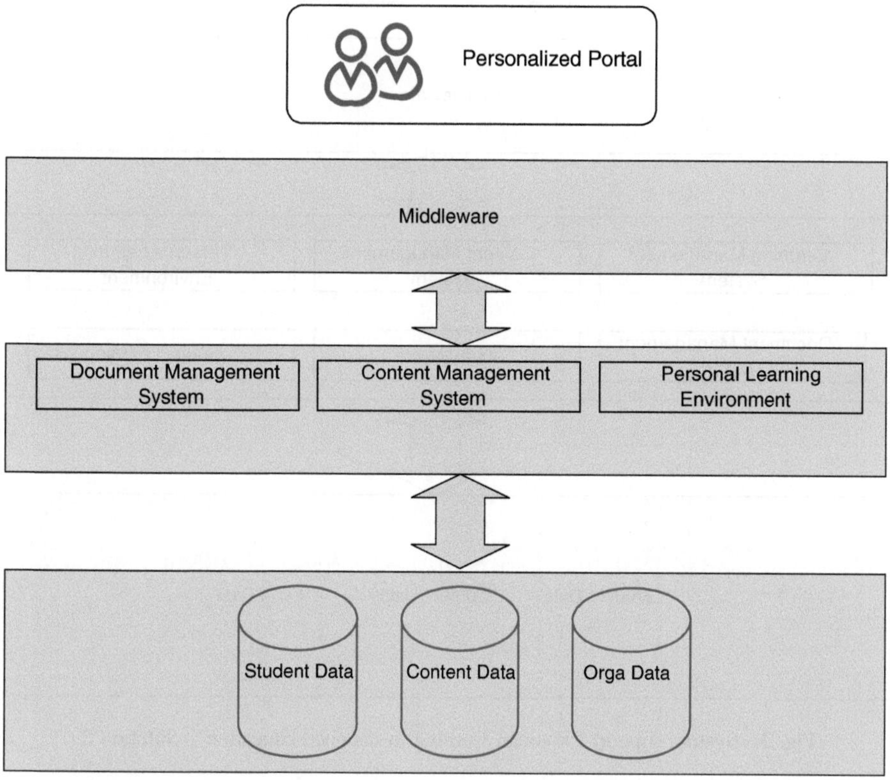


**Fig. 2.** System support for social learning in distance education – Solution 1

**Solution 2 –** In this scenario, we will add necessary new learning support systems for social learning by suitable ones:

The advantage of this solution is the comfortable access for current users, but the variety of the different systems could lead to the fact, that most users will not know about the systems and therefore not use it (as shown in our study [1, 2] nearly half of our students do not know, that the university runs two different learning management systems!). Another problem is the manageability of the system. The more complex system architecture is, the more complex is the administration of the whole system. Even by now, we do have a lot of problems with all the different application interfaces (Fig. 3).

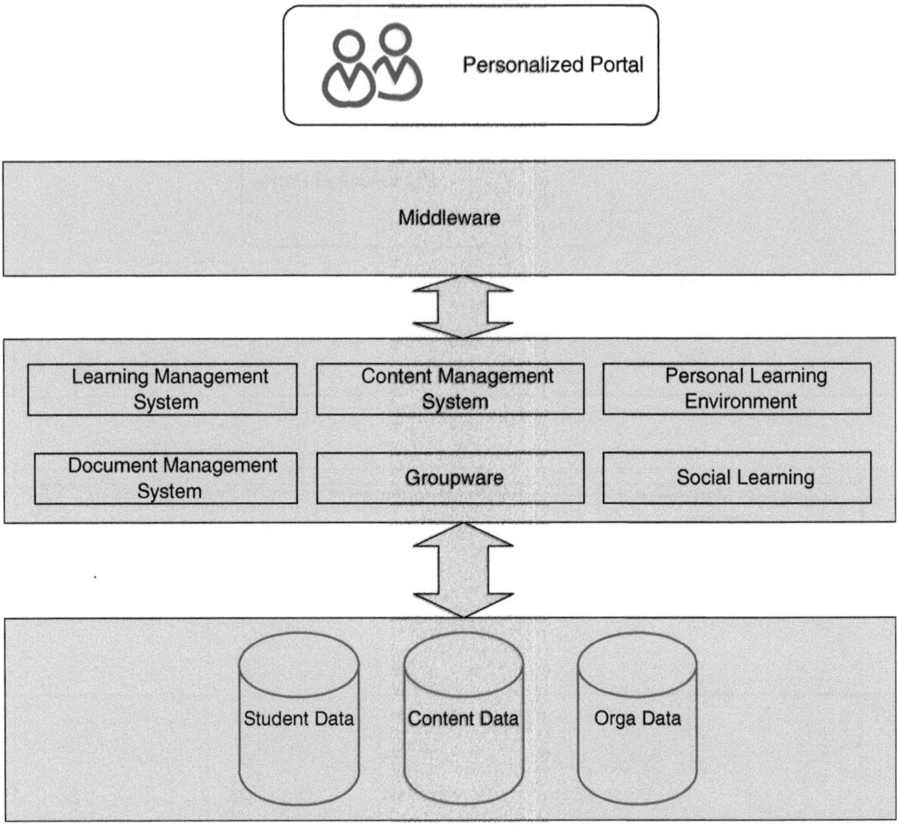


**Fig. 3.** System support for social learning in distance education – Solution 2

## 5 Conclusion

The students' needs are clearly identified [3, 4, 10, 13] by now and the task of the university is to improve the current situation according to the given suggestions. It is of utmost importance to restructure the current learning environment with a strong focus on the support of communication and interaction processes by installing community oriented features as described above. Not content and organizational functionalities are central, but finding adequate communication partners and being part of a group as early as possible and as long as possible. Becoming part of a group is useful even before enrolment. Students, teachers and staff should form a virtual community for learning and teaching, supported through adequate technology. This platform must provide easy to use functionality for

- organizing, discussing and publishing content collaboratively
- discussing and solving specific problems together
- creating different types of groups.

To achieve this goal, it is necessary to develop a new learning portal according to the students' needs. First suggestions are given in this paper. Currently, an ongoing discussion process throughout the university is discussing the different solutions. The author started out a couple of different feasibility projects in small courses to test the different possibilities. The experience so far favored the first solution. The detailed description of this new environment (architecture, features, interface, necessary restructuring) of this Social Learning Support System of the doctoral thesis of the author.

## References

1. Feldmann, B.: Two decades of e-learning in distance teaching – from Web 1.0 to Web 2.0 at the University of Hagen. In: Uden, L., Sinclair, J., Tao, Y.-H., Liberona, D. (eds.) LTEC 2014. CCIS, vol. 446, pp. 163–172. Springer, Heidelberg (2014)
2. Feldmann, B., Franzkowiak, B.: Studying in Web 2.0 - What (Distance) Students Really Want. EdMedia, Orlando (2011)
3. Feldmann, B.: Studying in Web 2.0 – Virtual University as Virtual Community. IARIA, Lissabon (2011)
4. Feldmann, B.: Group Types in Group Types in e-Learning Environments – Study Team, Working Team and Learning Team. Auckland (2010)
5. Feldmann, B., Schlageter, G.: Five years virtual university – review and preview. In: Proceedings of the WebNet 2001, Orlando, AACE (2001)
6. Becking, D., Betermieux, S., Schlageter, G.: Virtualising online seminars entirely - a variation of the variables. In: Proceedings of the HCI 2005, Las Vegas (2005)
7. Fritsch, H.: Aktiv und Online [Active and Online, German publication], ZIFF-Papers, University of Hagen, p. 10(2004)
8. Koch, M., Gross, T.: Computer Supported Cooperative Work. Oldenboury, Munich (2007)
9. Kerres, M.: Multimediale und telemediale Lernumgebungen [Multimedia and Telemedia Learning Environments – German publication]. Munich (2001)
10. Glowalla, U., Glowalla, G., Kohnert, A.: Studierverhalten in Online-Bildungsangeboten [Study Behaviour in Online Education Environments – German publication]. In: Issing, L. H., Klimsa, P. (eds.) Information und Lernen mit Multimedia und Internet [Information and Learning with Multimedia and Internet – German publication], pp. 359–372. Weinheim (2001)
11. Leh, A.S.C.: Computer-mediated communication and social presence in a distance learning environment. Int. J. Educ. Telecommun. **7**(2), 109–128 (2001)
12. Palloff, M., Pratt, K.: The Virtual student: A Profile and Guide to Working with Online Learners. Jossey-Bass, San Francisco (2003)
13. Kleimann, B., Özkilic, M., Göcks, M.: Studieren im Web 2.0 [Studying in the Web 2.0 – German publication], HIS Projektbericht (2008). https://hisbus.his.de/hisbus/docs/hisbus21.pdf
14. Kreijns, C.J., Kirschner, P.A., Jochems, W.M.G.: The sociability of computer-supported collaborative learning environments. J. Educ. Technol. Soc. **5**(1), 8–22 (2002)
15. Haake, J., Schwabe, G., Wessner, M.: CSCL-Kompenium. Oldenbourg, München (2004)
16. Andriessen, J.H.E.: Working With Groupware: Understanding and Evaluating Collaboration Technology. Springer, New York (2004)

17. Tajfel, H., Turner, J.C.: The social identity theory of intergroup behavior. In: Worchel, S., Austin, W.G. (eds.) Psychology of intergroup relations, pp. 7–24. Nelson-Hall, Chicago (1986)
18. Kerres, M., Nübel, I.: The status of e-learning at German higher education institutions. In: Dittler, U., Kahler, H., Kindt, M., Schwarz, C. (eds.) E-learning in Europe – Learning Europe: How have New Media Contributed to the Development of Higher Education? vol. 36, pp. 29–50. Waxmann, Münster (2005)
19. Schulmeister, R.: Lernplattformen für das virtuelle lernen: Evaluation und Didaktik [Learning Management Systems for Virtual Learning: Evaluation and Didactic] (2005)
20. Boyatt, R., Joy, M., Rocks, C., Sinclair, J.: What (Use) is a MOOC? In: The 2nd International Workshop on Learning Technology for Education in Cloud. Springer Proceedings in Complexity, pp 133–145 (2014)

# Using WCAG 2.0 and Heuristic Evaluation to Evaluate Accessibility in Educational Web Based Pages

Matjaž Debevc[1(✉)], Ines Kožuh[1], Simon Hauptman[1], Andrej Klembas[1], Julija Bele Lapuh[2], and Andreas Holzinger[3]

[1] Faculty of Electrical Engineering and Computer Science, University of Maribor, Smetanova ulica 17, SI-2000 Maribor, Slovenia
{matjaz.debevc,ines.kozuh,simon.hauptman}@um.si
andrej.klembas@gmail.com

[2] B2, Tržaška 42, 1000 Ljubljana, Slovenia
julija.bele@b2.eu

[3] Research Unit HCI-KDD, Institute for Medical Informatics, Medical University of Graz, Graz, Austria
andreas.holzinger@medunigraz.at

**Abstract.** In this paper, we presented an innovative way for a quick and comprehensive evaluation of different online educational websites by following and combining the Web Content Accessibility Guidelines 2.0, the standard ISO/IEC 24751 and heuristic evaluation approach. Five presentative web pages of the Learning Management System eCampus were evaluated by 14 participants classified into two groups with one usability expert in each group. Questionnaires containing twenty-five accessibility questions (=success criteria) were distributed among participants. Each participant was asked to evaluate only up to four success criteria. When completed, usability experts reviewed results and transformed them into final recommendations for improvements. Results revealed that none of five reviewed web pages reached level A for accessibility by the standard Web Content Accessibility Guidelines 2.0. On average, all five web pages reached the score 14 out of 25 in "pass" success criteria. In "fail" success criteria the average score was 4.80. The way of evaluation used in this study suggests possible implications in practice due to its simplicity and quickness.

**Keywords:** Accessibility · Usability testing · User experience · People with disabilities · E-learning

## 1 Introduction

Accessibility is defined as a standard by the ISO 9241-171:2008 »Ergonomics of human-system Interaction« which provides the usability for systems intended for all, regardless the type of impairment and environment [1–3]. It can also be used for educational web pages, where the multimedia learning material, delivering lectures and interactively testing the knowledge has to be suitably accessible for all.


L. Uden et al. (Eds.): LTEC 2015, CCIS 533, pp. 197–207, 2015.
DOI: 10.1007/978-3-319-22629-3_16

Even The European Union is aware that people with disabilities and elderly people are at risk of digital exclusion, due to factors such as lack of using Internet and computers skills. Therefore, they suggest to pass European i2010 initiative on e-Inclusion »To be part of the information society« as well as European directive on the accessibility of public sector bodies' websites [4]. The directive will influence not only the accessibility of public sector web pages, but also the accessibility of educational web pages.

To make the educational web pages accessible, they should be designed and adjusted according to the students' needs and requests, as defined in the standard ISO/IEC 24751 (Information technology – Individualized adaptability and accessibility in e-learning, education and training). This three-part standard offers the information about the needs and requests of learners with disabilities including the regulations on how to suitably adjust the digital lessons to this group of users [5–7]. The standard offers one of the possible ways of adjusting lessons, but it is demanding and comprehensive for evaluating [18, 20].

On the other hand, besides this standard, one could also use the standard ISO/IEC 40500:2012 (Information technology – W3C Web Content Accessibility Guidelines (WCAG) 2.0). It would help us check whether web pages follow the guidelines for wider range of people with disabilities and elderly people, including blindness and low vision, deafness and hearing loss, learning disabilities, cognitive limitations, limited movement, speech disabilities, photo-sensitivity and combinations of these. When using this standard for evaluation of web pages, all the suitably accessible web pages are marked with level A, AA and AAA [8, 9].

The comprehensive evaluation raises the question of how we can quickly and easily test different online educational documents, which include various multimedia and interactive elements, with the help of WCAG 2.0 guidelines and to draw closer to the requirements by the standard ISO/IEC 24751.

A number of studies exist on research conducted on multimedia environments. For instance, Richard Mayer defined 12 principles which help education providers improve multimedia learning when no traditional face-to-face interaction takes place [10]. Moreover, Sweller [11] focused on cognitive load theory which suggests that design of learning materials, if they are to be effective, should keep cognitive load of learners at a minimum during the learning process. Furthermore, significant research was also conducted by Sullins et al. [12].

Our paper presents an innovative way to evaluate online educational material regarding accessibility. First, we used WCAG 2.0 questionnaire for verifying the level A, later, in the process of evaluating, we partly used the principals and procedures typical for heuristic evaluation [13, 14]. Besides verifying web pages regarding the accessibility on level A, we also described problems and suggested changes/improvements. Accordingly, our aim was to form the basis for accessible online educational material.

Evaluation was performed on Learning Management System eCampus, which is a web application designed for learning, learning management and multimedia learning content creation which can be used regardless of the type of the device (PC, tablet, smartphone) and platform (Android, IOS, Windows) [17].

## 2 Heuristic Evaluation

One of the first set of usability rules developed for interface design was Jakob Nielsen's "10 Heuristics for User Interface Design" [15, 16]. The set was originally developed by Nielsen and Molich in 1990 [14] and was given a name heuristic evaluation. The list of 10 heuristics contains issues about visibility, user control, recognition, efficiency of use, error prevention and other heuristics.

The evaluating is generally performed with 5 to 8 experts, who emphasize in their reports the following three components:

- **Identification of problems** of the user interface considering suggested heuristics with the help of their own questionnaire.
- **Defining priorities** considering the difficulty of the problem, e.g.:
  - Example of best practice
  - Minor problem
  - Serious problem
  - Critical problem
- **Relate each issue and recommend solutions to screen shots of the user interface.** It enables the report readers to quickly see where precisely in the user interface the problem appears, without having to access the system we are evaluating.

Table 1 shows the example of the template for the heuristic usability report, which includes all three mentioned components. First, there is severity ranking with the title of the heuristic we are verifying, then follows the problem identification with its explanation. Recommendation for solving the problem follows. Finally, a screenshot is provided where problematic parts of the user interface are graphically marked, e.g. with circles or direction arrows.

**Table 1.** Example of the template for the heuristic usability report

| | |
|---|---|
| Severity rank | <Title of the heuristic> |
| Problem identification | <Explanation of the problem identification> |
| Recommendation | <Recommendation for solving the problem> |
| Figure | <Screenshot with graphically marked problematic parts of the user interface> |

In our study, we used the principle of above mentioned reporting, but instead of using the question for defining heuristics, we used the questions from the guidelines defined by the standard WCAG 2.0 for level A.

## 3 Accessible Web Content

Web Content Accessibility Guidelines (WCAG) are developed by World Wide Web Consortium (W3C), which also develops Web standards such as HTML, XML, CSS, etc. The current version of WCAG – WCAG 2.0, was published in 2008 and standardised in 2012 by the standard ISO/IEC 40500. WCAG is primarily intended for web content developers, web accessibility evaluators and others who need a standard for web accessibility. It includes 12 guidelines organised in 4 principles that should be followed:

- **Perceivable:** considering all three main sense organs which we need for interactive work: eye sight, hearing and feeling. It includes 22 success criteria.
- **Operable:** defining the manners of management (navigation and user interface) for persons with disabilities. It includes 20 success criteria.
- **Understandable:** defining the ways of correct interpretation of the content. It includes 17 success criteria.
- **Robust:** defining compatibilities with present and future technologies. It includes 2 success criteria.

Thus, the standard includes 61 success criteria, organised according to the three different levels of conformance:

- **Conformance Level A:** all Priority 1 checkpoints are satisfied – lowest priority. It includes 25 success criteria.
- **Conformance Level AA:** all Priority 1 and 2 checkpoints are satisfied – mid priority. Beside the criteria from the first priority, it also includes additional 13 success criteria.
- **Conformance Level AAA:** all Priority 1, 2, and 3 checkpoints are satisfied – highest priority. It includes the first two priorities and additional 23 success criteria.

When evaluating the web pages, the experts usually follow the first two priorities. However, only a few web pages generally reach the level AAA. For evaluation purposes experts need at least three comprehensive documents, WCAG 2.0 Guidelines (72 pages), Understanding WCAG 2.0 (165 pages) and Techniques for WCAG 2.0 (221 pages) [9]. All the documents have a total of 458 pages with 159.800 words.

## 4 Developing a Questionnaire for Accessibility Testing

We sought to identify whether there is a possibility to easily, quickly and simply get the first impression how accessible the web pages are, without additional comprehensive rules and regulations, because of large amount of material and problems with the evaluation.

First, we made a review of solutions for quick testing of the accessibility. McGrath [19] published on his web page freely accessible non-commercial questionnaires for the accessibility testing, following the standard WCAG 2.0. The first version of our questionnaire followed the source material by Luke McGrath. In the next version, the text in column Summary, which defines the standards of suitability of each item, was replaced by recommendations, which summarizes the questionnaire from the web page Web AIM [21].

The web page of the WCAG 2.0 [9] shows one more form of the questionnaire, which is divided into different guidelines and then combined regarding the levels of suitability (L1–L3). The difference from the previous two questionnaires is in an additional column for comments and its criteria of successfulness (Success Criterion).

After testing and transforming, we developed the questionnaires for level A, AA and AAA. Figure 1 shows the example of a question for level A.

**Checklist**

**WCAG 2.0 Checklist for Level A (Beginner)**

**Website url:** ____________________
**Webpage url:** ____________________
**Date tested:** ____________________

| Guideline | Recommendations | Pass |
|---|---|---|
| 1.1.1 Non-text Content | ○ All images, form image buttons, and image map hot spots have appropriate, equivalent alternative text.<br>○ Images that do not convey content, are decorative, or with content that is already conveyed in text are given null alt text (alt="") or implemented as CSS backgrounds. All linked images have descriptive alternative text.<br>○ Equivalent alternatives to complex images are provided in context or on a separate (linked and/or referenced via longdesc) page.<br>○ Form buttons have a descriptive value.<br>○ Form inputs have associated text labels.<br>○ Embedded multimedia is identified via accessible text.<br>○ Frames are appropriately titled. | |
| 1.2.1 Audio-only and Video-only (Prerecorded) | ○ A descriptive text transcript (including all relevant visual and auditory clues and indicators) is provided for non-live, web-based audio (audio podcasts, MP3 files, etc.).<br>○ A text or audio description is provided for non-live, web-based video-only (e.g., video that has no audio track). | |

**Fig. 1.** Example of the structure of a question for level A

The questionnaires for accessibility testing for level A include 25 main questions, which are taken from WCAG Guidelines. Figure 1 shows the Guideline "1.1.1. Non-text Content". As can be seen from Fig. 1, we added column "Recommendations", which broadens the guideline contexts and enables the examiners to define the most problematic items on a web page. In addition, we also provided a link to a comprehensive explanation, which is placed in the same document. What is more, there are additional links to documents in the original WCAG Guidelines.

This way, we designed gradual possibilities for the problem search for the examiners. Reading Guideline, e.g. "1.1.1. Non-text Content", experienced examiners will know what to search for and look at in the document. Less experienced will be appropriately directed to get additional information in the document, as well as in the original WCAG 2.0 Guidelines.

## 5 Methodology

The study started with the question: How can we quickly evaluate e-learning web pages on accessibility? From this question, another question arose concerning accessibility and usability: Can we combine heuristic evaluation methodology with accessibility questionnaire?

We chose five representative eCampus web pages, which were developed in order to provide online content for learning Business German and Business Mathematics. Learning materials are intended for students of Economy at a vocational college. The authors of web pages were not warned about the accessibility requests, which is why the aim of our evaluation was to find out whether there are the deviations from the standard recommendations, how the material can be improved and which guidelines should be given to the authors.

According to Nielsen and Landauer [14], three experts are sufficient to participate in such evaluation, because they find 60 % of problems in a particular system. Naturally, if we increase the number of experts, the number of problems found increases as well. For instance, if there were 10 experts, they would find 85 % of all problems.

In our study, we decided to perform evaluations with 14 participants. They were classified into two groups. In the first group, there were six final year faculty students and one mentor. In the second group, there were again six final year faculty students and one mentor who was also a usability expert with university degree.

Each group received a questionnaire for evaluating accessibility for level A and template for report preparation. They also received links to all five learning web pages. Each participant had its own account. In this way we assured that the changes made by participants' interactive work on one material did not reflect in the other participant's work. Accordingly, we reduced the risk that changes performed by one student could influence other participants' tests. They were given one week to evaluate these web pages.

Figure 2 shows screenshots of e-learning material, chosen due to the differences in the use of multimedia elements and interaction, and being evaluated by our participants. The first three screenshots are taken from the e-learning material for Business German and the other two from Business mathematics.

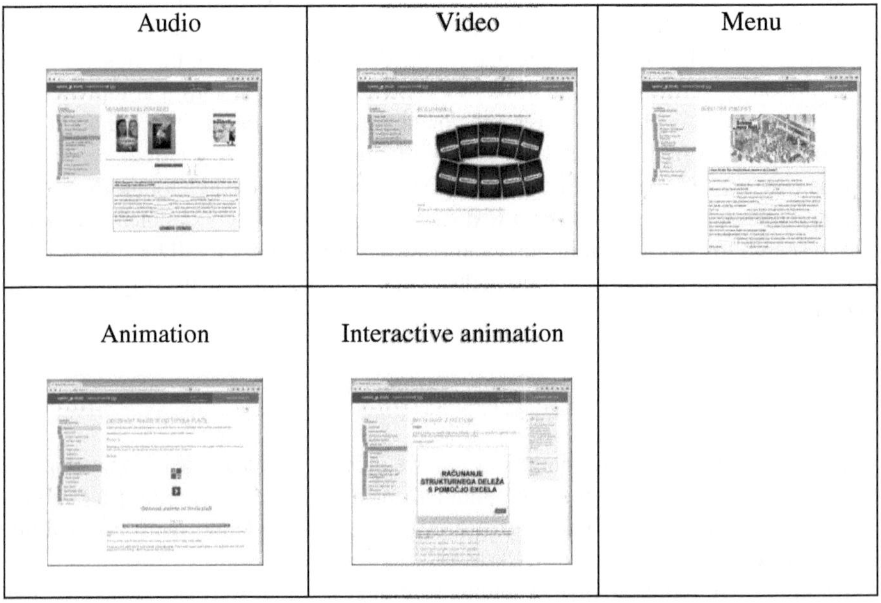


**Fig. 2.** Screenshots of 5 tested e-learning material

Web page in screenshot 1 includes an audio multimedia element, which is audio recording, and an exercise to insert the missing words.

Web page in screenshot 2 includes a video multimedia element with a role playing exercise.

Screenshot 3 shows interactive a web page with a menu, which includes the gap fill exercise with drop down menu.

Screenshot 4 shows a web page for Business mathematics featuring an animation multimedia element, which helps the author explain how the annuity depends on the payback period.

E-learning page shown in screenshot 5 also includes an animation from Business mathematics, which explains how to calculate structural shares and percentage. There is an interactive exercise to test the knowledge and there is also the key.

Participants evaluated five web pages (Fig. 2). Before evaluation, preliminary testing with two experts were conducted, where one web page was evaluated respecting all success criteria.

In evaluation session, twenty-five questions were distributed in a way that each group received 25 questions and not each individual. Accordingly, each participant had to evaluate up to four success criteria. The assignment had to be finished in one week.

## 6 Results and Discussion

After one week, participants were asked to hand in the reports. In two-and-half-hour meeting each participant had to present and explain their comments to other participants. Since there were two groups, we paid special attention to the answers, whether the success criteria (PASS or FAIL) were the same in both groups or not. The expert examined whether the success criteria were legitimately PASS or FAIL, discussed it with the participants and tried to find out the reason for different decisions. Table 2 shows the results in number of PASS, FAIL and different success criteria from all 25 success criteria.

**Table 2.** Results of pass, fail and different success criteria for both groups

| Web page | Audio | Video | Menu | Animation | Interactive animation |
|---|---|---|---|---|---|
| PASS | 12 | 13 | 14 | 15 | 16 |
| FAIL | 7 | 5 | 4 | 4 | 4 |
| Different | 6 | 7 | 7 | 6 | 6 |

Table 2 shows that all five web pages had an average of 14 pass success criteria, minimum 12 and maximum 16 pass success criteria. On the other hand, there were on average 4.80 fail success criteria and 6.40 different answers for success criteria.

On the whole, none of the web pages reached level A for accessibility by standard WCAG 2.0. Interestingly, the answers for each web page were similar and there were no greater deviations, which indicates the usability of methodology.

The greatest deviations in fail success criteria were at the following success criteria:

- 1.1.1 Non-text Content (img element missing alt attribute, when using images, specify a short text alternative with the 'alt' attribute.)
- 1.3.1 Info and Relationships (input element, type of "text" or "password", missing an associated label.)

- 3.1.1 Language of Page (Document language not identified, document has invalid language code.)
- 3.3.2 Labels or Instructions (Label text is empty.)

After a short discussion all the participants agreed on PASS or FAIL, which helped the expert responsible for the final report to quickly find out the critical success criteria. These were later presented in the final report which was also examined by the other usability expert, who added some comments. The number of all recommended changes for e-learning web pages is shown in Table 3.

**Table 3.** Number of recommended changes for each e-learning web page

| Web page | Audio | Video | Menu | Animation | Interactive animation |
|---|---|---|---|---|---|
| Number of changes | 13 | 12 | 11 | 10 | 9 |

| **Guideline** | 1.1.1 Non-text Content |
|---|---|
| **Cause** | ALT text is missing. No decorative or complex images and no description of form buttons and form inputs. Multimedia content has no identification description. First frame is appropriately entitled, other frames are not clear. |
| **Screenshot with emphasized areas** | 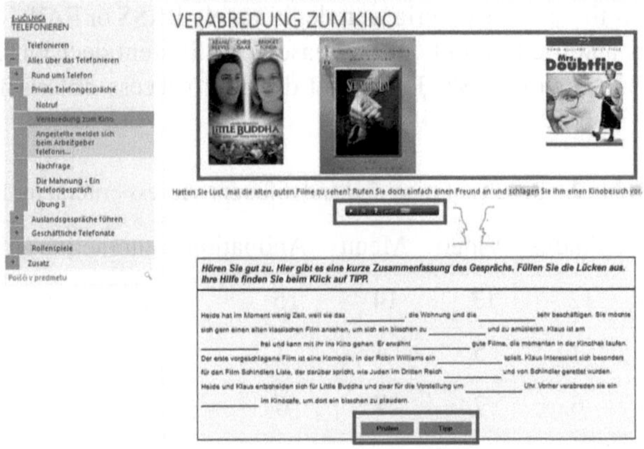  |
| **Code** | **Check 1: img element missing alt attribute.**<br>***Line 92, Column 110:***<br><img src="Statika/style/custom_templates/b2ic/img/b2ic_logo.png" /> |
| **Suggestion** | Insert text. Put the images in appropriate frames, which has to be included in the description. Add descriptions to form buttons and to multimedia. |

**Fig. 3.** Example of suggested change of e-learning web page

Figure 3 gives an example of suggested change of audio e-learning web page as published in the final report. It was written 14 days after the beginning of work. If we took into account the fact that each success criterion takes 30 min, then we would need 750 min for the whole level A and if we add to that the number of reviewed web pages, we end at a total of 63 h. Plus, up to 6 more experts, that means we would need as much as 47 people a day to review five e-learning web pages only for level A by the standard WCAG 2.0. Moreover, that would take three times longer if we checked level AA and level AAA as well.

The suggested method of testing with heuristic evaluation, where we divided questions in up to 4 questions per participant for level A, allowed us to shorten the time of testing and, despite that, offer results of good quality, so the editor could make suitable corrections.

## 7 Conclusion

Although the needs for accessibility greatly increase, the standard ISO/IEC 40500 with its WCAG 2.0 Guidelines unfortunately has not yet revived, like e.g. some new versions of HTML language. On the contrary, it seems that the developers avoid the development of accessible e-learning web pages due to complexity and comprehensiveness and they do not advertise them as accessible for people with disabilities and elderly people. This will definitely change with the new European declaration, which will request accessibility of public sector bodies' websites.

In this case, it is only a question of time how to quickly and easily test the accessibility of web pages. The presented method – 12 participants and two usability experts dealing with 25 questions for accessibility for level A for success criteria, each participant having up to four success criteria, and the results being checked and reviewed by both usability experts and then transformed into suggestions for changes – gives a chance for successful and quick testing of accessibility, which could also be used in practice. However, costs of evaluation also depend on number of sites being evaluated. For instance, when a large number of websites is being evaluated, the costs of evaluation may increase. It may accordingly affect also the performance of evaluation process we proposed.

Our study was limited in research method used as no flawless method exists. The websites could potentially be also evaluated as a combination of observation method and using log files of activities where wrong doings could be checked.

In future, our current methodology will be updated with the help of automatized tools, such as AChecker, Functional Accessibility Evaluator and Total Validator [22], which will give us additional quickly accessible results of testing reports of an individual participant.

**Acknowledgements.** This work has been partially supported by the European Union through the Tempus Programme project ECESM – Enhancement of cyber educational system of Montenegro, No: 544088.

## References


1. Batanero, C., Karhu, M., Holvikivi, J., Oton, S., Amado-Salvatierra, H.R.: A method to evaluate accessibility in e-learning education systems. In: Proceedings of the IEEE 14th International Conference on Advanced Learning Technologies (ICALT), Athens, Greece (2014). doi:10.1109/ICALT.2014.163
2. ISO 9241-171:2008: Ergonomics of Human-System Interaction - Part 171 Guidance on Software Accessibility. International Standard Organization, Geneva (2008)
3. Bevan, N.: How you could benefit from using ISO standards. In: Proceedings of the Extended Abstracts of the 32nd Annual ACM Conference on Human Factors in Computing Systems. ACM, Toronto (2014)
4. European Parliament: Proposal for a directive of the European Parliament and of the Council on the accessibility of public sector bodies' websites (COM(2012)0721 – C7-0394/2012 – 2012/0340(COD)) (2012)
5. ISO/IEC 24751-1:2008: Information Technology – Individualized Adaptability and Accessibility in E-learning, Education and Training - Part 1: Framework and Reference Model. International Standard Organization, Geneva (2008)
6. ISO/IEC 24751-2:2008: Information Technology – Individualized Adaptability and Accessibility in E-learning, Education and Training - Part 2: "Access for All" Personal Needs and Preferences for Digital. International Standard Organization, Geneva (2008)
7. ISO/IEC 24751-3:2008: Information Technology – Individualized Adaptability and Accessibility in E-learning, Education and Training - Part 3: "Access for All" Digital Resource Description. International Standard Organization, Geneva (2008)
8. ISO/IEC 40500:2012: Information Technology – W3C Web Content Accessibility Guidelines (WCAG) 2.0. International Standard Organization, Geneva (2012)
9. W3C: Web Content Accessibility Guidelines (WCAG) 2.0. http://www.w3.org/TR/WCAG20/. Accessed 20 December 2014
10. Mayer, R.E.: Multimedia Learning. Cambridge University Press, New York (2001)
11. Sweller, J.: Cognitive load during problem solving: effects on learning. Cogn. Sci. **12**, 257–285 (1988)
12. Sullins, J., Craig, S.D., Graesser, A.C.: The influence of modality on deep-reasoning questions. Int. J. Learn. Technol. **5**(4), 378–387 (2010)
13. Nielsen, J.: Finding usability problems through heuristic evaluation. In: Proceedings of the SIGCHI Conference on Human Factors in Computing Systems (CHI). ACM Press, New York (1992)
14. Nielsen, J., Landauer, T.: A mathematical model of the finding of usability problems. In: Proceedings of the ACM/IFIP INTERCHI 1993 Conference. ACM Press, New York (1993)
15. Nielsen, J.: Usability inspection methods. In: Conference Companion on Human Factors in Computing Systems, pp. 413–414. ACM (1994)
16. Holzinger, A.: Usability engineering methods for software developers. Commun. ACM **48**(1), 71–74 (2005)
17. Lapuh Bele, J., Hauptman, S., Kožuh, I., Debevc, M.: eCampus as a platform for ubiquitous learning. In: Proceedings of the IEEE Global Engineering Education Conference (EDUCON), Istanbul, Turkey (2014)
18. Gilbert, T.D., Machin, C.H.C.: Guidelines, icons and marketable skills: an accessibility evaluation of 100 web development company homepages. In: Proceedings of the International Cross-Disciplinary Conference on Web Accessibility (W4A 2012). ACM, New York (2012). doi:10.1145/2207016.2207024

19. McGrath, L.: What are the Web Content Accessibility Guidelines 2.0? http://www.wuhcag.com/web-content-accessibility-guidelines/. Accessed 20 December 2014
20. Michailidou, E., Mavrou, K., Zaphiris, P.: eInclusion @ cyprus universities: provision and web accessibility. In: CHI 2012 Extended Abstracts on Human Factors in Computing Systems (CHI EA 2012), pp. 1637–1642. ACM, New York (2012). doi:10.1145/2212776.2223685
21. WEBAIM: WEBAIM Checklist, WebAIM (Web Accessibility in Mind). http://webaim.org/standards/wcag/checklist. Accessed 20 December 2014
22. Oud, J.: How well do Ontario library web sites meet new accessibility requirements? Partnership. Can. J. Libr. Inf. Pract. Res. **7**(1), 1–17 (2012)

# An Implementation of Online Learning and Course Management System Based on Facebook

I-Hsien Ting[1(✉)], Wei-Jie Wu[1], Hao-Ting Kao[1], and David Wang[2]

[1] Department of Information Management, National University of Kaohsiung, No. 700, Kaohsiung University Road, Kaohsiung, Taiwan
iting@nuk.edu.tw, {joshot.ws, timothy820712}@gmail.com
[2] Syosset High School, 70 South Woods Road, Syosset, NY 11791, USA
djwang826@gmail.com

**Abstract.** In recent years, social networking websites play a very important role as the interactive platform between users as well as lecturers and learners. Thus, it would be a good idea if a learning management system can be built based on those social networking websites, such as Facebook. In this paper, we therefore proposed to construct an online learning and course management system, which can transform traditional learning management system functions to enable better interactions between lecturers and learners. Furthermore, the system has been implemented and the functions will be shown in the paper. We also concluded this paper with some future directions and suggestions about e-learning, learning management systems and social networking website.

**Keywords:** Social networks · Facebook · Online learning · Learning management system

## 1 Introduction

In recent years, online social networking websites have become a very popular type of platform in which WWW application allows users to interact and share with each other, such as Facebook, Google+, Twitter, Weibo, etc. More and more possible applications include fields such as marketing, politics, knowledge management and e-learning, etc. can be made in these websites. In knowledge management, many literatures have proved virtual community and online social networking websites as very ideal media and platform for knowledge management, such as "Community of Practice" [8]. For e-learning, these websites now also play a very important role as a platform of sharing, interaction, discussion and learning between lectures and learners [7, 12, 14, 18].

Cloud-learning now is a very hot research topic, especially when learning is based on social networking websites. Social networking websites provide lecturers and students with a platform for teaching and learning. With this platform, lecturers announce course information, discuss and answer students' questions and collect assignments. In Facebook, some lecturers even form a "Group" for a particular course, which is very similar to the functions provided by "virtual community" for Facebook users. Figure 1


L. Uden et al. (Eds.): LTEC 2015, CCIS 533, pp. 208–218, 2015.
DOI: 10.1007/978-3-319-22629-3_17

shows an example of a course group in Facebook, which allows students to upload and discuss the assignment directly.

According to the report of monthly active Facebook users worldwide as of 4th Quarter 2014, there are more than 1.39 billion active users now in Facebook. It means you almost can interact with whoever you want in Facebook [16]. Thus, it also means that the lecturers and learners can be reached with each other directly in Facebook without additional registration process. Furthermore, lecturers and learners don't need to install or launch extra software or websites for e-learning or course management. In addition to the functions that developed by Facebook, the developers are also allowed to design their own functions based on the data in Facebook via Facebook API (Application Program Interface).

Traditional e-learning and course management systems, such as Moodle (Modular Object-Oriented Dynamic Learning Environment) [10], has become well developed and enables most of learning activities to be transformed into online learning activities. However, some researchers found that a high percentage of users/learners usually stay in the system only for some particular tasks, such as uploading assignments. Moreover, it is not a good user experience for users to switch systems only for a particular task [9, 17].

According to the above reasons, it would be a good idea if we can develop an e-learning and course management system as a Facebook APP by applying the API provided by Facebook. Then, lecturers and learners can interact directly in Facebook without login/registration to another system. We also need to develop some basic functions for users to perform course activities to fulfill basic requirements. We expect the system helpful to improve users experience and to improve learning and course management performance accordingly. In addition to basic functions, we also hope this

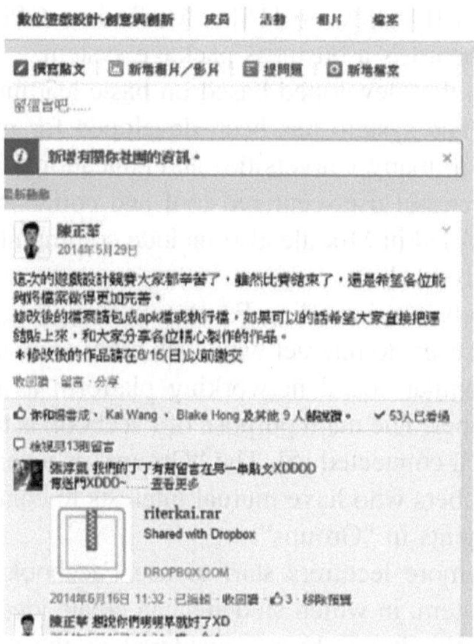


**Fig. 1.** A course group in Facebook (The course is "Digital Games Design")

system can provide some novel functions which can improve user interaction and learning and course management performance.

This article is divided into five sections. Section 1 provides an introduction to the background and motivation of the paper. Section 2 is the review of related literatures and works. In Sect. 3, the system architecture of the Facebook based e-learning and course management system will be introduced. The implementation of the system will be illustrated in Sect. 4 with the introduction to important functions of the system. In Sect. 5, we concluded the paper and provide future directions and suggestions.

## 2 Learning and Course Management Systems

Learning and Management System (LMS) is a software application that enable lecturers and system administrator to carry out administration, documentation, tracking, reporting and delivery of E-learning courses [19]. In some literatures, interaction is also described as an essential function that must be provided in LMS [2, 3, 13]. In the area of online social networking, some researchers shift their focus from traditional e-learning to social networking based e-learning, due to they believe it can provide better interaction function [14, 18, 20]. Currently three types of LMS are widely used for many courses: Moodle, Blackboard and customized system.

Moodle and Blackboard are two totally different oriented learning management systems by comparing to the course management approaches [1]. The full name of Moodle is Modular Object-Oriented Dynamic Learning Environment, which means the course management approach is modelized, dynamic and object-oriented. The course manager can add/remove the model of learning activities, which makes it is a very flexible learning management system. Comparing to Moodle, most of the functions in Blackboard system is not that flexible [15]. Moodle is a GPL open source learning platform whereas Blackboard is a business package system.

Moodle is a platform that developed based on basic learning functions and course management functions. The system has been developed for more than 10 years and therefore is widely used in many Universities and educational institutions. It has been considered as a very powerful user-centered tool and collaborative learning environment. The tools that provided in Moodle also include community tools such as forums, wikis, chats and blogs [10, 11].

Social networking websites, including Facebook, Google+, Twitter, Myspace, etc., are popular platforms for users to interact with each other. Among them, Facebook now is probably the most popular social networking platform as discussed in the introduction section of this paper. The main purpose of Facebook is to share and to make the world more open and well connected [5]. The "Groups" is a very important features of Facebook. It allows members who have mutual interests to connect with each other, to chat and to share documents in "Groups".

Recently, more and more lecturers start to use Facebook "Groups" as a formal learning management system, in which students can create ideas, share and learn from each other more efficiently. It has been considered as the main shortage of recent learning management systems, such as Moodle and Blackboard [4]. However, when using Facebook platform as the learning management systems, some problems could occur unexpectedly. For example, the students' responses are usually poor structured. In addition, it is usually time-consuming for lecturers to manage courses, privacy and security issue [4]. Therefore, It would be a good concept to develop a Facebook-based LMS in which we can keep the key features of the traditional LMS and improve its interaction function with the aid of the strength of Facebook. In the meantime, weaknesses of Facebook such as less-structured response, privacy and security issues should be considered to deal with.

## 3 System Architecture

In order to achieve the idea that mentioned in previous sections, we therefore proposed a system architecture to construct a Facebook based learning management system. The proposed system architecture is shown in Fig. 2. In the system, we will acquire the users data based on the API that provided by Facebook and to highlight the strength of Facebook, such as interaction and notification functions. The functions of the system and the architecture of the system will be discussed in detail. The implementation of the system will be introduced in Sect. 4 with some screenshots of the system.

**(1) User Login**

In this system, users can login to it by using their own existing Facebook account, and don't need to register to the system. This is considered as the strength of the system from users' experience. The login function is provided by Facebook and we only need to use the Facebook API for developing. After users logging in to the system, Facebook will assign a "Session" for our system to authorize the users. Alternatively, users can also sign in to the system by registering another account instead of that of Facebook. However, in that way, some special Facebook features will be disabled.

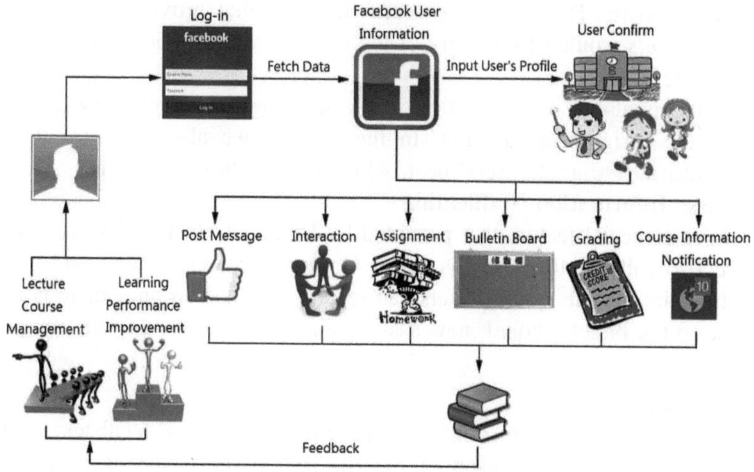


**Fig. 2.** The system architecture

**(2) Facebook User Information and User Confirmation**

After logging in to the system, user's data, to some extent, could be fetched under authorization depending on the extent to which the user is willing to expose by security setting. Normally, basic information of users, such as their names, email address, friend list, etc. is require. We will also need to get users' authorization to send them notification and post messages on their Facebook Timeline. Users finally can confirm their profile that listed on Facebook. They can edit and remove the information in the system.

**(3) Course Activities**

In the system, we provide major learning activities as well as some special features that provided by Facebook.

(i) **Message Posting**
This is one of the special features that provided by Facebook. The course administrator can send direct message to users/students. Some traditional learning management systems also provide similar function; however, they are not as efficient and real-time as the one provided by Facebook.

(ii) **Interaction**
The system also allows users and course administrator to have a better interaction by carrying out discussions and sending messages. The interact function that provided by Facebook is stronger than any other recent learning management system.

(iii) **Assignment**
Assignment is a basic function in the learning management system, which allows course administrator to create, edit and download assignment and users to view and upload assignment.

(iv) **Bulletin Board**
Bulletin board is also a very common feature that provided by the learning management system. Users will be notified of the information that posted in bulletin board. This is a very useful function that provided by Facebook to ensure users wouldn't miss any of the information in bulletin board.

(v) **Grading**
Grading is also a basic function in the learning management system together with the assignment function. In the system, we also authorize the course administrator to grade users' post, which is an optional function.

(vi) **Course Information Notification**
This is a special feature that provided by Facebook. In Facebook, the user can select to follow other users' (and/or Groups and Pages) posts and to receive notification. In the system, users can receive notification once there is any new post on the bulletin board, new assignment, new course material, etc. as well.

**(4) Feedback**

In the system, feedback function is designed to collect users' feedback, grades and experience. The data can be used to measure the performance of lecturer course management and the performance of learning improvement. We also keep the system and access logs of users for the analysis of users' behavior in the future.

# 4 Implementation and the System

In this section, we will illustrate the implementation of the system and show some screenshots of the Facebook-based learning management system to explain the features of the system.

We implement the system based on Facebook Graph API [6], the program language is PHP for web server side programming and JavaScript, CSS and JQuery for web front-end programming. The database that used in the system is MongoDB, which is a NoSQL database. The database is selected due to the system is a social network based system and NoSQL database has been considered as a good solution from many other experiences.

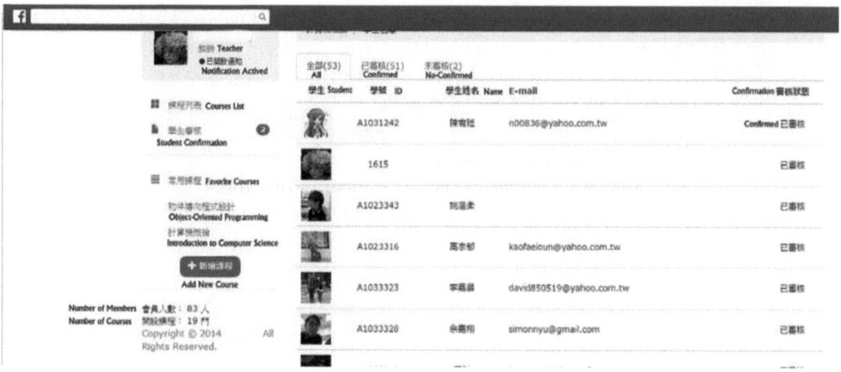

**Fig. 3.** The main interface of the system

Figure 3 is the main interface of the system. The language that used in the system is Chinese and we have translated some important words in the system into English near the original words. The interface is designed to be consistent with that of Facebook since it is a Facebook-based system.

In the interface, there are three main areas included. The function of the system is located on the top of the interface. On the left-hand side is the information of the user, the courses and system. The status of the user is shown near the picture of the user as "Teacher" or "Student". On the right-hand side is the main area of the system. Most of the course information and system manipulation are located here.

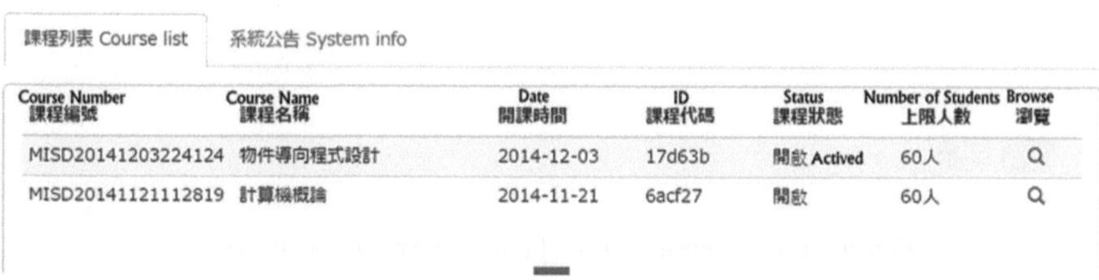


**Fig. 4.** The screenshot of course list

**Fig. 5.** The screenshot of course information

**Fig. 6.** The screenshot of the bulletin board of the system

Figure 4 is the screenshot of course list. All courses connected to the user will be listed, together with the course number, course name, the starting date of the course, the ID, current status of the course and the number of students (Fig. 5).

Figure 6 is the screenshot of the bulletin board of the system. The course administrator has the authorization to post message on the bulletin board. All users will receive a notification automatically by Facebook after the message has been posted (See Figs. 10 and 11 for the notification function).

Figure 7 is the screenshot of syllabus in which the course administrator can add, edit and arrange the events of the course. For each course event, different items can be added into the event, such as files, slides, documents, etc.

Figure 8 is the screenshot of assignments. Course administrators can add, edit and delete assignment for a particular course. Students can upload assignment for course administrator to grade. There are three types of assignments in the system including plan text assignment, question-answering assignment and file upload assignment.

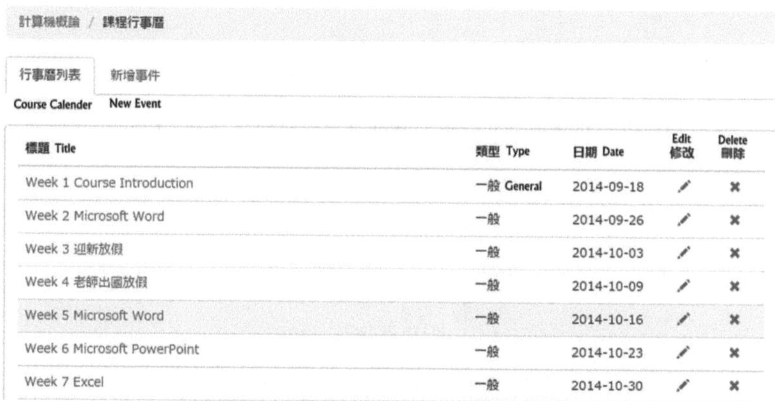


**Fig. 7.** The screenshot of course calendar

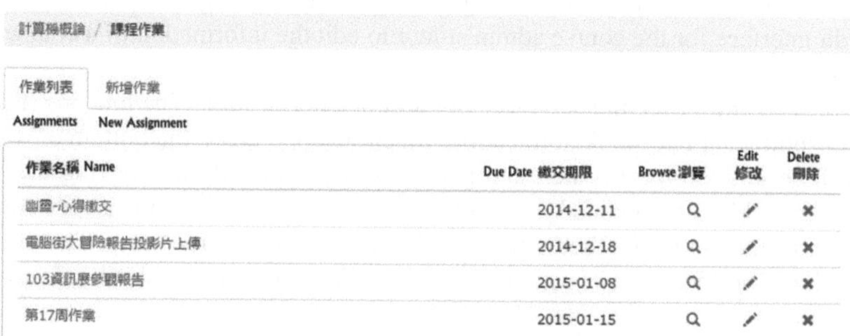


**Fig. 8.** The screenshot of assignments

**Fig. 9.** The screenshot of adding a new course in the system

**Fig. 10.** The screenshot of Facebook notification type 1

Figure 9 is the screenshot of adding a new course in the system. We designed an easy-edit interface for the course administrator to edit the information of a course more efficiently.

Figures 10 and 11 are the two types of Facebook notification. The first one (Fig. 10) is a very significant Facebook notification, which will pop up on the bottom of website. User will be notified by this alert and get the message directly by clicking the notification. Figure 11 is the second type of Facebook notification, which is a very common notification function in Facebook and is well known to Facebook users. The user also can check the notification by just clicking the notification. The notification feature is a

**Fig. 11.** The screenshot of Facebook notification type 2

special one comparing to other learning management systems and considered as the strength of the system for not letting users miss a single update and information.

## 5 Conclusion and Future Works

In this paper, we present a Facebook-based learning course management system in which we make use of strengths of the Facebook as a popular social networking website and in the meantime maintain fundamental functions in the traditional learning management system such as course editing, assignment and message posting etc. The special features of the system including include Facebook login, notification and student management. A series of screenshots are shown to demonstrate the implementation of the system.

Not only the possibility of combining the advantage of social networking website and traditional learning management system has been discussed above, we also turned the theory into reality with the illustration of the implementation of the system since it is just an idea and a trial to build a learning management system based on Facebook, a lot of works and researches should be done in the future. For example, the performance of course management or learning performance should be evaluated. The relationships between the system and knowledge management and innovation should also be appraised. In the future, we should improve the system by bringing in more useful interaction or social networking functions into the system. In the system, we also collected large amount of access logs and these data can be used for the analysis of users' behavior in the future. It is also a possibility to develop mobile application of the learning management system and the performance could be evaluated in the future.

## References


1. Blackboard: Blackboard platforms (2015). http://anz.blackboard.com/sites/international/globalmaster/Platforms/. Accessed 1 March 2015
2. Davidson-Shivers, G.V.: Frequency and types of instructor-interactions in online instruction. J. Interact. Online Learn. **8**, 23–40 (2009)
3. Du, Z., Fu, X., Zhao, C., Liu, Q., Liu, T.: Interactive and collaborative e-learning platform with integrated social software and learning management system. In: 2012 International Conference on Information Technology Software Engineering, Beijing, China, pp. 11–18 (2012)
4. Facebook in Education: Using a Facebook group as a learning management system (2015). https://www.facebook.com/note.php?note_id=10150244221815570. Accessed 1 March 2015
5. Facebook: Facebook page (2015). https://www.facebook.com/facebook/info. Accessed 1 March 2015
6. Facebook: Facebook graph API (2015). https://developers.facebook.com/docs/graph-api. Accessed 2 March 2015
7. Greenhow, C.: Online social network and learning. Horizon **19**, 4–12 (2011)
8. Kimble, C., Hildreth, P., Bourdon, I.: Communities of Practice, p. 444 (2008)
9. Machado, M., Tao, E.: Blackboard vs. moodle: comparing user experience of learning management systems. In: 37th Annual Frontiers in Education Conference, Milwaukee, WI, pp. S4J-7–S4J-12 (2007)
10. Moodle: Modular object-oriented dynamic learning environment (2015). https://moodle.org/. Accessed 25 February 2015
11. Moodle: About Moodle (2015). http://docs.moodle.org/26/en/About_Moodle. Accessed 28 February 2015
12. Moss, P.: Why learning through social networks is the future. In: TeachThought Staff (2013). http://www.teachthought.com/technology/learning-through-networks-is-the-future/. Accessed 28 February 2015
13. Al, N.A., Tang, A., Ahmad, A., Ahmad, M.S.: Learning management system using multi-agent technology: a proposed implementation strategy. Int. J. Asian Soc. Sci. **3**, 1878–1886 (2013)
14. Smith, F.: How to use social-networking technology for learning (2007). http://www.edutopia.org/how-use-social-networking-technology. Accessed 28 February 2015
15. SoftwareInsider: Blackboard learn LMS vs Moodle (2015). http://lms.softwareinsider.com/compare/83-226/Blackboard-Learn-LMS-vs-Moodle. Accessed 1 March 2015
16. Statista: Number of monthly active Facebook users worldwide 2008–2014 (2015). http://www.statista.com/statistics/264810/number-of-monthly-active-facebook-users-worldwide/. Accessed 25 February 2015
17. Unal, Z., Unal, A.: Investigating and comparing user experiences of course management systems: BlackBoard vs. Moodle. J. Interact. Learn. Res. **25**, 101–123 (2014)
18. Veletsianos, G., Navarrete, C.C.: Online social networks as formal learning environments: learner experiences and activities. Int. Rev. Res. Open Distrib. Learn. **13**, 144–166 (2012)
19. Wikipedia: Learning management system (2015). http://en.wikipedia.org/wiki/Learning_management_system. Accessed 28 February 2015
20. Wilson, C., Boe, B., Sala, A., Puttaswamy, K.P.N., Zhao, B.Y.: User interactions in social networks and their implications. In: 2009 ACM European Conference on Computing System (2009)

# Using Cloud-Based Applications for Education, a Technical Interoperability Exploration for Online Document Editors

Rocael Hernández Rizzardini[1,2(✉)], Christian Gütl[2,3], and Hector R. Amado-Salvatierra[1]

[1] GES Department, Galileo University, Guatemala, Guatemala
{roc,hr_amado}@galileo.edu
[2] IICM, Graz University of Technology, Graz, Austria
[3] SIS, Curtin University, Perth, WA, Australia
christian.guetl@iicm.tugraz.at

**Abstract.** Innovation in technology-enhanced learning (TEL) is constantly evolving, and social media, MOOCs and big data are some of the technologies improving education through cloud environments. A cloud education environment (CEE) uses external cloud-based applications for learning activities. This paper will explore on technical interoperability using a semantic web solution for cloud-based tools (CBT) in an educational setting. It will focus on the use case of online document editors for learning activities and present a proposed generic ontology for interoperability of online document editor tools. This work describes a proposal using Web APIs for integration and interoperability. The focus of this paper is to provide a description of the common characteristics of online document editor tools, such as their resources, operations, and properties, which will create a definition of a generic vocabulary for further interoperability.

**Keywords:** Ontologies · General Vocabulary · Moocs · Cloud-based tools · JSON-LD · Hydra · Interoperability · Cloud-based educational environment

## 1 Introduction

Technology-enhanced learning (TEL) has an evolutionary process of innovation, and a key area for improvement is interoperability. This paper will present a semantic interoperability solution for cloud-based tools (CBT) in an educational setting. It will define an ontology for an application domain type for online document editor tools using examples. A Hydra-based generic vocabulary [8] is derived from the ontology in this work. The proposed ontology is intended to be used together with JSON-LD [7] and Hydra [9] to describe a cloud-based tool, Web API. Once the Web API uses JSON-LD and Hydra, it will be discoverable, enabling machine processable Web APIs without a custom code for each tool. This work has a focus on online document editor tools, and intends to be developed based on previous work using mind map tools [4, 5].

The remainder of the paper is structured as follows: Sect. 2 gives an outline for Online Document editors. Section 3 offers a proposed ontology for interoperability related to Online Document editors for educational purposes. Section 4 presents a


L. Uden et al. (Eds.): LTEC 2015, CCIS 533, pp. 219–231, 2015.
DOI: 10.1007/978-3-319-22629-3_18

proposal for a General Vocabulary related to Online Document editors. Section 5 includes the discussion and presents conclusions and future work ideas.

## 2 Online Document Editors

Office productivity suites are one of the most mature software available at this moment, but still many new brands and versions come out to the market often. The evolution towards online document editors is a common technological trend, as an example, in office productivity suites such as Microsoft Office, they provide an online version of its desktop suite, known as Office Online and stored in OneDrive (formerly called Sky-Drive) [15]. Web based companies such as Google, initiated with its own suite of office productivity Cloud-Based Tools (CBTs), which is originally named Google Docs, and now is Google Drive [11].

As an initial exploration on interoperability with cloud education environments (CEE) [1, 2]; 12 tools providing web-based office productivity suites were identified and are shown in Table 1. An initial list of 21 tools was prepared, but several of these were not considered for interoperability tests because they are only desktop applications and do not have a Web API available.

**Table 1.** Group of 12 identified document editor tools reviewed

| Tool | Tool URL | Scope | API |
|---|---|---|---|
| Gdrive | https://drive.google.com | Web-based | Yes |
| Zoho | https://docs.zoho.com | Web-based | Yes |
| Onedrive | https://onedrive.live.com | Web-based | Yes |
| Etherpad | http://etherpad.org/ | Web-based | Yes |
| Hackpad | https://hackpad.com | Web-based | Yes |
| Crocodoc | http://personal.crocodoc.com/ | Web-based | Yes |
| Draftin | http://draftin.com | Web-based | Yes |
| Pangurpad | http://pangurpad.com/ | Web-based | No |
| Collabedit | http://collabedit.com/ | Web-based | No |
| Freeoffice | http://www.freeoffice.com/ | Web-based | No |
| WriteUrl | http://www.writeurl.com/ | Web-based | No |
| Firepad | http://www.firepad.io/ | Web-based | No |

Table 2 presents a group of four selected CBT that have an open accessible Web API. Some of them are standalone document editor, but others are full office productivity suites. These CBTs were classified in groups of three main interoperability features: interoperability response types (e.g., CSV, XML, or JSON), CBT API maturity level, and authentication mechanism (e.g., OAUTH, OpenID, Auth URL).

In terms of API maturity, CBTs were classified in four levels, with Level 4 (L4) the highest maturity level for an open API, allowing service consumers to do almost anything with the CBT, being able to manipulate almost anything within a document. Level 3 (L3) stands for an intermediate maturity level in which still has access to most

**Table 2.** Selected document editor CBTs with interoperability features.

| Supported features per resource or object for each CBT | | | Gdrive | Draftin | Etherpad | Zoho |
|---|---|---|---|---|---|---|
| User | Operation | Login | x | x | x | x |
| | | list files | x | x | x | x |
| | Properties | Id | x | x | x | x |
| | | Username | x | x | | x |
| | | email address | x | x | | x |
| | | picture url | x | | | |
| File | Operation | create and upload | x | x | x | x |
| | | Delete | x | x | x | x |
| | | update resource | x | x | | x |
| | | update content | x | x | x | |
| | | Copy | x | x | | |
| | | Get and download file | x | x | | x |
| | | share file | x | x | x | |
| | | export(plain text, html.) | x | x | x | |
| | Properties | Id | x | x | x | x |
| | | Title | x | x | x | |
| | | Labels | x | | | |
| | | Owners | x | x | x | |
| | | created date | x | x | x | |
| | | Editable | x | | | |
| | | last modifying | x | x | | |
| | | parent_id | x | x | | |
| API maturity level | | | L4 | L4 | L3 | L2 |

of the properties of a document, importantly has the ability to edit the content of the document itself and just a few properties are not accessible and the update resources operation is not available. Level 2 (L2) identifies a CBT that has access to the basic properties of a document and some of the basic operation, but it cannot update the content within a document. This is particularly important feature because allows to create specialized scenarios where is possible to automatically manipulate the content of the document, transferring content back and forth from the document to the VLE and other

CBTs. Finally, Level 1 (L1) implies a poor API, simple authentication, and a simple embed of html editor or player. There are no CBTs that classifies into this category.

Table 2 also presents the four CBTs characterized with the previously defined structure which have more features and are of further interest in the research. CBTs in Table 2 were classified based on two resources (user and file), including supported operations and properties.

## 3 Proposed Ontologies for Interoperability

Ontologies used for educational settings have been developed in different research and development projects. Initiatives as presented in the IntelLEO project defined a working reference framework with different ontologies, mainly the learning context [13] and activity ontology [14]. These ontologies were analyzed as building blocks to define ontologies to be translated to semantic technologies with the aim to complete interoperability between Tool Consumer (TC) and Tool Producer (TP).

A proposed general ontology for online editor is presented. The ontology formally models the possible operations that the CBT may have, represented as isolated classes. Additionally the resources that the CBTs are built on also are represented as classes, and the relations between the classes, including its corresponding properties. As expected, among the vast possibilities of CBTs brands and approaches, there are a large number of different operations and resources available for each provider (as depicted in Tables 1 and 2) therefore it has been decided to only represent those general and most common operations and resources that are in Level 4 interoperability API maturity.

The proposed ontology for an online editor is presented in Fig. 1 (using UML to represent OWL). This general ontology for online document editors models common resources, properties, operations, and relations identified in Table 2. The objective is to model online editors and their main resources such as paragraphs, text and users along with the correspondent properties for each resource. Finally, the operations are also represented.

An Application Domain Type (ADT) definition is a generic description of a Web API for a given application domain. Figure 2 presents the interoperability ontology for document editor ADT. This includes modeling the *User Class Resource*, with its properties. Then the *Document Class*, its properties, and further relation to the *User Class*. Then the six operations that are common and relevant for interoperability manipulation and automation.

This general ontology for document editor models common resources, properties, operations, and relations identified in Table 2. As in the previous ontology, this as well serves as a base to derive the General Vocabulary (GV).

## 4 Generic Vocabulary for CBT Interoperability

This section introduces the Generic Vocabulary (GV) developed for online document editors, based on the previously constructed ontologies in Sect. 3. To achieve that, it is necessary to select semantic Web technologies that support the outlined objectives.

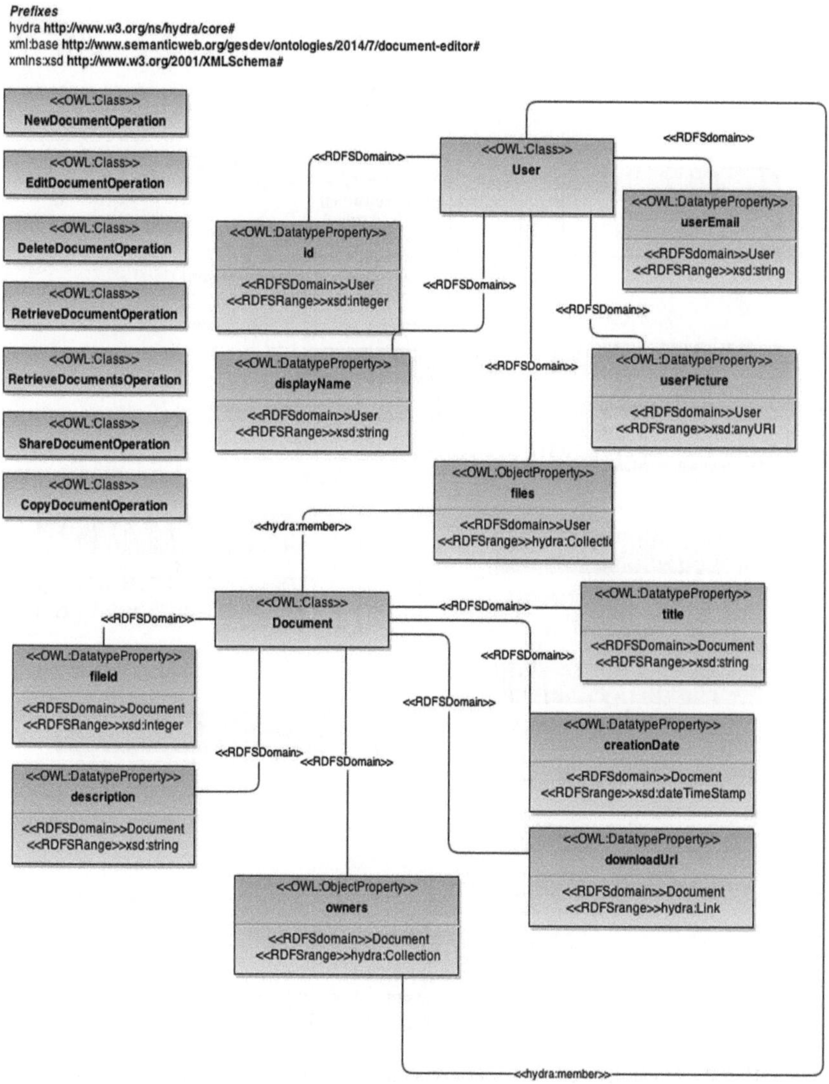


**Fig. 1.** Ontology for document editor for educational interoperability (OWL:Class is equivalent to rdf:Class).

JSON-LD [7] and Hydra [9] are selected to support the semantic model for Web interoperability. JSON itself is a widely used payload format thus is quite straightforward to further adoption of the proposed solution. Many Tool Providers (TP) already have JSON payload, then those TPs are able to adopt JSON-LD without too many changes over their existing Web API (for instance using the HTTP Link header for adding reference to other documents context). Furthermore RESTful services are highly common in Web APIs, thus supporting them correctly is necessary.

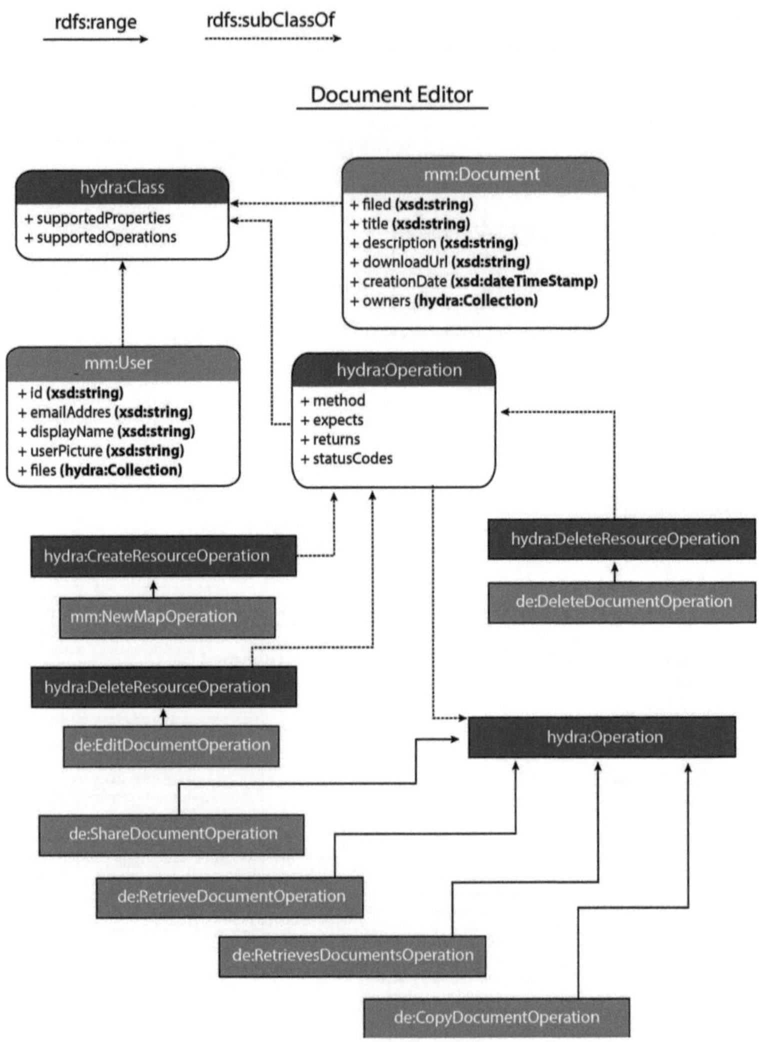


**Fig. 2.** Document editor generic vocabulary represented as class diagram

Hydra is a small but powerful addition to the current Web APIs to describe CBTs semantically using Linked Data and using a robust REST implementation. This is a powerful mechanism that enables discovery at run time of the Web API. Hydra provides the possibility to create generic descriptions of an Application Domain Type (ADT). In addition, Hydra also provides the flexibility for the TPs extend and support their own set of objects, operations and properties, a prerequisite to the flexible interoperability model.

Using Hydra [9] vocabulary it is possible to create self-descriptive, hypermedia-driven Web APIs. They can fully use Linked Data expressivity with REST's major benefits, such as scalability, evolution, and loose coupling. Hydra models represent resources, properties, and operations, among other useful classes for describing Web APIs. A GV is formed with subclasses of Hydra classes, and it is intended to model a specific ADT (i.e., an online documents GV can be used as a basis to model any online document CBT Web API). The ontologies presented in the previous Section are used, leading to create an online document GV that can describe basic properties and operations any online document editor CBT may have. This GV serves as the basis for interoperability while leaving CBT-specific details at implementation time.

```
{
    "@id": "de:title",
    "@type": "rdf:Property",
    "label": "title",
    "comment": "Document title",
    "range": {
       "@id": "xsd:string"
    }
} {
    "@id": "de:description",
    "@type": "rdf:Property",
    "label": "description",
    "comment": "Document description",
    "range": {
        "@id": "xsd:string"
    }
} {
    "@id": "de:owners",
    "@type": "hydra:Link",
    "label": "files",
    "comment": "Owners of file",
    "domain": {
        "@id": "de:Document"
    },
    "range": {
        "@id": "hydra:Collection"
    }
} {
    "@id": "de:Document",
    "@type": "hydra:Class",
    "label": "document",
    "comment": "General representation of a document",
       "supportedProperties": [
        {
            "property": "de:fileId",
            "readonly": "true"
        },
        {
            "property": "de:title"
        },
        {
            "property": "de:description"
        },
        {
           "property": "de:downloadUrl"
        },
        {
            "property": "de:creationDate",
            "readonly": "true"
        },
        {
            "property": "de:owners",
            "readonly": "true"
        }
       ]
}
```

**Fig. 3.** Document editor generic vocabulary, the main resource and some properties examples

The GV for a document editor is simpler compared to its equivalent to a mind map CBT [4, 5], because the main resource or object is the document itself. Thus as depicted in Fig. 2 the document resource has its set of properties. The GV also have the associated operations that can be performed towards a document, such as retrieve the document, new (create), edit and delete operations that inherit from the correspondent Hydra classes. It was purposefully left apart the management of folders (containers of documents), and document organization, because it is out of the scope of the research objective and suits better for a full description of the office environment, or to a storage CBT description.

Figure 3, presents a listing describing the initial part of the GV for a document editor. This part describes the *Document* as `de:Document`, and its properties that were define previous (e.g. title, description). It is also describe the *User*. Furthermore, it describes that a document can have multiple owners, which are users that have editor rights for the document.

The operations modeled for this General Vocabulary are described in listing in Fig. 4.: create a new document (`de:NewDocumentOperation`), edit (`de:EditDocument-Operation`), delete (`de:DeleteDocumentOperation`), share (`de:ShareDocumentOperation`). Also exist but not included in the listing presented in Fig. 4 `de:CopyDocumentOperation`, `de:Retrieve-DocumentsOperation` and `de:RetrieveDocumentOperation`.

```
    {
        "@id": "de:NewDocumentOperation",
        "@type": "hydra:Class",
        "label": "new-document",
        "comment": "Create a new document",
        "subClassOf": [
            "hydra:CreateResourceOperation"
        ]
      {
        "@id": "de:EditDocumentOperation",
        "@type": "hydra:Class",
        "comment": "Edit document",
        "label": "edit-document",
        "subClassOf": [
            "hydra:ReplaceResourceOperation"
        ]
      } {
        "@id": "de:DeleteDocumentOperation",
        "@type": "hydra:Class",
        "comment": "Delete a document",
        "label": "delete-document",
        "subClassOf": [
            "hydra:DeleteResourceOperation"
        ]
      } {
        "@id": "de:ShareDocumentOperation",
        "@type": "hydra:Class",
        "comment": "Share map",
        "label": "share-map",
        "subClassOf": [
            "hydra:Operation"
        ]
     }
    }
```

**Fig. 4.** Listing Document editor generic vocabulary operations

### 4.1 An Use Case with Draftin Online Document Editor

The General Vocabulary (GV) presented in the previous Section contains the common properties, data types and operations that a CBT may have. A Hydra API Documentation (API Doc) [9] describes all the current resources, operations, properties and data types that a CBT supports through its Web API. An API Doc first inherits from the GV the common operations and properties related to a resource (e.g. a *Document* or *User*). Thus the API Doc is defined for each specific online document editor CBT, it uses the GV to define its own classes. The API Doc describes the IRI, HTTP method, the expected data and return values when the TC requests an operation.

For the list of four online document editors presented in Sect. 2 (Table 2) a use case is presented for the online document editor, Draftin [12], the API Doc is depicted in Fig. 5. It describes the two resources of a document editor CBT: *User* and *Document*. A *User* resource (learners and teachers in this context) inherits from the GV class, for the *User* resource, the properties: `userId (id)`, `emailAddress (email)`. The `displayName` property is not supported, and instead it has its own substitution with

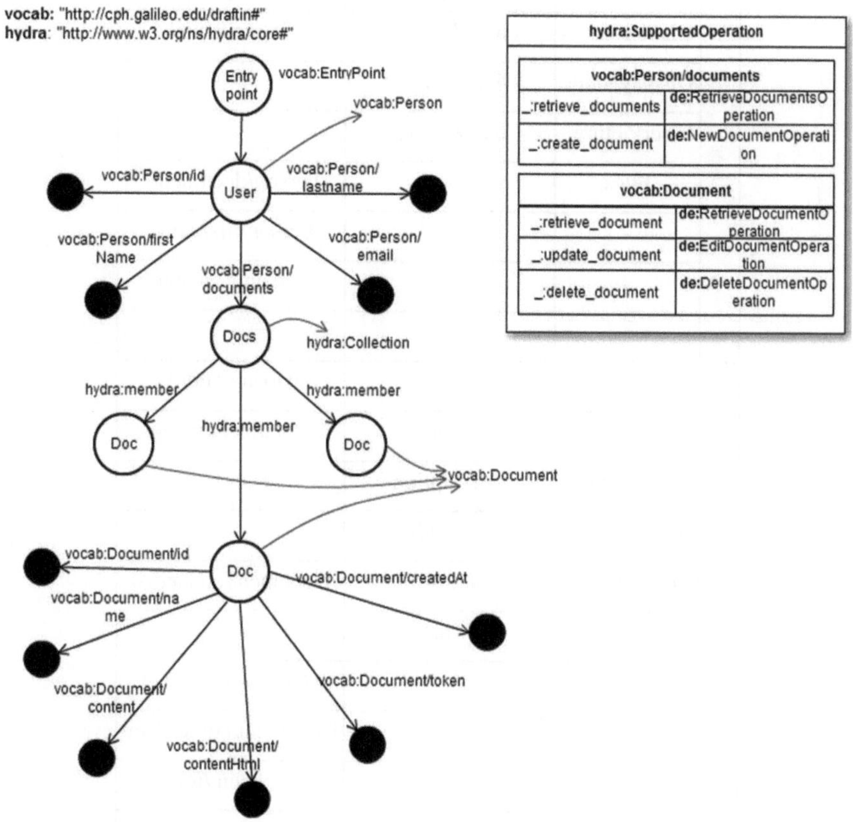


**Fig. 5.** Draftin Document Editor API Doc graph representation based on Hydra. "Doc(s)" as an abbreviation of Document (s)

firstName, lastname. The userPicture property that is defined in the GV is not available. Then it contains a collection of documents. A *Document* represents an instance of a *Document* resource, in the particular case of Draftin [12], this is named *File* instead of *Document*, that is because the real Web API uses different naming conventions but represents the same, therefore the GV serves to identify that it is the same type of the resource. The *User* resource there are two direct operations de: RetrieveDocumentsOperation and de:NewDocumentOperation both also defined in the correspondent GV.

A Doc has the properties of fileId (id), title (name), creationDate (createdAt). And is missing from the GV description, downloadUrl and

**Table 3.** Comparison of ontology, GV and API Doc available properties

| ONLINE DOCUMENT EDITOR | | | |
|---|---|---|---|
| | Ontology | General Vocabulary | DRAFTIN [12] |
| User | Id | Id | Person/id |
| | emailAddress | emailAddress | Person/email |
| | DisplayName | DisplayName | - |
| | userPicture | userPicture | - |
| | Files | Files | Person/documents |
| | - | - | Person/firstname |
| | - | - | Person/lastname |
| | - | - | - |
| Document | fileId | fileId | Document/id |
| | Title | Title | Document/name |
| | Description | Description | - |
| | downloadUrl | downloadUrl | - |
| | creationDate | creationDate | Document/createdAt |
| | owners | Owners | - |
| | - | - | Document/content |
| | - | - | Document/contetHtml |
| | - | - | Document/token |
| | - | - | Document/createdAt |

`owners`. But it has some other new introduced properties such as `content` and `contentHtml`. And the document resource has almost all the operations represented in the GV, but missing two operations: `de:CopyDocumentOperation` and `de:ShareDocumentOperation` operations.

Table 3 presents a comparison between the ontology, and the General Vocabulary (GV), and the CBTs API Doc implemented operations. In this Application Domain Type (ADT) it has not been used all the Web API available resources, and it is just focused on the necessary operations for supporting the use case. This is particularly notorious in the document editor ADT, because it conforms more than just a document editor, this includes other type of applications, such a presentations, file storage, spreadsheets, etc. The available operations comparison ontology, GV and CBT specific API Doc is depicted in Table 4.

**Table 4.** Comparison of ontology, GV and API Doc available operations

| ONLINE DOCUMENT EDITOR | | |
|---|---|---|
| Ontology | General Vocabulary | DRAFTIN |
| NewDocument | NewDocument | _:create_document |
| DeleteDocument | DeleteDocument | _:delete_document |
| EditDocument | EditDocumenht | _:update_document |
| RetrieveDocument | RetrieveDocument | _:retrieve_document |
| RetrieveDocuments | RetrieveDocuments | _:retrieve_documents |
| CopyDocument | CopyDocument | – |
| ShareDocument | ShareDocument | – |

## 5 Conclusions and Future Work

The General Vocabulary (GV) in conjunction with API documentation of Cloud-based Tools (CBTs) enable Tool Consumers (TC) to perform operations over the CBTs. A mandatory component in a Cloud Education Environment (CEE) is a public Web API from the CBTs. Currently, some of the CBTs support RESTful API and JSON payloads. But as Hydra is a new vocabulary, none of those CBTs uses it. This limitation makes it necessary to have an intermediate layer, such as the CBT proxy defined in LTIv.2 [3], with the capability to take a Tool Producer (TP) Web API and publish the translation in Hydra format. With this Hydra proxy, it is possible to take any Web API, create a proxy Hydra model of it, and enable the TC to process Hydra based Web APIs. And in the future, when the TP incorporates Hydra based responses, then the Hydra proxy will not be necessary.

While the Application Domain Type (ADT) CBTs available evolves, and the correspondent Web API become more mature, it is possible to enhance and expand the correspondent ontologies, therefore the GV has changes as well. For interoperability, using the presented Hydra approach, changes in Web API as described, have no impact in the interoperability with educational systems such as the Virtual Learning Environments (VLE) because a Hydra enabled run time environment has the capability to adapt to those changes, and administrators are able to choose whether to include or not certain features, etc.

The interoperability use case using JSON-LD and Hydra enables a high granularity management level of the VLE over the CBT, enhancing automation of course administrative task over the CBT (i.e. create a document of each group in a class, assign read permissions to comment over other group's document, etc.), and allows full access to the TP Web API. It requires only writing the definition of a Web API to include a new online document editor CBT. This can be achieved rapidly, without a large technical effort or complexity, although a big challenge is to convince web developer to use these technologies, providing SDK or programming languages libraries that easy the incorporation of these technologies might be a good approach.

When sharing CBT resources, for example an online document CBT, the teacher is able to manage a very granular set of properties and operations, for example, limit edition access to the document until a given assignment deadline, create role-based learning approaches, allow collaboration between learners, etc. This enables very custom designed learning experiences in a CEE looking forward to improve the learning experience and reduce attrition and increase motivation for learners [6, 10].

The approach of using a GV and the API Doc enables first to have generic services definition for an application type, while the TC (i.e. VLE) can choose to support only that predefined generic service resources, operations and properties (described in the GV) or allow to support extended features provided by the TP that are not described in the GV but in the API Doc.

There are other benefits of this approach, with the discovery at run-time of the application specific properties and operations, it can lead to automatically create user interfaces, input data validations, etc., which is an opportunity for future work, also include other tools implementations. The GV brings the benefit of a simple soft definition of the CBT at the design time. Thus leaving CBT specific interoperability details at the time of implementation, through a formal yet simple representation using the API Doc.

This interoperability approach for educational CBTs enhances and simplifies the integration of new CBTs in a VLE. The Hydra approach could enable further interoperability features such as the ones cited in this study, built on specifications such as IMS LTIv2 [3], or complementing its current capabilities.

## References

1. Hernández, R.: Cloud interoperability service architecture for education environments. Special issue on Massive open Online Courses: Combining Methodologies and Architectures for a Success Learning. J. Univ. Comput. Sci. **21**(5), 656–678(2014)
2. Hernández, R., Gütl, C.: Towards a flexible cloud education environment - a framework for E-learning. In: Fonseca, D., Redondo, E. (eds.) Handbook of Research on Applied E-Learning in Engineering and Architecture Education. Hershey: Information Science Reference. (2015, in press)
3. MS Global Learning Consortium: IMS GLC Learning Tools Interoperability Basic LTI Implementation Guide (2010)

4. Hernández, R., Gütl, C., Amado-Salvatierra, H.: Interoperability for cloud-based applications for education settings based on JSON-LD and Hydra: ontology and a generic vocabulary for mind map tools. In: Proceedings of the 14th i-Know Conference. ACM (2014)
5. Hernández, R., Gütl, C., Amado-Salvatierra, H.R.: Using JSON-LD and Hydra for cloud-based tool interoperability: a prototype based on a vocabulary and communication process handler for mind map tools. In: de Freitas, S., Rensing, C., Ley, T., Muñoz-Merino, P.J. (eds.) EC-TEL 2014. LNCS, vol. 8719, pp. 428–433. Springer, Heidelberg (2014)
6. Hernández, R., Gütl, C., Chang, V.: Must we be concerned with the Massive Drop-outs in MOOC? - An attrition analysis of open courses. In: International Conference on Interactive Collaborative Learning ICL (2014)
7. Lanthaler, M.: Model your application domain, not your JSON structures. In: Proceedings of the 22nd International Conference on World Wide Web, pp. 1415–1420 (2013)
8. Lanthaler, M.: Hydra: a vocabulary for hypermedia-driven Web APIs. In: Proceedings of the 6th Workshop on Linked Data on the Web (LDOW 2013) at the 22nd International World Wide Web Conference, WWW 2013 (2013)
9. Hydra W3C community group project. http://www.w3.org/community/hydra/. Last visit 12 February 2015)
10. Hernández, R., Gütl, C., Amado-Salvatierra, H.R.: Cloud learning activities orchestration for MOOC environments. In: Uden, L., Sinclair, J., Tao, Y.-H., Liberona, D. (eds.) LTEC 2014. CCIS, vol. 446, pp. 25–36. Springer, Heidelberg (2014)
11. Drive, G.: (2014). Accessed from http://drive.google.com
12. Draftin (2015). Accessed from https://draftin.com/
13. Jovanovic, J., Gasevic, D.: Learning Context ontology of the IntelLEO Ontology Framework (2011). http://www.intelleo.eu/ontologies/learning-context/spec/. Accessed 01 2014
14. Jovanovic, J., Gasevic, D.: Activities ontology of the IntelLEO Ontology Framework (2012). http://www.intelleo.eu/ontologies/activities/spec/. Accessed 03 2014
15. One Drive (2014): Accessed from https://onedrive.live.com/

# Interconnection of Information Systems in Academic Environment

## Case of University of Žilina in Žilina, Slovakia

Katarína Púčková[1], Lenka Tarábková[1], and Anna Závodská[2(✉)]

[1] Faculty of Management Science and Informatics, University of Žilina, Univerzitná 1, 010 26 Žilina, Slovak Republic
{katarina.puckova, lenka.tarabkova}@fri.uniza.sk
[2] University Science Park, University of Žilina, Univerzitná 1, 010 26 Žilina, Slovak Republic
anna.zavodska@uvp.uniza.sk

**Abstract.** Information systems play a crucial role in coordination of daily activities of academics. To maximize the effect of all information systems it is very important to interconnect them regarding their content. Moreover, it is very crucial to adapt them to new era which is continuously requiring implementing new information systems, e.g. filing hosting services, applications or social media into day-to-day life of academics. Since universities want to adapt to new technologies they implement various information systems which are becoming more complicated for understanding and subsequent use by academics. Therefore we focus our attention on analysing all the information systems at the Faculty of Management Science and Informatics and attempt of individuals to interconnect them. In our previous paper [22] we identified and analysed currently used KM tools at Faculty of Management Science and Informatics and proposed how these tools could be used more effectively or which ones could be introduced. In this paper we focus on information systems and investigate how they can be utilized even better than they are now.

**Keywords:** Information system · Academics · Knowledge sharing · Interconnection · University

## 1 Introduction

University of Žilina has several information systems which are used by all faculties. Most used systems are Moodle (for education purposes), Dawinci (for librarian purposes), economic system SAP (especially financial module) or Intranet (for internal communication among employees). We chose Faculty of Management Science and Informatics for the purpose of our paper because this faculty is most progressive and as it can be seen from its name it is focused on IT studies. Therefore, we suppose that this faculty would have the best experience with new systems, changing the obsolete systems for newer ones as well as unifying current systems. Based on our research we identified problems in using of information systems at this faculty and proposed solutions for effective merger of existing systems.


L. Uden et al. (Eds.): LTEC 2015, CCIS 533, pp. 232–242, 2015.
DOI: 10.1007/978-3-319-22629-3_19

Our paper is divided into 5 sections. First section describes information systems in general and their role in academic environment, while second section focuses on academic information systems in particular. Third section describes research methods and methodology. Fourth section focuses on analysis of information systems used at the Faculty of Management Science and Informatics and describes problems which are connected with these systems. The final section introduces proposal how to solve these problems based on interconnecting current systems. We conclude our paper with suggestions for further research.

## 2 Role of Information Systems at University

The knowledge management infrastructure is the foundation on which knowledge management resides. It includes five main components: organization culture, organization structure, communities of practice, information technology infrastructure, and common knowledge [4]. In this article, we concentrate on the role of information system (like a part of information technology infrastructure) in the knowledge management infrastructure at universities.

Since universities are knowledge intensive environments, and play a central role in knowledge creation, and dissemination, they should have an appropriate information system which provides the database, the information networks and the necessary functions by which the parts of the university communicate.

Information systems provide several benefits to an organisation. Information systems not only store and process data, they also produce information, which is the basis for good decision-making. Better information is available if data is properly managed in the information system, i.e. the data is available for processing, and is current, accurate, and secure [2]. Information systems operate at any time of the day or night and process data faster than humans. Furthermore, they make the work more productive in a shorter period of time [15].

The basic functionality of such an information technologies platform designed 'with knowledge management in mind' would comprise an integrated set of the following functions [8]:

- Communication: as well as coordination and cooperation, e.g. email, workflow management, newsgroup or list server.
- Document management: handling documents throughout their life cycle.
- Access: to various data sources, e.g. relational databases, document bases, file servers or Web servers.
- Search: basic search functionality.
- Visualisation.

Information systems and information technologies have many tools how they can support work with knowledge in the academic environment. Combination of knowledge can be supported by databases, web-based access to data, data mining, and repositories of information, web portals, best practices and lessons learned. Socialization of knowledge can be supported by video-conferencing, electronic discussion groups and e-mails. Externalization of knowledge can be supported by experts systems, chat groups, best practices, lessons learned and databases. Internalization of knowledge can be supported by computer-based communication and computer-based simulation. Exchange of knowledge can be supported by team collaboration tools, web-based access to data, databases, and repositories of information, best practices databases, lessons learned systems and expertise locator systems. Direction of knowledge can be supported by troubleshooting systems, case-based reasoning systems and decision support systems. Routines in work with knowledge can be support by expert systems, enterprise resource planning systems, management information systems [4, 7, 9, 14, 17, 21].

## 2.1 Development of Academic Information Systems at Slovak Universities

The internal environment of most universities is now undergoing rapid transition. The increasing number and demands of students, implemented credit system of studies, the expanding curricula and physical facilities and the introduction of computer-based information systems make university administration a most stimulating and challenging profession. These changes urge to upgrade and modernize the basic information systems at the university [19].

Integration of information systems [20] must support the basic goals of each organization - minimize the costs and maximize profits, and also gain a competitive advantage. Universities are more and more similar to companies and so they also need to integrate information systems to improve the operation. Integration of information systems can be done by the following approaches:

- sharing and exchange of data; the principle of shared data storage,
- shared services; the idea is to create integration interlayer between the integrated applications,
- integration by the user interface; this is the connection of a number of user interfaces of applications that these applications look like one unitary application.

Academic information systems deployed at every university interconnect users such as students, teachers, university/faculty management and broader community being public or academic. The purpose of information system in academic environment is to manage all three university degrees (Bachelor, Master and PhD.) and support the management of university science and research. Therefore, the majority of information systems at the universities are separated into administrative, teacher and research-oriented components [19]. Furthermore, an academic information system has to be interconnected with the librarian system where both students and researchers have an access to books, articles or journals.

In 2006 universities in Slovakia gradually started to implement economic information system SAP in order to centrally manage economic issues. This was done under the SOFIA project. The aim of the project was to have economic and administrative processes standardization at all universities. Until 2006 every university had different economic software and information systems which were not entirely suitable for academic environment in terms of functionalities, maintenance, support or technical requirements. Nevertheless, attempts to interconnect various economic and administrative software and integrate them into current academic information systems at universities started in 1998–2000 at conference UNINFOS. Furthermore, these attempts were supported by the Ministry of Education, Science and Sport of the Slovak Republic by means of the central development IT project [12].

Nowadays, every public university in Slovakia has an academic information system. However, many of these systems have some imperfections, such as excessive complexity of the platform. Usually, these information systems are developed at academic ground (information system AiS2 is a successor of the Academic Information System AIS developed at University of Pavol Jozef Šafárik in Košice in the period from 1997 to 2007) or in the cooperation with a software company (modular academic information system MAiS as joined development programme of Technical university of Košice (TUKE), University of Trnava and company Dupress-Consulting, limited) [11]. Some universities use university information system (UIS) developed by software company IS4U, s.r.o. Brno or have their own developed academic information system.

AiS2 has been gradually implemented across 14 universities, while MAiS has been implemented at three universities. These systems are for non-commercial purposes and available to any university which needs to deploy central information system to interconnect various systems, software of workflow processes.

## 2.2 Information Systems Found at University

***Moodle*** (acronym for modular object-oriented dynamic learning environment) is a GPL open-source learning platform also known as a learning management system, or virtual learning environment employed in education, training, development and business environment. It can be used to create a private website for dynamic online courses with a focus on interaction and collaborative construction of content, to interact with other students and teachers [13].

***Dawinci*** is an automated librarian system which integrates the state-of-the-art elements in the field of server applications, database systems and file management. It is complex multimedia system which automates information flow and processes of a library [5]. The system was created by Slovak company SVOP. First it was introduced to professional public at a symposium INFOS 2001 and is a part of a broader alike named project. The aim of the project is to create complex librarian system and build, support and cover other subprojects. The basic structural element is modular architecture with three level architecture of client/server type. There are these modules:

- Module Catalogue.
- Module Borrowing.
- Module Administrator.
- Module On-line Catalogue (Online Public Access Catalogue).

***SAP*** is an economic software to manage business operations and customer relations developed by German multinational software corporation SAP SE. SAP applications, built around their latest R/3 system, provide the capability to manage financial, asset, and cost accounting, production operations and materials, personnel, plants, and archived documents [18]. University of Žilina has been managing its economic issues in SAP system since 2005. The implementation of central economic system for all Slovak universities was conducted within project Sofia [12].

A ***ZyXel NSA 320*** has been introduced at the Department of management theories. It is a file server where participant can upload, download and manage various documents and files. It is fast, stable and accessible via the Internet.

***Dropbox*** is a free file hosting service operated by Dropbox, Inc. It allows users to create a special folder with documents, photos or other multimedia on their computers, which Dropbox then synchronizes so that it appears to be the same folder (with the same contents) regardless of which computer is used to view it. Files placed in this folder are also accessible via the Dropbox website and mobile apps [6].

***OneDrive*** (previously *SkyDrive, Windows Live SkyDrive* and *Windows Live Folders*) is a file hosting service that allows users to upload and sync files to a cloud storage and then access them from a web browser or their local device. It is part of the suite of online services formerly known as Windows Live and allows users to keep the files private, share them with contacts, or make the files public [16].

***Attendance records application WATT*** is used to record and automatically process attendance and actual periods of service by using attendance cards. Not only does a user record their attendance, they can learn whether a colleague is at work.

***SharePoint*** is a web application platform created by Microsoft (the latest available version is SharePoint 2013). It is built upon previous releases in 2007 and 2010 to better support Big Data, mobile users and public-facing websites [10]. SharePoint comprises a multipurpose set of Web technologies backed by a common technical infrastructure [1]. SharePoint can be used in a business as an intranet where employees can elaborate, upload, download and edit various documents in real time and across multiple devices (smartphones, tablets, iPads, Android, BlackBerry, Windows Phone, etc.). It connects people across the business and enables them to share important information, new ideas or best practice. Furthermore, it provides a central workspace for projects where team members can organise particular work tasks on ongoing projects or manage schedules.

## 3 Research Approach and Methodology

Qualitative research was used as core approach for data collection. This approach has involved the case study method (analysing, summarizing and evaluating the current state of the information systems at the Faculty of Management Science and Informatics), semi-structured interviews with 5 individuals from this faculty in order to gain knowledge about their experience with all faculty information systems (we asked them if they know all the faculty systems, if they use them, in which situation they use them, what are their experience with these systems, what are the pros and cons of these systems, if they know how to work with them, if there is anything missing in these systems), and analysis of all features of Share Point system.

Data was collected over the three-month period. Through the process of triangulation we used various types of evidence to examine the practices for best interconnection of academic information systems. We examined many different systems in order to solve problem of fragmented information systems.

The main purpose of this research was to find out if the interconnection of information systems at the Faculty of Management Science and Informatics was effective and brought value to its users.

Case study approach was chosen to demonstrate how IS are interconnected at the Faculty of Management Science and Informatics and what problems raised from this interconnection as well as how this process of interconnecting can be improved.

## 4 Analysis of Information Systems Used at Faculty of Management Science and Informatics

The university has its own integrated information system which serves students, teachers, the university/faculty management, study officers and operational staff. Particular subsystems are interconnected by a ***university Intranet.*** Nevertheless, there are several problems when it comes to their daily usage. This is caused also by the fact that there are several systems which are used at the same time. In this section we describe systems which are used the most and which usage could be the most beneficial and time-effective if they were interconnected.

**Moodle.** E-learning platform Moodle is a part of the integrated information system. To work with the system, every user is allowed to use those data and functions, which are needed only for the particular task (e.g. a student has access to those subjects he enrolled for) [3].

***Activities which students use:***

- Information about particular subjects and lesson schedules.
- Information about student cards used at the university.
- Information about formalities regarding diploma/dissertation thesis.
- Enrolling for exams and checking exam results.

***Activities which teachers use:***

- Assignment submissions.
- Quizzes as part of students' assessment.
- Grading of students.
- Adding content and re-organising the course.
- Surveys related to subject evaluation.

***Activities which students do not use:***

- Forums and discussions.
- Database, glossary, wiki and workshop.
- Surveys.

***Activities which teachers do not use:***

- Forums and discussions.
- Database, glossary, wiki and workshop.
- Gamification.

***Problems:***

Students as well as teachers have the opportunity to use discussions and forums or blogs to share information. However, these activities are used rarely and even if used, the responses are late resulting in not very continuous conversation. Interestingly, every subject has its own blog, which would provide students with related information and instant feedback. It is not so long that surveys to evaluate subjects by students have been introduced. Therefore, this activity requires more time for students to get used to it.

**Share Point.** Every doctoral student and employee of the faculty has access to the Share Point, which is currently in testing mode.

***Activities (store documents related to):***

- Research projects, research outcomes and citation of research in other databases.
- Statistics data regarding documents for accreditation purposes.
- Publications of employees and doctoral students (which are uploaded from the university librarian system).
- Internal documents relating to doctoral individual study programmes, application for doctoral exams and thesis defence.
- List of preparatory seminars for writing master thesis and students' papers relating to their topics.

***Problems:***

Despite all functions and their potential contribution to academic work, Share Point is not so widespread and used at the faculty. One of the most important reasons is the fact, that it is easy to get lost since the structure of sites is complicated. Furthermore, insufficient administrative support and lack of information how to use it, make users feel lost and frustrated. Other contributing factors could be labelled as low awareness of the Share Point among doctoral students and teachers and unwillingness to change until-now used means of communication (email communication).

**Dropbox.** Students and employees can share their folders with colleagues via Dropbox.

***Activities:***

- Create folders on own computer, which can be accessible via the Dropbox website and mobile apps.
- Share folders with colleagues.

***Problems:***

- It is not possible to work on documents with colleagues in the same time.
- Paid service if a person needs more space.

**Onedrive.** File hosting service, which has similar functions like Dropbox.

*Activities:*

- Upload and sync files to a cloud storage, which are accessible via web browser or local device.
- Share folders with contacts.

*Problems:*

- Users and their colleagues have to have Windows live account.

## 5 Recommendations for Improving Unification of Information Systems at the Faculty of Management Science and Informatics

Analysis has shown that there are several problems not only in usage of each particular information system but also the faculty attempt to interconnect these systems via Share Point failed. Share Point can connect all information systems in one and therefore it can be an interface for all the existing systems. However, at the Faculty of Management Science and Informatics they allowed and encouraged users to use only one feature for document sharing and therefore this system is not fully functional and consequently causing problems.

Share Point was created at the Faculty of Management Science and Informatics over a year ago. Since that time its features have not been fully exploited. It was undoubtedly good step in interconnecting information systems at the faculty, however, academics are not familiar with this system yet, which is decreasing its value added. By adding more features to existing system as well as training of faculty employees to use it effectively, this system can provide beneficial platform for plenty of academic activities.

Furthermore, Share Point can be fully customizable. Computer scientists are able to make any changes in Share Point as well as add whatever features they like.

We recommend faculty administrators to include following Share Point information/features to be used more effectively:

- detailed profiles of faculty employees, not only list of courses they teach but also their description, field of research, list of publications, etc.,
- discussion forums,
- possibility to share documents on which employees can collaborate at the same time,
- wiki with explanation of various terms, correct translations of english words approved by experts,
- ask and answer system,
- expert locator system,
- databases of contact persons at various institutions that faculty is cooperating with including universities as well as research institutions or commercial partners,

**Table 1.** Share Point features comparing to other information systems features

| Processes | Share Point feature | IS this Share Point feature currently implemented? | Currently most used IS at the Faculty of management science and informatics |
|---|---|---|---|
| Sharing | Storing documents in OneDrive | yes | Google Drive, Dropbox, ZyXel NSA 320 |
| | Sharing documents | | Google Drive, Dropbox, ZyXel NSA 320, email |
| | Groups and communities | x | Facebook |
| | Social feeds | x | Facebook, Twitter, LinkedIn |
| Organizing | Task management | | Podio, Asana |
| | Sites | x | Blogs |
| | Site mailbox | | Outlook |
| Discovering | Data visualization | x | |
| | Search tools | | Google (external search) |

- simplifying the work with Share Point, it should be an interface for all systems (e.g. librarian system, attendance system, SAP), well interconnected with one login,
- database of upcoming conferences, events as well as any other useful links.

In the following table we present how the features of Share Point can encompass all existing systems currently used at the Faculty of Management Science and Informatics (Table 1).

**Sharing Information and Documents**

**Cloud storage:** Dropbox, Google Drive or ZyXel NSA 320 are helpful online tools for creating and storing various types of documents. They can all be replaced by Microsoft OneDrive which is part of Share Point.

Social networking is available at Share Point by participating in discussions via social feeds or groups and communities where academics can share all relevant knowledge and information. There can be placed a question where other academics can give their answer. This feature can fully replace Facebook and LinkedIn in this particular case.

All the excel sheets, documents, presentations, etc. can be stored and updated in Share Point. Moreover, it is possible to collaborate on one document by more people at the same time.

**Organizing work**

Task management tools are an integral part of Share Point, therefore there is no need for separate installation of any other tools. This can fully replace the usage of any external task management tools like Podio or Asana.

Mailbox is interconnected with Outlook which is most used email service by academics at the Faculty of Management Science and Informatics as well as commonly used personal information manager so there is no problem with, e.g. learning to use different system, fear of losing data from previous one, fear of creating another account, etc.

**Discovering**
Moreover, this system provides features that any other currently used information system does not provide, e.g. data visualization, sites or social feeds or various advanced search tools.

## 6 Conclusion

A crucial activity of academics is knowledge sharing. One important mean by which it is very effective, easy and fast to share knowledge is information system. Academics use several types of academic information systems because they have many types of targeted audience they want to share information with: students, colleagues, bachelor, master or doctoral students they are tutoring, public, etc. as well as various types of purposes they want to use information systems for. Because technology is quickly advancing and new information systems are continuously arising universities are facing problem with too many information systems they possess but do not necessarily use.

This paper, therefore, investigates the present set of information systems, provided for academics at Faculty of Management Science and Informatics. This investigation shows that even though faculty has provided their academics with a wide range of information systems, these information systems are not as beneficial to academics due to their lack of knowledge in using them, lack of interconnectedness and obsolescence. We found out that academics consider information systems crucial for their work. They provide them opportunity to optimize their work and thus improve their outcomes. By using information systems academics can save time, focus on core problem and find the best available sources and experts worldwide. Based on the analysis, we proposed relevant interconnection of all IS that can be used by academics at the Faculty of Management Science and Informatics. This interconnection can lead to better orientation in wide range of features needed by academics as well as all-in-one-place system.

Share Point as a user interface interconnecting systems such as Moodle, the librarian information system, attendance system and data storage systems or faculty web page, would ease administrative pressure as well as looking up information related to current projects at the faculty, research activities, etc.

This presented information system was implemented a year ago and it is not widely spread between academics. However, its modification can lead to several benefits that can be explained to academics and if they are trained, this system can be used more effectively. The benefits of our recommendations need further examination. Nonetheless, there are no doubts that they can be very helpful.

**Acknowledgements.** This paper is supported by the following projects: Research park of the University of Zilina (ITMS: 26220220184) supported by the Research & Development Operational Programme funded by the European Regional Development Fund, VEGA n. 1/0363/14 - Innovation management, VEGA n. 1/0621/14 Marketing management in cooperation environment.

## References


1. Adsoft solution - official page: What is sharepoint. http://www.adsoft-solutions.com/what-is-sharepoint
2. Alter, S.: Information Systems: A Management Perspective. Addison-Wesley, Reading (1999)
3. Akademický informačný systém e-vzdelávanie Žilinskej univerzity. www.uniza.sk/document/ais_popis.doc
4. Becera-Fernandez, I., Sabherwal, R.: ICT and knowledge management system. In: Encyclopedia of Knowledge Management. Idea Group Inc. (2005). ISBN 9781591405740
5. Dawinci - home page. http://www.dawinci.sk/dawinci.aspx
6. Dropbox - Wikipedia. http://en.wikipedia.org/wiki/Dropbox_(service)
7. Franco, M., Mariano, S.: Information technology repositories and knowledge management processes: a qualitative analysis. VINE **37**(4), 440–451 (2007). ISSN: 0305-5728
8. Galandare-Zile, I., Vinogradova, V.: Where is the Border Between an Information System and a Knowledge Management System? http://www.fm-kp.si/zalozba/ISSN/1581-6311/3_179-196.pdf
9. Gray, P.M.D., et al.: KRAFT: Knowledge Fusion from Distributed Databases and Knowledge Bases. http://citeseerx.ist.psu.edu/viewdoc/download?doi=10.1.1.31.635&rep=rep1&type=pdf
10. Hassel, J.: 7 Things About SharePoint 2013 All IT Pros Should Know. http://www.cio.com/article/2388447/collaboration/7-things-about-sharepoint-2013-all-it-pros-should-know.html
11. MAIS - home page. http://www.truni.sk/sk/o-projekte
12. Martiško, B.: Slovenské univerzity majú centrálny ekonomický systém. http://arl1.library.sk/arl-umb/m-sk/detail-umb_un_cat-0051967-Slovenske-univerzity-maju-centralny-ekonomicky-system/
13. Moodle - home page. https://docs.moodle.org/28/en/Activities
14. Morey, D., Maybury, M.T., Thuraisingham, B.M.: Knowledge Management: Classic and Contemporary Works. MIT Press, Boston (2002). ISBN 9780262632614
15. Nickerson, R.C.: Business and Information Systems. Prentice Hall, Upper Saddle River (1998)
16. Onedrive - Wikipedia. http://en.wikipedia.org/wiki/OneDrive
17. Patton, M.G.: Evaluation, knowledge management, best practices, and high quality lessons learned. Am. J. Eval. **22**(3), 329–336 (2001)
18. Tom Payne, T., Roets, C., Schlanderer, D.: SAP. http://searchsap.techtarget.com/definition/SAP
19. Siegmanm, R.M.: Information Systems in Universities. http://eric.ed.gov/?id=ED032098
20. Szigeti, G.: Integrácia informačných systémov – pohroma alebo prínos? http://www.itnews.sk/tituly/infoware/2009-10-20/c129737-integracia-informacnych-systemov-pohroma-alebo-prinos
21. Sharif, M.N.A., Zakaria, N.H., Ching, L.S., Fung, L.S.: Facilitating Knowledge Sharing Through Lessons Learned System. http://www.tlainc.com/articl82.htm
22. Závodská, A., Šramová, V., Púčková, K., Kocifajová, L.: Knowledge management tools and their role in doctoral studies. In: Uden, L., Oshee, D.F., Ting, I.-H., Liberona, D. (eds.) KMO 2014. LNBIP, vol. 185, pp. 145–156. Springer, Heidelberg (2014)

# STEM

# An Implementation of a Classroom Lighting System for the Improvement of Learning Efficiency

Hwa-Soo Lee[1], Sook-Youn Kwon[2], Kil Hee Kim[3], Kee-Sun Lee[4], and Jae-Hyun Lim[1(✉)]

[1] Department of Computer Science and Engineering, Kongju National University, Cheonan-si, Korea
{zooey,defacto}@kongju.ac.kr

[2] Green Energy Technology Research Center, Kongju National University, Cheonan-si, Korea
sookyoun@kongju.ac.kr

[3] Department of Architectural Engineering, Kongju National University, Cheonan-si, Korea
kimkh@kongju.ac.kr

[4] Department of Advanced Materials Engineering, Kongju National University, Cheonan-si, Korea
kslee@kongju.ac.kr

**Abstract.** Existing LED-based classroom lighting systems too were designed to adjust color temperature and intensity of illumination, etc. for visual pleasantness and concentration of the teacher and students, but most of them are controlled manually, which causes inconvenience to users. To address this problem, it is necessary to develop an intelligent lighting control system that recognizes the locations and behaviors of the teacher and students automatically by means of sensors; grasps the current class context; and creates appropriate lighting environments accordingly. Thus, this study suggests a classroom lighting system to grasp the current class context to create appropriate lighting environments in recognition of the locations and behaviors of the teacher and students by means of sensors. Based on existing research findings, a standard index for lighting illumination effective for concentration depending on the subjects is designed. LED lighting whose color temperature, intensity of illumination, and on/off switch are adjustable in addition to hybrid sensors for context-awareness is produced. In addition, such elements as learning schedule, current class context, and lighting illumination are monitored real time on a user interface screen, or the lighting combination that the teacher desires is recreated with the learning schedule modifiable accordingly.

## 1 Introduction

Recently, existing fluorescent lamps have been replaced with LED lightings to improve classroom lighting environment, enhance learning efficiency, and reduce energy consumption. LED is a next-generation luminous source that features high efficiency, low power consumption, long lifespan, and eco-friendliness [1–4]. This is highly valuable


L. Uden et al. (Eds.): LTEC 2015, CCIS 533, pp. 245–254, 2015.
DOI: 10.1007/978-3-319-22629-3_20

in that it provides a lighting environment suitable for contexts within a classroom with such factors as color tone, color temperature, and intensity of illumination under precise control.

As for existing fluorescent lamps installed in classrooms, the lifespan is likely to be shortened in proportion to the frequency of blinking while the costs for replacement increase as a result. When used for a long time, fluorescent lamps involve a blackening phenomenon, which lowers the output intensity of illumination or makes the distribution of light imbalanced. As a result, various problems occur such as the deterioration of students' concentration and increase of myopia [5, 6]. Further, as the focus is on improving the intensity of illumination to secure visibility among students, design and construction become standardized, which limits the functional and psychological pleasantness of a lighting environment [7, 8].

Existing classroom lighting systems by means of LED luminous sources make it possible to freely adjust color temperature, intensity of illumination, etc. depending on the types of subjects, as well as enhance the intensity of illumination. In this case, visual pleasantness and concentration are basically improved although the manual controlling method causes inconvenience to most users and disturbs the general flow of classes. Some institutions have demonstrated through experimental researches that providing different lighting environments depending on the subject is effective for better learning efficiency, but the standard index of color temperature ranges appropriate for each class context is not absolute with only few study cases examining the optimal combinations of color temperature and intensity of illumination. Another problem is the lack of technical elements to automatically recognize various possible contexts within a classroom without a user's intervention, which is supposed to minimize the inconvenience of manual control and maximize learning efficiency by reorganizing the lighting environment [2, 6].

This study suggests a classroom lighting system to create the appropriate lighting environment depending on the class context by designing the classroom lighting environment index and learning schedules including such variables as day, time, and subject type and by recognizing the locations of the teacher and students by means of sensors. First of all, the lighting environment indexes such as color temperature, intensity of illumination, etc. are designed depending on the subjects and class types based on existing research findings [2, 6, 9]. Sensors and gateways are created to recognize various class contexts and white LED lightings that can adjust color temperature, intensity of illumination, and on/off switching. In addition, learning schedules that change depending on the day or time, current class contexts that change depending on the occupants' location and behaviors, and light characteristics that change dynamically are monitored real time. Likewise, the teacher may reorganize the combinations of lighting or adjust the learning schedule by means of the user interface functions.

## 2 Classroom Lighting System

The USN(ubiquitous sensor network)-based classroom lighting system suggested in this study consists mainly of the three parts as shown in Fig. 1: the sensor part that recognizes contexts, the LED lighting controlling part, and the monitoring part to check

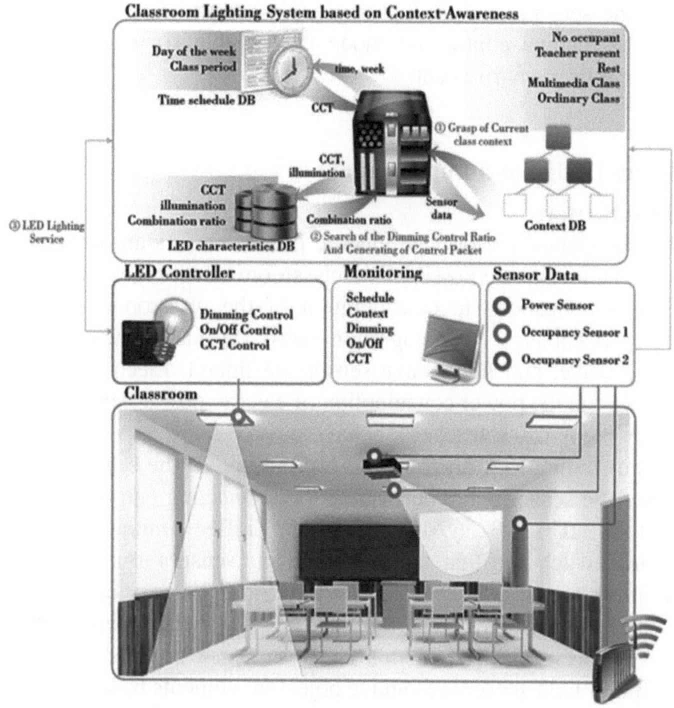


**Fig. 1.** Diagram of the classroom lighting system

the object's lighting environment. The sensor part is divided into the occupancy sensor to grasp the movements of the teacher and students around the blackboard and seats, and the electric power sensor that recognizes the teacher's behaviors by measuring the electric power consumption of devices such as the beam projector. The LED lighting controlling part applies electric signals to lighting fixtures, depending on the packet data transmitted by the server, and controls the lighting environment including color temperature, intensity of illumination, on/off, etc. The communication interface between the controller and sensor of the classroom lighting system is based on ZigBee wireless communication.

To provide the lighting environment services depending on the class context, the suggested system ① grasps the current class context based on the packet data collected from sensors as well as class schedules. ② It searches for the lighting environment standard indexes suitable for the current context such as intensity of illumination, color temperature, etc. from the database, generating controlling packets that include illumination controlling rates corresponding to the indexes from the lighting environment DB of intensity of illumination and color temperature that may change depending on the dimming steps of LED lightings. ③ The generated controlling packets are transmitted to the LED controller and then the intensity of illumination and color temperature changes depending on the lighting environment information contained in the packets. Lastly, the monitoring part checks the learning schedule, the class context as recognized by the sensors, and the lighting environment being currently represented. Additionally, the manual controlling mode is available so that a user can directly reorganize the lighting environment.

## 2.1 Hardware Design and Implementation

### 2.1.1 Hybrid Sensors

In this study, occupancy sensors and electric power sensors are utilized to recognize various class contexts that are possible in a classroom environment. Occupancy sensors are set at selected locations in consideration of the classroom area and structural characteristics. To enhance the recognition rates, various elements such as infrared light, ultrasonic wave, and microwave sensor are linked. Electric power sensors are employed to measure the power consumption of electric power devices such as lighting fixture and they recognize a teacher's behaviors.

Figure 2 shows the block diagram and a prototype of the sensor board for human body detection. The sensor board consists of the connecting part of various occupancy sensors, 32 bit AT32UC3B0256 MCU of Atmel, ZigBee communication part, context indicator, setting switch part that supports adjusting sensors to a switch type, and the power distribution part of a DC constant power and 9 V batteries.

Table 1 shows the hardware characteristics of the infrared light, ultrasonic wave, and microwave sensors utilized in this study to sense occupants' movements in a classroom. Infrared light sensors recognize object movements based on the temperature difference between recognized objects and surroundings. Although they are widely utilized because of the easiness of manufacturing and low costs, the recognition rates might not be sufficient when an object's movement is insignificant or there is little difference in temperature from the surrounding. Further, as shown in Fig. 3, the sensing angles and distances may be varied depending on the types of Fresnel lenses, and thus the lens types need to be selected in consideration of the object space's area and characteristics.

Figure 3 shows the block diagram and a sample of the electric power sensor designed to recognize a teacher's behaviors and measure the power consumption of lighting fixtures. The electric power sensor receives control commands from the server through Zigbee communication interface, processes them by means of 32 bit

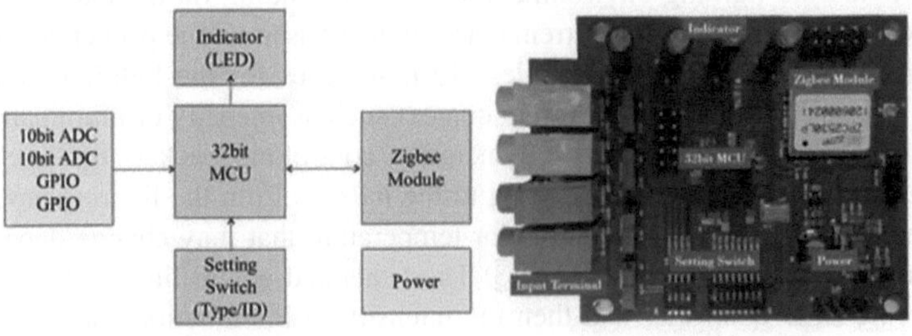


(a) Block Diagram (b) Prototype

**Fig. 2.** An occupancy sensor board

**Table 1.** Hardware characteristics of occupancy sensors

| Type | Photo | Model Name | Range of Recognition | Voltage or Frequency | Temper-ature |
|---|---|---|---|---|---|
| Infrared light sensor | 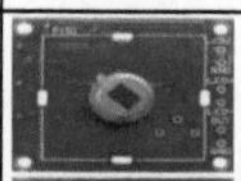 | APS002 | (Angle) 100°<br>(Distance)7m | 3V - 6V | -20° to +75° |
| Ultrasonic sensor |  | NT-TS601 | (Distance)<br>2cm-3.3m | 40hKz | -0° to +70° |
| Micro-wave sensor |  | DNS-010 | (Distance)<br>8m-15m | 5V | -20° to +55° |

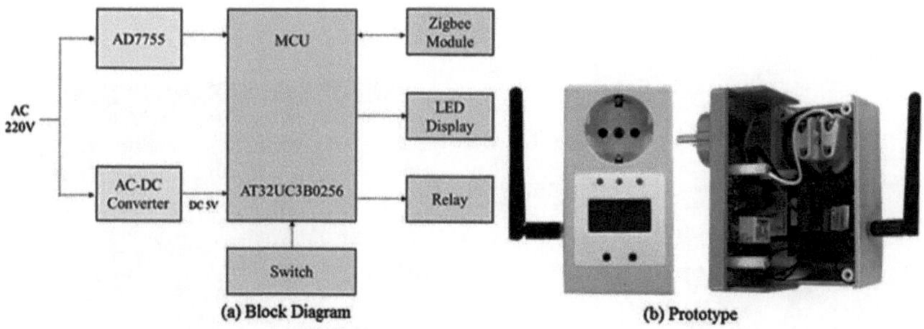


**Fig. 3.** Behavior-recognizing electric power sensor

AT32UC3B0256 MCU of Atmel and AD7755 chip of Energy Metering IC, and turns the electric devices on/off by means of a relay.

### 2.1.2 LED Lighting and Controller

In this study, LED lighting fixtures and controller are designed and produced for optical characteristics such as color temperature and intensity of illumination, as well as on/off switching, so that various classroom lighting environments can be created. Table 2 shows the hardware characteristics of LED lightings designed in this study. 256 Warm White LED luminous sources and 256 Cool White LED luminous sources in total are designed and produced. The intensity of illumination ranges from 0 to 1,089 lx, along with color temperature from 2,635 to 5,718 K.

Figure 4 shows the block diagram and a sample of the LED lighting controller. Luminous sources are controlled in the way of Pulse Width Modulation (PWM), which features easy control as the current output of a controller is in a linear proportion to the duty ratio. A controller's MCU generates pulse signals upon a user's lighting controlling command, delivers the signals to two channels (Warm White LED and Cool White LED) and the LED driver, and thus controls the lighting fixtures and luminous

**Table 2.** Hardware characteristics of white LED lighting fixtures and controller

| Class. | Detail | Photo |
|---|---|---|
| Types of Luminous Sources | Warm White LED and Cool White LED |  |
| Quantity of Luminous Sources | Warm White LED 256ea, Cool White LED 256ea | |
| Controlling Elements | Color temperature, intensity of illumination, On/Off | |
| Controlling Range | Intensity of illumination 0-1,000lx<br>Color temperature 2,000-6,000K | |
| Power Type | Double 50W SMPS, constant power supply | |
| Installation Type | fixed on the ceiling | |

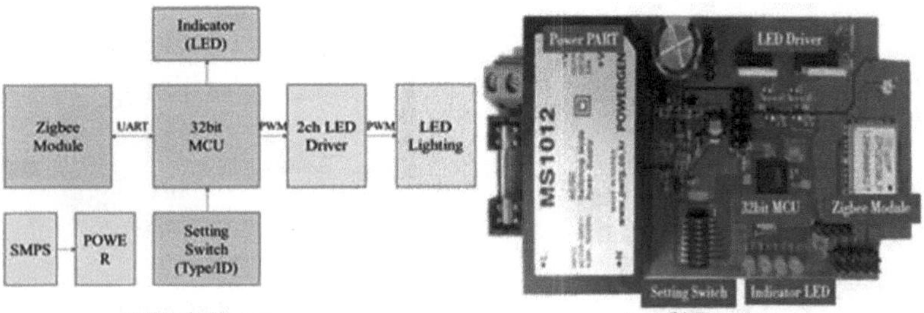


(a) Block Diagram (b) Prototype

**Fig. 4.** A LED lighting controller

sources. It is possible to check the data transmission through LED Indicators. The types of object LED luminous sources are also set by means of the Setting Switch.

In this study, an actual measurement experiment is conducted in a lighting cabinet of 1.28 m × 1.28 m × 2.08 m to save in a database white LED lighting fixture conditions that will change depending on dimming steps such as intensity of illumination and color temperature. Figure 5 shows the patterns of intensity of illumination and color temperature that change as the dimming levels of the Warm White LED and Cool White LED luminous sources are changed at intervals of 10 from 0 to 255. The intensity of illumination ranges from 0 to 1,089 lx, along with the color temperature from 2,635 to 5,718 K. As shown in the graph, as the dimming steps of Warm White LED luminous sources increase depending on the characteristics of the luminous source, the intensity of illumination increases accordingly while the color temperature decreases. As the dimming steps of Cool White LED increase, both the intensity of illumination and color temperature increases.

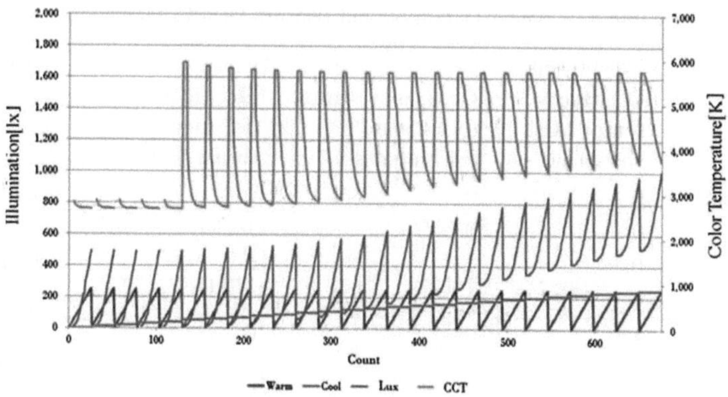


**Fig. 5.** Changes in the intensity of illumination and color temperature depending on the dimming steps of LED lightings (Color figure online)

## 2.2 Lighting Environment Indexes and Sensing Data Combination

In this study, the lighting environment indexes, as shown in Table 3, are designed in consideration of KS Illumination Standard [10], Kruithof's Comfort Curve [11] and existing research findings, in reference to the 2009 Amendment of the Education Act, and for subjects under different categories: language/memorizing (Korean, social studies/ ethics, English), mathematics (mathematics, science/practical courses), Physical Education (P.E.), arts (music/fine arts), and resting time. As for the language/memorizing area, the color temperature was set to 4,000 K – 5,000 K and an intensity of illumination of 400 lx; as for mathematics, a color temperature of 5,000 K – 6,000 K and an intensity of illumination of 600 lx; and as for arts and resting time, a color temperature of 3,000 K – 4,000 K and an intensity of illumination of 300 lx to ease the tension and create relaxed atmospheres.

**Table 3.** Lighting environment indexes of the suggested system

| Area | Subject | Color Temperature [K] | Intensity of Illumination [lx] |
|---|---|---|---|
| Language/Memorizing | Korean | 4,000–5,000 | 400 |
| | Social Studies/Ethics | | |
| | English | | |
| Mathematics | Mathematics | 5,000–6,000 | 600 |
| | Science/Practical Courses | | |
| P.E. | P.E. | | |
| Arts | Music | 3,000–4,000 | 300 |
| | Fine Arts | | |
| Rest | Break Time | | |
| | Lunch Time | | |

**Table 4.** Context Definition and Sensing Data Combination

| Context | Sensor Type | | | Service |
|---|---|---|---|---|
| | Occupancy sensor (desk and chair) | Occupancy sensor (blackboard or teaching desk) | Electric power detection sensor (beam projector) | |
| No occupant | 0 | 0 | 0 | Light Off |
| | 0 | 0 | 1 | |
| Teacher present | 0 | 1 | 0 | Ordinary lighting |
| | 0 | 1 | 1 | |
| Rest | 1 | 0 | 0 | Context lighting |
| Class (multimedia) | 1 | 0 | 1 | Context lighting and some light off |
| | 1 | 1 | 1 | |
| Class (ordinary) | 1 | 1 | 0 | Context lighting |

Table 4 below defines five possible situations in a classroom: no occupant, a teacher present, rest, class (multimedia), and class (common class). It also shows combinations of sensor data sets to recognize such contexts. When a sensor fails recognizing teachers' or students' movements, it is interpreted that there is no object within the classroom that needs lighting service and thus all lightings are turned off. In this case, as devices such as beam projector may be still on even if there is no occupant, the service is stopped with this viewed as an exceptional situation. When only a teacher's movement is recognized with no students sensed, it is viewed as a context other than a class and the common lighting is provided: 5000 K of color temperature and 400 lx of the intensity of illumination. When only students' movement is recognized, it is viewed as "rest" in reference to the learning schedule while a comfortable lighting environment is created to ease the tension. When both a teacher's and students' movements are sensed, a class context is signaled. Thus, a lighting service for the current class context is provided in reference to the learning schedule and lighting environment indexes. When the electric power sensor recognizes beam projector operation, it is viewed as a class context of multimedia-based video watching or presentation and the lightings over the blackboard and teaching desk are turned off with lighting environment suitable for multimedia-based watching.

## 2.3 User Interface

The user interface screen of the suggested system includes the real time monitoring of the current lighting environment, LED control function for manual adjustment of lighting environment according to a user's input, and learning schedule setting timetable that specifies such variables as day, time, and subject (See Fig. 6). The monitoring tab displays real time subject types, current class contexts, and lighting environment

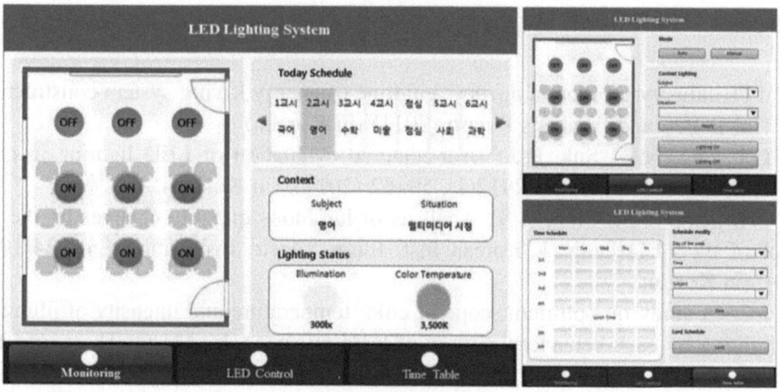


**Fig. 6.** User interface of classroom lighting system

information such as changing color temperature and intensity of illumination based on learning schedule information. The LED control tab provides the dual –automatic and manual –mode so that the lighting environment can be adjusted not only by the automatic control system but also manually by a user. The timetable tab includes the function for a user to modify the learning schedule, as well as other basic functions such as addition, edition, and deletion of certain days, times, and subjects.

## 3 Conclusions

This study aims to design and embody a classroom lighting system to recognize locations and behaviors of a teacher and students in a classroom environment according to the learning schedule and to provide appropriate lighting environment. To this end, lighting environment indexes, such as color temperature and intensity of illumination, are designed depending on the subject and class types in reference to existing research findings. A hybrid type of sensors for context-awareness, white LED lighting fixtures that can control color temperature, intensity of illumination, and on/off switching, controller, and gateway for data transmission are developed. In addition, the current subject type, class type, and lighting environment (color temperature, intensity of illumination) are monitored real time through the user interface screen. A user can adjust the lighting environment and learning schedule as he/she wants. In the future, not only the lighting environment but also learning achievement of students should be evaluated in application of the suggested system to actual classroom contexts. In addition, researches on lighting environment indexes in consideration of various age groups of students need to be conducted.

**Acknowledgments.** This research was supported by Basic Science Research Program through the National Research Foundation of Korea (NRF) funded by the Ministry of Education (2009-0093825). This work was supported by the National Research Foundation of Korea (NRF) grant funded by the Korea government (MSIP) (No. 2014R1A2A1A11054509).

## References


1. Natural IT industry promotion agency: guidline of energy saving system construction based on IT. In: Policy and Analysis Report (2011) (in Korean)
2. Park, G.L., Na, N.R., Suk, H.J.: User-centered evaluation of LED lighting in classroom. Proc. Korea Soc. Public Des. **2012**(1), 59–62 (2012). (in Korean)
3. Jang, I.H., Kim, Y.S., Choi, A.S.: Analysis of luminous quantity changes by the dimming control of the LED lamp. J. Korean Inst. Illum. Electr. Installation Eng. **24**(10), 13–20 (2010). (in Korean)
4. Jung, J.C.: A study on optimum scope of color temperature and intensity of illumination of LED lighting by each behavioral pattern of learning space. In: Master Thesis of Chungnam University (2012) (in Korean)
5. An, Y.K., Choi, H.K., Lee, G.M., Park, S.W., Yoon, C.G., Lee, J.E.: Fluorescent lighting equipment which has a lamp shift timely display device. Proc. Korean Inst. Illum. Electr. Installation Eng. **24**(10), 13–20 (2008). (in Korean)
6. Jee, S.D., Kim, C.B.: Subjective evaluation on the color temperatures of LED illumination in the classroom. J. Korean Inst. Illum. Electr. Installation Eng. **25**(1), 30–41 (2011). (in Korean)
7. Kim, J.G., Kim, H.: A study on the analysis of relations between classroom illumination and variation of the students' eyesight and improvement of the classroom illumination in primary school. J. Korean Inst. Illum. Electr. Installation Eng. **19**(1), 15–23 (2005). (in Korean)
8. Im, K.M., Lim, J.H.: Context lighting system for intelligent self-regulation process control. J. Green Home Energy Technol. Kongju Natl Univ. **2**, 51–57 (2012). (in Korean)
9. Philips: SchoolVision (2010) http://www.lighting.philips.co.uk/
10. Gil, J.S., Kim, H.: A study on the concept of classroom simple lighting platform lighting system. Proc. Korean Inst. Illum. Electr. Installation Eng. **2012**(5), 3–4 (2012). (in Korean)
11. Chain, C., Dumortier, D., Fontoynont, M.: A comprehensive model of luminance, correlated colour temperature and spectral distrubution of skylight:comparison with experimental data. J. Solar Energy **65**(5), 285–295 (1999)

# E-learning Intervention for Stem Education: Developing Country Case Study

Hitendra Pillay[1(✉)] and Werner Kappus[2]

[1] Queensland University of Technology, Brisbane, Australia
h.pillay@qut.edu.au
[2] Education Consultant, Apia, Samoa

**Abstract.** This paper reports an innovative and systemic approach to implementing ICT intervention to support enhancement of teaching and learning of STEM subjects in developing countries. The need for adopting ICT was 2 fold: a lack of availability of qualified STEM secondary teachers and a lack of quality teaching and learning resources to assist teachers and students. ICT was seen as being able to impact on both issues. The intervention involved developing sustainable network design including equipment choices, providing high quality e-learning resources and human resource development including teacher training. The intervention has gradually been accepted by teachers, students, and parents and institutionalized as a key feature of the secondary STEM education in the case study country.

**Keywords:** Electronic learning · Learning center design · E-learning resources · New learning technology

## 1 Global ICT Trends and Background

E-learning is thought to be one of the fastest growing industries and has been frequently heralded as a transforming influence on education systems globally [1]. The challenge of adoption, diffusion and exploitation have been explored by Martin et al., [2] by drawing on an increasingly influential body of management literature on the absorptive capacity (ACAP) of organizations to acquire, assimilate and use new technologies and ideas. One of the key recommendations of Martin et al., is to adopt a systematic approach involving the unique organization of forms, ideas and human resource development approaches into an integrated education ICT system. While dispersed models, adopting a bottom-up approach such as project-based and teacher-led interventions seen in many ICT for education development projects [3], can be useful as a complementing approach, they may not be sufficient to sustain and grow a nationwide, equity-based e-learning system. Thus, there is a need to consider a coordinated, top-down as well as bottom-up intervention. Further, such intervention must support organic capacity development and engagement and be supported by international and national empirical research and evidence-based practices.


L. Uden et al. (Eds.): LTEC 2015, CCIS 533, pp. 255–267, 2015.
DOI: 10.1007/978-3-319-22629-3_21

## 2 Context of the Case

The case study site is a pacific island nation with a population of approximately 190,000 people. It has 40 secondary schools, all of which offer science and mathematics subjects. Historically, attracting good STEM teachers has been a challenge for the case study country due to unattractive job conditions, including remunerations. This is confounded by the small number of local science graduates entering the workforce each year. It creates a high demand for science graduates with better work conditions (including graduate science teachers) across all sectors including private sector employers. The government has tried directly recruiting STEM teachers from abroad (India and Philippines), using the US peace-corps volunteers, and using international donor support to convert teachers from other subject specializations to teach STEM subjects. All these efforts have had limited success. The high turn-over of well qualified teachers and limited availability of STEM teaching/learning resources further aggravates the situation. Given the innovations in interactive design and the versatility and ubiquity of ICT, a robust ICT system can provide interactive learning opportunities and simulations of complex STEM concepts in a user-friendly manner to supplement the teaching of STEM students and also help teachers to continuously upgrade their own STEM knowledge. Students can use the same e-resources for self-directed learning to practice and rehearse their learning. Often ICT interventions in development projects target only teachers, whereas it is imperative that the focus is on the students and their learning in order to improve students learning outcomes. Teachers are important, but they are only a means to an end; dispositions like self-directed and lifelong learning are the hallmarks of $21^{st}$ century education and its important that both teachers and student develop this new learning dispositions. The main objective of the intervention described in this report was to enhance the quality of STEM secondary education at this site and improve students' learning outcomes. This was achieved through the ubiquity of ICT-based learning and well-thought-out, systematically embedded ICT in the teaching and learning of STEM subjects to directly improve STEM learning outcomes.

## 3 Units of Analysis Within the Case

Against the above background, the approach adopted for the present case study was influenced by global contemporary ICT intervention research and implementation experiences. It is apparent that ICT intervention goes through a series of phases, as noted by Pillay [4]. Plomp et al. [3], also report similar trends in the country-specific chapters of their edited book. Figure 1 illustrates the key factors (ICT equipment and devices, access to connectivity such as WAN and internet, educators—teachers, curriculum e-resource developers, e-learning resources, etc.) and their progressive influence from 2005 to 2009 on the adoption of ICT in school education. This pattern is continuing and, in recent years, has attracted both private and public sector stakeholders in developing e-learning resources, which proves to be the most significant influence on the adoption of ICT in schools. These factors were used as units of analysis in the case study.

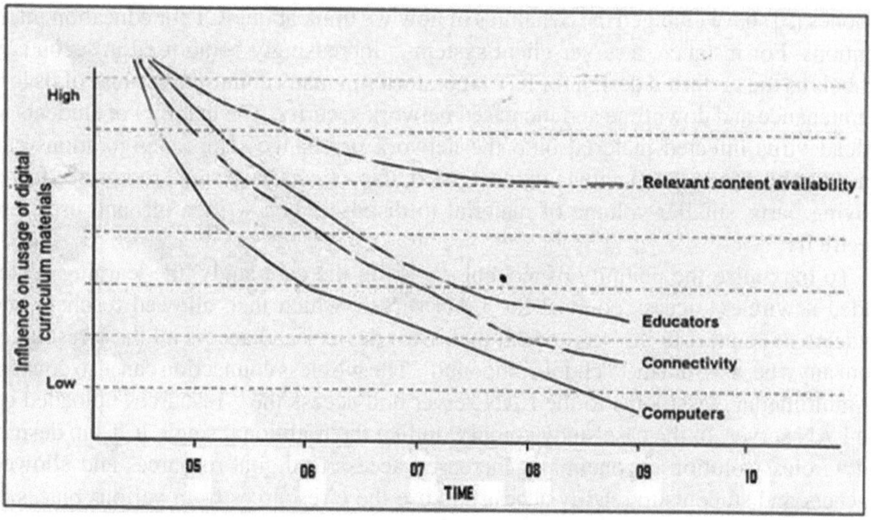


**Fig. 1.** Influence of key ICT factors on use of e-learning/digital learning. Adopted from Pillay [4]

The next sections discuss how the four units of analysis were adopted into secondary school teaching and learning globally and their influence on the adoption of ICT for STEM education in the present case study.

# 4 Computer Equipment for the Laboratory

The first unit of analysis is the provision of computer equipment in school laboratories. Traditionally, the supply of ICT equipment meant the provision of desktop computers, connected either as peer-to-peer or as a LAN, in a laboratory. Access/supply of equipment is gradually increasing through various means such as direct government interventions like student loan schemes, tax incentives and subsidies to teachers, diaspora and international community support, INGO and NGO support, private sector donations when upgrading in-house equipment, and international donor partners. In the case study country, the availability of access devices has increased exponentially in recent years, triggered by cheap communication options through emails and VoIP. The large diaspora living in neighboring countries like Australia, New Zealand and the USA often provide personal ICT devices to relatives in the case study country to stay connected with families.

Furthermore, innovations in new IT product development and increased competition has seen the ICT landscape changing rapidly in the island nation since 2011. There are three telecommunication providers and about a dozen IT equipment retailers on the island which have helped bring down prices of ICT equipment considerably and have led to new ways of providing access to e-learning. IT equipment and technology solutions through wireless connectivity within and across school ICT learning centers (in addition to new models of classroom setups such as server-client design, tablet and iPhones [5]) have changed the dynamics of how we think about ICT for education interventions. For instance, a server-client system is increasingly being used in secondary schools as the preferred design for ICT laboratories in many countries because of its low maintenance and downtime and increased network security. The inability of students to upload virus infected material onto the network or change setup configurations can considerably lower the maintenance cost. Also, *thin-clients* have small footprints, fewer moving parts, smaller volume of material to dispose when written off, and uses less electricity.

To maximize the ubiquity of technology [5] in the case study, the learning center added a wireless access point at the LAN server, which then allowed teachers and students to connect to the server with their own devices and access all the e-resources from anywhere within the 'school compound'. The wireless connection can also connect all multimedia classrooms to the LAN server and access the e-resources uploaded on the LAN server. In the case study country, unlike the traditional single ICT lab design, the wireless solution exponentially increased access to digital resources and allowed teachers and students to readily access and use the e-resources from various places in the school other than the ICT learning center.

Similarly, ICT display solutions are now increasingly using LCD monitors rather than traditional multimedia projectors. The decreasing cost of LCDs, low power consumption and low maintenance all make the LCD monitors the preferred option. Mobile device such as mobile thin-client, laptops, tablets etc., can be used to connect access and display e-resources on the LCD monitors.

After undertaking considerable desk-research on ICT systems deployed for schoolnet, community learning centers, and rural ICT hubs for businesses in Africa, South and South East Asian countries, the case study country adopted the server-client system for the school ICT learning centers. After 3 years since the procurement and setting up the chosen of ICT system has confirmed its robustness as there were minimal teaching issues and the system has been running extremely well.

## 5 Connectivity

This brings us to the second unit of analysis, which is connectivity. E-learning/digital learning can be delivered through either LAN, WAN or through an internet-based network. Internet connectivity becomes necessary when you need to access materials from the World Wide Web (WWW), which is a global database of all types of information. A LAN and WAN also require connecting to a database where the e-resources are stored, but this database can be located at either the school level (LAN) or at central Ministry of Education level (WAN). Both of these may be achieved without going through the internet, which makes it more cost effective and can significantly increase the access speed. Given the similarity of the two ICT environments (LAN and Internet) the skills developed when using LAN can be easily transferred to the internet environment. Access to the internet in most developing countries is generally low (but is steadily improving), has varied quality of service, and is expensive. The International Telecommunication Union report [6] notes that, apart from the internet penetration being low in most developing country, it was concentrated only in the larger metropolitan areas and the quality of service was still varied. Therefore when designing for connectivity certain key questions were asked.

- What is the purpose of connectivity?
- What and how information will be accessed and used by teachers and students?
- Where and how will the e-learning materials be hosted?
- How do you want to access the information - synchronous/asynchronous?
- How many people will access simultaneously?

As noted in the ICT equipment unit of analysis, if a LAN system is adopted connectivity can be extended beyond the learning center via wireless access to cover the school compound thus access can be exponentially increased. If rural teachers and students have to access e-learning resources from a server in capital cities via a slow speed internet, it could be very slow and frustrating, making it impractical. However, if rural schools have electricity, it should be sufficient to run a LAN and let children enjoy the use of e-learning.

Therefore, when considering connectivity with regard to ICT for education, it is necessary to be mindful that connectivity is not about providing access to internet - that should be the aim of the Ministry for Telecommunication, not the education sector; the education sector should focus on providing e-resources to enhance student learning.

Figure 2 illustrates the LAN network design adopted by the case study country. To extend the LAN to a WAN a simple internet access point may be connected to he server which will open access to the internet from all thin client terminals. The value in opened access to the internet and WAN will be dependent upon the cost and

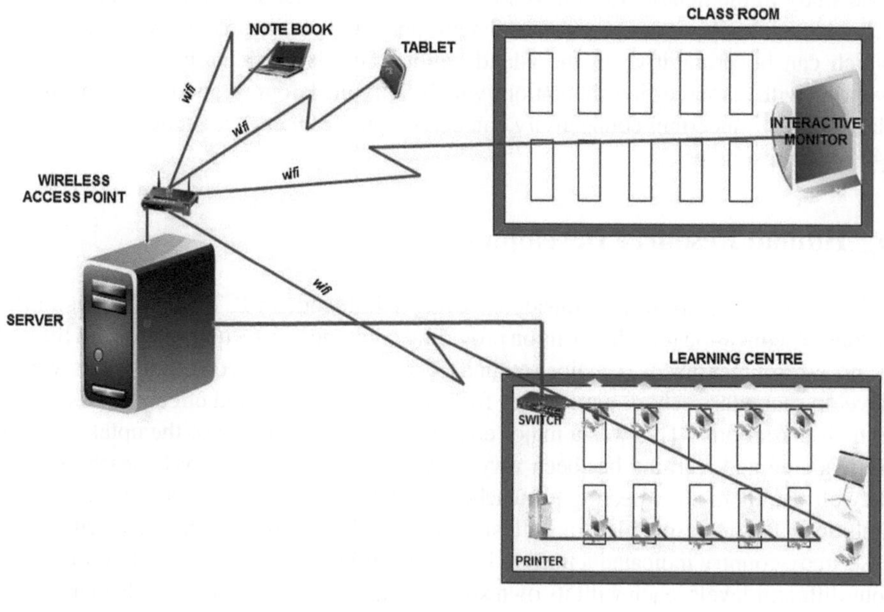


**Fig. 2.** The LAN design

quality of service. For the case study site WAN was a possibility but internet costs were very high.

Another advantage of setting up a LAN or a WAN is that access to the Internet can be managed and monitored. Using a Star WAN network design, all traffic on the WAN comes to a single gateway to access the internet. This assists the Ministry of Education and schools in their duty of care to ensure children are not exposed to undesirable sites on the WWW. Providing access to the internet needs to consider risks and parental anxiety regarding the types of sites their children could be accessing. In the case reported here, community consultation workshops were held to explain how the LAN/WAN systems operated separately to the internet. This approach eventually relaxed the strong resistance to using e-learning. The Star design allowed firewalls and filters to be set at the single gateway to manage and monitor access to undesirable sites.

A common confusion with e-learning is that it is often aligned with 'internet'. The strengths of digital learning and e-resources can be found in the new teaching learning processes such as *visualization, simulation, interactive, repetition and practice, and self-directed learning.* The internet has plenty of information that may be useful to secondary teachers and students, but equally there is a vast amount of information that is not useful at all. Even in developed countries, teachers lack the time or the funds for extended hours to surf the internet to collect appropriate teaching learning resources [7]. The issue of internet access from rural areas and the speed of connectivity also confound the issue of internet access. All of the above constraints were evident in the case-study country. Consequently, the above noted LAN design, with all e-resources uploaded to a server in every individual school, was implemented and found to be very successful in terms of stability of the system, speed and ease of access to the learning materials.

In light of the above discussions, and in consultation with IT industry experts, the case study implementors agreed to host the learning material on a LAN server at the school level. It allowed easy access and high speed without incurring any internet costs, which can be prohibitive in the island nation. This is particularly important when working with resource-rich simulations which are typical of most good e-learning materials. Slow or uncertain connectivity can demotivate teachers and students from using e-learning resources.

## 6 Human Resource Development

ICT equipment is no longer considered a major influence in ICT interventions in the secondary education thus the focus on providing computer labs (equipment) with limited or no e-resources needs a major rethink [3, 4]. It was assumed that teachers would develop secondary school e-resources for respective subjects and effectively use them in their classrooms. This was a major error in judgement and hence the uptake of ICT for teaching and learning has been very slow. All teachers do not write textbooks but they all use them so expecting all teachers to develop their e-learning resources was ambitious and unreasonable. An analysis of the baseline human resource capacity in the case study country indicated a need to have appropriately qualified human resources at four different levels, each with its own specific training needs. These levels include the teachers' competency in using e-learning resources in the classroom (teachers are not expected to develop e-resources); the head teachers' ability to manage e-learning facilities effectively to maximize utilization, community awareness, and IT administrators to provide 'back-end' maintenance support.

The main capacity development that occurred in the majority of the ICT intervention programs was in the basic ICT skills, like the International ICT driver's license (very basic computer skills to familiarize teachers with the functions of a computer and some exposure to productivity software applications such as MS Word, MS Excel). This type of basic IT skill training is rapidly becoming obsolete, as was the seen in the case study country. The teacher training in the case study focused on how to use ICT resources in their classrooms rather than basic IT skills. The delivery modalities of the training program have also evolved due to the one-off, intensive training provided in most ICT intervention programs often causing 'information overload' and not being considered effective [8]. A hard or soft copy of the training manual may help as reference material for reflection when the teacher returns to their school after intensive group training. In the case study country, the training was not sufficient given the teachers' low level of STEM knowledge and skills. Regular school-based coaching was provided over a 2 year period to supplement the intensive training.

The training for school-level ICT administrators is critical for the sustainability of the investments, but it is often overlooked. It is a necessary capacity development at the school level and the training is about first level technical trouble shooting and not pedagogical issues. Consequently, in the case study this was developed and delivered by people who have deep ICT knowledge in maintenance and backend support. This training is not intended for all teachers, it is for a selected two or three teachers from each school who have sufficient base knowledge of ICT 'systems' and can do the basic level of trouble shooting. The ministry of education in case study country anticipates that, as school libraries transform to information hubs, this role will be integrated with the school librarian.

The community awareness training sessions were necessary to obtain the support of the parents and the school community and were conducted as workshops to encourage open conversations. The case study country has a strong Christian ethos and the church is a major stakeholder (manages 20 % of the secondary schools in the country), with significant influence on education policy issues including adoption of e-learning. These workshops were conducted on the different islands and villages to illustrate the security built in the design, the value of the e-resources (in terms of both cost and for learning outcomes) and the need for financial planning to ensure sustainability. A cost modeling was undertaken to provide a medium-term expenditure framework to illustrate the cost implication to the community and to secure their continue support. The cost modeling was also used for advising the Ministry of Education for appropriate budget allocations.

Traditionally, ICT learning centers (LC) become computer laboratories for teaching computer science. To change the mindset to the ICT learning center as a library with interactive e-resources for all STEM teachers requires capacity-building of school principals in order for them to maximize the use of the ICT learning centers. In the case study, the principals were shown ways to encourage the use of LC and the use of e-resource during the allocated teaching times for STEM subjects plus making the learning center accessible during lunch and after school. Teachers volunteered to keep an oversight during non-class times. This is a huge shift from the traditional practice of closing the school after school day finishes or keeping children out of the LC during their free time. The above was possible only after considerable capacity development of the school principals and, toward the end, the LC were heavily subscribed by both STEM teachers as well as students. This was only possible after the principals were convinced that there was value in changing the traditional rules and opening access to the learning centers.

Perhaps the most significant and continuous capacity development was with the STEM teachers. As noted earlier, the STEM subject content knowledge of the teachers was very limited. Thus, the training was not merely focused on using e-resources, but developing all subject content competencies. A team of coaches were recruited who visited schools on a regular basis to work in situ with teachers, embedding the e-resource in their regular classes. This approach was found to be more effective than the traditional approach of bringing the teachers to a central site and provide a 2/3 weeks training. This situated learning approach [9] helped the knowledge to be directly linked to their everyday practices. It also prevented the removal of teachers from their classrooms when, often, there are no replacements and children lost 2/3 week of learning opportunities. The regular visits provided constructive feedback and optional strategies for teachers to trial in their classrooms. Initially, only a few schools and teachers were keen to participate, but after 2 years of support from the coaches, the majority of the schools and teachers incorporated class activities that used e-resource in their teaching and learning.

## 7 e-Resources, Digital Content, e-Learning Materials

The final unit of analysis noted in Fig. 1 is the learning content. This is often interchangeably referred to as e-resources, digital content, e-learning materials and e-learning content. Unfortunately, despite the high influence learning content has on adoption of e-learning [10], the majority of the intervention projects have not given much attention to this. Many projects adopt and advocate teacher-led development of e-resources [11]. As note earlier, while this may be good to empower and build teachers' confidence, the resources will not be as good as those developed by professionals[1] and will not be comprehensive enough to be adopted by a national repository. Teacher-developed digital content, and other open source materials, can be uploaded onto a common national repository as supplementary material. A review

[1] E-learning resources are now replacing textbooks and other commonly used supplementary teaching and learning materials. Publishing companies and other private sector ICT content development companies are now involved in developing high quality e-learning resources organized as a repository indexed to the secondary school curriculum. They contain general instruction on respective topics, simulations, experiment and interactive activities, quizzes etc. These c-learning materials can be used as teacher facilitated activities, self-learning, group and peer learning etc., and the design is underpinned by new teaching learning processes such as visualization, simulation, interactive, repetition and practice, self-directed.

of countries that supported teacher-developed digital content revealed, as expected, simple and very limited material, the majority perhaps appropriate for an individual teacher's needs. Furthermore, in most developing countries teachers are not given sufficient time to produce digital content and they have had limited exposure to examples of high quality e-resources. Even if teachers have ICT skills, tools, and time, limited access to more specialized software can severely hinder the progress which, in turn, can hinder the country's progress in the significant integration ICT in secondary education. It can take many years before an acceptable quality of repository can be developed from teacher-developed resources. This could disadvantage generations of secondary school students—particularly in light of the shortage of STEM teachers.

Developing a high quality, comprehensive repository of e-learning resources is not easy and requires specialized skills. It is not simply a collection of materials developed by teachers and/or materials collected from the internet. The material needs to be standardized, have simple and consistent operational interface, and be indexed to school curriculum. The repository is deliberately and professionally developed and takes advantage of the special ICT capacities such as visualization for abstract concepts; simulations for dynamic and interactive learning; new, student centered and self-learning pedagogies; and mapping appropriate content for the various subjects and topics from the secondary school curriculum.

In recognition of the above, there is an increased interest in developing repositories for specific purposes [12]. Specific purpose repositories also help to efficiently deal with the exponential growth of information (varified plus opinions) on the WWW. Spending hours shifting through the vast information and yet not finding useful information can be demotivating and slow the uptake of e-learning. There are open access and proprietary repositories available for secondary school STEM subjects which can be negotiated and procured for very cost effective prices. The adoption of creative commons licensing agreements provide options for legally using e-resource development by others. Reinventing the wheel is no longer necessary and neither is it efficient or effective.

The hosting platform of these repositories are also complex. Good propriety platforms have flexibility to accommodate other high quality and relevant e-learning materials sourced from the internet and adapted for local context, plus quality assured teacher-developed materials. An example of a national repository procured and adapted for the case study country is shown in Fig. 3. As can be seen, there is no clutter, it save teachers time, and teachers and students can go directly to the e-learning materials—which is the central purpose of this e-learning repository. It has a mix of professionally developed propriety materials, which are listed on the far right side of the simulation box. Materials collected from other sources such as the PhET interactive simulations [13], English language materials acquired from the British Council, school text books, and past examination papers and quizzes are uploaded to the same repository.

After considerable discussion the Ministry of Education and local ICT stakeholders it was agreed that a high quality repository or e-resources should be procured adapted and provided to all secondary schools. The comprehensive repository of e-resources increased teachers motivation and leap-frogged the ICT inventions in teaching and learning in this particular case study country.

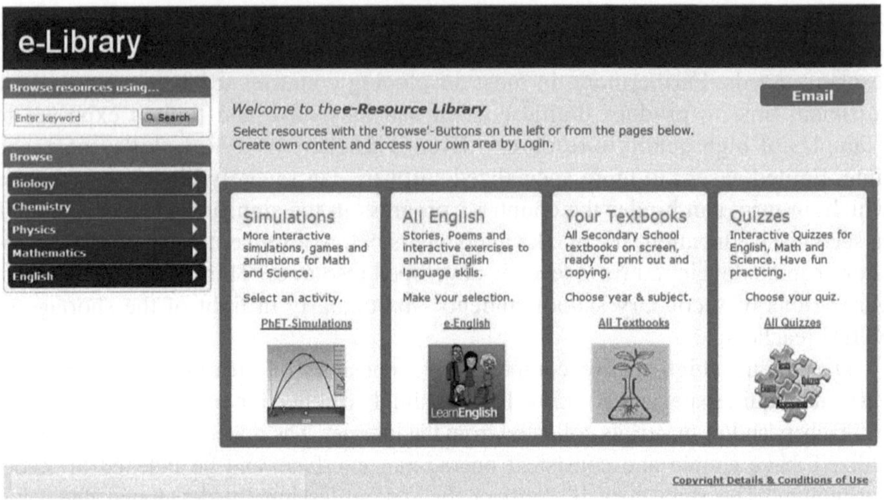


**Fig. 3.** National e-Library repository

Furthermore, the learning content in the e-library above is indexed to topics from the national secondary STEM curriculum, by grade level, organized by subject and topic level to avoid teachers having to navigate through huge amounts of information. It is all carefully organized in a single repository which is uploaded to the school LAN server to ensure quick and easy access. The screen capture (Fig. 4) shows the scope and coverage of the e-learning resource used in the case study. There are two more sub layers of e-resource for each topic noted in the screen capture. Each folder has a list of sub areas as shown for the topic 'Forces', which is further deconstructed into specific e-learning activities. Each specific e-learning activity includes instructional materials,

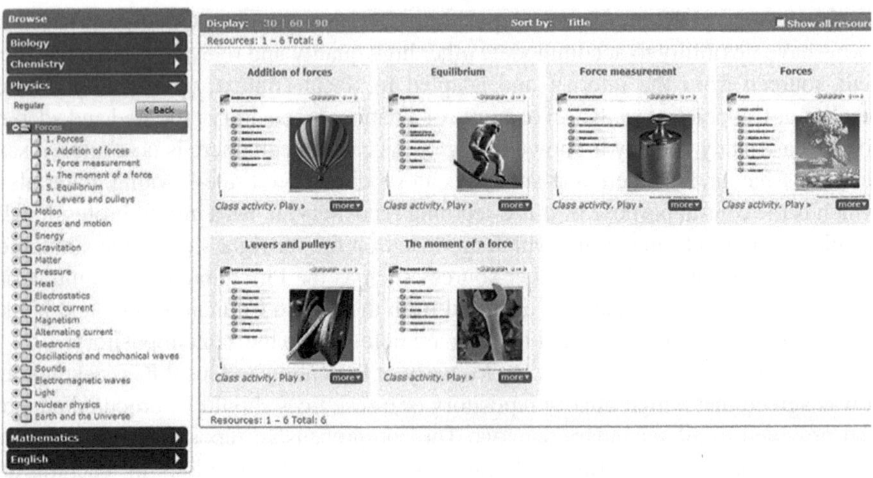


**Fig. 4.** Example of the topic 'forces'

simulations, activities, tests etc. Considering the limited discipline knowledge of the local STEM teachers, such organized and one-stop-shop design was found to be very useful for teachers to rehearse their knowledge and prepare classroom teaching.

## 8 Cost Analysis and Procurement

Most governments in developing countries provide text books at a cost to the government. E-Resources are no different. However, the return on investment in e-resource is far greater than text books. The e-resources can be used by several cohorts of secondary students (grade 9–12), whereas test books typically last 2 years in rainy, humid climates. If one computes the unit cost of the e-resources when 2–3 cohorts of grades 9–12 student have used it, it is very low. In the situation of the case study country it was approximately $2.50 per child.

There are various options regarding how one may procure a commercial e-resource repository.[2] Many curators are willing to give online access, but the internet cost and the quality of service prevented the case study country accepting this option. Instead a perpetual server license was considered. It involves a one-time cost but the repository can be uploaded to the servers only. It cannot be accessed via the internet[3] and often cost may be determined by the number of servers you wish to upload to. A perpetual license means after the one-time cost, the government will own the e-resource subject to the use policy agreed under the procurement contract.

## 9 Final Thoughts

The ubiquitous nature of learning and the rapidly evolving technology present a complex and often confusing challenge for education sector development. ICT for education has many, more direct, educational values other than using the internet to access the vast information available on the WWW. Instead of waiting for internet with reasonable speed and affordable pricing, a staged approach as illustrated in this case study, using LAN and progressively linking to WAN and the internet, as connectivity gets better can be started immediately. This can happen in rural areas as well as long as there is electricity. As noted in Fig. 1 the connectivity is a means to and end the limited education resources available to children, particularly in rural areas even on a LAN can be a huge asset in improving access and equity to secondary education.

The intervention has been driven by theoretical knowledge and lessons learned for previous ICT for education interventions and the preliminary evaluation after three years since implementation, based on observations and login-in data, has been positive. Using

---

[2] http://www.litespeed.com.sg/2_products/prod_cw_secondary.html; http://yteach.com/.

[3] Since commercial e-resource repositories are governed by intellectual property rights procuring the rights to host it on the WWW means you will be making it accessible to everyone in the world. This undermines the commercial company's ability to sell the repository to others, which means the right to do so can be very expensive. Internet based access. However, if you upload on to local servers and make it available to student and teachers it will be much cheaper.

the unit of analysis, equipment and laboratory design has shown to be resilient. The downtime caused by equipment breakdown and/or software corruption has been very low, electricity and consumable costs have been lower then expected and are now integrated into the annual budget of ministry of education. Regarding connectivity, the initial LAN setups are now linked up as a WAN with monitored access to the internet. The WAN has also helped to perform remote maintenance on/or upload new resources. This adds efficiency and also supports the school IT administrators who have been the weak link in the design. To enhance communication between the schools and the central Ministry VoIP phone has also been installed to maximize the use of the network. The capacity development for community members and the head teachers very perhaps the most effective considering the level of reluctance to integrate ICT in education found during the baseline study. With the exception of ten principals, all others made changes to the school management procedure and embraced the option of opening the learning center during lunch and after school. The most encouraging was the engagement of teachers and students which was very slow initially, but increased exponentially toward the end of the intervention. The log-in data collected from the each school corroborated with random observations and indicated a very high use of the e-resource by the teacher and students. Almost all STEM teachers in the country were using the e-resource in some part of their teaching. However, considering the base level capacity of these STEM teachers, they still have long way to go. The impact of the intervention on student achievement is not yet evident, but considering the base level resource available to teachers and students in the case study country, the ICT intervention can only help to improve student learning outcomes. A more rigorous study after at least five years of use of the ICT resources and continued support for the teachers should be undertaken to assess the sustainability and impact of the intervention on student learning outcomes.

## References

1. Bonk, C.J.: The World is Open: How Web Technology is Revolutionizing Education. Wiley, New York (2009)
2. Martin, G., Massy, J., Clarke, T.: When absorptive capacity meets institutions and (e) learners: adopting, diffusing and exploiting e-learning in organizations. Int. J. Training Dev. **7**(4), 228–244 (2003)
3. Plomp, T., Anderson, R.E., Law, N., Quale, A. (eds.): Cross-National Information and Communication Technology Policies and Practices in Education. IAP, Charlotte (2009)
4. Pillay, H.: Case Study on the use of New Technologies in Teacher Education/Training. UNESCO PROJECT. Ref: 133.32.60/ac/625/00 (2009)
5. Sampson, D.G., Isaias, P., Ifenthaler, D., Spector, J.M. (eds.): Ubiquitous and Mobile Learning in the Digital Age. Springer, New York (2012)
6. International Telecommunication Union Report. http://www.internetworldstats.com/stats3.htm. Accessed 12 December 2012
7. Hartshorne, R.: Teacher Education Programs and Online Learning Tools: Innovations in Teacher Preparation. IGI Global, Hershey (2012)
8. Mooij, T., Smeets, E.: Modelling and supporting ICT implementation in secondary schools. Comput. Educ. **36**(3), 265–281 (2001)

9. Lave, J., Wenger, E.: Situated Learning: Legitimate Peripheral Participation. University of Cambridge Press, Cambridge (2012)
10. Beetham, H., Sharpe, R.: Rethinking Pedagogy for a Digital Age: Designing for 21st Century Learning. Routledge, Abingdon (2013)
11. Khan, A.R., Hadi, R.S., Asraf, M.: Impact of ICT on education: a study on rural schools. Commun. Inf. Sci. Manag. Eng. **3**(8), 367–373 (2013)
12. Pinfield, S., Salter, J., Bath, P.A., Hubbard, B., Millington, P., Anders, J.H.S., Hussain, A.: Open-access repositories worldwide, 2005–2012: past growth, current characteristics and future possibilities. J. Am. Soc. Inform. Sci. Technol. **65**(12), 2404–2421 (2014)
13. PhET Interactive Simulations, University of Colorado, Boulder, USA (2014). https://phet.colorado.edu/

# Engineering Active Learning in 3D Virtual Worlds

Michael Vallance(✉), Kenta Ibayashi, and Yuta Goto

Department of Media Architecture, Future University Hakodate, 116-2 Kamedanakano, Hakodate, Hokkaido T041-8655, Japan
michael@fun.ac.jp

**Abstract.** To advance education in the 21st century, experts in neuroscience argue for more 'active learning' through experience. A practical implementation for such active, experiential and, we propose, multi-disciplinary learning is for students to consider, analyze, solve and make personal meaning from engaging problems. Collaborative problem-solving promotes communication involving creative and interpretive meaning-making, analysis and reflective judgement. Due to advances in computer technologies, educators can now consider a wider range of collaborative problems and extensive solutions which can be implemented in both real and virtual worlds. This paper will summarise five scenarios of virtual worlds from our research project: Second Life, OpenSim, OpenQwaq, Unity 3D and Unity 3D with Oculus Rift. In each virtual world participants from Japan, UK and USA have been engaged in remote collaborations to solve problem-based tasks requiring the programming and manouvering of virtual robots and real-world LEGO Mindstorms robots. Robot Mediated Interactions are analyzed to determine robot task complexity, student learning and task immersion. We have determined that for effective active learning involving 3D virtual worlds specifically focusing upon the development of beginner programming knowledge, the challenge is for educators to design tasks of zero (or close to zero) Task Fidelity and for students to become fully immersed within the tasks. The paper explains how this has been achieved, summarizes the benefits, obstacles, limitations and challenges of 3D virtual world implementations, and suggests future directions in educational research to engineer active learning in 3D virtual worlds.

**Keywords:** Computer science education · Virtual worlds · Robot task complexity · Learning

## 1 Introduction

Our research has been designed to collate data of students collaborating in 3D virtual worlds to program LEGO robots to successfully navigate mazes from start to completion in both the physical world and simultaneously within the 3D virtual spaces. This is implemented by students remotely located in Japan, UK and USA: (i) designing circuits that necessitate the use of robot maneuvers and sensors; and (ii) collaborating in a virtual world to solve pre-determined tasks. The task solutions necessitate the use of programming skills, collaboration, communication, and higher-level cognitive processes. It is


L. Uden et al. (Eds.): LTEC 2015, CCIS 533, pp. 268–282, 2015.
DOI: 10.1007/978-3-319-22629-3_22

posited that these experiences lead to personal strategies for teamwork, planning, organizing, applying, analyzing, creating and reflection.

As a consequence of our implementations we are developing an evidence-based framework of tasks of measurable complexity in virtual worlds. This is undertaken by collecting data of collaboration: (i) capturing students' procedural processes as they work through the task solution; and (ii) capturing students' learning reflections during and after completion of tasks. From this data we then associate specific cognitive instances within the task process to a taxonomy of cognition. The aim is to develop students' programming knowledge, technology skills, design aptitude and communication competency. The affective aim is to develop students to be more independent, responsible, and reflective learners. It is proposed that this will lead to a better understanding of tasks performed in a 3D virtual world in which we can expect specific learning to occur. Our research question is: How can learning be determined when students collaborate in a 3D virtual world?

The paper is organized as follows. A rationale for active learning using robots and 3D virtual worlds is first provided. It is determined that robot programming enables tasks in the real world and virtual worlds to be quantified in terms of task complexity (summarized in Sect. 2). The use of robots consequently set the context for our active learning, which we call Robot Mediated Interaction (summarized in Sect. 3). Following this, Sect. 4 then explains our task metric, termed Task Fidelity. To complement the interactions and robot task metric we also gather data on students' immersion within each task, as explained in Sect. 5. Section 6 then illustrates five virtual world scenarios and the technologies utilized in the research project since 2010. The Results section summarizes data collected in one these scenarios; namely the OpenSim project. We conclude the paper with an acknowledgment of the limitations of our research to date and how we will remedy these in our future research.

## 2 Learning and 3D Virtual Worlds

Anderson *et al.* [1], furthering the work of Bloom [2], has proposed a hierarchy of knowledge consisting of factual knowledge (relating to a specific discipline), procedural knowledge (techniques and procedures), declarative knowledge (relationship between concepts) and meta-cognitive knowledge (knowledge of demands, strategies and one's limitations). However, in accordance with the views of Dewey [3] on education, Hase [4] believes more is required: "The acquisition of knowledge and skills does not necessarily constitute learning. The latter occurs when the learner connects the knowledge or skill to previous experience, integrates it fully in terms of value, and is able to actively use it in meaningful and even novel ways" (p. 2). Experts in neuroscience additionally argue for more 'active learning' through experience [5].

It is recognized that learning is an extremely complex process that occurs within the learner, is unobserved, occurs in random and chaotic ways and is a response to a personal need and, often, occurs to resolve some ambiguity. It is associated with making new linkages in the brain involving ideas, emotions, and experience that lead to new understandings about self or the world. Research has revealed that this can be undertaken by implementing a constructionist environment where students are 'active producers' of learning [6]. A practical implementation for such active, experiential and, we propose, multi-disciplinary learning is for students to consider, analyze, solve and make personal meaning from engaging problems. Problem-solving which necessitates multi-disciplinarity presents opportunities for reciprocation between declarative and procedural knowledge in which personal input and collaborative efforts support connections which in turn can lead to understanding of concepts and theories in multiple contexts (i.e., meta-cognitive knowledge). Additionally, collaborative problem-solving promotes communication involving creative and interpretive meaning-making, analysis and reflective judgment [7]. Accordingly, due to advances in computer technologies, educators can now consider a wider range of problems and extensive solutions, which can be implemented in both real and virtual spaces.

An approach is required then which encourages exploration, procedural knowledge, iterative, recursive and logical thinking, structured task breakdown, and dealing with abstraction. An instructivist pedagogy does not support such an approach, so an alternative has to be sought. Barr and Stephenson [8] point to successful projects which have involved simulation and robotics. For instance, beginner programming concepts can be introduced and experienced using the graphical LEGO Mindstorms software which has been shown to support programming through its drag-and-drop graphical user interface [9]. Consequently, LEGO NXT and EV3 Mindstorms robots and software were used in our research as tools to mediate the communication of the students. Tasks were provided that necessitated the programming of robots to navigate circuits, often with the use of sensors.

## 3 Robot Mediated Interaction

In the first iteration of our research from 2010 to 2012, in order to quantify each task complexity the programming of our LEGO robot required a determination of an action and a vector [10]. As circuits became more challenging, the LEGO Mindstorms programming became more complex. We found that the logic of assigning task complexity to circuits was inadequate. This was especially the case when we needed to add sensors to maneuver around and over obstacles We re-named our initial Task Complexity as 'Robot Task Complexity' (RTC) because the task focuses upon the robot and what the human has to do to manipulate that robot. We call this the 'product' of a robot task. We appreciate that Human-Robot Interaction (HRI) is the 'intelligent interaction' between a human and a robot but the word 'interaction' assumes that the human and the robot are engaged in two-way communication. We call this the 'process' of a robot task. Although there is feedback from the robot in our tasks we would not necessarily claim that there is any intelligent interaction; it is simply feedback. Therefore, we consider the collaboration between the students to be an example of Robot Mediated Interaction (RMI) where humans act upon feedback provided by both robot and other humans. Consequently, we define Robot Mediated Interaction as any human communication that occurs when engaged in the deployment of robots.

## 4 Task Fidelity

As stated, our project encourages students to communicate in a virtual world when programming a robot to follow pre-determined tasks. The students' aim is to effectively communicate solutions to problems that involve the programming of a LEGO robot to follow the specified circuits. This is undertaken by (i) designing circuits which necessitate the use of robot maneuvers and sensors; and (ii) experiencing collaboration in a virtual world with other, remotely located, students. However, to give meaning to the students' experiences over a series of task challenges, we need to quantify each task's complexity. Common metrics allow for benchmarking within a particular domain. For instance, road transportation such as cars, motorcycles and trucks can be compared by the metrics of top speed, acceleration, engine capacity, fuel economy, transmission and price. However, this is not the case with robots. When discussing robots that undertake specific maneuvers, some researchers provide a common metric labeled as Task Complexity, where tasks are defined as physical action units that are undertaken by a robot, and the designation 'complexity' is used to characterize the intricate parts of a task. Murphy and Schreckenghost [11] conducted a meta-analysis of twenty nine papers that proposed metrics for human-robot interaction (HRI). Forty two metrics in total were determined. They found though that HRI metrics were often not measured directly, but most often were 'inferred' through observation. Although the paper identified proposed HRI metrics, it was recognized that they "have no functional, or generizable, mechanism for measuring that feature" [*ibid*]. After conducting a review of the literature, Vallance *et al.* [12] determined that a gap in the research existed so proposed a new metric for robot-mediated tasks, termed Task Fidelity.

Task Fidelity is defined as an indicator of the complexity of the circuit compared with the complexity of the program to complete the circuit. For instance, in designing the task challenge, Circuit Task Complexity (CTC) equals the number of directions + number of maneuvers + number of sensors + number of obstacles.

$$\mathrm{CTC} = \Sigma(\mathrm{d} + \mathrm{m} + \mathrm{s} + \mathrm{o})$$

For example, if a robot has to maneuver past 2 obstacles in order to reach its target, the number of directions to be programmed can be 4, the number of maneuvers is 3, and the number of sensors is 2 (i.e. two touch sensors), then CTC = Σ (4 + 3 + 2 + 2) = 11

We then modified our task complexity to be determined by the LEGO Mindstorms EV3 program solution rather than the circuit to be navigated. We call this Robot Task Complexity (RTC), which is measured as:

$$\mathrm{RTC} = \Sigma \mathrm{Mv}_1 + \Sigma \mathrm{Sv}_2 + \Sigma \mathrm{SW} + \Sigma \mathrm{Lv}_3$$

where M = number of moves (direction and turn); S = number of sensors; SW = number of switches; L = number of loops; v = number of decisions required by the user for each programmable block ($v_1 = 6$, $v_2 = 5$, $v_3 = 2$)

A LEGO Mindstorms EV3 program solution for our example above has RTC = 66.

In order to compare the data from all tasks, for the Circuit Task Complexity values we took the maximum CTC value of all our tasks and divided it into each task's CTC value. Similarly, for the Robot Task Complexity values we took the maximum RTC value and divided it into each RTC value. All values are thus represented between 0 and 1. As a result, the complexity of the task can now be quantified by a new metric which we term Task Fidelity; where. Task Fidelity = Circuit Task Complexity - Robot Task Complexity (TF = CTC − RTC). A more detailed development of Task Fidelity contextualized by our research has been published in Vallance *et al.* [12, 13].

## 5 Immersion

Task Fidelity is a useful indicator of the complexity of a task. However, a cognitive determiner of Task Fidelity can be immersion: a cognitive phenomena also referred to as 'flow' [14]. To record immersion, data was collected from the students during and after each task, and we utilized Pearce *et al.'s* [15] flow criteria of task challenge and skill: "Amongst the various studies researching flow, an ongoing issue has been to find a method for measuring flow independently from the positive states of consciousness (such as enjoyment, concentration, control, lack of self-consciousness, lack of distraction). One solution has been to use a measure of the balance between the challenge of an activity and the participant's perception of their skill to carry out that activity" (*ibid*, p. 250). In order to capture this data immediately after the completion of a task and while still in communication with their virtual collaborators in the virtual world, the students reported on the task's challenge and their skill in attempting the task. The assumption is that with optimal parameters for challenge and for skill relationship, students become 'immersed' in the Robot Mediated Interaction (RMI) tasks. The calculation of immersion is beyond the scope of this paper but is detailed in Vallance *et al.* [13].

## 6 Implementations

Five virtual world scenarios will next be summarized. Each scenario has been developed by researchers and students involved in the project since 2010. A descriptive analysis is offered. References to published articles detailing the research outcomes are provided in each scenario.

### 6.1 Robot Mediated Interaction and Second Life

The initial research, from 2010 to 2012, utilized the Second Life virtual world and LEGO NXT Mindstorms robots. Details of the research may be found at Vallance *et al.* [10]. The design of the virtual learning space by participating students enabled individual avatars to place and move blocks on a virtual floor (see Fig. 1). These blocks were graphical representations of the NXT Mindstorms software blocks required to build the program required to maneuver the LEGO robot in pre-determined task circuits. On the sides of the virtual structure were images of the NXT configuration panels. These were displayed so that students could point and focus on specific configurations that needed to be inputted in order to program specifically detailed operations of the robots. Once this virtual learning space had been built, sixteen (16) tasks were implemented: the initial seven (7) were utilized for practice; data was collected from the remaining nine (9). Each iteratively more difficult task aimed to challenge students to communicate a construction process leading to a successful outcome; that is, program a LEGO robot to follow a specified circuit of movements and turns. Communication between participants (in this case, N = 8) was supported by the virtual world chat facility and the behavior of participants' avatars in the environment. Each team had to design the maze of an identical robot on the floor of their laboratory using adhesive tape. Next, one team's task was to act as 'learners' and create a robot program (using the Mindstorms software) to follow the maze that the other (teaching) team had designed. The learning team used the information provided in an attempt to solve the robot programming problem. Over 60 h of video capture of participants communicating in the real world was recorded, transcribed and analyzed [10]. Given the steadily rising level of task difficulty and students' increasing mastery of the more challenging tasks as evidenced by their ability to complete them with fewer errors and in less time, Anderson *et al.* [1] suggest that some developmental pattern should be expected to emerge as the procedural knowledge required to complete the task came to be more effectively applied and as student accomplishment increased. However, the relative frequency with which particular kinds of cognition appeared in the data (e.g. 'applying procedural knowledge') was not patterned as tasks progressed and difficulty increased. Moreover, the relative frequency with which the different elements of cognition appeared in the data (e.g. 'applying conceptual knowledge') did not present itself as a linear or rising percentage of what might have been expected in a developmental sequence but more often was discontinuous. In other words, despite the linear complexity of the tasks, the students' learning outcomes were neither linear or patterned [10].

**Fig. 1.** Interactions in Second Life

## 6.2 Robot Mediated Interaction and OpenSim

Open Simulator, commonly referred to as OpenSim, is an open source multi-platform, multi-user 3D application server. Our learner-centered design approach enabled a number of innovative tools to be created and customized by the students in OpenSim: for instance, the ability to move a graphical representation of the LEGO robot object and leave a trace of the circuit in-world. Also, media objects in-world (known as prims) can display live streamed video from the lab in Japan (using the online UStream service) and also from an iPhone attached to the front of the LEGO robot (using the Bambuser iPhone App). Virtual noticeboards can be updated with text and images to aid communication (see Fig. 2). Although programming is mostly undertaken using the Mindstorms NXT and EV3 software, a LabView VI has been developed to enable communication directly between an in-world prim and the physical LEGO robot [16]. In this project, from 2013 to 2014, the participants were undergraduate students studying Media Architecture in a Systems Information Science focused Japanese university (N = 6) and A-level students in UK studying science-based subjects (N = 10). Of the 16 participant students 2 were female, 14 were male, all are aged between 17 and 19, and none had prior experience working with the project's technologies. Some tasks involved Japanese students collaborating with other remotely located Japanese students and some with Japanese students collaborating with UK students. Tasks included maneuvering around obstacles using distance and turn commands, using touch sensors to find ways around

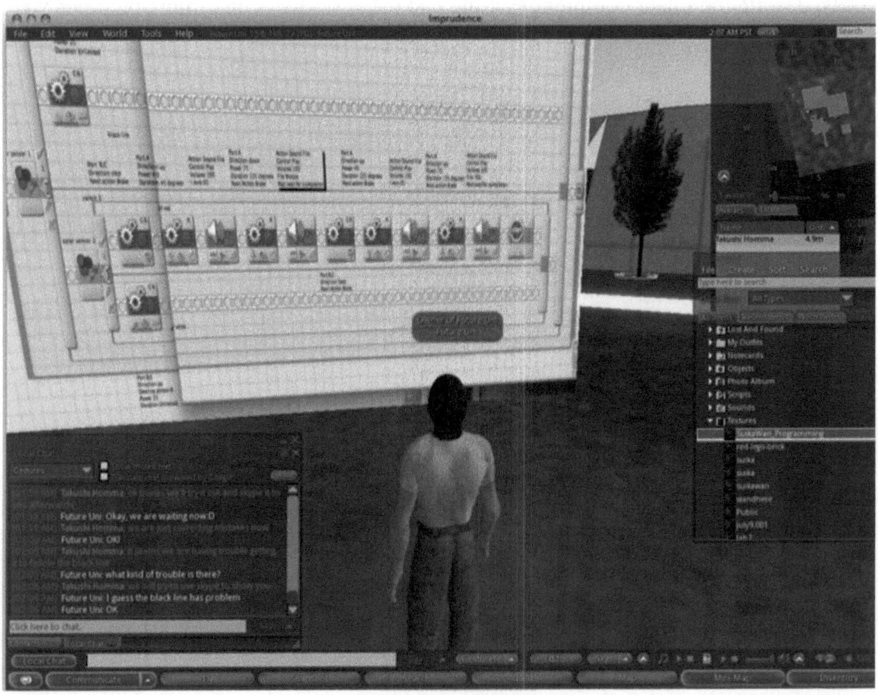


**Fig. 2.** Interactions in OpenSim

obstacles, constructing a bridge and using touch sensors to move over obstacles, using light sensors to avoid obstacles, using sensors to locate items, and manipulating the telerobotic controls to virtually maneuver our LEGO robot within the virtual space as part of 'search and rescue' simulations. Communication between students required the use of virtual world tools such as text panes, voice, live video streaming of respective real-world labs, and 3D presentation boards where Mindstorms program images were deposited. The use of avatars in-world also enabled students to remotely maneuver a real-world robot (tele-robot communication). Data from 39 tasks is summarized in the Results section below. A more comprehensive analysis is available in our International Journal of Learning Technology paper [13].

## 6.3 Robot Mediated Interaction and OpenQwaq

During 2014 a global virtual team collaboration project between first year university students in the United States (N = 20) and Japan (N = 7) utilizing the OpenQwaq 3D virtual environment was implemented. Students in both locations met together synchronously within the 3D virtual space over the course of four weeks, and were challenged with collaborating to discover solutions to robot tasks. One location each week designed a robot task that was shared with the other classroom at the start of the online meeting. The class that was challenged could ask questions of the other location to help them understand the build, programming, and use of the LEGO robot sensors to complete the task. A 3D virtual environment, built upon the OpenQwaq platform, was used to host the online collaboration meetings. The OpenQwaq forum supported several beneficial

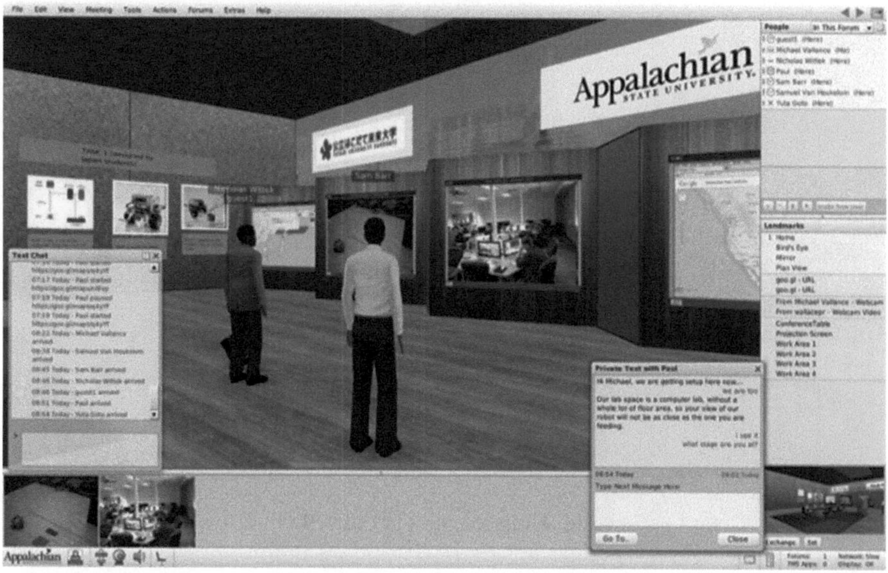


**Fig. 3.** Interactions in OpenQwaq

tools for virtual team collaboration, including text chat, synchronous audio, and video feeds from both locations. The physical layout of the 3D space resembled a real-world conference room, where panels were placed on the walls to display live video camera feeds from each site, such as a full-room view and a close-up view of the robots performing the tasks (see Fig. 3). A discussion panel was used to provide a text chat for students to use in asking and answering questions. This short project has been summarized in a presentation by Wallace and Vallance [17].

## 6.4 Robot Mediated Interaction and Unity 3D

To present a more realistic scenario we have created a virtual Fukushima nuclear plant using a Unity 3D-based technology called JIBE (see Fig. 4). In this space we can view reactors plus four cooling towers. We have a meeting space where we can upload images to a presentation board, and a glass structure for developing future learning spaces. We are currently programming a virtual robot to move within the Fukushima space and its maneuvers replicated in our real-world lab. As the project matures we would like children and adults to gain hands-on experience moving around our simulated virtual Fukushima space and observe a physical robot simultaneously moving at a remote location (e.g. in a scaled mock-up of a hazardous building such as the reactor). It is anticipated that such user-accessible simulations with citizens controlling the virtual robot will create an awareness and understanding of disaster recovery, and not simply rely upon retrospective information from unprepared experts. As well as capturing data for analysis of cognitive processes, we also aim to familiarize students and the public with the complexities of nuclear power; given that there is much confusion about the situation at present in Japan [13, 18].

**Fig. 4.** Interactions in Unity 3D

### 6.5 Robot Mediated Interaction and Unity 3D with Oculus Rift

To engage our learners in the active design and construction of their learning environment both in the 3D space and the real world lab, we commissioned a consultant Unity programmer to design an abandoned factory as our virtual space [19]. The rationale is to combine a 3D simulation space for real world collaboration; in our case we are teaching the programming of robots contextualized by simulating a robot navigating in a restricted area. We then present participants with the following scenario:

> Four children have been admitted to hospital with apparent radiation sickness. They were playing in the old abandoned factory complex belonging to NEPCo (Nuclear Energy Production Company). Upon inspection, the factory area recorded a radiation value of 4.00 Sv/h. This measurement is the same value as the Fukushima Reactor 1. Note that a dose of 0.75 Sv/h can be enough to induce radiation sickness. Therefore, it seems it is too dangerous to enter the factory complex. It is estimated there are 5 radioactive bins within the complex. We are not sure where the radioactive bins are located and do not yet know why they have been dumped in the old factory complex. Your mission is to maneuver the Unity robot and drone, locate the 5 radioactive bins, and return them to the designated safe area. Be careful! One wrong move can cause an explosion ... and disaster!

Students can maneuver the virtual robot using the built-in controller (see Fig. 5) to locate and pick up the radioactive bins. The project has also been developed to be viewable via the Oculus Rift and utilizing the hands-free Leap Controller (see Fig. 6). Data is currently being collected as students in Japan participate in tasks requiring collaboration and communication.

**Fig. 5.** Interactions in Unity 3D with robot

**Fig. 6.** Interactions in Unity 3D and Oculus Rift

## 7 Results

This section will summarise the results of data collected from the Robot Mediated Interaction tasks undertaken within OpenSim (see Sect. 6.2 above). Details of all tasks, the methodology utilized, and more a comprehensive discussion of results are available in our International Journal of Learning Technology paper [13].

Briefly, we conducted tasks of various specifications over three semesters and for each task we measured Circuit Task Complexity (CTC) and Robot Task Complexity (RTC). In order to compare data from all the tasks for the Circuit Task Complexity values we first took the maximum CTC value and divided it into each task's CTC value. Then we looked at the program solutions by our students and calculated the Robot Task Complexity. Similarly, for the Robot Task Complexity (RTC) values we took the maximum RTC value and divided it into each task's RTC value. All values could thus be represented between 0 and 1. Finally, we could calculate Task Fidelity as explained in Sect. 4 above.

A total of 53 LEGO robot tasks have been undertaken to date. The Task Fidelity for Tasks 40 to 53 have yet to be calculated. The zero line in Fig. 7 indicates ideal Task Fidelity; or, in other words, ideal task complexity. Data plotted above the zero line indicate that the robot program was more complex than the circuit the robot had to maneuver. Data below the zero line indicate that the circuit was more complex than the robot program required to successfully navigate it. Ideally, the instructor should provide a task commensurate with the expected successful outcome to be developed by the learners; i.e. tasks along the horizontal zero line illustrated in Fig. 7. But there are differences, and we measure the difference as Task Fidelity.

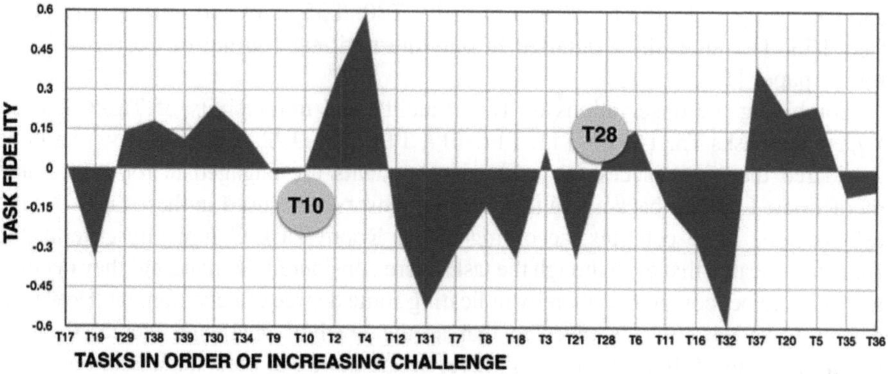


**Fig. 7.** Task Fidelity

We have also attempted to detail the 'flow' or immersion of students within each task. Given that data from Tasks T10 and T28 were 'optimal tasks' we revisited the additional data and increased the flow metrics; see Fig. 8 where Tasks T10 and T28 are still within Carli *et al.*'s [20] immersion quadrant but are located as 'arousal' and 'control' respectively. Task which would fall within a state of 'flow' are tasks

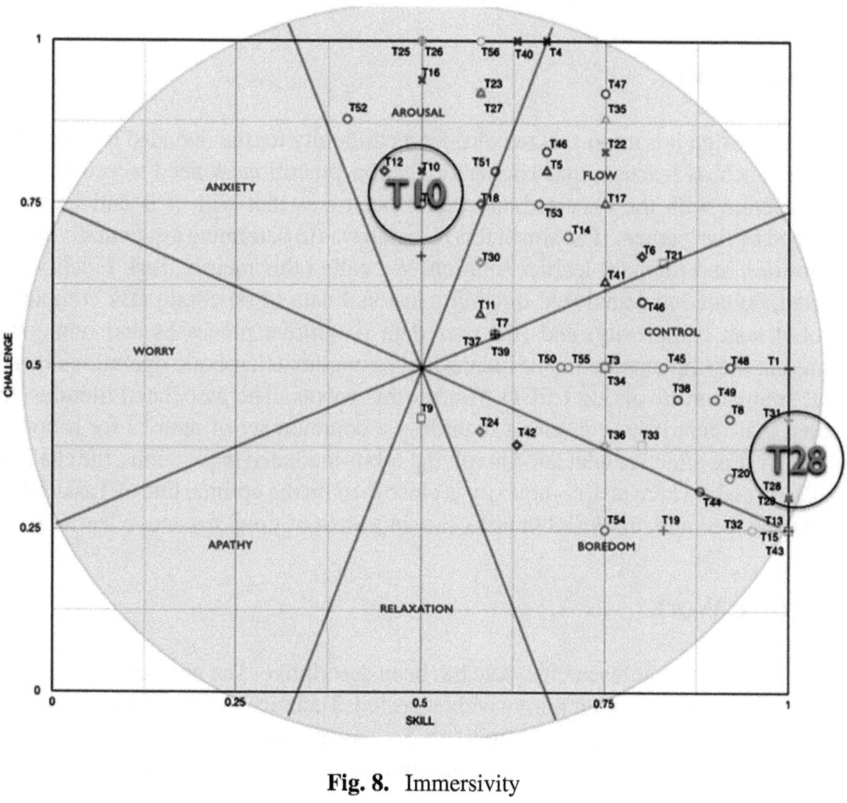


**Fig. 8.** Immersivity

T5, T6, T7, T11, T14, T17, T18, T21, T22, T30, T35, T39 and latterly T47, T46, T41, T53. The analysis is detailed in our International Journal of Learning Technology paper [13].

Combining the observations of Task Fidelity and immersivity of Tasks 1 to 39 suggest that tasks T5, T6, T7, T11, T14, T17, T18, T21, T22, T30, T35, T39 would be considered the most successful tasks when students are engaged in robot-mediated interactions. Looking back at the task details, sensors were used in these tasks. As the tasks became more complex, according to our Robot Task Complexity criteria, the students indicated that even though the tasks were considered 'demanding' they deemed their skills to be 'competent' thereby indicating some degree of development. However, in later tasks the students revealed that as the level of challenge increased (from 'manageable' to 'difficult'), their skill level in attempting to seek successful outcomes decreased (from 'competent' to 'reasonable'). Looking at the task communication transcripts and screen captures, it appeared that the students had to utilize different procedural knowledge involving, for instance, programming a touch sensor to coordinate with a motor action. These latter tasks required students to 'analyze' and 'create' unique solutions based upon their prior task experiences and were thus deemed most challenging. The increased task complexity necessitated a higher level of programing skill incorporating sensor variables and loops. Even though students' post-task reflection data revealed that they found sensor related tasks difficult, being immersed in a task led to more 'active learning' and, in turn, led to greater student success [21].

## 8 Conclusion

In any task design it is important to consider its difficulty for the intended learners. Task designers such as teachers and Higher Education practitioners need to provide tasks commensurate with the expected successful outcomes that will, it is anticipated, be developed by the learners. The aim of this research was to determine a quantitative metric of robot task and (human) learner solution. We called this metric 'Task Fidelity'. We collected, collated and analyzed three-dimensional data of (i) circuit task complexity, (ii) robot task complexity, and (iii) user data (cognitive processes and immersion) captured in the implementation of increasingly complex telerobotic operations in a 3D virtual simulation involving LEGO Mindstorms robots. The associated literature has revealed that there is no consensus regarding a common set of metrics for robot task complexity. For effective education involving robot-mediated interactions, the challenge is to design tasks where task complexity is close to or on the optimal line of Task Fidelity and students become immersed in tasks (i.e. in a state of flow) for active learning.

## 9 Future Work

It is recognized that our research to date has been descriptive. The number of participants has been quite low and rather purposively selected. Technical barriers to the implementation of 3D virtual worlds also persist in Secondary and Higher Education. Due to increased funding and institutional recognition of the value of our research, the next phase will involve a causal, quantitative, evidence-based approach of learning within a 3D virtual space. An increased number of participants will be randomly assigned to a control group and an experimental group. Psychometrics will be adopted and quantitative statistical data will be reported for each dependent measure of learning outcome.

**Acknowledgments.** This study is funded by Future University *tokubestsu kenkyuhi* special research funds with the project number 2014E02 and JAIST kakenhi grant no. 15K01080. Many thanks to participating colleagues and students at Future University Hakodate, Appalachian State University, USA, Hull University, UK, University of South Wales, UK and Mountain Ash Comprehensive School (MACS), UK.

## References

1. Anderson, L.W., Krathwohl, D.R., Airasian, P.W., Cruicshank, K.A., Mayer, R.E., Pintrich, P.R., Raths, J., Wittrock, M.C.: A Taxonomy for Learning, Teaching and Assessing: a Revision of Bloom's Taxonomy of Educational Objectives. Longman, New York (2001)
2. Bloom, B.S. (ed.): Taxonomy of Educational Objectives, the Classification of Educational Goals. Handbook 1: Cognitive Domain. McKay, New York (1956)
3. Dewey, J.: Experience and Education. Touchstone, New York (1938)
4. Hase, S.: Learner defined curriculum: heutagogy and action learning in vocational training. Southern Institute of Technology J. Appl. Res., Special Edition: Action research and action learning in vocational education and training. http://sitjar.sit.ac.nz/SITJAR/Special. Accessed 16 August 2014
5. Battro, A.M., Fischer, K.W., Lena, P.J.: The Educated Brain: Essays in Neuroscience. Cambridge University Press, UK (2011)
6. Harel, I., Papert, S.: Constructionism. Ablex publishing, USA (1993)
7. Tarricone, P.: The Taxonomy of Metacognition. Psychology Press, New York (2011)
8. Barr, V., Stephenson, C.: Bringing computational thinking to k-12: what is involved and what is the role of the computer science education community? ACM Inroads **2**(1), 48–54 (2011)
9. Lui, A.K., Ng, S.C., Cheung, H.Y., Gurung, P.: Facilitating independent leaning with LEGO Mindstorms robots. ACM Inroads **1**(4), 49–53 (2010)
10. Vallance, M., Martin, S.: Assessment and learning in the virtual world: tasks, taxonomies and teaching for real. J. Virtual Worlds Res. **5**(2), 1–13 (2012)
11. Murphy, R., Schreckenghost, D.: Survey of metrics for human-robot interaction. In: Proceedings of the 8th ACM/IEEE International Conference on Human-Robot Interaction, Tokyo, pp. 197–198 (2013)
12. Vallance, M., Yamamoto, T., Goto, Y., Ibayashi, K.: Task fidelity: a new metric for measuring task complexity involving robots. IEEE Comput. Soc. Tech. Com. Learn. Technol. **15**(4), 22–25 (2013)
13. Vallance, M., Martin, S., Naamani, C.: A situation that we had never imagined: post-Fukushima virtual collaborations for determining robot task metrics. Int. J. Learn. Technol. **10**(1), 30–49 (2015)
14. Csikszentmihalyi, M.: Flow: the Psychology of Optimal Experience. Harper, USA (2008)
15. Pearce, M., Ainley, M., Howard, S.: The ebb and flow of online learning. Comput. Hum. Behav. **21**, 745–771 (2005)

16. Controlling Robots 6,000 Miles Away? No Problem! Posted by Laura_Arnold on 15 March 2012 at National Instruments Developer Zone. https://decibel.ni.com/content/groups/sweet-apps/blog/2012/03/15/controlling-robots-6000-miles-away-no-problem. Accessed 24 March 2015
17. Wallace, P., Vallance, M.: Global virtual team collaboration utilizing a 3D virtual environment. In: Proceedings of the Asian Conference on Technology in the Classroom (actc), Kobe, 30 April 2015–3 May 2015
18. Vallance, M., Naamani, C., Thomas, M., Thomas, J.: Applied information science research in a virtual world simulation to support robot mediated interaction following the fukushima nuclear disaster. Commun. Inf. Sci. Manage. Eng. (CISME) **3**(5), 222–232 (2013)
19. Gabriel, C.: personal communication, 9 December 2014. gabriel.campitelli@gmail.com
20. Carli, M., Delle Fave, A., Massimini, F.: The quality of experience in the flow channels. In: Csikszentmihalyi, M., Csikszentmihalyi, I.S. (eds.) Optimal Experience: Psychological Studies of Flow in Consciousness. Cambridge University Press, New York (1998)
21. Vallance, M., Naamani, C.: Experiential learning, virtual collaboration and robots. In: Jerry, P., Tavares-Jones, N., Gregory, S. (eds.) Riding the Hype Cycle: The Resurgence of Virtual Worlds. Inter-Disciplinary Press (2013)

# Integrating Synthetic and Analytical Aspects of Geometry Through Solving Problems Using a DGS

Carolina Guerrero-Ortiz, Aaron Reyes-Rodriguez(✉), and Hugo Espinosa-Perez

Ciudad del Conocimiento de la UAEH, Carretera Pachucha-Tulancingo Km. 4.5, Mineral de la Reforma, 42184 Pachucha, HGO, Mexico
aaron.reyes.rdz@gmail.com

**Abstract.** In this paper we document and analyze the extent to which the systematic use of a Dynamic Geometry System (DGS) in problem solving activities can become a means to integrating the synthetic and analytical aspects of geometry. We analyze some solution paths for a task of geometric construction, implemented by three participants at a problem-solving seminar. We identify limitations of purely analytical approaches as well as the usefulness of integrating analytical and synthetic techniques to construct or justify a solution path. We observed that solving problems of geometric construction without the support offered by digital technology reduces the opportunities that a solver has to interpret algebraic procedures from a geometric perspective and to construct meaning for mathematical ideas and concepts.

**Keywords:** Geometry · Problem solving · Understanding · Connections · DGS

## 1 Introduction

The development and wide variety of technological tools has challenging to educational experts, in order to improve learning scenarios. Thus, has become important to know in depth how new ways of learning are developed in technological environments. To understand how an individual build knowledge in a digital context, it is necessary to analyze and document how individuals interact with the technological environment in order to achieve a goal. In the teaching and learning of mathematics, the coordinated use of digital tools provide to teachers and students extensive resources to construct meaning for mathematical concepts, and to organize instructional scenarios aimed to foster learning with understanding [1]. On the other hand, with more people involved in the virtual world there are more opportunities for all to generate and share human knowledge and creativity [2]. Design teaching activities, in an age where technological development is too fast, where students are able to obtain information from everywhere in the web, is not an easy task. It demands from teachers to previously know how the students can address different paths to obtain some answer.

A widely accepted line of research in the mathematics education community is related to the construction of connections as a relevant indicator of mathematical understanding [3]. In the research literature we identified some proposals whose aim is to


L. Uden et al. (Eds.): LTEC 2015, CCIS 533, pp. 283–297, 2015.
DOI: 10.1007/978-3-319-22629-3_23

identify paths which can help students to connect naturally synthetic and analytic geometry, and to relate tools from both areas as a mean to construct connections between geometrical ideas and procedures [4, 5]. For instance, Gascon [6] argues that some epistemological and pedagogical characteristics of analytical techniques can complement synthetic approaches to solving geometry problems, since the latter are characterized by offering simple and intuitive proofs of mathematical facts.

Other studies have explored the role of Dynamic Geometry Systems (DGS) as a tool to promote the use of algebraic resources to justify results or conjectures that emerge during the exploration of relationships within dynamic configurations, whose initial elements are lines, segments or circles. For instance, Santos-Trigo et al. [7] argue that simple mathematical objects such as lines, segments, circles, perpendicular bisectors or angle bisectors can be used as springboards to develop students' mathematical reflection supporting them to build platforms to identify and explore relationships among objects such as conic sections. The authors showed the way in which students use the coordinate system embedded in a DGS allowed them to construct algebraic arguments to justify that a locus is a parabola, and to analyze the properties of conic sections using a combination of synthetic and analytical techniques.

Santos-Trigo et al. [7] also provide evidence that the use of a DGS can support students' explorations of properties of objects embedded in a dynamic configuration, which can lead them to the discovery of serendipitous results. The discovery of mathematical results is enhanced by questioning the relationships among objects such as lines, circles, segments, angles, etc. In this context, we hypothesize that a digital tool such as Geogebra allows to problem solvers making sense of analytical procedures based on the meanings and interpretations that emerge through integration of visual aspects of loci with their corresponding algebraic representation.

## 2 Conceptual Framework

Addressing problem solving with a DGS demands that learners think about geometric objects in terms of their basic properties, and that they consider problems as a set of dilemmas which they have to approach by mean of mathematical tools: How are the objects involved in a problem defined? Is there any relation between those objects? What are the characteristics, if any, of those relationships? A key element to promote the construction of connections among mathematical ideas, when students work with a DGS environment, is to take advantage of visualization and exploration affordances offered by the tool to explore properties of mathematical objects, to formulate and justify conjectures, to communicate results and pose new problems [8]. It is well known that ways of represent data in a problem are crucial for the generation of solution routes, as are strategy selection, prior knowledge and the tools used to organize a solution path [9].

The use of digital technologies in mathematics classroom involves not only change ways that students use their resources and organize their ideas, it is not only an efficiency tool, compared to a paper and pencil setting, but also a mean that promotes cognitive reorganization of students' mental structures [10]. A DGS, as a tool to solve problems, facilitates the construction of meaning for mathematical objects, since the tool affordances that mediate between mathematical knowledge and the student's cognitive system defines the characteristics of knowledge that an individual construct [11]. A DGS is not only an environment to develop straightedge and compass constructions, it allows us carry out arithmetic calculations or sketch graphs by typing an algebraic expression; but also constitute an mean to help problem solvers to build relationships between prior knowledge and new ideas or concepts. Through experimentation and the exploration of invariants the individuals can be able to articulate synthetic and analytical geometric knowledge.

Solving problems with the support of digital technology allow students to develop particular forms of interaction with mathematical objects, which differ from those that can be developed in a pencil and paper environment. When students solve problems using a DGS, the geometric objects, generally considered as ideal, intangible and imperceptible, acquire a tangible existence on the computer screen [11]. Some researchers refer to these ideas as the generation of a new mathematical realism [12, 13]. Within a DGS environment, the conceptual objects of mathematics are "materialized", and therefore can be operated and manipulated in an analogous form to physical objects using the mouse, stylus or finger.

In this line of thinking, the existence of objects such as conic sections or functions is no longer virtual for students, since the representations of those objects do not only occur in the students' mind but also on the computer screen. The objects on the screen become manipulable models of the mathematical objects subjected to the geometric rules (axioms) implicit in the software. Drawing a parabola in GeoGebra is an externalized cognitive act, in the sense that the action changes from being in the mind of the operator, to being externally executed on the computer screen. Thus, the software not only provides the means of representing mathematical objects externally, but can also lead students to reflect on the information provided by the computer system, as a result of operating representations of geometric objects provided by the tool [13].

One aspect that we cannot ignore as teachers or researchers, when students work with a DGS such as GeoGebra, is that the tool can foster the development of meanings directly related to the semiotic context of the artifact and the evolving character of meanings derived from the students' ability to use the tool, their ability to visualize relationships or sub-figures and their prior knowledge of geometric facts. Therefore, the process of solving problems with a DGS is deeply affected by the resources used to represent, manipulate, and associate the different representations offered by the system to problem solver.

The introduction of a DGS as a tool to solve geometric problems invariably changes the way in which the tools of synthetic geometry are employed to analyze geometric problems and consequently, increments students' opportunities to understand expressions, theorems and procedures. Resources offered by a DGS become part of an axiomatic system (which differs in several aspects from the Euclidean axiomatic system) whose properties are gradually integrated into the individual's cognitive system. Eventually, potentialities of the tool in conjunction with the geometric knowledge of students are structured as a dialectic human/tool system, in which both elements are deeply interwoven. As will be shown latter, without the support of Geogebra the objective of problem solvers was reduced to obtain a single response, while the use of the tool promoted that the task became a springboard to generate mathematical knowledge.

A DGS allows students to recognize relationships and invariants, through the exploration of the properties of objects that integrate a dynamic configuration; relationships that eventually strengthen the network of meanings associated with geometric and algebraic objects. The problem solving activity helped learners to integrate prior knowledge about mathematical objects (which presents different levels of articulation) in a structured network of knowledge, supporting of this manner the construction of a more robust meaning of a concept. This structuring process requires understanding of the epistemological role of digital tools when they are integrated into the cognitive structure of an individual.

By using a DGS, the students' actions are necessarily linked to the representational context of the computational environment, so that their observations and reflections are expressed in terms of the resources provided by it. In this regard, it is important to question whether when students work on a DGS a proof of mathematical results, from a didactic point of view must retain its axiomatic-deductive character in the classical sense or if it can be developed based solely on the tools offered by the DGS [13]. Our view is that both are complementary in achieving mathematical ways of thinking. In response to the claim that geometry must not be taught independently or separated from other areas of mathematics, we exemplify a way to address geometric situations that lead to the integration of different concepts and ideas through synthetic and analytic geometry tools during problem solving.

## 3 The Research Context

The task proposed in this paper was discussed in a context of problem-solving seminar, which involved participation of mathematics teachers, mathematicians and mathematics educators. All they were teachers in high school. The seminar's aim was to reflect on teaching and learning of mathematics, the participants discussed on forms of thinking and reasoning developed when they were engaged in the construction of paths to approach non-routine tasks.

The discussion was developed in three-hour weekly sessions for 16 weeks during one semester. The authors of this report coordinated the sessions whose main goal was to introduce the participants to the use of digital technology to work problems of geometric construction. Some of the approaches to the task emerged during three sessions and the others were proposed or resulted from the participants' work done out of the sessions. To work on the task, the participants initially discussed results and properties about a parabola and their elements such as foci, vertex or focal axis.

The task analyzed in this paper was: Given two lines $m$ and $t$, and a point $T$ on line $t$, construct a parabola such that the vertex $V$ is on line $m$ and such that lines $m$ and $t$ are tangent to the parabola at points $T$ and $V$, respectively.

During the seminar, a process of discussion on the proposed solution routes was addressed. We analyzed the solution routes developed by three participants: Jacob, John and Arthur, who were chosen because they showed the ability to clearly explain and justify their solution processes, and were willing to answer our questions about the thinking used to solve the problem. It is important to note that even though the participants were free to use a DGS to solve the problem only Arthur used it. The analysis of the solution paths is focused mainly on the strategies and heuristics used by the participants. We also determined the scope and limitations of the different approaches as well as their cognitive characteristics and pedagogical implications.

The task discussed in this article is representative of a broad class of situations of geometric construction in which the use of linked dragging [14] can conduce to the generation of families of conics as loci of some points in a dynamic configuration. Data analysis led us to reflect on learning with understanding [3] and the forms of mathematical thinking developed in activities where participants focus on doing mathematics [15]. We also reflected about the ways to promote an inquisitive approach to problem solving [7]. The paths of solution proposed by the participants included both synthetic and analytic approaches. We realized that the use of the DGS to approach problems of geometric construction promoted building connections to articulate the synthetic and analytical aspects of the geometry, and allowed us to identify and contrast the advantages and limitations of working within DGS with respect to a pencil and paper environment.

### 3.1 Preliminary Analysis of Solution Routes

A useful heuristic to follow in solving this problem is to consider the problem as solved. That is, assuming that the solution to the problem exists, in order to determine the properties that such a solution should have [16]. How can you construct a parabola that satisfies the conditions of the problem? GeoGebra has a command that allows you to construct a parabola given the focus and the directrix. Then, a line $n$ and a point $F$ are drawn, and a parabola is constructed based on those initial objects. A perpendicular line passing through F is then drawn. The intersection of the parabola with the perpendicular line is the vertex V. Now, we draw a line m, parallel to the directrix and passing through V. An arbitrary point T is then selected on the parabola, and a tangent line t to the parabola through T is traced using the “tangent” tool.

We now have a configuration that satisfies the conditions of the problem. The next step is to identify some relationships between the configuration elements that allow us to construct the parabola given the lines $m$ and $t$, and the point $T$. To find some relationships between the objects in a dynamic configuration, it is often useful to add auxiliary elements. However, the question of what objects must be added is not a simple one; the answer depends on each particular problem. For example, in this case, it was useful to draw the line $t'$, perpendicular to line $m$ at point $T$, as well as points $G$ and $J$, the intersections of $t$ and $t'$ with the line $m$, as shown in Fig. 1.

Is there any useful relationship between point $J$ and segment $VG$? If $G$ and $J$ are known, is it possible to determine $V$? Can we draw the point $G$ starting from point $T$ and line $m$? The answers to these questions will help us to obtain the information required to locate the parabola’s vertex knowing the point $T$ and lines $t$ and $m$: Given the lines $m$ and $t$ and the point $T$, we draw line $t'$, perpendicular to $m$. Then, point $G$ is the intersection of the lines $t'$ and $m$. We draw the vertex $V$ as the symmetric point of $G$ with respect to $J$. The line $p$, perpendicular to $m$ passing through $V$, necessarily is the focal axis of the parabola. We must now ask: which point on line $p$ is the focus of the parabola? One could choose an arbitrary point $F$ as the focus, and then draw $F'$ symmetrical to $F$ with respect to $V$ and obtain the directrix (line $n$) and draw the respective curve using the "parabola" tool.

If the point F is moved on the parabola's axis, we obtain a family of parabolas that partially satisfy the problem conditions, since line $m$ is tangential to $V$, but $T$ is not a point on the parabola. However, when we vary the position of F, there is a position where $T$ is on the curve (Fig. 1). So far, we can consider the problem partially solved. The challenge now is to locate the position of the point $F$, such that $T$ is a point on the parabola.

In Fig. 1, point $G'$ (the intersection of lines $t'$ and $n$) is included. What do we know about distances $G'T$ and $TF$? What is the definition of parabola? What kind of triangle is $G'T$ ? Is there any relationship between line $t$ and triangle $G'T$ ? What line can help us to obtain the focus of the parabola? If one recognizes that line $t$ is a perpendicular bisector, height or median of the triangle $G'T$, then reflecting the line $t'$ about line $t$, and finding the intersection of this new line with line $p$, will give us the location of the point $F$, the focus of the parabola (Fig. 2). The construction of the directrix, only requires us to obtain point $F'$, symmetrical to $F$ with respect to $V$ and, at this point to draw the line $n$ perpendicular to the axis of the parabola and finally employ the "parabola" tool to visualize the curve that satisfies the conditions of the problem (Fig. 2). This solution path has shown us how the use of different heuristics was useful to observe some basic properties of synthetic geometry. We also stand out the expertise required using the software to gather relevant information that allowed problem solver to design a solution route.

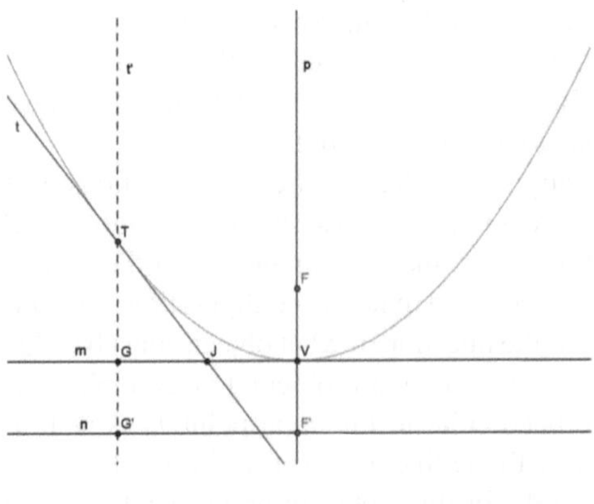


**Fig. 1.** The parabola seems to satisfy the conditions of the problem.

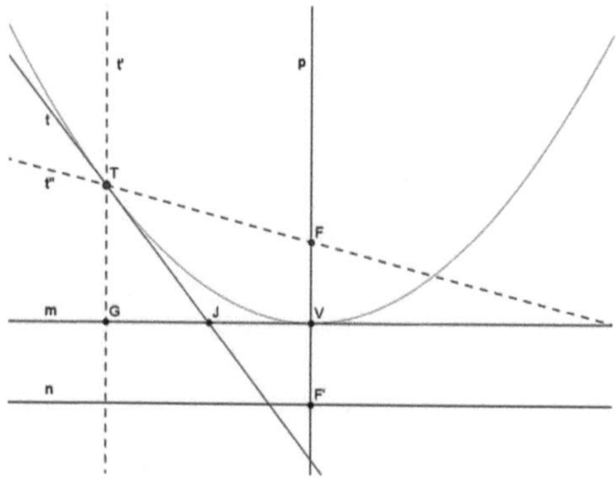


**Fig. 2.** The parabola that solves the problem.

### 3.2 Extending the Initial Problem - in Search of New Relationships

By changing the slope of line *t*, the geometric objects in the configuration will maintain the properties under which they were constructed, i.e. when we change the slope of line *t*, this line will remain tangential to the parabola at point *T*, and its vertex will be on line *m*. The following question can be formulated: What is the locus of the foci of that family of parabolas? To answer this question, a slight variation to the previous configuration will be introduced. In order to have control over the slope of line *t*, we draw a circumference *c* of arbitrary radius with center T, and then we draw a point *R* on circumference *c*. The line *t* was drawn connecting the points *T* and *R*. The idea of using auxiliary objects to control the movement of some element of a configuration is a heuristic characteristic of a DGS environment which we have named "controlled movement". The controlled movement heuristic is useful for solving and formulating new problems. Thus, when point *R* moves on the circumference, the slope of line *t* changes; in this situation, the geometric objects are moved in such a way that they maintain the properties assigned to the objects during the construction process. Can we imagine the locus that describes the parabolas' foci? The GeoGebra´s "Locus" tool can be used to visualize the path of point R (Fig. 3).

Using the "Locus" tool has been considered as a heuristic when it is used intentionally identifying the path described by a point in a dynamic configuration. In this case, one can conjecture that the curve described by the foci is another parabola whose focus is the point *T*, and the focal axis and the vertex are line $t'$ and point *G* respectively. What arguments can be provided to validate this conjecture? If the locus is a parabola, we must show that the segment *TF* is congruent to a segment perpendicular to the line m, and which segment can be considered?

Let us observe Fig. 4. The points $G'$ and *E* are located on the bottom semi-plane defined by line *m*. It can be seen that triangles *TGJ* and *EJV* are congruent and hence the conjecture is true. It should be noted that segments *GJ* and *JV* are also congruent. Furthermore, the angles in *G* and *V* are right-angles (by construction) and angles *GJT* and *VJE* are also congruent (because they are opposed at the vertex *J*). These facts allow us to establish that triangles *TGJ* and *EJV* are congruent (ASA criterion). Therefore,

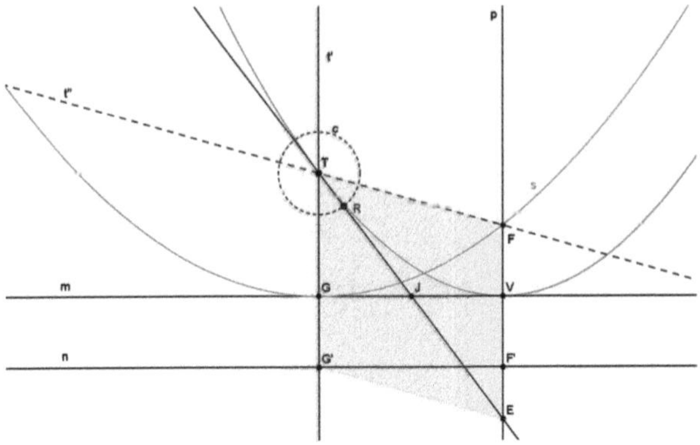


**Fig. 3.** Points G' y E are intersections of lines t' and p with line m.

segments *GT* and *EV* are congruent, *GG'* and *FV* are also congruent, and triangle *TG'F* is isosceles. Segment *TF* is then congruent with the segment *TG'*, but *TG'* is congruent with *FE*. Thus, the curve generated by moving the focus of the family of parabolas is a parabola also.

So far we have used DGS to show different alternatives for exploring and solving the problem. We will now try to show the scope of the use of algebraic tools in the solution. The intention is to provide an overview of how different representations are integrated to solve a problem. Below we discuss the solution routes constructed by three participants at the problem solving seminar, one of them with expertise in mathematics research, an undergraduate mathematics student and a mathematics educator. Beyond making a pictorial representation of the problem, the first two participants tried a similar strategy to that undertaken in previous sections. In order to visually illustrate their algebraic operations, the solution process of these participants is complemented with a geometric explanation.

### 3.3 Jacob's Solution

Jacob assigned general coordinates to points *T* and *V*, and he obtained the equations of lines *t* and *m*, *m*: $m_1x + b_1$ and t: $m_2x + b_2$. In order to get the coordinates of vertex V ($h$, $k$), Jacob used the equation of line *m* to determine the equation $m_1h + b_1$, so, the coordinates of vertex *V* can be written as ($h$, $m_1h + b_1$). Jacob assumed T($r$, $s$) like a fixed point and a tangent point; he replaced *r* in the equation of line *t*, with the aim of obtaining the coordinates of the tangent point $T(r, m_2r + b_2)$, and used the equation of the parabola, assuming that its axis is parallel to the vertical axis of the coordinates, to find *p* analytically as follow:

$$\begin{aligned} (x-h)^2 &= 4p(y-k) \\ p &= \frac{(x-h)^2}{4(y-k)} \end{aligned} \quad (1)$$

He, then substituted the values of $h$, $k$, $r$, $s$ in $p$ to obtain:

$$p = \frac{(r-h)^2}{4(m_2 r + b_2 - (m_1 h + b_1))} \tag{2}$$

Since he assumed that the axis of the parabola is parallel to the vertical axis of the coordinate system. Then, the coordinates of the focus are $(h, k+p)$:

$$\left(h,\ m_1 h + b_1 + \frac{(r-h)^2}{4(m_2 r + b_2 - (m_1 h + b_1))}\right)$$

**Comments.** In considering the points V and T on the line, in the way Jacob did, we can see that the position of these points will depend on the position of the coordinates h and r, respectively. That is, the coordinate k depends on h, and the coordinate s depends on r, and not of the slope of the lines. Jacob also considered these points as independent from each other, which is wrong; since both points belong to the parabola. The expression of the parabola given by Jacob suggests that it has a vertical axis, and the directrix of the parabola should be parallel to the horizontal axis of the coordinate system; thus, the line m from which the vertex belongs should be perpendicular to the axis of the parabola. The graphical representation of the solution process used to solve the problem is as follows: When we draw a perpendicular to the directrix of the parabola (in this case unknown) at point T, then the directrix should be parallel to the horizontal axis. So we must draw from T the perpendicular line t′ to the axis X, and at V we must draw a parallel line r to the horizontal axis. The lines r and t′ intersect at point Q. Moreover, the tangent t to the parabola cuts line r at a point N (Fig. 4).

If $V$ is the parabola's vertex, $N$ necessarily should be the midpoint of the segment $QV$. However, it can be verified that it is not the case. This would be a sufficient argument to discard Jacob's approach. This result is due to the consideration of

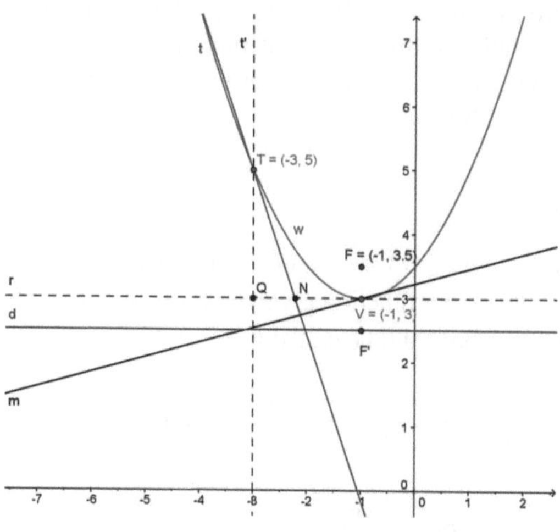


**Fig. 4.** The parabola does not satisfy the problem conditions.

points as independent from each other. If we follow the procedure described by Jacob, the focus of the parabola should be $F$ (–1, 3.5), which has been calculated under the conditions of the expression obtained for the focus with the coordinates $T$ (–3, 5) and $V$(–1, 3). If $F$ is the focus, then the directrix passes through $F'$, the symmetrical point $F$ with respect to $V$. The curve $w$ is the parabola, where $F$ is its focus, it has vertex $V$ and the directrix is line $d$ (Fig. 4).

In conclusion, the vertex of the parabola is the point $V$ but the line t is not a tangent to the parabola at point $T$. However, the problem is solvable under the conditions that the vertex is on the line $m$ and the parabola is vertical. This solution is shown below (Fig. 5). We have seen that the vertex is not any point on line m. Let us consider a point $V'$ on line m such that $V'$ moves on it. The idea is to find the position where the point V′ corresponds with the vertex of the parabola, having $t$ as tangent at point $T$.

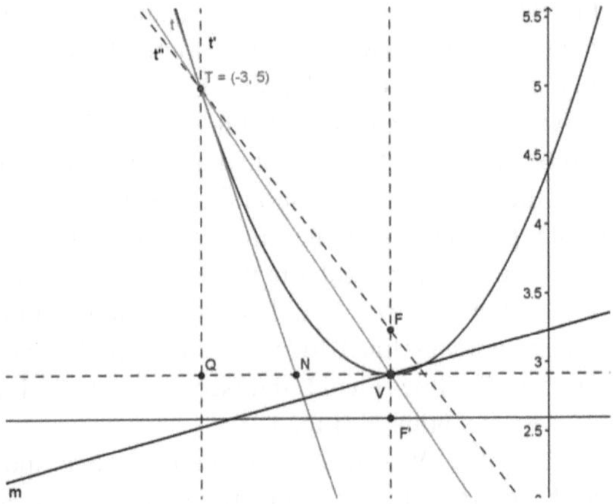


**Fig. 5.** The parabola satisfies the condition of being tangent to the line t at T, but not to m at V.

When Jacob's procedure was analyzed with the help of the DGS, we found that in this way it is only possible to solve the problem partially, since the conditions that the parabola is tangent to the line $t$ at $T$ and the vertex is on the line $m$ are satisfied, but the parabola is not tangent to line $m$.

## 3.4 John's Solution

John started proposing equations for each of the lines t and m as follow: t: $y = m_1x + b_1$ and m: $y = m_2x + b_2$. Then, the function given by t was integrated to obtain the form of an expression for the parabola and he called it $P$.

$$\int m_1x + b_1\,dx = \frac{m_1x^2}{2} + b_1x + k_1 \tag{3}$$

$$P\!: \; y = \frac{m_1x^2}{2} + b_1x + k_1 \tag{4}$$

He completed squares to write the equation of the parabola, and he obtained an expression for the parabola with axis parallel to the vertical axis, where he identified the vertex (h, k), given by $h = -b_1/m_1$ and $k = k_1 - (b_1^2/2m_1)$. As the vertex lies on the line m, he replaced it to find $k_1$, the constant of integration. Thus, similarly to Jacob, John obtained an expression that could represent a parabola with its vertical axis in terms of the intercept with vertical axis ($b_1$ and $b_2$) and the slope of the initial lines.

$$\begin{aligned} k_1 - \frac{b^2{}_1}{2m_1} &= m_2\left(-\frac{b_1}{m_1}\right) + b_2 \\ k_1 = m_2\frac{b_1}{m_1} + b_2 + \frac{b^2{}_1}{2m_1} &= \frac{b_1}{m_1}\left(m_2 + \frac{b_1}{2}\right) + b_2 \end{aligned} \quad (5)$$

**Comments.** It may be observed that John's procedure is based on the assumption that the parabola has its vertical axis looking very similar to Jacob's hypothesis. This shows how John attempts to relate his knowledge of calculus with his knowledge of analytical geometry, but without a graphical and dynamic representation to help him to explore the problem; such understanding is insufficient to find the solution.

### 3.5 Arthur's Solution

This participant assumed that line m is the horizontal axis of the coordinate system. Moreover, he assigned coordinates (a, b) to point T, and slope n to line t. Then, he determined the equation of the line t as $y = n\,(x–a) + b$. Since m is the horizontal axis, the vertex of the parabola has coordinates $V(c, 0)$ and its equation is $y = k\,(x–c)^2$. The slope of the tangent line at the point (a, b) to this parabola is $n = 2\,k\,(x–c)$. In addition, the parabola must go through the point (a, b), and thus $b = k\,(a–c)^2$. In order to find the values of parameters k and c, Arthur solved the system of equations.

$$\left\{ \begin{aligned} n &= 2k(a-c) \\ b &= k(a-c)^2 \end{aligned} \right. \quad (6)$$

Isolating $a–c$ from the first equation of (6), we have that $a–c = n/2\,k$ by substituting into the second equation of (6) we have that $b = k\,(n/2\,k)^2$ and hence $k = n^2/4b$ and $c = (an–2b)/n$. Then, the equation of the parabola with vertical axis and vertex on the X-axis is given by:

$$y = \left(\frac{n^2}{4b}\right)\left(x - \frac{an-2b}{n}\right)^2 \quad (7)$$

In order to obtain additional evidence that the solution is correct, Arthur constructed a dynamic configuration in GeoGebra, in which the values of a, b and n were defined as sliders, and from these values he calculated the values of k and c, and then he drew the parabola that satisfies the conditions of the problem. Now, the coordinates of the focus of the parabola are $((an–2b)/n,\, b/n^2)$ and it follows that the parametric coordinates of the locus described by the focus, considering the slope parameter n are:

$$\begin{cases} x = \frac{an-2b}{n} \\ y = \frac{b}{n^2} \end{cases} \quad (8)$$

By solving n in both equations and equating the resulting expression we obtain that $y = (1/4b)\,(x-a)^2$, the equation of the parabola that describes the focus when the slope of line t varies (Fig. 6).

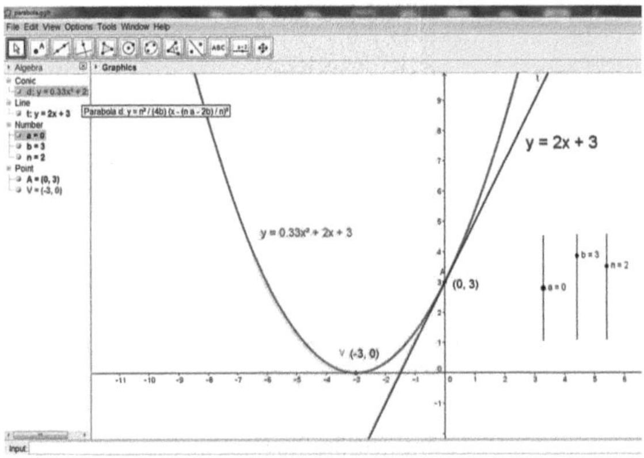


**Fig. 6.** Arthur's dynamic configuration.

**Comments.** Arthur first conducted the algebraic procedure to obtain the equation of the parabola that satisfies the conditions of the problem; however, to be certain that the solution was correct he used GeoGebra to develop a dynamic configuration in which the problem data were defined as sliders, and from the data he obtained the equation of the parabola for a particular case. Moreover, he built a family of particular solutions as a means of verifying that the algebraic solution of the problem was correct.

## 4 Final Remarks

We obtained evidence that the use of a DGS can enhance the emergence of a wide range of heuristics, some of which are specifics to this type of environment, such as controlled movement and locus heuristics. In formulating new problems in the context of DGS, problems that cannot be solved with only synthetic tools emerge. This constitutes an example of the potential of the technological environment to expand the field of exploration into the study of more complex problems. It should be noted that in order to progress in solving problems as we have shown, where the transition from solving a particular problem to exploring more general qualities as possible, the active participation of problem solvers is required, while maintaining the conviction that finding a solution to the problem is not the only purpose. Therefore, it is desirable for the individual to maintain an exploratory vision that allows him/her to seek different strategies for solving a problem and identifying mathematical relationships underlying in the configurations used to approach the problem. In order to improve opportunities of learning mathematics by using material and applications available on the web, the previous aspects should be considered; and in making decisions when we think on teaching mathematics in a technological environment.

The review of the work done by the participants shows that when algebraic procedures are not coordinated with a geometric representation they can lead to solutions that do not satisfy all the conditions requested in the problem statement. This fact is congruent with Duval [17] who claims that the use of a single representation is a limiting factor because it provides little information on the most relevant mathematical relationships in the problem statement.

In this regard, we note that conducting algebraic calculations without tools that help students to understand algebraic procedures, could degenerate into blind work, thereby limiting the development of mathematical knowledge. We have shown some of the relationships that can be established in order to improve the understanding of the concepts involved. Thus, the identification of the relationships in a geometric configuration, together with the potential offered by the tool for the exploration and construction of loci, are structured into a new knowledge construct to be incorporated into the mathematical knowledge of the student [12].

We found that the discussion process of different problem solution paths promoted the construction of knowledge regarding the nature of mathematics and discipline learning, emphasizing the connections between synthetic and analytic geometry that can be exploited in the search for the construction of knowledge related to the analytic geometry and supported by the use of more basic skills. Moreover, as noted in previous sections, the three participants directed their work towards finding the equation of the parabola with vertical axis without considering other cases. This fact could be due to the influence of school practices, which restrain the potential of students to explore and inquire the veracity of the solution and to query whether the found solution is unique. This aspect suggests the need to incorporate classroom activities that encourage students to develop metacognitive skills. In order to support students' construction of mathematical sense, it is necessary that teachers are aware of the thought processes that are developed to solve problems in a dynamic geometry environment, that they know the mistakes arising with software usage and that they know the forms of interaction that emerge in the classroom [18]. Thus, the research results showed in this paper can be a means to influence the design of technological learning environments.

In the same vein suggested by Santos-Trigo and Reyes-Martinez [1], we concluded that the use of digital technologies for enhance learners' mathematical understanding involves the collaboration of experts' communities working on different fields and determine what are important elements in the users' appropriation process of the tool. Thus, designers of instructional activities should consider or rely on information about how users employ digital technologies as instrument to solve problems. Finally, our results contributes to the research field offering information about what type of mathematical reasoning and knowledge problem solvers construct as a result of using digital tools in their learning experiences.

Finally, we remark one possible route to implement the task analyzed in this paper in a sequence teaching, it should consider: (1) A learners' open discussion on what the statement of the task involves, emphasis should be on how students make sense of the problem statement and what ideas, concepts, and relationships come to their mind related to a parabola and a tangent line; (2) a list of concepts and relationships provided by learners should be the departure point to start thinking of possible ways to construct the parabola. For example, they might be asked about properties of objects related to the parabola such as foci, focal axis, vertex, directrix, and so on; (3) a relevant task approach involved the construction of a dynamic model. Thus, it is important that learners engage in experiences to move objects within the geometric configuration and observe their behavior. Relaxing initial conditions of tasks and adding auxiliary objects becomes crucial strategies to control objects' movements and explore their behaviors; and (4) the approaches to solve the tasks proposed in this paper provide information that teachers can transform into a set of questions to guide and adjust to the development of their instructional materials.

## References


1. Santos-Trigo, M., Reyes-Martinez, I.: The coordinated use of digital technologies in learning environments. In: Uden, L., Sinclair, J., Tao, Y.-H., Liberona, D. (eds.) LTEC 2014. CCIS, vol. 446, pp. 61–71. Springer, Heidelberg (2014)
2. Schmidt, E., Cohen, J.: The New Digital Area: Reshaping the Future of People. Nations and Business. Random House and Google Inc., New York (2013)
3. Hiebert, J., Carpenter, T.P., Fennema, E., Fuson, K.C., Wearne, D., Murray, H., Olivier, A., Human, P.: Making Sense: Teaching and Learning Mathematics With Understanding. Heinemann, Portsmouth (1997)
4. Contreras, A., Contreras, M., Garcia, M.: Sobre la geometría sintética y analítica. La elipse y sus construcciones. Rev. Lat. Inv. Mat. Educ. **5**(2), 111–132 (2002)
5. Ancochea, B.: Las funciones de las calculadoras simbólicas en la articulación entre la geometría sintética y la geometría analítica en secundaria. In: Bosch, M., Gascon, J., Ruiz, A., Artaud, M., Bronner, A., Chevallard, Y., Cirade, G., Ladage, C., Larguier, M. (eds.) Un panorama de la TAD III Congreso Internacional sobre la TAD, pp. 533–551. Centre de Recerca Matemàtica, Barcelona (2010)
6. Gascón, J.: Evolución de la controversia entre geometría sintética y geometría analítica. Un punto de vista didáctico-matemático. Dis. Mat. Sem. Mat. Fund. **28**, 1–21 (2002)
7. Santos-Trigo, M., Espinosa-Perez, H., Reyes-Rodriguez, A.: Constructing a parabolas' world using dynamic software to explore properties and meanings. IJMEST **12**(3), 125–134 (2005)
8. Santos-Trigo, M., Reyes-Rodriguez, A., Espinosa-Perez, H.: Musing on the use of dynamic software and mathematics epistemology. TEAMAT **26**(4), 167–178 (2007)
9. Polya, G.: How to Solve It. Princeton University Press, Princeton (1945)
10. Pea, R.D.: Cognitive technologies for mathematics education. In: Schoenfeld, A. (ed.) Cognitive Science and Mathematics Education, pp. 89–122. Erlbaum, Hillsdale (1987)
11. Drijvers, P., Kieran, C., Mariotti, M.A., Ainley, J., Andresen, M., Chan, Y., Dana-Picard, T., Gueudet, G., Kidron, I., Leung, A., Meagher, M.: Integrating technology into mathematics education: theoretical perspectives. In: Hoyles, C., Lagrange, J.-B. (eds.) Mathematics Education and Technology: Rethinking the Terrain. New ICMI Study Series, vol. 13, pp. 89–132. Springer, New York (2010)

12. Balacheff, N.: Computer-Based Learning Environment in Mathematics. In: Bishop, A.J., Clements, K., Kilpatrick, J., Laborde, C. (eds.) International Handbook of Mathematics Education. Kluwer International Handbooks of Education, vol. 4, pp. 469–501. Springer, Heidelberg (2010)
13. Moreno-Armella, L., Sriraman, B.: Structural stability and dynamic geometry: Some ideas on situated proofs. ZDM Math. Educ. **37**(3), 130–139 (2005)
14. Arzarello, F., Olivero, F., Paola, D., Robutti, O.: A cognitive analysis of dragging practices in Cabri environments. ZDM Math. Educ. **34**(3), 66–72 (2002)
15. Schoenfeld, A.H.: Learning to think mathematically: Problem solving, metacognition, and sense-making in mathematics. In: Grouws, D. (ed.) Handbook for Research on Mathematics Teaching and Learning, pp. 334–370. MacMillan, New York (1992)
16. Schoenfeld, A.H.: Mathematical Problem Solving. Academic Press, Orlando (1985)
17. Duval, R.: Sémiosis et pensée humaine: Registres sémiotiques et apprentissage intellectuels. Peter Lang, Berne (1995)
18. Ruben, K., Hennessy, S., Deaney, R.: Constructions of dynamic geometry: A study of the interpretative flexibility of educational software in classroom practice. Comp. Educ. **51**(1), 297–317 (2008)

# The Use of Digital Technology in Extending Mathematical Problem Solving Reasoning

Manuel Santos-Trigo(✉), Isaid Reyes-Martínez, and Daniel Aguilar-Magallón

Centre for Research and Advanced Studies, Cinvestav-IPN, Mexico City, Mexico
msantos@cinvestav.mx

**Abstract.** The incorporation of digital technologies (both multiple purpose and mathematics action technologies) in mathematical learning environments can foster and extend discussions among learners and teachers even beyond class time. That is, learners not only keep reflecting on mathematical ideas or problems; but also they can review or consult related online resources. Similarly, the use of dynamic geometry systems provides affordances to construct dynamic models of tasks where learners can analyse how objects move within the configuration and formulate mathematical relations. In this report, we discuss three exemplars to characterize ways in which the use of technology extends mathematical reasoning in problem solving approaches. This information becomes important for teachers to value and frame the incorporation of technology in learning environments. At the end, some limitations of this approach are discussed.

**Keywords:** Digital technology · Mathematical problem solving · Tool affordances and mathematical reasoning

## 1 Introduction

School systems worldwide face a challenge to consistently incorporate the coordinated use of digital technologies in curriculum proposals and learning environments. In this context, it is important to discuss what changes the use of technology brings into contents, structure, and ways of reasoning that learners could develop about concepts and problems solving competencies. For example, with the use of a dynamic geometry system, students can construct models where parameters or elements can be moved to visualize and explore behaviours of mathematical objects. Similarly, learners can access online information that includes concept definitions and explanations (https://www.khanacademy.org), problem examples, and in some cases solutions of typical course problems. As results, teaching/learning environments should not only guide students to select and analyse pertinent online resources; but also to incorporate that information into the learning activities. Mobile devices such as tablets o smart phones can extend learning environments to support peers communication or interaction almost anytime. That is, the use of technology becomes important to structure extended conversations among students and teachers to frame and foster problems solving


L. Uden et al. (Eds.): LTEC 2015, CCIS 533, pp. 298–309, 2015.
DOI: 10.1007/978-3-319-22629-3_24

experiences. Walling [1] pointed out "this Digital Age shift in schools is not, or should not be, about hardware and software. It should be about teaching and learning in new and exciting ways that expand learning opportunities for all students" (p. xiii). How can mathematics teachers design and implement learning activities where students rely on the use different technologies to develop mathematical knowledge and problem solving experiences? To delve into this question, we review the role played by the coordinated use of digital technology in students' development of mathematical knowledge. Furthermore, we present and discuss exemplars that illustrate ways in which learners could formulate problems, transform routine tasks into a set of opportunities to develop deep mathematical knowledge and engage in collaboration projects to comprehend, refine, and apply mathematical concepts.

## 2 Background and Conceptual Framework

In the traditional teaching/learning environments the teacher is the only responsible to select mathematics tasks and to coordinate the implementation of learning activities. In general terms, the way teachers and students interact during class activities has remained consistent over the years. This model has been criticized in terms that its success depends mainly on the teacher's individual competencies to select and implement learning activities, the lack of motivation that students often experience during the development of the course, and the limited options for students to discuss curriculum contents beyond syllabus and courses goals. What type of innovations should learning environments incorporate in order for students to rely on online resources and technologies to develop mathematical thinking? Alagic and Alagic [2] pointed out that digital technologies offer teachers and learners affordances to provide a learning environment that fosters collaboration and direct interaction with peers. Thus, teaching environments need to be adjusted to take into account and incorporate the use of diverse technologies in students learning of mathematics. Barbeau [3] argues that in the process of learning, students face challenges that "often involve explanation, questioning and conjecturing, multiple approaches, evaluation of solutions for effectiveness and elegance, and construction and evaluation examples" (p. 5). Nowadays, it is recognized that learning involves a maturation process that requires time for students to develop an increasingly complex network of connections of concepts and problem solving strategies. "To learn mathematics more meaningfully, students need to build connections over time through a coherent learning progression with adequate support for the affective challenges of maintaining interest and engagement" [4] (p. 34). Mathematical tasks play a crucial role for students to develop awareness of technology affordances as a means to comprehend and develop problem-solving competencies. Tasks are given to students to engage them in thinking in order to experience shifts in their focus and structure of their attention. Mason [5] stated: …"Tasks are provided for students to initiate activity, which provides experience and, in order to learn effectively from experience, it helps to adopt a reflexive stance" (p. 12). With the use of technologies students continuously reflect on what ways of reasoning about concepts and problems that are important to detect invariance and to support mathematical relationships. It is recognized that different digital technologies offer distinct opportunities for learners to engage in mathematical thinking. Thus, the existence of several types of technologies makes necessary to identify what a particular technology can offer to learners during the process of comprehending mathematical ideas and solving problems.

Artigue and Mariotti [6] characterize a conceptual framework as a structured but dynamic entity that articulates research questions, methods to address those questions, data collection, and interpretation of research results. In this perspective, our research inquiry is framed around three related fields: mathematical problem solving, digital technologies, and subjects' construction of mathematical knowledge [7]. In the problem solving domain, our interest lies on orienting and discussing learners behaviours and activities in terms of three constructs: (i) the importance of goals (what do mathematics learning and problem solving activities involve?), (ii) orientations (what do learning experiences, beliefs, values, and resources teachers or learners bring into learning environments?) and (iii) the decision making process involved in dealing with mathematical tasks [8]. In the field of digital technologies, we identify changes to the content and learning environments that the use of technology brings to the students' construction of mathematical knowledge. In particular, we emphasize and make explicit the potential and opportunities that the coordinated use of digital technologies offer to subjects to reason about mathematical concepts and problems. Furthermore, the subjects' comprehension of mathematical ideas and the development of problem solving competencies can be framed and structured around a problematizing principle. Problematizing means that students develop and practice an inquisitive or inquiring approach to delve into concepts, to identify relationships among data and to solve mathematical tasks. Likewise, the coordinated use of digital technologies appears relevant throughout all problem-solving episodes that include problem formulation, comprehension, representation, exploration, generalization, and communication of results. In this perspective, learners engage in continuous problem solving activities that involve:

- Looking for information related to the themes or contents in study through online books, Wikipedia and WolframAlpha computational knowledge machine. In this process, students rely on methods and strategies that help them select, analyse, summarize and contrast the use of available information.
- Learning and fostering several ways to work on problems within a community that shares and discusses ideas as a part of a group or teams where it is important for students to listen to others during problem solving approaches.
- Using different digital tools to represent, explore, solve and communicate results, in particular, the construction and analysis of dynamic models of problems.
- Identifying and discussing partial results that might appear during the solution process of tasks and share them with other students.
- Looking for different and novel ways to represent and explore problems. In this process, students are encouraged to find creative solutions to problems.

# 3 Exemplars

We present three exemplars to illustrate how the use of technology becomes important to construct dynamic models of problems in order to engage learners in the process of recognizing patterns, in looking for arguments to support mathematical relations and in presenting and communicating results. For each exemplar, we comment on features of mathematical reasoning that emerges during the solution process of the task. It is important to mention that the tasks are part of the activities that we have been implementing in a problem-solving seminar with high school teachers. One goal of the seminar is to analyse the process that teachers get involved during the tool appropriation and to examine ways of reasoning that they exhibit to represent, explore and solve the tasks. In this report, we focus on identifying features of mathematical reasoning that appear during the solution of the tasks associated with the use of the tools. We argue that teachers themselves need to get involved in problem solving experiences in order for them to develop resources and strategies to efficiently use technology affordances in the problem solving approaches. Although the approaches the problems represent part of the work that high school teachers have shown during the problem solving sessions, we do not intend to analyse in detail how teachers individually contributed to each task solution; rather, we aim at characterizing what types of reasoning became involved during those approaches as a group.

## 3.1 The Construction of Dynamic Models

The goal is to represent mathematical tasks dynamically. To this end, learners are guided to develop resources and strategies to construct or build dynamic configurations of tasks where objects can be moved within the model. Thus, moving points or objects orderly becomes a crucial strategy to construct dynamic models. Güçler et al. [9] argue that the use of a dynamic geometry system "allows students to reason quickly from the specific to the general, from concrete to abstract, from example or illustration to concept and idea (p. 99). Figure 1 shows triangle ABC and a perpendicular bisector of side BC. Circle centred at A is a heuristic strategy to move side AC on the plane by moving point P along the circle. It is observed that a family of triangles is generated when point P is moved along the circle. What is the locus of point Q when point P is moved along the circle?

Figure 2 shows that the locus of point Q seems to be a hyperbola. It also shows that for different positions of point Q it is true that |d(A, Q) – d(Q, B)| is a constant (2.37). That is, it holds the definition of the hyperbola with foci points A and B. Another argument to show that the locus is hyperbola involves recognizing that point Q is on the perpendicular bisector of side BC, then, d(Q, C) = d(Q, B) and d(A, Q) = d(A, C) + d(C, Q). Therefore, d(A, Q) – d(Q, B) = d(A, C) which is constant (side AC).

What happens if point B is moved along line AB? Figure 3 shows that at one position the hyperbola becomes an ellipse. Point Q generates de locus and is on the perpendicular bisector of BC. Then, d(A, Q) + d(Q, B) = d(A, Q) + d(Q, C) = d(A, C). That is, the sum of the distances from Q to foci A and B is constant (definition of ellipse).

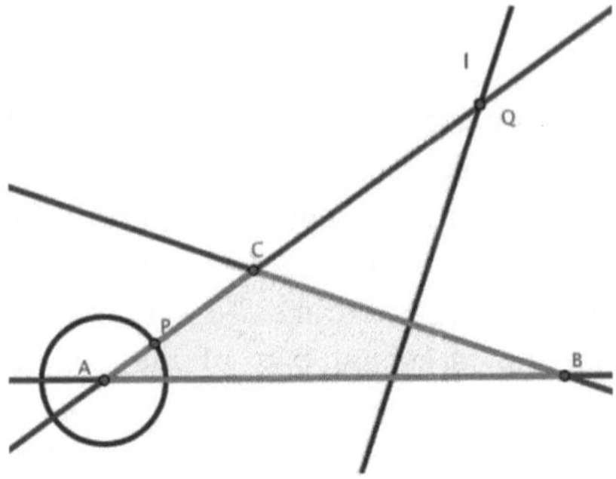


**Fig. 1.** Triangle ABC and the perpendicular bisector of side BC.

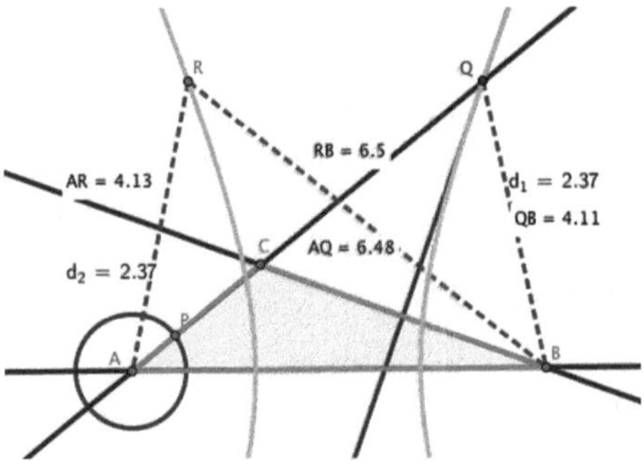


**Fig. 2.** An empirical argument to show that the locus of Q is a hyperbola.

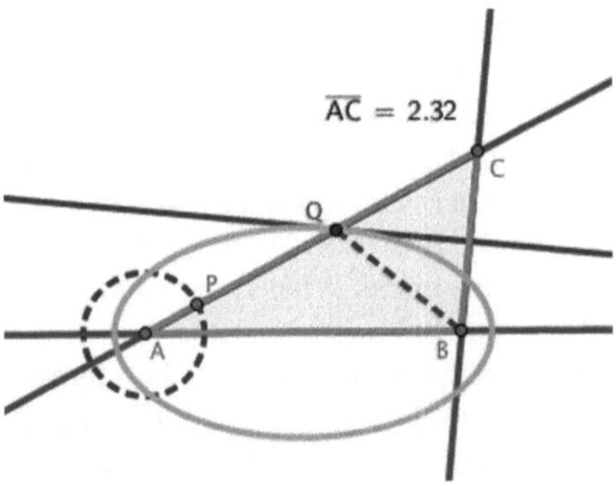


**Fig. 3.** The generation of an ellipse within the dynamic model.

**Comment:** A key activity in mathematical practice is to examine objects or models in order to identify patterns or invariants. To this end, the use of a dynamic geometry system (such as GeoGebra) offers affordances for learners to explore the behaviour of mathematical objects as a result of moving others elements within the model or dynamic configuration. In this case, a triangle is a model or platform to identify objects that appear in an analytic geometric course. The construction of a perpendicular bisector becomes instrumental to generate and justify properties the conic sections. The objects dynamic exploration involves examining a family of triangles by moving a particular point (P) and looking for arguments to explain relationships among the objects. Similarly, finding loci of points is another important strategy to find mathematical relations.

### 3.2 Patterns' Recognition

In general terms, a pattern is a rule or way to describe certain type of behaviour of a finite or infinity family of objects. It can be described verbally or via a formula or symbolic expressions. There are different types of patterns that might appear in the study of numbers, shapes, motion, or mathematical objects behaviours. Steen [10] points out that mathematics is an exploratory science that aims to identify different types of patterns found in nature phenomena or even patterns created by analysing the behaviours of other patterns.

> …[Thus] patterns can be either real of imagined, visual or mental, static or dynamic, qualitative or quantitative…They can arise from the world around us, from the depths of space and time, or from the inner working of the human mind [11] (p. 3).

The process involved in the identification of patterns includes ways to observe what is important in the situation or phenomenon and to think of what mathematical resources are need to express it. What tools or resources and ways of thinking do students need to develop in order to identify and explore different types of mathematical patterns? What type of problems or tasks should teachers discuss with their students in order to explore, identify, and communicate mathematical patterns? Addressing these types of questions implies analysing and reflecting on what features of mathematical thinking are relevant in the process of looking for and examining the behaviours of mathematical objects. We argue that students not only should deal with a variety of situations to find and explore patterns; but also teachers should discuss overly with students what tools and questions become important to recognize and analyse how the patter behaves.

Within a variety of patterns, the concept of recursion is essential in mathematics, computers science, biology and even language. Recursion definitions are used to characterize something in terms of itself. For example, the factorial function is defined as $1! = 1$ and $N! = (N - 1)!(N)$ for $N \geq 2$, N integer. Cuoco [12] pointed out that recursive thinking is a key problem solving approach to build spreadsheet analysis to explain how banks figure out the monthly payment on a house or car loan. What types of resources and ways of reasoning should students develop and exhibit to approach recursive tasks? We use a task that involves a recursive sequence to illustrate that the use of GeoGebra provides a means for learners to make sense of the task and to initially explore the sequence behaviour.

**The task:** Let the real numbers $a_0$ and $a_1$ be given. Define the sequence $\{a_n\}$ by $a_n = \frac{a_{n-2}+a_{n-1}}{2}$ for each $n \geq 2$. Prove that $\lim_{n\to\infty} a_n$ exists and determine its value [13] (p. 77).

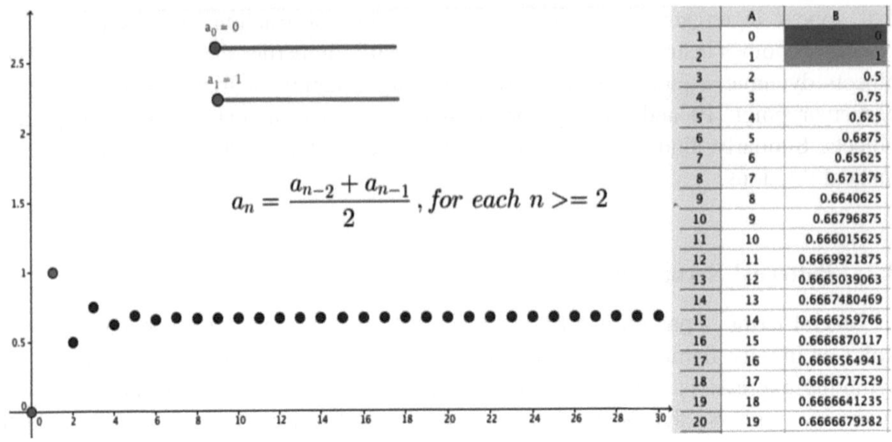


**Fig. 4.** Visualizing the behaviour of some elements of the sequence

To focus on particular cases in order to make sense of and explore the sequence behaviour is a common strategy in pattern recognition. The issue is then how the problem solver decides and implements what a special case to consider or try in order to shed light on its solution. In this problem, Schoenfeld recommends to evaluate the sequence for $a_0 = 0$ and $a_1 = 1$ and (as special case) to observe the involved pattern. Figure 4 shows a dynamic model of the sequence where $a_0 = 0$ and $a_1 = 1$. In http://www.geogebratube.org/student/m139246 the initial values are associated with two sliders whose values can be changed by moving the points on the sliders. Visually, the behaviour of the sequence, for $a_0 = 0$ and $a_1 = 1$, converges to $0.666\ldots = 2/3$. How can we get a closed form for the general term $a_n$?

We can also begin by finding some of its particular values. The list of terms of the sequence includes both rational and decimal representations.

$$a_n = \frac{a_{n-2} + a_{n-1}}{2}$$

The initial conditions are $a_0 = 0$ and $a_1 = 1$, then, some terms of the sequence are:

$$0, 1, \frac{1}{2}, \frac{3}{4}, \frac{5}{8}, \frac{11}{16}, \frac{21}{32}, \frac{43}{64}, \frac{85}{128}, \ldots$$

These terms expressed in decimal form are:

$$0,\ 1,\ 0.5,\ 0.75,\ 0.625,\ 0.6875,\ 0.65625,\ 0.671875,\ 0.6640625,\ \ldots$$

If we continue writing more terms, we can observe that after certain number of terms of the decimal part includes the digit 6 (looking for patterns). That is, we get expressions such as 0.666…Here are some examples:

$$a_{10} = \frac{341}{512} \approx 0.666015625$$

Or

$$a_{20} = \frac{349525}{5124288} \approx 0.6666660308$$

Examining the behaviour of the decimal expression let us to conjecture that the limit of the sequence is $0.666\ldots = {}^2/_3$.

**Comment:** Exploring dynamically the sequence behavior via the use of digital technologies (GeoGebra) offers students not only a way to visualize graphically the behavior of the sequence elements associated with the special case; but also (through the use of sliders) others cases can be visualized. In addition, the use of others technologies (CAS) became important to carry out numeric and symbolic calculations to delve into the pattern sequence. Making sense of task statements is essential to recognize and express patterns that are involved in recursive tasks. Cases that are easy to handle ($a_0 = 0$ and $a_1 = 1$) often provide useful information to recognize and explore patterns. Rational and decimal representations of results offer different angles to detect invariance. For instance, the decimal representation of the generated elements for the special case led us to visualize the limit; while the rational form led us to focus on the differences $a_{n+1} - a_n$. Looking at the difference is also an important strategy to detect patterns. Similarly, expressing the sequence terms in different manners is another useful to identify interesting behaviors. Table 1 shows some patterns that emerged from the list of some element of the initial sequence.

**Table 1.** Some patterns involved in the terms of the sequence.

| Elements of the sequence | Representation involving power of 2 |
|---|---|
| $a_2 = \frac{a_0+a_1}{2}$ | $a_2 = \frac{(2^0)a_0+(2^0)a_1}{2}$ |
| $a_3 = \frac{a_1+\frac{a_0+a_1}{2}}{2} = \frac{a_0+3a_1}{2^2}$ | $a_3 = \frac{(2^0)a_0+(2^1+2^0)a_1}{2^2}$ |
| $a_4 = \frac{\frac{a_0+a_1}{2}+\frac{a_0+3a_1}{2^2}}{2} = \frac{3a_0+5a_1}{2^3}$ | $a_4 = \frac{(2^1+2^0)a_0+(2^2+2^1-2^0)a_1}{2^3}$ |
| $a_5 = \frac{\frac{a_0+3a_1}{2^2}+\frac{3a_0+5a_1}{2^3}}{2} = \frac{5a_0+11a_1}{2^4}$ | $a_5 = \frac{(2^2+2^1-2^0)a_0+(2^3+2^2-2^1+2^0)a_1}{2^4}$ |

### 3.3 Making Sense and Conjecturing

The task involves analysing properties and relationships associated with linear and quadratic functions.

**The task**: Based on a given linear function $f$, find another linear function $g$, such as the graph of the product function $h = f.g$ is tangent to both linear functions. The task is an adjusted version of a problem used by Wilson and Barnes and it can be found in: http://jwilson.coe.uga.edu/Texts.Folder/tangent/f(x).g(x)%3Dh(x).html

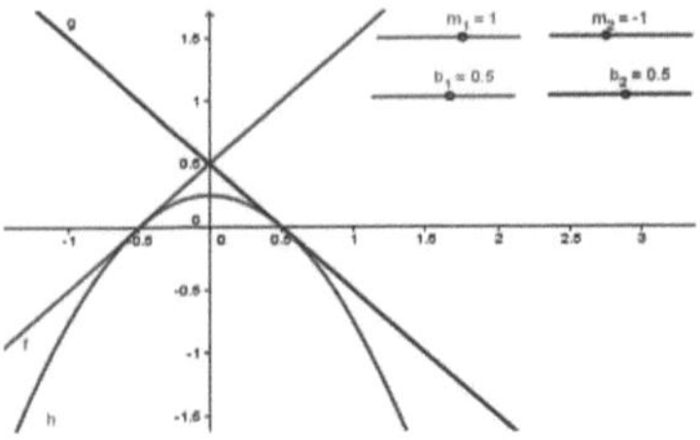


| | | |
|---|---|---|
| 1. $f(x) = -x + 0.5$, | $g(x) = x + 0.5$, | $h(x) = -x^2 + 0.25$ |
| 2. $f(x) = -2x + 2$, | $g(x) = 2x - 1$, | $h(x) = -4x^2 + 6x - 2$ |
| 3. $f(x) = x + 2$, | $g(x) = -x - 1$, | $h(x) = -x^2 - 3x - 2$ |
| 4. $f(x) = -2x + 4$, | $g(x) = 2x - 3$, | $h(x) = -4x^2 + 14x - 12$ |
| 5. $f(x) = -x - 2$, | $g(x) = x + 3$, | $h(x) = -x^2 - 5x - 6$ |

**Fig. 5.** (a) Finding function $g$. (b) Examples of some solutions.

To make sense of the task, we can begin with a particular case, that is, "given the function $f(x) = x + \frac{1}{2}$, find a linear function $g$ such as the graph of $h = f.g$ is tangent to $f$ and $g$". Some questions might help learners understand the task: What does it mean two linear functions are each tangent to its product? Can we sketch some examples? Is it always possible to find those functions holding the condition? What properties or how the product of two linear function behave? The use of GeoGebra provides affordances to represent and explore graphically a family of linear functions and their product by changing through a slider the slope and y-intercept point. Figure 5a shows a visual solution to the task, and Fig. 5b shows others examples that satisfy the conditions.

Based on this empirical information, some conjectures emerge:

(i) *For two given linear functions $f(x) = m_1x + b_1$ and $g(x) = m_2x + b_2$ when the graph of the product $f(x).g(x)$ is tangent to both $f$ and $g$ then $m_1 = -m_2$ (same slope with opposite sign) and also $b_1 + b_2 = 1$.*

(ii) *The function $f$ intersects the quadratic function $h = h(f(x).g(x))$ at one or two points and one them (in case that there are two) $B(x_1,f(x_1))$ also holds that* $g(x_1) = 1$. This is because at the intersection point it is true that $f(x_1) = h(x_1) = f(x_1)$ *and therefore $g(x_1) = 1$. Likewise, when a linear function became tangent to the parabola, then intersection points between the product function and the linear function coincide (Fig. 6).*

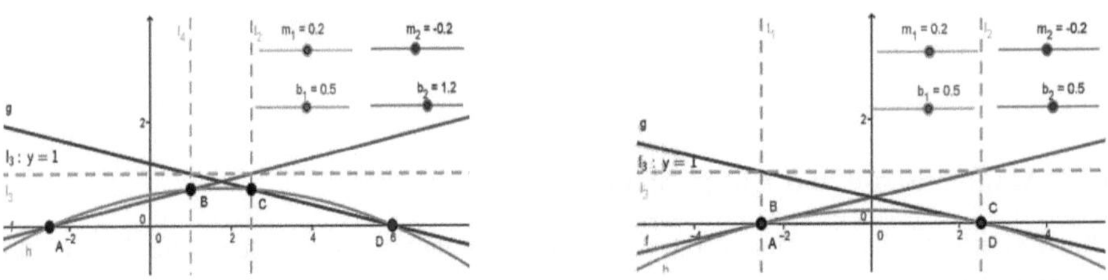


**Fig. 6.** The intersection points of the linear functions and the product function coincide when the lines are tangent to the product function.

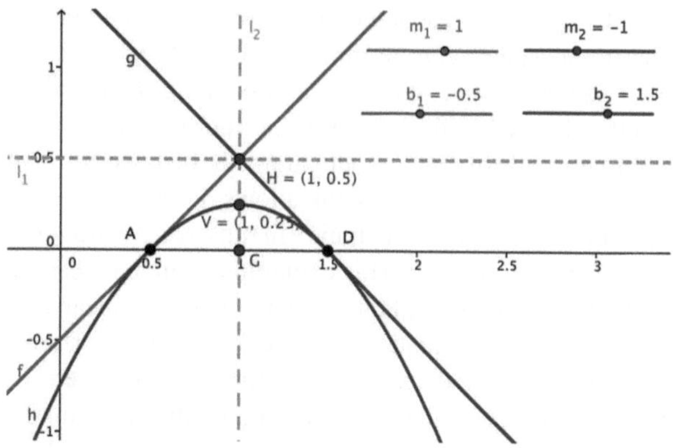


**Fig. 7.** Identifying the axis of symmetry and the intersection of $f$ and $g$.

(iii) *When both lines are tangent to the parabola, then the parabola vertex and the intersection point of both lines (point H) are on the axis of symmetry of the parabola and the point H, intersection of* $f$ and $g$, *is located at the intersection point of the axis of symmetry and line* $y = 0.5$ *(Fig. 7). Furthermore, the intersection of function product and the axis of symmetry is the vertex (V) of the parabola.*

**Comment:** Making sense of the task is a crucial step for learners to represent and explore possible ways to solve it. The use of GeoGebra, in this case, became instrumental to associate the sliders with the graphic representation of the linear and quadratic functions. In this process, the analysis of a particular case provides useful information to formulate a set of conjectures not only to solve the task, but also to explore others related properties. In addition, the graphic and empirical information can be used to construct an algebraic approach to the task.

## 4 Discussion and Final Remarks

A powerful mathematical activity that get heightened with the use of digital technology, such as a dynamic geometry system, is making explicit the implicit dynamism of reasoning about mathematical objects behaviours. The first exemplar illustrates how a dynamic model of a simple figure (triangle) can be used to generate and explore properties of the conic sections. Likewise, the dynamic exploration not only involves analysing family of objects via dragging; but also the identification of new concepts such as the perpendicular bisector and loci to generate those conic sections. In this context, a new route to study and structure an analytic course emerges. Furthermore, the use of the tool affordances could play an important role to explore visually the behaviour of recursive sequence, second exemplar, and this exploration again provides useful information to analyse both decimal and rational representation of the sequence values. In addition, the visual representation can easily be extended to analyse a family of cases where the initial values can be modified. It is observed that problem solving strategies such as "examining special cases" or "assuming the problem as solved" can be implemented and enhanced with the use of the tool because it is possible to coordinate visual and numeric information about parameter behaviours. The third exemplar illustrates that a dynamic geometry system allows learners to explore graphically properties of functions (linear and quadratic, in this case) through changing slider values that represent main parameters. This exploration can lead learners to formulate a set of conjectures and patterns to explain relations between linear functions and their product. In general terms, the systematic use of technology offers learners not only a set of affordances to make sense and explore concepts or objects embedded in mathematical tasks; but also offer them an opportunity to identify new mathematical results. It is also important to recognize that teachers need to develop some kind of expertise in the use of digital technologies and a possible path to develop it is to engage themselves in problem solving activities as a part of a community that recognize and value strengths and limitations in the use of technologies. In addition, teachers should also discuss what new heuristic strategies (dragging, finding foci, quantification of attributes, etc.) emerge during the construction of tasks dynamic models. It is clear that a limitation in a technology problem solving approach is to work on and follow up a well-structured curriculum that often includes course and contents sequences. In this context, a new flexible proposal to organize contents and fundamental concepts in which the systematic use of digital technologies appears as important in fostering students' mathematical thinking and peer collaboration.

Finally, all approaches to the tasks can be put online and all students can access and continue their analysis and discussion anytime. Thus the tools are used to keep the discussion alive even outside of classrooms.

**Acknowledgements.** The authors would like to acknowledge the support received from projects Conacyt-168543 and Plan Nacional I+D+I del MCIN, Reference EDU2011-20328 during the preparation of this article.

## References

1. Walling, D.R.: Designing learning for tablet classroom. Innovation in instruction. Springer, New York (2014)
2. Alagicc, G., Alagic, M.: Collaborative mathematics learning in online environments. In: Martinovic, D., Freiman, V., Karadac, Z. (eds.) Visual mathematics and cyberlearning, pp. 23–48. Springer, New York (2013)
3. Barbeau, E.: Introduction. In: Barbeau, E.J., Taylor, P.J. (eds.) Challenging mathematics in and beyond the classroom: the 16th ICMI Study. Springer, New York (2009)
4. Roschelle, J., Courey, S., Patton, C., Murray, E.: Dynabooks: supporting teachers to engage all learners in key literacies. In: Mouza, C., Lavigne, N. (eds.) Emerging Technologies for the Classroom, Explorations in the Learning Sciences, Instructional Systems and Performance Technologies, pp. 31–46. Springer, New York (2013)

5. Mason, J., Johnston-Wilder, S.: Designing and Using Mathematical Tasks. Tarquin Publications, St. Albans (2006)
6. Artigue, M., Mariotti, M.A.: Networking theoretical frames: the ReMath enterprise. Educ. Stud. Math. **85**(3), 329–355 (2014)
7. Santos-Trigo, M.: Problem solving in mathematics education. In: Lerman, S. (ed.) Encyclopedia of Mathematics Education, pp. 496–501. Springer, New York (2014)
8. Schoenfeld, A.H.: How We Think: A Theory of Goal-Oriented Decision Making and Its Educational Applications. Routledge, New York (2010)
9. Güçler, B., Hegedus, S., Robidoux, R., Jackiw, N.: Investigating the mathematical discourse of young learners involved in multi-modal mathematical investigation: the case of haptic technologies. In: Martinovic, D., Freiman, V., Karadac, Z. (eds.) Visual Mathematics and Cyberlearning, pp. 97–118. Springer, NY (2014)
10. Steen, L.A. (ed.): On the Shoulders of Giants: New Approaches to Numeracy. National Academies Press, Washington, DC (1990)
11. Devlin, K.: Mathematics the science of patterns. Scientific American Library, New York (1994)
12. Cuoco, A.A.: Mathematics as a way of thinking about things. In: Mathematical Science Education Board, National Research Council (ed.) High school mathematics at work, pp. 102–106. National Academic Press, Washington, DC (1998)
13. Schoenfeld, A.H.: Mathematical Problem Solving. Academic Press, New York (1985)

# Author Index

MIX
Papier aus verantwortungsvollen Quellen
Paper from responsible sources
FSC® C105338

If you have any concerns about our products,
you can contact us on
**ProductSafety@springernature.com**

In case Publisher is established outside the EU,
the EU authorized representative is:
**Springer Nature Customer Service Center GmbH**
**Europaplatz 3, 69115 Heidelberg, Germany**

Printed by Libri Plureos GmbH
in Hamburg, Germany